Race and Morality

*How Good Intentions
Undermine Social Justice
and Perpetuate Inequality*

CLINICAL SOCIOLOGY
Research and Practice

SERIES EDITOR:

John G. Bruhn, *New Mexico State University*
Las Cruces, New Mexico

CLINICAL SOCIOLOGY: An Agenda for Action
John G. Bruhn and Howard M. Rebach

HANDBOOK OF CLINICAL SOCIOLOGY (Second Edition)
John G. Bruhn and Howard M. Rebach

THE LIMITS OF IDEALISM: When Good Intentions Go Bad
Melvyn L. Fein

THE PARTNERSHIP MODEL IN HUMAN SERVICES: Sociological
Foundations and Practices
Rosalyn Benjamin Darling

RACE AND MORALITY: How Good Intentions Undermine Social Justice and
Perpetuate Inequality
Melvyn L. Fein

A Continuation Order Plan is available for this series. A continuation order will bring delivery of each new volume immediately upon publication. Volumes are billed only upon actual shipment. For further information please contact the publisher.

Race and Morality
How Good Intentions Undermine Social Justice and Perpetuate Inequality

Melvyn L. Fein
Kennesaw State University
Kennesaw, Georgia

Kluwer Academic / Plenum Publishers
New York, Boston, Dordrecht, London, Moscow

Library of Congress Cataloging-in-Publication Data

Fein, Melvyn L.
   Race and morality: how good intentions undermine social justice and perpetuate
inequality/Melvyn L. Fein.
      p.   cm.—(Clinical sociology)
   Includes bibliographical references and index.
   ISBN 0-306-46513-2
     1. United States—Race relations—Moral and ethical aspects.   2. Social justice—United
States. I. Title. II. Series.

E185.615 F395 2001
305.8′00973—dc21

                00-049776

ISBN 0-306-46513-2

©2001 Kluwer Academic / Plenum Publishers, New York
233 Spring Street, New York, N.Y. 10013

http://www.wkap.nl/

10 9 8 7 6 5 4 3 2 1

A C.I.P. record for this book is available from the Library of Congress

Printed in the United States of America

To Lizzie Tarriff,
for her example of courage.

Preface

After I had finished my presentation, a colleague and I sat rocking on the hotel porch to discuss its merits. It was a picture-perfect fall day in Jekyll Island Georgia, and he was a friend. Yes, he explained, what I was saying seemed to be true. And yes it probably needed to be said, but why did I want to be the one to say it? Wasn't I, after all, a tenured professor who didn't need to make a fuss in order to retain his job? Didn't it make sense to just kick back and enjoy the easy life I had earned? The topic of our tete-à-tete was my speculations about race relations and he was certain that too much honesty could only get me in trouble. Given my lack of political correctness, people were sure to assume that I was a racist and not give me a fair hearing.

This was a prospect I had previously contemplated. Long before embarking on this volume I had often asked myself why I wanted to write it. The ideological fervor that dominates our public dialogue on race guaranteed that some people would perceive me as a dangerous scoundrel who had to be put in his place. Because they would not be amenable to conclusions that differed from their own, and might interpret the mere mention of unpleasant facts about race as an assault on those whom they were pledged to defend, they might even try to get me fired. As a black student in one of my graduate courses made clear, unlike her, these others had not spent a full term with me and would not have the context within which to judge my views. She was certain that I genuinely wanted to improve race relations, and agreed with many of my assessments regarding the nature of the problem, but other African-Americans were sure to take offense. They would look at my observations as put-downs. "Be careful," was her final counsel.

Why then have I blundered ahead? Why have I sought to publish such a controversial analysis? It is not, as some seem to imagine, that I enjoy a vigorous fight. Indeed the contemplation of being condemned by others fills me with dread. Although experience has taught me that I can hold my own in debate even with determined adversaries, I find no pleasure in these encounters. Infinitely preferable are those quiet conversations in which the pros and cons of a defined issue are systematically examined. It is from these that I ultimately learn the most. No, I proceeded on this course because I believed I had no other choice. By now hundreds of students have informed me of how valuable they have found my views on the subject. They have literally thanked me for my honesty and bemoaned the fact that a similar candor was not available outside the classroom. I could not let them down.

But more than this, I too have been disturbed by our national lack of candor regarding race, and this, more than anything else, has impelled me compile the current volume. When my students first urged me to write my observations down, my apprehension gave me pause, but it was a recognition of these qualms that eventually convinced me to move forward. That well-intentioned attempts at honesty could jeopardize one's career struck me as a dreadful commentary on our current social situation. That I should personally be influenced by this prospect struck me as a dreadful commentary on myself. It implied a level of cowardice I found appalling. Although I have never considered myself particularly brave, the notion that I was afraid to tell the truth on a public stage violated my self-image in a way I was unprepared to accept.

Then too, it seemed to me that I had something to add to our discourse on race. Were this true, why would I want to deny people access to my ideas? Given the fact that so much pain has been caused to whites, as well as to blacks, wasn't it my duty to make an effort at amelioration? Wasn't it even a matter of self-interest, i.e., of promoting the kind of color-blind, democratic, free-market-oriented society that I favor? The upshot is that the chapters which follow represent an act of love and of obligation. Far from wishing to injure anyone, I perceive myself as offering a gift of hard won insights. Those who might profit from them, be they few or many, will be privy to a part of my innermost self. In a sense, I am embarrassed by my impulse to rescue others. Nevertheless I hope that the provenance of my efforts will be recognized and approved, at least by some.

I must also add that there have been some encouraging trends in recent years. One of these has been the greater recognition that cultural factors have been receiving, even among sociologists. It may no longer seem strange to be advocating the existence, and importance, of a "culture of slavery." There has also be more research into biological factors of the human condition and greater acceptance of the positive aspects of the middle class. Perhaps the pieces are finally starting to come together for an honest and accurate assessment of our race-based problems.

Acknowledgements

As is usual, no work of this scope is an isolated accomplishment. Among the many people who have helped in its realization are my immediate colleagues at Kennesaw State University. During the past year we have been establishing a separate department of sociology, geography and anthropology, and the experience has been exhilarating. In the process, Samuel Abaidoo, Vasilli Economopoulos, Barbara Karcher, Lana Wachniak, William Wallace, Wayne Van Horne, Betty Smith, Garret Smith, Harry Trendell, Mark Patterson, Lynn Moss, and Donna Walls have demonstrated a level of collegiality that is atypical. I trust that they know they are appreciated. Other colleagues such as Linda Noble, Nuru Akenyemi, Akenmu Adebayo, Christina Jeffrey, Jack Moran, Helen Ridley, Christina Tanner, Bridget Doss, Gina Harmon, Alan Wolfe, Michael Hoover, Berverley Cuthbertson-Johnson, Melodye Lehnerer, David Kallen, Jonathan Freedman, Phil Robinette, Michael Capece, Fred Zampa, and John Bruhn, have been especially helpful in providing both commentary and support. So too have been the editors at Kluwer Academic / Plenum, especially Eliot Werner and Felix Portnoy. Nor can I forget the contributions of former colleagues such as James Harris, Bruce Stewart, Carole Milano, Noel Martlock and Sandra Cottingham. I must likewise express my gratitude to the many ordinary students in my sociology classes at Kennesaw State. The discomfort they expressed with purely conceptual accounts of social issues made it imperative that I find more effective ways to proceed. Ultimately what worked best was storytelling. Because examples drawn from my personal experience so captivated them, this encouraged their utilization in a work intended for broader consumption. Finally the many clients with whom I worked over the years, in sharing of themselves, made me privy to facts that I could have learned in no other way.

Contents

Race and Morality

How Good Intentions
Undermine Social Justice
and Perpetuate Inequality

Chapter 1

Moral Invisiblity

> *I am an invisible man. No, I am not a spook like those who haunted Edgar Allan Poe; nor am I one of your Hollywood-movie ectoplasms. I am a man of substance, of flesh and bone, fiber and liquids—and I might even be said to possess a mind. I am invisible, understand, simply because people refuse to see me. Like the bodiless heads you see sometimes in circus sideshows, it is as though I have been surrounded by mirrors of hard, distorting glass. When they approach me they see only my surroundings, themselves, or figments of their imagination—indeed, everything and anything except me."* Ralph Ellison, *Invisible Man* (1947)

MORAL VERSUS STATUS INVISIBILITY

I had been looking forward to the presentation. It was a crisp November morning at Lake Lanier Islands in northern Georgia and the annual conference of the Georgia Sociological Association was drawing to a close. Outside the hotel the resort's Christmas display was already on view, but inside we were discussing the business of teaching sociology. The panel's opening paper, as noted in the meeting summary, was *Man, How Can You Teach This Class: Being White and Teaching Race in an Integrated Classroom.* As a white person teaching race in an integrated classroom, I was naturally curious about what approach the presenter would recommend in the face of what he described as the "many visceral, hot button issues raised in the class." Because I had only at the last moment been appointed discussant, I had not received a copy of his essay and was intrigued by the promise that there were

1

"ways in which an environment of openness can be created and maintained while examining issues which are emotional at a gut level."

Whites who teach about race quickly learn that their credentials are apt to be challenged. Black students, in particular, tend to question the legitimacy of a professor who cannot discuss the black experience from a first-hand perspective. "How do you know what it feels like?" they demand. "You've never been black!" If, in response, I refer to my own background and suggest that being Jewish has exposed me to prejudice, they find this amusing and insist it is not the same thing—which it certainly is not. In the end, most listen politely, but some always persist in rejecting the exercise—contending that they possess an understanding no amount of schoolroom erudition can supersede. How, I wondered, would the speaker handle this dilemma? Had he uncovered a technique for breaking through this curtain of skepticism?

The presenter began encouragingly enough by summarizing a familiar situation, namely his discomfort at having his expertise dismissed by these tyros. Despite his possession of a doctorate, their tendency to snicker made him uneasy. But this, he assured us, did not last long. Having discovered a means of neutralizing their suspicions, these evaporated once he spelled out some pivotal truths. Most significant among these was his declaration that there was only one race, that is, "the human race." Since the concept of "race" was illegitimate, it must be eschewed and all social groupings dealt with from the same standpoint. When white students protested this maneuver, he confronted them with an assurance that racial divisions were scientifically invalid; that is, that "race" did not, in fact, exist.[1] Challenged by such scholarly testimony, they were said to have backed off.

Patiently trying to absorb this, I grew increasingly restless. Having undergone similar discussions, I found this scenario disingenuous. In my experience, when asked how many races there were, someone—usually an earnest white teenager—chimed in that there was only one. Initially startled by this rejoinder, I soon realized that the social science version of race had become conventional wisdom among the politically correct.[2] When I subsequently inquired as to why the student believed this, the reply tended to run something like this: "We are all basically the same and therefore whatever differences exist are trivial." "Well then," I would respond, "what is the shouting about? If there really is only one race, how can there be such a thing as racism?" The response to this was generally a perplexed hush.

At the GSA conference the professional comeback to a similar query was more emphatic. Most of my peers scowled, and the presenter was taken aback. Indeed, as soon as he realized I was in disagreement, he became offended. Rather than give reasons why I was wrong, he insisted he was correct and when the session ended, pointedly walked past me without proffering the usual handshake. Had he been less discomfited, he might have responded as many textbook writers do. Martin Marger,[3] for instance, declares that "the idea [of race] is essentially devoid of significance...because there is virtually no scientific agreement about how many races exist, what the distinguishing features of races are, and what bearing race has on human behavior traits." Prince Brown,[4] in an even stronger denunciation, writes that "It is not possible to classify people by 'race.'" He alleges that because "no particular set of traits is limited to any one group or 'race'...and all groups are able to produce children with members of any other group.... absolute 'racial' categories" are impossible. Richard Dyer[5] goes further yet, underscoring the illegitimacy of the concept by noting that "Race is something only applied to non-white people" by whites. It is only through their discriminatory eyes that "they... function as a human norm."

Marger, to his credit, allows the concept of race a modest area of meaningfulness, admitting that its "sociological importance...lies in the fact that people have imputed significance to [it] despite its questionable validity." Adalberto Aguirre and Jonathan Turner[6] make a similar point by noting that "Even though biological differences are superficial and difficult to use as markers of boundaries between peoples, they are important sociologically. For if people believe that others are biologically distinctive, they tend to respond to them as different." At the GSA I might have seconded these sentiments had I been afforded the opportunity, but settled instead for being quietly ostracized.

Back on my home campus, once my reservations regarding the existence of race became known, several colleagues[7] tried to persuade me I was wrong and attempted to explain why the notion made no physiological sense. Since we human beings were obviously not separated into isolated breeding populations, no specific communities could be characterized by unambiguously identified features. Clearly, as modern transportation systems eroded the geographical barriers dividing peoples, everyone was operating within a "genetically open system." In fact, the differences between those identified as belonging to the same racial stock were often greater than between those identified as being from a diverse group.

My reaction to these arguments was: "Sure, but so what?" Such quasi-scientific precision misunderstood the ordinary use of the concept. While I agreed that the races glided imperceptibly into each other, and that their purported number fluctuated with the motives of those doing the enumerating, race was fundamentally a social category. Biological precision was never intended, hence its absence could not invalidate it. Thus, for example whether American Indians or Polynesians constitute discrete groups, or are merely branches of the same Mongoloid line, was to some extent arbitrary, but not, on this account, meaningless.[8] Similarly, whether the United States preserved a "one-drop" rule whereby anyone with a "smidgen" of visible African heritage was considered black or rejected this formulation and developed a new one in which some people were deemed to be of a "mixed race" was an important and substantial decision. To question its validity because it was inexact or subject to social modification was to misconstrue what is going on.[9]

Ordinary concepts are inherently imprecise. Science may seek to reduce their uncertainty through operational definitions that specify how they are to be applied, but in normal life people live with the ambiguities. They know, for instance, that some tables have more in common with chairs than with other tables, but are unperturbed by this. Stools may be closer in shape to end-tables than to wicker rockers, but most of us do not insist that the notion of "table" makes no sense—that all these objects are actually the same, namely "furniture."[10] Nor do people, because they sometimes encounter hermaphrodites, claim that there are no differences between men and women.[11] They understand that biological differences do exist and are sufficient to support a linguistic distinction. In the case of race, there are likewise sufficient differences. Although, to cite Jon Entine,[12] race is a "fuzzy" concept, the man on the street rarely has any difficulty distinguishing a Swede from a Nigerian, or a Korean from an Australian Aborigine.[13] Indeed, recent DNA studies make it clear that some populations are more closely related than others; that despite eons of migrations and interbreeding, there remain gene pools more concentrated in some places than others.[14] An "out-of-Africa" hypothesis may contend with a "multiregional" school of thought about how best to explain the means by which these biological differences arose,[15] but there is little dispute that there are differences. Some are even inclined to argue that the between-population variance is greater than the within-population variance.[16] The result is that those who would adopt a newly minted scientific definition of "race" that denies these factors in actuality undermine the study of the complex ways in which human communities are related.

But this is not the primary issue for the anti-race partisans. Whether they admit it or not, in maintaining that racial distinctions do not exist, they, in essence, endeavor to render them invisible. The reason they assert that they should not be recognized is their fear that they will be invidiously employed. Such an attitude may be compared with that found in the famous opening paragraph of Ralph Ellison's[17] *Invisible Man*. Among the best known works of contemporary literature, this novel alerted a generation of Americans to the liabilities under which most blacks labor. As Ellison wrote, those such as he—at the time called Negroes—had to contend with a myriad of others who looked through them when they passed on a street or rubbed elbows on a queue. Considered insignificant enough to ignore, even when they were overtly acknowledged, this acceptance was generally to the white person's advantage. Somewhat bitterly, nevertheless accurately, Ellison observed that liberals too, despite their declarations to the contrary, perceived blacks as "causes" to be fought over or "trophies" to be exploited, rather than as sentient individuals to be valued on their own account.

This circumstance may be described as "status" invisibility. It is a byproduct of social stratification and helps maintain these ranking systems. Ellison attributed the proclivity to "a peculiar disposition of the eyes of those with whom I come into contact. A matter of construction of their *inner* eyes, those eyes upon which they look through their physical eyes upon reality." In truth what his tormentors detected was a "social reality." For whatever reasons—including their physical attributes—those regarded as different were judged inferior and hence lost their title to humanity. Another example of this propensity was vividly portrayed in Richard Lester's irreverent cinematic remake of *The Three Musketeers*. In this rollicking comedy the hero, Dumas' swashbuckling D'Artagnan, in his haste to recover the French Queen's jewels, seeks permission to advance past an officious sentry. After handing the guard a written warrant, he is told that he cannot proceed because the authorization is for one person only, not the two obviously present. "Oh," D'Artagnan responds incredulously, "he's a servant," and the pair are immediately allowed to continue. In the social milieu of the seventeenth century servants were not considered real people. If they slept at the foot of one's bed while one was having sex, or clumsily removed a chamber pot immediately after its employment, one need experience no embarrassment, for their opinions, observations, and physical propinquity simply did not count.

There is, however, another sort of invisibility, one whose operation is even less often acknowledged. Usefully designated "moral invisibility," it is the sort that was exhibited by my sociological colleagues. While it too can result in an inexplicable refusal to accept reality, its cause is less self-seeking. Typically appearing among those dedicated to promoting goodness, its apostles decline to perceive unpleasant facts. Engaged either in outright denial of reality or in fiction building, they may believe, for instance, that things are as wonderful—or terrible—as they imagine they should be. Just as with Dr. Pangloss in Voltaire's *Candide*, a "see-no-evil" approach allows them to portray their friends as righteous, their enemies as misguided, and the world as amenable to their idealizations. Moreover, since they find it inconceivable that justice might not triumph, they discern no contradiction in denying evidence indicating otherwise.

A modest illustration of this is recounted by Stephan and Abigail Thernstrom.[18] In *America in Black and White*, they write that, "In December 1995 black employees at the Library of Congress forced the closing of an exhibit about slave life on southern plantations. 'I was so upset I couldn't look at the rest of the exhibit,' reported an employee who had glanced at an 1895 photograph depicting an armed white man on a horse looking down on black cotton pickers." Just like a child who cannot bear to stare directly at a detested medicine, she apparently hoped that if she closed her eyes, the offending incident would no longer exist. She evidently further hoped that if she could force others to close their eyes as well, an unfortunate epoch in history might itself be expunged.

This same tactic is evident in the assertion that there is a single human race. Its logic is clearly that we can eliminate racial differences by refusing to acknowledge them. The belief seems to be that this will also banish the mischief inherent in treating people disparately. But this is no more than a form of word magic based on the premise that if we change what we say, the facts on the ground will mutate to fit our desires. Unfortunately this is not an isolated effort. Many other attempts to neutralize morally unpalatable behavior also rely on manipulating language. An astonishing instance is provided by the widespread claim that black people *cannot* be racists. Though common sense would seem to indicate otherwise, a strict construction of the term is said to preclude the possibility. Thus, Joseph Lowery, the former head of the Southern Christian Leadership Council, has asserted that "If a person is powerless, he is just prejudiced. Racism [entails] the exercise of power." In other words, since only whites have power, only they qualify.[19] The problem with this thesis is that it assumes power to be an absolute. Lowery, in effect, assures us that blacks are so weak there is nothing they can ever do to injure whites. The black nationalist Molefi Kete Asante[20] goes beyond this. He writes that, "There is no such thing as black racism against whites; racism is based on fantasy; black views of whites are based on fact."

In matters of race, moral invisibility has become remarkably prevalent. White transgressions, especially those of conservatives, emerge as fair game for condemnation, whereas those of blacks (or their allies) are passed over in silence. Because picking on the latter's faults might give comfort to the "bigots," it is not tolerated. Out in the real world, this translates into people refusing to perceive what is morally unflattering. I am reminded of a graduate school seminar wherein two black classmates confidently asserted they had "to work twice as hard in order to get half the credit." Sitting opposite them, I winced, for I was aware of their actual work habits. Yet chiding them for this would have been construed as offensive. It would have been depicted as casting aspersions on all blacks. Fortunately, the professor in charge was Joyce Ladner[21] who was later to become acting president of Howard University. As a black woman, she could (and did) chuckle over their conceit. Absent this, the rest of us of a paler complexion would have had to pretend nothing was amiss.

The quasi-invisibility of black transgressions often seems to emanate from a consciousness of the unfairness African-Americans have had to endure. People render themselves deaf and dumb, not from malice, cupidity, ignorance, or even guilt, but from a desire to rectify past wrongs. That this might deprive them of information needed to accomplish their goals does not occur to them.[22] The belief seems to be that trying to do good guarantees one will do good. And so they blunder along banging into walls and stumbling over their own feet. Even when the bruises and broken bones accumulate, they continue to attribute these misfortunes to the malevolence of their foes, not to their own omissions.

A WHITE PROBLEM

As outré as it has become to suggest that African-Americans contribute to their own on-going problems, it has become just as obligatory to blame whites for being the prime instigators of these difficulties. Not only is white turpitude open to endless scrutiny, but attacking Caucasians is frequently regarded as a mark of virtue. Because European-Americans are the putative authors of American racism, they are regarded as liable for all the tragedies that have befallen their one-time bondsmen. Thus it is that from the moment the first slave ship landed to the latest example of police brutality, their conduct is susceptible to reproof and demands for full and immediate rectification.

This tendency toward one-sided blame was evident when Jane Elliott appeared as a guest speaker on the Kennesaw State University campus. Each year the school's Chautauqua Society invites prominent lecturers to present their views. The funds for these are provided by the institution, but the selections are made by a committee of students. Among the luminaries who have appeared are Jesse Jackson, Naomi Wolf, N. Scott Momaday, Joycelyn Elders, James Earl Jones, and Beverly Sills. Although the college is located in the deep South, in notoriously conservative Cobb County, there is a distinctly liberal bent to these choices. Even when a conservative is invited, a countervailing voice is usually brought aboard, presumably to prevent the corruption of the innocent. Thus, when Charles Murray[23] of *The Bell Curve* fame appeared, he was teamed with Harvard psychiatrist Alvin Poussaint so that the latter could debunk his alleged thesis that a deficiency in IQ underlay black academic failures.

An excellent indicator of student concerns, the series, to judge from its offerings, has settled on racial and gender issues as a high priority. The choice of Elliott was especially revelatory. Less well known than most invitees, she possessed a lingering fame because of her views on race. Back in the 1960s, following the Martin Luther King assassination, she had devised a classroom exercise that became nationally celebrated and kept her in demand. As Elliott was to explain, she had been deeply pained by the King murder and determined to demonstrate to her third graders in tiny Riceville, Iowa just how vicious discrimination and prejudice can be. Dividing her students into blue-eyed and brown-eyed groups, she first instructed one, and then the other, to treat the disfavored half as their inferiors. Members of the subordinate body were required to wear identifying arm bands, to sit at the back of the room, and to refrain from playing with their superiors. They were even ordered to accept leftovers in the school lunchroom. When her students protested, Elliott explained that this was because the inferior ones were confirmed troublemakers. Less intelligent or agreeable than their peers, they deserved less. The repercussions of this division were so wrenching that when written up in the local paper, they caught the eye of a former Iowa native named Johnny Carson, who invited her to appear on his late night television show. This led, in turn, to a series of documentaries on the ABC television network.[24] The upshot was that Elliott's technique converted her into a nationally recognized expert on racism.

A blurb in *Inside KSU* drove this point home by introducing Elliott as a "nationally known diversity trainer" who was so effective in thwarting racism, sexism, homophobia, and ageism that "the story of her life and work [would soon] be featured in an upcoming Disney film starring Susan Sarandon." Thus acclaimed, what was Elliott's message? As her audience was soon to learn, she explicitly, emphatically, and unambiguously alleged that our nation's race problems derived from a single source. According to her, the propensity of whites to judge blacks as inferior based solely upon skin color accounted for all the horrors of intolerance. Were white people to discard this absurd predilection, the barbarities associated with it would promptly disappear. Just as eye color was a ridiculous indicator of personal worth, so was skin color, and it was long overdue that European-Americans accepted this truth.

The effect of this denunciation was electrifying. As affirmed by the indelible glints in their eyes, most of those in attendance enthusiastically endorsed this thesis. Thus a video designed to illustrate Elliott's technique, in presenting images of young children sulking as they were shunted aside by their former friends, elicited a palpable current of empathy that was reinforced when a middle-aged black woman blurted out, "That happened to me too."[25] A guttural moan literally filled the room as she settled back into her seat with tears streaming down her cheeks. Indeed, in the almost three hours it took for Elliott to elaborate upon her point, not a word was raised in contradiction of anything she said.

Though she did not allude to it, Elliott's theory encapsulates what has been called the "Civil Rights vision." In its raw form, this was brought to public awareness by the noted black economist Thomas Sowell.[26] In brief, this conception has three central premises.

1. That "Statistical disparities in incomes, occupations, education, etc., represent moral inequities, and are caused by 'society.'"

2. That an alleged "Innate inferiority explains policies and practices of differential treatment, whether expressed in overt hostility or in institutional policies or individual decisions...." And

3. That "Political activity is the key to improving the lot of those on the short end of differences in income [and] 'representation' in desirable occupations or institutions...."

Stated slightly differently, the Civil Rights ideal affirms that prejudice and discrimination are the pivotal causes of African-American misery and hence their resultant anguish can be alleviated only by governmental interventions that outlaw such immorality. Because whites are responsible for the poverty, frustrations, and hopelessness blacks experience, they must stop doing what they have been doing. Furthermore, because whites are responsible for having ruptured the social fabric, they are obligated to repair it. At minimum, they must understand, and show deference to, their victims. It is only fair that as the perpetrators of a horrendous wrong, they recognize its implications and treat those who have borne its brunt with the sensitivity they deserve.

The obverse of this thesis is that society's racial difficulties are not a specifically black problem. As the targets of abuse, African-Americans have done nothing that it is their duty to rectify. On the contrary, it is their responsibility to demand reform. No longer must they allow themselves to be victimized. Thus, should the perpetrators of their predicament have the temerity to resist, they must apply force to bring them into compliance. Simple justice demands that evil-doers be compelled to recant. Nor are blacks obligated to understand whites. Rather, as the victims of discrimination, they possess a first-hand knowledge it is their duty to share with their oppressors. Since experience with racism can be acquired only on the receiving end, it is with this that they must be concerned. Therefore, when black students in white-run college courses object to the ignorance of their teachers, they are correct in questioning how anyone can understand them without having faced the bloody end of the lash.

Obviously the Civil Rights perspective is at its core a moral perspective. Though conceived of as empirically neutral, it indubitably presents the difficulties it assails in ethical terms. Specifically, whites are enjoined, as a matter of decency, to renounce the injustices to which they are prone. The snub of a co-worker who ignores a black colleague and the lynching of a teenage boy are alike condemned as social atrocities only the morally corrupt would sanction. This moralism may seem transparent, but its ramifications are rarely worked through. On the contrary, it has become customary to regard the "factual" nature of our race problems as settled and therefore beyond discussion. This has had the effect of consigning some potential solutions to the realm of conventional wisdom and others to a nether world of inattention. The rightness or wrongness of the civil rights policies, in particular, are not submitted to analysis. Because they are deemed moral, they are to be accepted in toto.

But why should this be? Shouldn't moralistic answers receive an especially close inspection? The importance of their implications would seem to merit it. In point of fact, are the disparities between the races exclusively caused by white society? Are black social liabilities, indeed, created entirely from a belief in the inferiority of blacks? Finally, is Civil Rights legislation the best instrument for correcting these abuses? None of the answers to these questions is a matter of logical certitude. Insisting on their moral necessity may seem to foreclose the issue, but it cannot. However persuasive this tactic, if the facts belie it, in the long run it cannot stand.

THE PROBLEM MISUNDERSTOOD

Race problems have long been viewed in Manichean terms—with a set of good guys arrayed against a host of bad ones. Locked in mortal combat over how to treat the downtrodden, they seem destined to confront each other until the inevitable victory of the former. And since prejudice and discrimination are unmitigated evils, decent people have no choice but to agree. Unless they commit themselves to destroying bigotry, they inadvertently align themselves with the forces of depravity. This sort of interpretation was promulgated by abolitionists before the Civil War, by Civil Rights marchers during the 1960s, and it remains in vogue today. Perhaps its clearest expression is found in the writings of Gunnar Myrdal.[27] A Swede who two generations ago investigated America's race problems, he came to the conclusion that they were essentially moral in nature. In his seminal *An American Dilemma*, he identified these as encompassing a congenital contradiction that was gnawing at the country's innards and prophesied that they must be resolved before the country could fulfill its destiny.

According to Myrdal, the central conundrum was an "ever-raging conflict between...valuations on the general plane which we shall call the 'American Creed'...and...the valuations on specific planes of individual and group living...." Whereas most Americans, including Southerners, genuinely subscribed to the words of the Declaration of Independence and fiercely believed that "All men are created equal," they did not necessarily respect this equality in the concrete case of African-Americans. Yet if everyone possessed an inalienable right to "life, liberty, and the pursuit of happiness," why not they? Although a neutral observer must conclude that Negroes were human, all around him Myrdal met with evidence of their aggressive exclusion from the fruits of democracy. How would Americans reconcile these disparities? Could they continue to maintain their devotion to freedom and equality, and deny these to millions of their fellow citizens? Time would tell.

World War II, the very struggle during which Myrdal's book appeared, was to prove a watershed. The racist excesses of the Nazi regime, as revealed in stomach-turning newsreels from the concentration camps, so appalled the average American citizen that it became increasingly difficult to justify domestic racism. Even those who hated blacks—or Jews—did not want to be associated with these fascist atrocities. Thus, when legal challenges to school segregation culminated in a Supreme Court decision that "separate is inherently unequal," a grass-roots movement was ignited that questioned all aspects of racial discrimination. By the end of the 1950s, the central figure in these proceedings was Martin Luther King, Jr. As the head of the Southern Christian Leadership Conference, he led a series of boycotts to demand nonviolent change. A Baptist minister and a disciple of Mohandas Ghandi, he regarded this as a moral crusade, the chief objective of which was to persuade whites of the virtues of fairness.

By the 1970s and 1980s, the moral basis of these appeals was taken for granted. As research by Reynolds Farley,[28] the Thernstroms,[29] and Paul Sniderman[30] attests, most Americans, including white Americans, now regard racism as a moral catastrophe. Indeed, to deny a request for eliminating it has become the equivalent of sin. There has likewise evolved a moral game in which blacks are considered good and whites bad. Besides making it virtually impossible to evaluate race-related proposals on their merits, this has rendered it impossible for whites accused of bigotry to defend themselves without sounding bigoted. Stepping into this fray has been Shelby Steele,[31] who contends that African-Americans have been exploiting this circumstance to everyone's disadvantage. His central proposition is that blacks have been portraying themselves as innocent victims to induce guilt in whites. This maneuver enables them to seize the moral high ground, while simultaneously excusing them from competition on equal terms with others. In other words, instead of using their individual abilities and characters to earn the success they deserve, they collectively invoke a deference due them in light of ongoing weaknesses.

Steele vociferously objects to this gambit. As a black man, he wants to be appreciated for his own attributes. More importantly, he wants his children to be so judged. His vision, which he argues is the same as that championed by Dr. King, is that success should derive from one's character and competence, not from group affiliation. In Steele's view, if interracial relations are interpreted entirely in ethical terms, with one group owing the other moral restitution, then winning is not worth the candle. As he sees it, those who seek apologies or compensatory advantages undercut their own position by implying that they cannot make it on their own. Ironically, by arguing that their weaknesses earn them a social promotion, they force themselves to cling to archaic infirmities, thereby ensuring that their successes will be self-limiting.

What Steele has demonstrated is that a strictly moral construction of race relations has grave implications. Beyond this, however, a moralistic mindset seems to conceive of the solution to our race problems as tantamount to "getting religion." What is envisioned amounts to little more than a quasi-*conversion* process in which an evil person progresses out of darkness and into the light. Like St. Paul on the road to Damascus, the "bigot" is expected to have the scales fall from his eyes. In the end, this convert will be reborn as a good guy and the moral universe thereby delivered from an imminent slide into destruction.

This moralistic scenario, it develops, assumes a fairly determinate progression. First it asks the potential convert to recognize his wrong. As the perpetrator of a series of misdeeds, he is held responsible for acknowledging his culpability and required to endure the humiliation of exposing his inferiority. Second, the miscreant must see the light. Incumbent upon him is a move beyond error and toward the correct course. He must, in short, distinguish between right and wrong and endorse the right—not merely acknowledge the wrong. Third, he must, whatever else he does, terminate his illegitimate behavior—and do so instantaneously. An admission of fault and an embrace of virtue are deemed insufficient if they have no consequences in action. Fourth, the former malefactor must make positive efforts to actualize his insights. It is not adequate to refrain from what is unjust; justice itself must be promoted. "Actions," as the old adage has it, "speak louder than words"; hence only positive performances can confirm a reformed status.

Yet there are problems here. The difficulty with this scenario is not a lack of clarity, or of allure, but the fact that it is grossly misleading. It is, to be blunt, dangerously wrong. The racial problems with which so many of us wrestle are not fundamentally moral and to assume that they are is to be led astray. To assume, specifically, that blacks are essentially weak and that whites are essentially sinners is to convert our universe into a kabuki dance. It is to dress people up in garish masks, and then imagine that their exaggerated features reflect reality. But worse than this, it is to seduce people into asking the impossible. To imagine that once whites are converted away from their presumed transgressions, they will be able to "rescue" blacks from the dilemmas engulfing them is to endorse a fantasy. The painful truth is that however well-intentioned whites may become, they will never have the power to save blacks from a predicament that is partly of their own making.

According to the redemption scenario whites are required both to supply emotional supports for and concrete services to African-Americans. As employers, they must change their hiring practices to provide more high-paying jobs for them; as politicians, they must earmark higher budgets to support inner city schools; as television programmers, they must make sure there are sufficient positive black role models on the airwaves; as community leaders, they must lobby for the Martin Luther King holiday and against flying the Confederate battle flag over the state house. They must also endorse economic opportunity zones, contractual set-asides, school quotas, hiring goals, and intracity busing schemes. What they must never do is use the N-word or in any way suggest that blacks and whites are different. Thus, they must never attribute the extraordinary feats of modern black athletes to biological advantages.[32] Rather, they must be prepared to honor the race card whenever it is played and even to dismiss offending individuals from their jobs if they so much as appear to be racist. At minimum they must be willing to send someone such as the Atlanta Brave's John Rocker to sensitivity training so that he will no longer utter opinions abhorrent to minority group members.

All this, unfortunately, flies in the face of how the world works. Salvation projects have a way of not succeeding. They are notorious for promising what they cannot deliver. To date no government or religion has come close to effecting its utopian projections. As tens of thousands of helping professionals have learned, it is almost impossible to rescue people from the quagmires pulling them down, even when these are not of their own making. Indeed novice counselors often find themselves betrayed by their personal sympathies. When confronted by a human being in obvious pain, the impulse to reach out and fix the problem can be overwhelming. Those newly exposed to intrapersonal torment quite naturally want to hug this other person, to dry his tears and to fill his belly. They may even wish to invite him home to share a warm drink before a hot fire. But then come the warnings from the old pros. Be careful, they will say, lest when you reach out to grasp the drowning man you are not the one who winds up submerged.

Years of experience invariably teach those who make a career of assisting others that there are limits to what they can do.[33] A substance abuser who has not made an internal commitment to stop using drugs can only temporarily be cleaned up, while generally speaking a patient suffering from schizophrenia cannot learn to manage independent living without keeping to a strict medical regimen. Even when it is clear that a client's uncontrollable anger has roots in a childhood of inconceivable brutality, it is the person himself who must make the Herculean efforts necessary to overcome his past. Much to their regret, helping professionals regularly discover that they can only aid others in achieving their ambitions. They can facilitate change, but the doing must come from the person in distress.

But if race problems are not fundamentally moral, then what are they? And if they are not amenable to redemptive strategies, then how are they to be repaired? To begin with, we must acknowledge some unpleasant truths. At their core, our race problems are stratification dilemmas; that is, they are problems concerning the distribution of interpersonal power.[34] Racial conflicts do have a moral dimension, but it is a derivative one. When the abolitionists, or Dr. King, insisted on a reform of moral rules, they were not deluding themselves. But the changes they demanded, though necessary, were not the most crucial. By themselves these modifications could never bring about the circumstances they desired. Only an opportunity for blacks to compete for social status on an equal footing with others can accomplish this. Only this can reorder their relationships in ways that satisfy their needs for interpersonal achievement. In short, because social rank is an accomplishment to be attained, not an advantage to be conferred, its potential beneficiaries are the ones who must strive for it.

We need, therefore, to launch a serious investigation into the nature of social stratification. As we shall see, what it is and how it operates make all the difference in what is possible. In general, stratification is an hierarchical arrangement wherein some people are accorded more power and resources than others. Those involved in seeking social standing literally fight it out to see who will emerge on top, with the winners gaining a reputation for being stronger, and more worthy, than the losers. This subsequently provides an on-going advantage that has momentous implications for their well-being. Social class is probably the most fundamental form of stratification in modern societies. Mass-market oriented communities, such as our own, rely on distinctions based on wealth, occupation, and style of life to organize their social space. Although these comparisons tend to be imprecise, they have enormous import. Unlike sports—where the rankings can shift rapidly—once social class standings have been achieved, they are difficult to rearrange. Nor are the contests in which these evolve "games." Because the life chances of the players are inextricably entwined with how well they do, the rivalries can become deadly. Deception, coercion, and manipulation are all brought to bear, though not necessarily consciously. This means that whatever qualities or relationships furnish an advantage may be exploited and that few players will chivalrously defer to the weak or poorly connected. Social class strife tends therefore to be not only confusing, but quite nasty.

Unfortunately, African-Americans have been gravely handicapped in this social class struggle. More than any other group, they have been subjected to obstacles that come close to being insurmountable. Sociologists, such as Pierre Bourdieu,[35] speak of "cultural capital" when they seek to understand why some individuals have an advantage over others. They observe that the social status one is born into and the skills one acquires along the way can provide leverage in contests with others. In the case of most blacks—unlike their peers—their American sojourn began in the sub-basement of the stratification system. Starting out as slaves, they were physically denied the normal opportunities for advancement.[36] Slavery, and the ensuing Jim Crow era, created the equivalent of a caste system.[37] In a caste system, an entire group of people, by reason of their birth, are forced to remain subservient. Both ideology and coercion are utilized to "keep them in their place." In India, the caste system was enforced by a belief that karma destined each individual to a particular moral standing. By comparison, in the United States, the subordinate condition of blacks was sustained by a belief in their innate inferiority. Both religion and Social Darwinism[38] were called upon to certify that Negroes did not possess the ability to manage their own affairs. If this did not work, threats of physical harm were directed at those deemed "uppity." Plantation overseers, the Ku Klux Klan, a sharecropping system, and ultimately the law itself were utilized to maintain segregation and economic subjugation. Even if an African-American did manage to become successful, he was not accorded the respect granted others. It thus took an act of political bravery for Theodore Roosevelt to invite Booker T. Washington[39] to the White House. Despite the latter's accomplishments, most of his fellow citizens did not regard him as equal to the meanest white.

It is this rigid submergence that makes racism insidious. Prejudice and discrimination, while repugnant, are only a part of the problem. It is their role in creating the moral stigmas that prevent upward mobility, rather than their offensiveness, that must command our attention. Few would deny that any solution to our racial dilemmas must enable the descendants of slaves to rise to whatever social level their abilities entitle them. As Steele affirms, merit, not skin color or previous condition of servitude, should be the decisive factor. Often labeled "meritocracy," this strategy, while it does not exist in pure form, offers a vision of fairness worthy of aspiration.

As long ago as the beginning of the nineteenth century, Thomas Jefferson[40] called for an aristocracy of merit, while at the same time Alexander Hamilton sought to erect an economic edifice in which individual mobility was protected. Both, in their own ways, sought to establish the republican institutions that persist into our own times. If the United States is now universally regarded as a "free country," it is because their commitments have here attained a state of realization granted few other societies. Centuries of evolution have produced a surfeit of what Robert Putnam[41] has designated "civic capital." In his groundbreaking study of democracy in Italy, he determined that it was only in those provinces with a history of interpersonal trust and habits of public association that representative government took effective root. In the United States, as de Tocqueville[42] documented more than one hundred and fifty years ago, these have a long and honored pedigree.

Yet this remarkable feat has not produced uniform benefits. Easily the most swindled have been black Americans. The real question thus becomes how to bring them into the fold. Paradoxically, an excess of moralism can interfere with this effort. While consigning a segment of our population to predestined failure is, in a real sense, pernicious, too narrow a fixation on this iniquity can be counterproductive. Intense moralizing may be a natural response to such abuses, especially when one is their victim, but it can prevent people from seeing what needs to be seen, saying what needs to be said, or accomplishing what must be accomplished. Wallowing in self-righteousness may be a temporary anodyne to generations of pain, but it is not the best guide to locating an egress. What is necessary instead is an ability to recognize what has gone wrong and a dedication to planning strategies that work.

As we have seen, when people feel virtuous, their tenacity in denying the undeniable can prompt them to assert such nonsense as that there are no distinctions between the races or that black persons are incapable of racial bias. Much as a self-righteous sense of entitlement once enabled plantation owners to reject their kinship with the human beings they owned, contemporary moralists cannot see what is in plain sight. Yet, to obscure unpleasant facts is to reduce one's options. When one's eyes are fixed on a vision that exists only in one's imagination, it is easy to aspire to the impossible. Hope becomes confounded with actuality and is not relinquished despite persistent failures. Ironically, what is insisted upon is often itself immoral and would be recognized as such were not the players dazzled by a fatuous idealism.

Today an excessive moralism with regard to race tends to demonize whites, while exalting blacks. In the end, as a black slave in Ken Burns' documentary on the Civil War was quoted as saying when he encountered his former master on the way to a prisoner of war camp, "Bottom rail on top now." The problem with this sort of role reversal is that it rekindles the very sort of enmity it seeks to eliminate. Merely to exchange positions of arbitrary power only turns around who injures whom and who feels justified in hating whom. Instead of fostering a genuinely open class system, it encourages reprisals and disguised forms of racism. But preventing this sort of foolishness is not easy. We humans are emotional creatures. When our visions are held in place by powerful feelings, we tend to act without conscious control. Nor are our conflicts of interest prone to summary repeal. Virtually all of us are so intent on winning that we find rationalizations for keeping others from doing so. This applies to reformers as well as to bigots.[43] It therefore takes courage to oppose the inertia of ostensible reforms once they have begun rolling. A daunting riptide of taunts, threats, and derision confronts anyone with the temerity to question their validity. In the present case, it is the radical civil rights agenda that is regarded as divine. Honesty and candor, though abstractly endorsed, are, in fact, given short shrift.

THE LONG VIEW

When Bill Clinton convened his national town meetings on race, he saw to it that the majority of speakers shared his ethical positions. These earnest assemblages of high school students, ministers, and professional athletes were asked to instruct their fellow Americans, not because they had unique insights, but because their hearts were in the right place. Although such exercises advertise themselves as efforts at public education, the participants bring no special knowledge to the endeavor. Nor is it thought necessary that they should. When moral issues are on the line, the only expertise believed necessary is good intentions. As long as one's soul is pure—which is typically decided by an agreement with those doing the choosing—he or she can be trusted to make the right choice. Technical knowledge, far from being valued, is suspect. By diverting attention from the moral core, it might prevent people from subscribing to an "essential" truth.

As noted earlier, blacks, in particular, are thought to command an unparalleled expertise based on their life experience.[44] Centuries of having to fend off majority depredations theoretically confer a finely tuned awareness of what makes whites tick. If, therefore, an individual African-American asserts white immorality to be the source of his troubles, this judgment must occupy a privileged position. The evidence, however, indicates otherwise. A study by Diane Ravich and Chester Finn[45] suggests that black teenagers, at least, know relatively little about white society. On almost every level, except that of black history, they scored significantly less well than whites. If this seems paradoxical, there is a meaningful body of evidence suggesting that lower class persons understand less about those above them than the other way around.[46] Having less familiarity with the world of their superiors and possessing less power to pry into their affairs, they are not as apt to acquire an accurate a picture of things outside their immediate purview.

There is also the fact that blacks are likely to be more unhappy with whites than vice versa.[47] Intense anger, even when warranted, has a way of obscuring one's vision.[48] Instead of calmly calculating what is occurring, it obstinately seeks revenge and refuses to be instructed regarding distasteful truths. This means that many blacks are not able to distinguish what they, or their white tormentors, contribute to their mutual dilemma. As such, their recommendations regarding the best cure may not be particularly enlightened.

In a recent survey of middle-class American values, Alan Wolfe[49] uncovered a striking manifestation of this phenomenon. The opinions expressed by his respondents revealed that black anger was, in general, not reciprocated by whites. He thus concludes that "The language of accusation is different between the races...[with] no [white] counter anger...[declaring] that racial justice has moved too quickly to match the anger among blacks that it has not moved quickly enough." In short, "For the most frustrated blacks...[the] language is anger; for the most conservative whites..., it is resignation." This suggests that some blacks may not see things very objectively. Drawing on his experience as a newsman, James McBride[50] provides another illustration of this fact. He reports that black journalists at *The Washington Post* often refused to perceive the world from the point of view of their white editors and instead strode around the newsroom "wielding their race like baseball bats." Regularly gathering in cliques to reaffirm their grievances, they raucously rejected all those who disagreed with them.

What is apparent in all this is a need for more racial balance. In *The Souls of Black Folk* W.E.B. DuBois[51] states that "It is not enough for the Negroes to declare that color-prejudice is the sole cause of their social condition, nor for the white South to reply that their social condition is the main cause of prejudice." It is "Only by a union of intelligence and sympathy across the color-line...[that] justice and right [shall] triumph." In his later years DuBois became embittered by white intransigence, but in the flush of his youth, with his optimism intact, he recognized that fairness is an interactive feat requiring reciprocal contributions.

If our racial difficulties are more about social stratification than moral turpitude, this fact must be appreciated in context. To facilitate the transition from a caste to a class system, we must take the long view and recognize the nature of social stratification in historical terms. This means we must perceive its causes, consequences, and modes of transformation in stark detail. Of particular concern must be the cultural practices that preserve destructive behavioral patterns. Culture is a universal and highly conservative component of human societies. As the sociological pioneers William Ogburn[52] and Robert Park[53] understood, it can lag behind other factors, especially technological ones, and in the process wreak havoc. Comprised of learned and shared ways of life that guide people in selecting their actions— including those toward people of a different race—when culture fosters compassion and fairness, its tenacity can be a bulwark against injustice. If, however, it prevents people from being fair or flexible, it can be the instrument of continued distress. As it happens, in America, both white and black cultural patterns—with their origins in slavery—conspire to relegate blacks to an inferior status. Long established inclinations toward prejudice and discrimination, as well as tendencies toward violence and paternalism, make it difficult for rationality to prevail.

Nor is the attainment of power, when it has for centuries been denied, a simple procedure. Despite rhetoric to the contrary, this entails much more than one group stepping aside and letting the other assume its rightful place. Because contests over authority are ubiquitous, priority over others is not in anyone's province to bestow. Power is a capacity that must be earned and exercised; it cannot be unambiguously inherited or conferred.[54] This means that those who would acquire it must develop personal qualities that enable them to hold their own in competition with others who themselves wish to occupy positions of superiority. Psychologically, intellectually, and emotionally a person must aspire to become the sort of individual who is perceived as strong, even when he or she is challenged. But this sort of strength is not gained overnight or by the uncomplicated expedient of aspiring to it. Those who think it is thereby impede their quest for it.

With all these roadblocks strewn along the path toward a color-blind system, it should come as no wonder that rearranging patterns of social stratification can be a lengthy and painful process, one entailing what we later call "natural resocialization." Counter to what many activists believe, neither impassioned exhortation, nor politically organized social engineering, nor clinically inspired interventions can do the job. Far from being a matter of converting the depraved, this sort of social restructuring is normally a multigenerational, and even a multicentury, undertaking. A hundred years ago, the influx of masses of immigrants stimulated a desire for a melting pot in which everyone would quickly become part of one people. In retrospect, this can be perceived as wishful thinking.[55] Experience has demonstrated that culturally diverse minorities take three or more generations to become un-self-consciously American. In the case of former slaves and their progeny, these difficulties have been compounded. Their assimilation into the mainstream, being energetically opposed, has required greater adjustments. As a result, long established social institutions must shift their channels so dramatically that the dislocations dwarf the Mississippi when it changes course.

Chapter 2

Moral Enemies

> *The poisonous atmosphere surrounding any attempt to debate issues involving race and ethnicity is demonstrated in many ways. In addition to the usual ad hominem attacks and overheated rhetoric, there has also developed a fundamental disregard for the truth, which has become widespread not only among journalists, but is even beginning to creep into scholarly publications. Not since the days of Senator Joe McCarthy has the drive to discredit so overridden every other consideration. Lies out of whole cloth are not uncommon and straw men dot the landscape.* Thomas Sowell, *Civil Rights*

WHITE DEPRAVITY

The effects of excessive moralism can be severe. Not merely a matter of being too strident, in dividing the universe into villains and heroes—into racists and nonracists—it creates frictions that undermine the resolution of important issues. Those singled out for defamation resent the obloquy to which they are subject, while those showered with unearned praise develop a distorted self-image. Either way, this moral warfare increases the probability of misconstruing essential information. Because of the nature of morality, people fail to perceive the obvious or misinterpret it so badly they are led astray. In the case of race relations, this has resulted in America being trapped in a collective impasse for some decades now.

Enter Jane Elliott. When on October 30, 1997 she stepped on stage to address KSU's Chautauqua Society, she received a warm greeting from the hundred or so persons present. Having just been lauded by a faculty member who attributed his own racial awakening to her, and facing a self-selected and largely integrated group of students, she was expected to expose racism for

23

the despotism it truly is. She began, however, by noting that she stood before a Southern audience and was therefore speaking to what amounted to the enemy. This was, after all, the part of the country most responsible for creating and perpetuating bigotry. It was also a citadel of religious conservatism and hence the headquarters of those opposed, in principle, to enlightenment. As a bastion of the Bible Belt, Cobb County was unquestionably the home to tens of thousands of closed-minded Southern Baptists who had no intention of treating black people with the decency they deserved. How could she, she wondered, expect a fair hearing in such an environment?

Surveying the crowd, Elliott observed that her listeners seemed to be taking her diatribe in good spirits. At this her face grew stern and she warned them not to smile too broadly because she was just warming up. Next she proceeded to lambaste Southerners in general, and Baptists in particular, for their presumed allegiance to pro-life politicians such as Newt Gingrich. When this onslaught too failed to draw a critical response, she pointed to her own short hair and commented on the tendency of strangers to identify her as a lesbian. Because sexism is as abhorrent as racism, she now predicted that most of her hearers would reject her in the mistaken belief that she was a homosexual. In fact, no one was offended. No matter how coarse the insults hurled their way—and many of these were voiced in obscene language—they were taken in stride. Indeed, many chuckled over the extravagance of her verbiage.

Shortly thereafter Elliott asked a white female student and a black male faculty member to join her on stage. Both were beaming, but nervous. Unsure of what was going to happen, they were determined to be cooperative. Elliott proceeded to point to one and then the other and asked the audience if they could tell the difference between them. When no answer was forthcoming, she turned to her subjects and posed the same question. Because they too were perplexed, she offered to explain herself. Conservatives, she commented, had recently taken to claiming that ours should be a color-blind society.[1] But this was ridiculous; anyone with two eyes could discern a difference in pigmentation betwixt blacks and whites. To this her chosen assistants nodded in assent. Soon the larger assembly joined in and began shaking their heads in vigorous agreement. Yes, there was a difference and they clearly saw it. Anyone who denied it must obviously be a fool and a bigot into the bargain. Conservatives thus stood indicted as hypocrites because they favored color-blindness.

Seated in the midst of this chorus, I felt as if I were attending a revival meeting. When I looked behind me, a sea of upwardly tilted faces were adorned with glistening eyes and beatific smiles. Yes, racists were dunderheads, but they, her listeners, were not. Much as the members of an evangelical congregation might exult in the thunderbolts hurled at them by a fire and brimstone preacher, this KSU gathering identified with Elliott and cheered her on. In *The Color of Water* James McBride[2] recounts how his Jewish mother reacted to the inception of the black power movement. Though often the only white face at civil rights meetings, she was convinced she belonged. "When Malcolm X talked about 'the white devil' Mommy simply felt that those references didn't apply to her." These Kennesaw students evidently had a similar reaction.

Several months later, on April 14, 1998, in the same auditorium, the African-American Student Alliance sponsored a presentation by SST Communications, a Chicago-based theater group that specialized in touring the country to perform programs with a multicultural message. Taking turns role-playing fictional characters, members of the troupe strove to re-create the flavor of contemporary race relations. Two thirds of the way through, one of their number assumed the role of a white bigot. Thrusting forward both his chin and chest, with great bravado he related how he and a group of his buddies responded when they encountered a white girl dating a black boy. After cornering them in an alley, they decided to teach her a lesson and launched into a gang rape in which he too participated. Performed with gusto and violence, this was deemed an appropriate punishment. Only later—but now reported with great sorrow—was the speaker to discover that the girl he had so violated was his own daughter. Because her face had been obscured by the dress raised over it, he did not realize who she was. As he bemoaned this tragedy, his self-selected audience found their loathing of racism confirmed. With eyes constricted in sympathetic horror, their appreciation of the message was in no way diminished by a calculation of how unlikely the incident would be. Bigots were terrible people who deserved to be shunned, ridiculed, and denounced. Any comeuppance they received was surely deserved and participating in doling it out only marked one as a person who would not tolerate racism in any of its guises.

In common with Elliott, though with greater subtlety, the SST people assumed that bigotry per se must be debunked. And what better way to demonstrate its nauseating character than to equate it with sexual perversion. Though the recitation was not based on an actual case, the attitude was nevertheless deemed appropriate. Moreover, since the ravages of racism were exclusively of white origin, blaming whites was perfectly proper. The images might be harsh, but excess had to be repulsed with excess. How else could immoral people be expected learn?

In both the cases of Elliott and SST, whites were attacking other whites for an alleged moral turpitude, yet it has also become common for blacks to lead such assaults. The result is that ordinary whites can now anticipate a multitude of such reproaches. Whatever their private opinions, if they find themselves in the wrong place the most contemptible motives may be attributed to them. An improbable illustration of this occurred at the Denny's restaurant chain. Caught in numerous acts of discrimination, and forced to pay out a multimillion dollar settlement, the corporation brought in a new CEO to turn things around. From the beginning, he made it plain that he would not tolerate discrimination and immediately changed the hiring policies. He also implemented a training program to inculcate the requisite sensitivities.

After this directive had been in place for awhile, Leslie Stahl and a *Sixty Minutes* crew showed up to report on their progress. Sitting in on several training sessions, Stahl was surprised to discover that the waiters and waitresses were being instructed to set down plates in a slow and choreographed manner. When she inquired as to why, the response was that too a quick a delivery might be interpreted as evidence of a racist desire not to serve a particular customer. Stahl was incredulous. Years of eating in restaurants, she explained, had taught her that busy servers were sometimes brusque because they were in a hurry. Indicating that she took no offense at this, on camera she turned and asked her black production assistant how she would react to such a situation. This young woman admitted that she would indeed have drawn a racist conclusion. She also agreed that, as Denny staffers were being informed, failing to place change directly in a black patron's hand would be construed as a sign on not wanting to touch her. It was thus better to take no chances and make direct contact with all customers.[3]

These sorts of assumptions are not limited to transactions in public establishments. The academic world too has fallen prey to them. The reaction to Dinesh D'Souza's[4] book *The End of Racism* made this abundantly plain. In an attempt to demonstrate that racism is no longer the primary impediment to black economic and social progress, he approved a title that was perhaps too enthusiastic. Understanding, as he and his publishers surely did, that a provocative cover brings additional readers, they selected a phrase that seemed to state that racism no longer exists. But the text was unequivocal in establishing that this is was not what D'Souza had in mind. What he actually asserted was more subtle. It was that much of what seems discriminatory is really a rational response to environmental factors; that is, to dangers that are sometimes real. He also argued that discrimination, though unpleasant, is less harmful to blacks than many cultural factors currently operative within their communities.

One of D'Souza's examples of "rational discrimination" is cab drivers who refuse to pick up black male passengers. Noting that "The U.S. Labor Department...reported that driving a cab is the riskiest job in America, with occupational homicide rates higher than those for bartenders, gas station attendants, and policemen," he contends that it is not unreasonable to shun fares that have a high likelihood of being dangerous. Since, in fact, black males are more apt to commit violent crimes, they qualify as passengers to be avoided. Quoting FBI statistics, he elaborates on how although blacks constitute only 13 percent of the population, they represent "39 percent of those arrested for aggravated assault, 42 percent of those arrested for weapons possession, 43 percent of those accused of rape, 55 percent of those arrested for murder, and 61 percent of those arrested for robbery." Even assuming these figures to be distorted, the preponderance of black criminality is so substantial that potential victims have a right to be concerned. Although many scholars deny the connection, those on the receiving end cannot afford such equanimity.[5]

D'Souza goes on to cite the myriad accusations of white racism emanating from persons as diverse as anthropologist Johnetta Cole, Coca Cola executive Charles Morrison, legal scholar Richard Delgado, philosopher Cornel West, Civil Rights activist Roger Wilkins, columnist Anthony Lewis, and sociologist Jennifer Hochschild. His response to this deluge is that when someone such as Kimberle Crenshaw finds "Racism is the central ideological underpinning of American society" this is a flagrant distortion. Acknowledging that "the end of racism" remains more a hope than a fact, he nonetheless insists that the deleterious consequences of family breakdown, endemic patterns of communal violence, and paternalistic social arrangements are real and debilitating. In his view, a "pathological" culture that celebrates dependence on government, repudiates achievement as a form of "acting white," and converts street thuggery into a cult of "coolness"[6] is bound to have difficulty promoting conventional forms of success. Describing this tradition as "oppositional" in nature, D'Souza regards it as frequently "vicious, self-defeating, and repellent." Predictably, such language has not endeared him to those to whom it might apply. Not surprisingly, in their haste to distance themselves from him, they display what D'Souza has summarized as "a reflexive tendency to blame racism for every failure, even those that are intensely personal."

One of those offended by D'Souza's analysis was the respected economist Glenn C. Loury.[7] Usually regarded as a black conservative, he was sufficiently incensed to write a harsh review in *The Weekly Standard*. Essentially accusing D'Souza, a man of East Indian descent, of naked bigotry, he complained that he "is utterly determined to place poor urban blacks outside the orbit of American civilization." Loury opined that he personally rejected "wholeheartedly and with intense fervor, [this] effort to draw a moral line down through the heart of my country, placing those...deem[ed] civilized on one side, and leaving the barbaric to the other." Reacting in turn to this denunciation, Richard Monk[8] came to the conclusion that Loury assumed that "Unlike other minority members, Blacks [were being] viewed as less than human....[which] to Loury, is racism." Monk then observed that Loury may have too readily perceived a negative message about blacks as an insincere effort to be helpful; that, like many African-Americans, he was prepared to believe the worst of others when it came to a non-black offering an unflattering depiction of blacks.

This tendency to perceive as villainous even well-intentioned attempts to examine racial issues has visited me in my classroom. When I provide dramatic illustrations of controversial points, or choose too inflammatory a word to make a case, I am in danger of being accused of insensitivity. In a maneuver sufficiently prevalent to have been labeled "playing the race card,"[9] some students pronounce themselves mortified by the baseness of a specific statement. One such incident arose during a course on social theory. In discussing the writings of W.E.B. DuBois, I mentioned that racism were remarkably prevalent during the nineteenth century. The notion that some groups were morally and biologically superior to others was so common that many groups, not just blacks, were impeded in their efforts to join the mainstream. Even the Irish,[10] today thought of as a branch of WASP society, were treated as social outcasts. To give some flavor of how vicious these put-downs could be, I noted that one of the things said—something that gratuitously slurred two groups for the price of one—was that the Irish were just "niggers turned inside out."[11]

Much to my chagrin, my use of the N-word drew the ire of one member of the class. Although initially not a ripple of dissent was heard, two weeks later my chair called me in to share a letter angrily alleging that I had irresponsibly uttered the proscribed term. When I observed that I had not directed my remarks at the class—that I had merely reported a historical fact—and that moreover the student in question had just badly failed an examination, she was satisfied. He, on the other hand, was not and proceeded to forward his accusation to the Dean. This too required an in-person explanation, which fortunately was again found sufficient. Only now did the student confront me face to face. With understandable hesitancy, the two of us squared off upon meeting in a hallway. He then explained that he found the use of the word personally abhorrent and would appreciate a retraction. When I responded that I had not been making a personal declaration and was depending upon the odium of the word to drive home the seriousness of the offenses against both blacks and the Irish, he refused to be placated. The term, he insisted, bothered him and was evidence of an unconscious racism. Besides, he had a "right" not to be offended by his teachers. In return for his tuition, he was entitled to an education consistent with his sensibilities.

Perhaps the apotheosis this inclination to excess sensitivity is exhibited in the criticisms leveled at persons of color who are perceived as allied with whites. Foremost among these has been Thomas Sowell. His rejection of the radical Civil Rights agenda has brought special attention from those intent on demonstrating the corrupt nature of his motives. In *Civil Rights: Rhetoric or Reality*, he[12] writes that on more than one occasion what he has said has been so flagrantly distorted as to depict him upholding the opposite of what he believes. Among the examples he gives are of CBS correspondent Lem Tucker describing him as being a supporter of the racial inferiority of blacks when the reverse is true, of the sociologist Christopher Jencks reviewing his book *Ethnic America*[13] as "in effect" about affirmative action when its index shows a "grand total" of two mentions of the subject, and of syndicated columnist Carl Rowan portraying him as opposing the government giving "any lazy bastard anything," when, in reality, he has gratefully acknowledged receiving the benefits of many government programs, including the G.I. Bill.

Sowell also relates "an almost comic example" of setting him up as a straw man. It seems that in *The Washington Post* he once "argued that some blacks from the old elite, which denigrated and discriminated against other blacks, were now exhibiting the extreme reactions typical of reformed sinners and being blacker-than-thou. Among the examples was Patricia Harris Roberts, once a member of a sorority which refused to admit darker-skinned college girls." For the temerity of publicizing this hypocrisy, he was soon denounced as "criticizing Mrs. Harris for being light skinned." Icons of the black liberal establishment, among them Roger Wilkins and St. Clair Drake, felt no compunctions about piling on and accusing him of "an almost paranoid preoccupation with a non-existent 'light skin elite.'"—such an absorption, no doubt, revealing a latent self-hating racism.[14]   Ward Connerly, the businessman/politician who spearheaded the drive to pass Proposition 209 to eliminate racial preferences from the admissions policies of the California University System, has experienced similar censure regarding his alleged unwillingness to assist members of his race. Some have suggested that his financial success or his white wife must have convinced him that he was really white and, therefore, free to indulge in the same injustices as they.

Those who engage in this sort of slander apparently believe themselves above the fray. Self-defined racial paladins, they regard European-Americans and their fellow travelers as legitimate targets of abuse. Because, in their eyes, little has changed since the days of the antebellum South, the need for vigorous moral conflict remains. Unless white villainy is identified for what it is—and assailed when, and wherever, it occurs—they would feel complicit in sustaining it. The result, unfortunately, is that whites can do little to defend themselves against such calumnies.[15] However they decide to behave, unless this echoes the black party-line, they are regarded as anti-black. Proof of this is delivered to my office virtually every week. Each term, the mail coming over my transom brings an unending stream of racial indictments. Because I teach race, publishers regularly send me brochures about their books on the subject, most of which are skewed toward proving white culpability. One of these, for example, informed me that if white toy manufacturers produce only white dolls, they are insensitive, but if they make dolls with black features, they are patronizing.[16] I have similarly learned that if whites fail to hire blacks for middle management positions, they are prejudiced, but if they start hiring them, they are practicing tokenism. No matter what the surveys show, and they do show a striking reduction in white hostility,[17] racism is said to be so entrenched that it is everywhere, lurking under even the most benign facades.[18]

The virulence of such attacks is epitomized by a publication of the National Education Association asserting that "All white individuals in our society are racists." Even if whites are totally free from all conscious racial prejudices, they remain racists, for they receive benefits distributed by a white racist society through its institutions. Our institutional and cultural processes are so arranged as to *automatically* benefit whites, just because they are white."[19] In other words, no matter how fair or dedicated to self-reform the individual Caucasian, to be white is inevitably to be racist.

BLACK INNOCENCE

The other side of the extreme moralization of race relations is that blacks are habitually depicted as innocents.[20] To the degree that whites are thought solely at fault for what has befallen our society, to that same degree blacks are exonerated of complicity. As the perpetrators of slavery, discrimination, and prejudice, whites are branded guilty of crimes against humanity, whereas the recipients of these violations are adjudged to have little or nothing of which to be ashamed. With no reason to feel contrite, they must nonetheless guard against being blamed for problems they did not create. The upshot has been a flood of denials of moral responsibility. The mere suggestion that blacks cause their own difficulties is greeted with vehement cries of derision and tortured explanations of why they are not.

Not long after I began teaching about race, a political science colleague passed by my classroom. Through the open door he heard something of which he did not approve and decided to set me straight. An activist noted for his outspoken candor, later that day he quietly pressed into my hand the copy of an article from *Ebony*[21] magazine that he recommended I read. Entitled *Who Get's Welfare?*, it purported to show that blacks were mistakenly accused of dominating the welfare rolls. The authors (the magazine's editors) emphatically announced that racist motives lay behind the widespread belief that African-Americans were taking advantage of the system, whereas hard evidence clearly demonstrated that "Whites not Blacks make up the bulk of clients on these public aid programs; a fact that dispels the notion that Blacks are scheming for a free lunch courtesy of the American taxpayer."

Utilizing statistics identified as coming from the 1990 Census, the article contained a table summarizing the total number of recipients of a variety of programs ranging from Social Security, Medicare, Ceterans Disability and Supplementary Security (SSI), through Aid to Families with Dependent Children (AFDC), food stamps, Medicaid, public housing, and educational aid. Although few would regard Social Security and veterans benefits as welfare, the editors brushed this potential quibble aside with the observation that "The federal government defines welfare as all entitlement programs funded through taxes." They then placed Social Security at the top of their list, with veterans benefits ranked third. Boldface figures alongside these proclaimed that 88.7% of the recipients of the former and 86.3% of the latter were white. Toward the middle of the chart, other figures indicated that only 39.7% of those on AFDC were black, as opposed to 38.1% who were white.

Similarly 50% of those living in public housing and 56.7% of those receiving educational aid were black compared with 29% and 32% for whites. Amazingly, this was described as incontrovertible verification that "Whites get the biggest chunk of public aid dollars" with the "real story" that "Some 61 percent of welfare recipients are White, while 33 percent are Black...."

Buried deep in the text was an acknowledgment that welfare critics argue that since blacks comprise only 13% of the population their 39.7% share of AFDC was disproportionate. This observation was, however, quickly dismissed with a citation to the effect that "Racism is at the heart of the standard-of-living gap." Overlooked was the implication that individual blacks were five to six times more likely to be on welfare than individual whites. A similar maneuver occurred at a recent meeting of the Southern Sociological Society. After a panelist mentioned the large number of whites on welfare, an audience member attempted to correct him by indicating that proportionately blacks were many times more likely to be on welfare. At this the moderator, a professor of sociology at a major university, declared with an air of finality that "Percentages don't matter." Although the room was packed with professional sociologists who theoretically should know that percentages do matter, no one rose to challenge this fiat.

Indeed, the denial of shameful black behavior and the affirmation of unique black benefits have become a cottage industry. Rather than admit African-Americans are responsible for behaviors that might be considered immoral, the focus is shifted onto whites. A typical version of this ploy was printed in *U.S. News & World Report*.[22] Under the title *Whites' Myths About Blacks*, it argued that Caucasians erroneously believe blacks lack a work ethic, are given to violence and crime, and refuse to take responsibility for their problems. Approvingly reprinted in sociology texts,[23] the article notes that "A 1990 NORC poll found that 62 percent of whites rated blacks as lazier than whites, and 78 percent thought them more likely to prefer welfare to being self-supporting." This was immediately countered by another NORC poll in which 80% of blacks said they prefer to work and by the reputed "fact" that for most of this century an overwhelming majority of blacks have been employed at rates commensurate with those of whites. What was not mentioned was that most of the blacks polled also thought African-Americans were lazy. Nor was there reference to the fact that, in the absence of an extensive welfare system, until the latter part of the century most blacks had no recourse but to work.

As to crime, the NORC survey was cited as having discovered that more than half of all whites believe blacks are prone to violence. This was immediately labeled fallacious because even though "blacks account for roughly 45 percent of all arrests for violent crime...the disparity...results partly from the fact that blacks *ask* police to arrest juveniles and other suspects more often than whites do." Moreover, "The vast majority of victims of black crime are blacks themselves...." Why this latter was construed as diminishing the extent of black crime, or demonstrating white error, is something of a mystery. With blacks committing five, six, or even seven times the proportion of homicides as whites, and with whites now more likely to be murdered by a black than by a white, the real question is, Why is black violence thought to be a myth?

Moving on to the supposed unwillingness of blacks to take personal responsibility for their condition and to blame others for their problems, the NORC revealed that 57% of whites subscribe to the belief that blacks have "worse jobs, income and housing" because they don't have the motivation "to pull themselves up out of poverty." In this case, a Gallup poll was cited to disprove this allegation. It reported that two out of three blacks believe they should "solve their communities' problems themselves" and that 30% thought "black poverty was the fault of blacks themselves." What the authors failed to note is that this refutation, like those that preceded it, depended heavily on the self-proclaimed attitudes of the respondents. But if these were merely socially acceptable responses, even if honestly proffered, they might not accurately reflect real-world conduct. To uncritically accept them thus revealed more about the author's desire to exonerate blacks than the truth about white perceptions.

The Rodney King trial, as well as the events that surrounded it, tell a similar tale.[24] Though the LAPD officers who beat King senseless surely covered themselves with no glory, King's own innocence was never established. People, both white and black, gave credence to what they thought they saw, namely an unprovoked assault, but the investigative journalist Lou Cannon[25] has revealed there were facts never observed. Besides the police chase that led up to the beating, the first thirteen seconds of the videotape were not televised. Deleted by the networks on the grounds that they were not of broadcast quality, they clearly showed King charging at the police. Although the first jury did see this material, it was the truncated version that the public viewed—and viewed many thousands of times. As a consequence, despite his criminal history and aggressive behavior, King came off as blameless.

The initial police acquittal, of course, triggered the worst American riots in more than a century. Whole sections of Los Angeles were set aflame and over fifty persons killed in an explosion of brutality that millions scrutinized on their home screens. After the fires were extinguished and the dust cleared, they also witnessed a stream of politicians visiting the rubble and promising to repair the damage. Most of these expressed their abhorrence at what had occurred, but this was tempered by a recognition that many blacks thought the violence justified. Interpreted as a political protest, the damage was depicted as unfortunate, but unavoidable. Ordinary blacks were reinforced in this conviction by Maxine Waters, the local congresswoman, who explained to admiring crowds that it was essential thousands of innocent citizens not be lumped together with a few vandals. This was not, she insisted, a "black riot" and hence blacks must not, as a community, be blamed. She therefore abstained from condemning the many hundreds of ordinary people who had impulsively taken advantage of the disorders to burn and loot. Although images of men, women, and children breaking windows and carrying out electronic equipment were still vivid in the public psyche, she warned against making them scapegoats for larger social problems.

This willingness to disregard the liability of those responsible was dramatically corroborated in the Reginald Denny trial. Caught on camera by a helicopter circling overhead, Daimian Williams unquestionably participated in using a brick and a claw hammer to fracture the skull of a hapless trucker, but his lawyer argued that he should not be held accountable because he was himself in the clutches of a mob enthusiasm. The emotional contagion of the riot had presumably been so potent that he could not restrain himself. Astoundingly, this justification was accepted by a jury that found Williams guilty of a lesser charge. So taken was it by the theory that social victims cannot be victimizers, it could not bring itself to realize that it is precisely in moments of temptation that a community must demand self control. Something comparable seems also to have happened in the O.J. Simpson trial, but more of this later.

Likewise coming to us from California, but admittedly of less import, was an incident that occurred at Stanford University. Not so much a blanket exoneration of black conduct as a defense of their right to claim a monopoly on "goodness," it too exposes a privilege not granted others. At the end of the 1980s Stanford decided to transform itself into a beacon of multicultural enlightenment. In the midst of this effort, there occurred a remarkable piece of theater. As David Sacks and Peter Thiel,[26] then students at the institution write, on Sept. 29, 1988, at Ujama House, a university-sponsored residence, a conversation occurred between two white freshmen and a black sophomore. In a discussion of race relations, the sophomore, B.J. Kerr, declared that "All music is black" and that "All music listened to today in America has African origins." When a white bystander asked "What about classical music? Beethoven?" Kerr responded that, as verified by a book he had seen in the Ujama library, Beethoven too was black.[27] Incredulous, the freshmen, Gus Heldt and Ben Dugan, challenged this assertion, but were immediately rebuked for interpreting things from a white point of view.

"The following evening, Ben noticed a Stanford Symphony recruiting poster featuring a picture of none other than Beethoven himself....Inebriated, Gus and Ben used crayons to color in the Beethoven flier with the stereotypical features of a black man...and then posted the flyer on a 'food for thought' bulletin board adjacent to B.J.'s door." The black residents of the house were not amused. Far from regarding this as a justifiable, if tasteless, exercise in satire, they pronounced themselves to be "outraged and sickened." In a series of house meetings and protest marches, they demanded that the offending freshmen be expelled from the college, or at least from the house. As summarized in a subsequent investigation by the Dean's office, this culminated in a confrontation so emotional that "people were 'crying, screaming,' 'hysterical' and distraught.'" Comparing the event to mass hysteria, the participants were said to be "holding hands and crying, [with] tears running down." Kerr himself was described as being so wound up that "he was groaning and flailing his arms."

What got lost in this pandemonium were the questions of whether Beethoven was really black and whether it was acceptable for white persons to comment on the matter. The uproar over the appropriateness of the caricature so thoroughly obscured the initial provocation that no one thought to reprimand Kerr for attempting to promulgate an incorrect version of history. A more celebrated illustration of this same proclivity is apparent in the recent tendency to overlook groundless boasts of blacks priority. As classicist Mary Lefkowitz found, breaking this taboo can get even respected scholars in trouble. A nationally known author, she became so disturbed by Afrocentric books that claim Africa as the wellspring of Western civilization that she wrote a volume to refute them.[28] Among the exaggerations that most distressed her was that Aristotle obtained many of his seminal ideas by cribbing them from texts in the Alexandria library. Noting that, its African location not withstanding, Alexandria was a Greek city, she made the even more telling observation that it, and its library, had come into existence only after Aristotle had completed his major works. Indeed, the city's founder, Alexander the Great, had been a student of Aristotle's. About a year after her exposé came out, I happened to catch a panel discussion on the topic on C-

Span. A lonely white figure on the dais, Lefkowitz sat stone-faced as several black scholars castigated her for not knowing enough about African history to make valid observations. Rather than challenge her on specific facts, one of her tormentors asked if she had ever personally visited Africa. When Lefkowitz admitted that she had not, the questioner issued an exultant sigh that seemed to gloat, "See, I told you so."[29]

This tactic would not have surprised Arthur Schlesinger.[30] An historian, academic, and lifelong liberal, he became alarmed as multiculturalism spread its tendrils into politics and education. Though strongly in favor of tolerance and mutual understanding, he became convinced that "ethnic cheerleading" and a propensity to mythologize black history were destroying the ligatures holding our society together. High on his list of the instruments helping to disunite the country were the *Portland Baseline Essays*. Put forward as a curriculum guide, these taught that the roots of Western civilization, including those of math and science, lay south of the Sahara. While admitting that black history has been egregiously omitted from American classrooms, Schlesinger nevertheless contends that attributing all good things to an African birthplace is not only wrong, but an impediment to improved intergroup relations.

Nor would Shelby Steele[31] have been astonished. Though he too considered himself a liberal, in breaking ranks and suggesting that blacks might not be total innocents, he came to be regarded as a traitor and a conservative.[32] Observing that the principal element of Martin Luther King's civil rights strategy was to seize the moral high ground, he concluded that King's very success had seduced many of his peers into taking this modus operandi too far. They had moved beyond King's emphasis on nonviolence and passive resistance and insisted that blacks were *inherently* innocent. In capsule form their argument was that, never having been slave owners, the relative powerlessness of blacks conferred a moral superiority that entitled them to re-educate whites. Yet, submitted Steele, this claim was a double-edged sword. To sustain it, blacks had to remain comparatively weak and therefore to limit their horizons. Furthermore, in granting whites no vestige of innocence, "it [denied] their moral capacity and then [demanded] that they be moral." This was nothing less than trying to have one's cake and eat it too.

THE NATURE OF THE MORALITY GAME

Let us assume for a moment that race relations have indeed been deeply moralized. The question remains, Have they been unduly so? And if so, has this moralization created problems? What, indeed, are the implications of people being immersed in a never-ending ethical debate over race? Are there, for instance, factors associated with morality that make it less likely that they will achieve their goals? If this is the case, the irony would be enormous. If in trying to do the right thing, people actually increased the likelihood of doing something wrong, more than a few of the "devout" would be "hoist by their own petards."

In fact, extremism and immorality are inherent in the nature of morality. The idealizations and conflicts that are part of the "morality game" are virtually guaranteed to lead people astray when indulged in with too much vigor. A negotiation/emotion paradigm[33] reveals that far from being a set of uniquely uncontaminated facts, morality is a social process. As Francis Fukuyama[34] affirms, "The creation of particular rules of behavior...is frequently the result of a process of horizontal negotiation, argument and dialogue among individuals." But because these principles are constructed in a social cauldron, when the pot overheats, it can prevent people from recognizing what they are doing. As Richard Ellis[35] warns, even the most noble goals can be perverted by fanaticism. "Before we praise radical egalitarians for their noble if unrealizable ideals, we do well to remember that noble ideals can themselves be the source of ignoble actions....It is not enough to declare an idea noble and one's hands clean; one needs to ask what will happen to that uplifting ideal when people behave not like angels but like fallible, biased human beings." This is particularly true when dealing with the civil rights agenda. Since much of its counsel is regarded as off-limits to serious investigation, it can go grievously amiss.

Morality has long been a source of social contention. For as far back as we have records, people have been arguing about it and not coming to settled conclusions. Despite millennia of effort, they seem not to understand how the process operates. Instead of producing progress, inquiries into its mysteries seem only to have deepened the confusions. The reason is that morality is a very peculiar enterprise with a constitutional propensity for concealing its tracks. Though few realize it, the rules at its core, and their modes of creation and enforcement, are such as to be inherently difficult to comprehend. The complexity of what is regulated, combined with the vehement desire of the players to impose their individual wills, ensure that it remains cloaked in doubt.

Most people, for instance, believe that moral rules are short declarative statements. When asked for instances, they regularly conjure up examples drawn from the Ten Commandments. Precepts such as "Thou shalt not lie" and "Thou shalt not kill" seem to capture what is involved. The irony is that ever obedient to the lessons of their childhood, even adults fail to recognize that moral imperatives are more like highway speed limits than instructions on how to assemble a bicycle. Were they to examine how they behave, they would soon realize that their most cherished principles are *informal* prescriptions. Like speed limits, these may seem exact, but are not. First they would have to acknowledge that although the official speed maximums are enshrined in legislative enactments and on highway signposts, the limits people really live by are not explicitly stated. A drive down any interstate makes it plain that most people cruise at speeds substantially higher than those theoretically allowed. If anything, traveling at the prescribed rate is regarded as deviant.

Most people may be loath to acknowledge it, but a similar situation prevails with regard to moral rules. "Thou shalt not lie" may seem unambiguous—as if it forbids every lie—but virtually all grown-ups, and most children, know that this is not the case. They realize that the dictum is fraught with exceptions and qualifications. In fact, the concept of "white lies" is acquired before kindergarten and that of "tact" is achieved not long afterwards, with most of us learning that to be "indiscreet" is no virtue. Later on, when we join the world of work, we encounter the concept of "puffery" which converts inflating claims about products for sale into a normal business practice. Likewise we learn not to be too candid with our bosses if doing so might endanger a promotion. In short, what constitutes a lie requires an act of interpretation.[36] The same is equally true of prescriptions that seem unambiguous. Thus, our rule against killing, although apparently absolute, is modified by a variety of exceptions that make it allowable to extinguish a life in self-defense or when serving as a soldier during war-time. Once articulated these deviations may seem obvious, but others are not. In point of fact, many change over time. To illustrate, despite the fact that killing slaves was once considered unobjectionable, it now seems barbaric, whereas imposing the death penalty on cold-blooded murderers continues to arouse dispute.

Who then instructs people as to which interpretations are valid? How indeed do any of us discover the specific qualifications built into our rules if these are rarely affirmed out loud? The answer can be detected in how we learn about speed limits. The unofficial standards, that is, the real ones, are usually internalized from examples of who the police pull over. It is experience on the road, not authoritative pronouncements, that establish what is required. In other words, we learn informal rules by observing them in action. Rather than a myriad of variations being crammed into the few sacred words, we depend on numerous concrete instances to flesh out the particulars.

Correspondingly, with moral rules, it is tangible examples that provide the necessary guidance. They serve as models of what is intended. Wolfe[37] notes that "Middle class Americans develop their moral philosophy anecdotally: they listen to the news and read newspapers to find stories that underscore virtuous and selfish behavior." The same is essentially true of all Americans, including the youngest. Their exemplars may not always come from current events, but they utilize everyday gossip and normal interpersonal sanctions in the same way. This means that for children it is what mommy and daddy in fact punish that matters. Does stealing a cookie result in being grounded? Will little sister's lie get her in trouble? These are what count. In adult life the stakes are higher, but who is promoted, ostracized, or praised still determines what is required.

The paradigmatic quality of moral rules also results in the extensive use of object lessons. Those who wish to be effective in making a moral point quickly discover that it is better show people what is wanted than to state it in injunctive form. If someone can be depicted as the epitome of good or ill, and castigated or rewarded accordingly, others are more or less likely to follow his or her lead. This then is the role of heroes and villains, of scandals and mythologies. People simply respond better to stories than to lectures— hence the fairy tales told children and the fictions purveyed in novels and on the silver screen.[38]

Also pregnant with consequence is how moral rules are created. There is a tendency to believe that what these standards represent is eternal and beyond human manipulation —that they are either ordained by God or the laws of nature—but they are in actuality social constructions. One of the triumphs of modern sociology was its discovery that societies establish their own realities through shared social processes. Emile Durkheim,[39] writing a century ago, demonstrated that religious truths obtain their potency by partaking in the projected strength of a community. In the case of morality, universalistic rules arise from a similar source, that is, they emerge as a result of interpersonal negotiations. People literally wrangle with one another over what their common principles should be. Whether the issue is the legitimacy of abortion, the propriety of prohibition, or the validity of abolitionism, they contest the particulars until an informal settlement is reached. Thus, in the case of abortion, pro-life and pro-choice factions have for years disputed what is acceptable. Only now, at long last, does a compromise appear to be emerging, namely that abortion should be legal, but nontheless semi-immoral.

One of the more notable aspects of this process is how ferocious it can be. Morality may encourage gentleness and compassion, but its lineaments are forged in fire. Elsewhere I have described these negotiations as comparable to hardball played without an umpire.[40] People fight, often savagely, to impose their version of the rules, but do so without the benefit of a neutral observer to moderate their passions. Left to their own devices, they attempt to prevail by any means necessary, including the unreasonable and the extreme. This tends to produce polarized contests in which the participants disguise their efforts lest too open a declaration of intent undermine their objectives. There thus arises a good guy/bad guy mentality in which all of the players are divided into two mutually exclusive teams. Regardless of their personal preferences, they are assigned to one or the other, with an escape into nonpartisanship forbidden.

Once these sides have come into existence, each views the other as an enemy to be overcome or converted. A "you-are-either-for-me-or-against-me" mentality defines the middle ground as empty and invites each faction to celebrate the motives and qualities of its adherents, while denigrating those of its opponents. The upshot is that the best possible construction is placed on everything associated with one's allies and the worst on that associated with one's adversaries. Good guys obviously do good things and bad guys bad ones. Similarly, good people have only good intentions. Kind and loving souls, they care about the well-being of others and give generously of their time and treasure to promote their advantage. Bad people, in contrast, have bad intentions. Their mean and cramped souls spur them to inflict injury on others. Moreover, good guys are knowledgeable, trustworthy, and fair, whereas bad ones are ignorant, irresponsible, and biased. If, therefore, a good guy tells you a lie, it is because he is defending a noble cause, whereas if a bad one tells you the truth, he is deviously attempting to seduce you into abandoning your allegiance to what is just. As a consequence, it is the responsibility of all right thinking people not to listen to bad guys or even examine the arguments they make. With justice entirely on one side, there is nothing to be gained from giving the other a fair hearing.

Moreover, the views of each side tend to be extravagant. In order to generate constituencies and to motivate partisans, they must encompass unclouded issues and copious promises. Only positions that seem unambiguously beyond reproach can elicit the necessary passions. Subtleties are thus unacceptable. Nor is it allowable to be sympathetic to the other side's truths. To do so might dilute one's own.

With such profound suspicions so prevalent, it is no wonder that moral rivalries degenerate into blame games. Whenever something goes wrong, each team is primed to insist on the culpability of the other. Whether or not there is evidence of a causative connection, they contend that if the "bad guys" just reformed their behavior, the evil would vanish. Since it is up to these others to "clean up their act," it is only fitting that good guys pound on them until they do. Whatever defenses bad guys offer must be recognized as rationalizations. The opposite side of this coin is that "good guys" must not be allowed to change their minds. For them to do so would be to slip into error. The end result is that each side establishes an orthodoxy it rigorously enforces. Subtlety and creativity may be valued in other human endeavors, but in morality it is faithfulness that is venerated.

Yet another vital aspect of morality is its intense emotionality. Both the negotiations that create its rules and the sanctions that enforce them depend on strong feelings for their substance. When trying to develop a consensus regarding a particular rule, and even earlier when trying to decide what standard to support, people rely on their emotions to evaluate its desirability. Because moral rules are essential to achieving personal and communal needs, and because feelings play a crucial role in determining what is satisfying, emotions are central to weighing the functionality of particular rules. That which we love or hate generally provides the best guide as to what will make us happy. It is this ability which enables—nay, requires us—to utilize emotions in prioritizing our goals both as individuals and as groups.

After a rule has been negotiated, our emotions are equally critical in seeing that it is respected. Moral principles are not optional recommendations, but mandatory prescriptions. However uncertain their genesis, once agreed upon, they are enforced—and foremost among our enforcement agents are our passions. This may sound outlandish, as if it is impossible for something as exalted as morality to depend on something as arbitrary as feelings, but moral anger is nothing to be laughed at. Its ferocity can be so potent that it reduces grown men to tears and drives entire nations to wage righteous warfare. Generally relabeled moral "indignation," it may not at first be recognized for what it is, but it is nothing other than intense animosity harnessed for social purposes.

Moral anger, which also gets repackaged as moral "outrage," is probably the pivotal moral emotion, but it is not alone. Among its more important partners are guilt, shame, and disgust. Guilt is an internalized form of anger that disciplines people from the inside when they flout a standard to which they are committed. It tortures them with doubts until they comply. Shame, in contrast, shapes external performances. Usually experienced as embarrassment, it makes people uncomfortable when they display unacceptable behaviors. In essence, it discourages them from acting as models of immoral conduct. Disgust, though having a different source, commands a similar outcome. Often described as "contempt," the aversion it promotes may have its origins in our reaction to ripe excrement or rotted foods, but when applied to conduct, makes it likely that it will be shunned.

Unfortunately strong emotions also reinforce extremism. Intense, and often too inflammatory to be examined, they easily slide into irrational vehemence. Anger becomes rage, guilt inner torment, shame an inexplicable immobility, and disgust a loathing that need not be explained. Deemed normal, they may demand the impossible and/or impose the bizarre without a twinge of regret.

Besides helping determine what the rules will be and ensuring that they will be honored, strong emotions are crucial in effecting moral change. Their role as enforcement and prioritizing agents can prevent transformations or push them in particular directions, hence their position at the cusp of our reorganized commitments. Although sometimes proceeding gradually; these moral modifications are often engulfed in firestorms of emotion. In biological evolution this pattern has been dubbed a "punctuated" equilibrium.[41] When translated into a moral framework, the pivotal moments may be termed "crises." These are instants in history when people are wrenched out of their comfortable certainties and thrust into an unfamiliar order that in time will metamorphose into a restructured certainty.

PLAYING THE GAME

The most cursory inspection discloses that contemporary disagreements over race are *morality games* that display all the markers of such games. Can it be doubted that the awful things said about whites, or the excuses made on behalf of blacks, are part of a moral negotiation? Their good guy/bad guy character screams out for notice, as do their intense emotionality and extremism. Both sides are convinced that they are fighting to save the world and will not rest until they succeed. Even when they declare that they are seeking honesty and reconciliation, as was the case in President Clinton's race initiative, the true objective is moral conversion. When confronted with the "facts," those on the other side are expected to realize the error of their ways and to collaborate in instituting reforms.

Probably the most explicit statement of this moralism has been that of Steele.[42] His observation that African-Americans have been playing a "victim game" in which claims of innocence are traded for white restitution is a classic description of a moral negotiation. Attempts to induce guilt over past transgressions reveal nothing less. "Victims" are, in fact, moral players who automatically qualify as good guys because of their suffering. Their pain presumably purifies them and confers the right to set our moral agenda. The victimizers, however, having forfeited the moral high ground, can redeem themselves only by enduring the cleansing anguish of profound remorse. Having, as it were, previously been turned to the "dark side," they must either perish or submit to the authority of their betters.

Those on the correct side of the moral divide, in their eyes at least, have an obligation to instruct those who would otherwise remain lost. Furthermore, because people learn moral lessons by example, they regard it as their duty to provide object lessons on how not to behave. This is the point of most of the criticism of white behavior. It was certainly the intent of those who singled out the Stanford University freshmen for having posted an objectionable caricature of Beethoven. When they pronounced themselves to be "outraged and sickened" by the action, it was to make sure that no one missed the point, that is, that those who put up the offending sign were bad guys who deserved to be punished. It was also the goal of Elliott's exhortations at KSU, the SST company's heated performances, and the demonizing of the LAPD during the Rodney King affair. Conversely, *Ebony* magazine's denial that blacks have exploited welfare, Maxine Waters polite disregard of the depredations of Los Angles looters, and the numerous school systems that have taught mythological black accomplishments as historical fact all represent object lessons in black purity. In these cases, it is a lack of culpability that is the point.

More than five decades ago, in their massive ethnographic study of Chicago's black community, Cayton and Drake[43] observed that there was a "cult of race" in which "Negroes feel impelled to prove to themselves continually that they are not the inferior creatures which their minority status implies." Today this impulse is often expanded into a rejection of all that is white. The breadth of this rejection was epitomized at KSU by a so-called

"Dialogue on Race" held in conjunction with Clinton's race initiative. In preparation for this campus-wide meeting, the organizers circulated a memorandum calling for the implementation of a "multiculturalism" that would surmount "white, male, eurocentric norms." The endpoint, as they envisaged it, was a world in which "prejudice and discrimination [are] constantly confronted publicly and negatively sanctioned. —Alternative norms are publicized and embraced. —[And] white, male, and eurocentric symbols are changed." Phrased somewhat differently, they proposed to eliminate white models of conduct and replace them with prototypes drawn from a minority rootstock. Acclaimed as being "inclusive," this strategy relied almost exclusively on black and hispanic examples rather than the traditional European ones.

Had this procedure been questioned, a blame game was likely to ensue in which to defend white behaviors, or to challenge black ones, would have been prima facie evidence of bigotry. Because in blame games the benefits of specific standards are not evaluated according to their merits, but in conformity with the moral faction with which they are aligned, one's enemies are not given the benefit of the doubt and are reflexively assumed to be seeking hegemony. D'Souza could no doubt testify to this. Irrespective of the rich documentation he brought his essay, given his conclusions, he was treated as a unidimensional pariah who lacked the wit to recognize that blacks have gotten a raw deal. Charles Murray could also elaborate on pitfalls of being on the wrong side of an issue.[44] When he and Richard Herrnstein decided to collaborate on *The Bell Curve*, they did so in the belief that they had little to lose. Already written off as enemies of liberalism, they expected to be tarred with a familiar brush. The outcome bore this out. Despite the fact that only one of their chapters dealt with racial variables—the infamous Chapter thirteen—and despite the fact that it essentially came to an agnostic conclusion, they were lambasted as racists. Ironically, many of those who joined in this calumny had not read the work. This was true at KSU, where an informal survey of those attending a reception in Murray's honor revealed that I alone had done so. This, however, did not deter his critics from loudly expressing their rejection of his arguments.

The situation is worse still for those supposed to be allies of blacks. If they do not actively espouse the orthodox position, they are attacked as renegades. Cayton and Drake, a half century ago, identified the "proper" stance for African-Americans. They were expected to be "race men," or better still, "race heroes." The former were proud of their race; the latter actively fought on its behalf. This evidently disqualifies Steele. He may have fancied himself as advocating a position that is practical and moral, but because it rejects affirmative action and demands that blacks prove themselves, he is branded anti-black. Sowell, notwithstanding his pioneering work on ethnicity and race, has endured the same reaction. For the sin of identifying the "Civil Rights vision," he is summarily ejected from the pantheon of prominent black academics and his work hardly ever cited by fellow African-Americans.

Of special import when contemplating the impact of moralism on race relations has been the role of *crises*. The emotional cataclysms of our moral universe, these events are essential to mobilizing the passions necessary for dramatic change. This is so because if people are to relinquish long-established modes of conduct, or to adopt new ones, they must be sufficiently indignant. That which was once regarded as normal must come to seem so sinister that it can no longer be tolerated. Often, this reaction is intentionally aroused by making a situation appear as offensive as possible. The more quickly and abrasively it is thrust before a target audience, the more probable that it will provoke their irritation. And the greater the irritation, the greater is the likelihood that an emotional contagion will push its members in a desired direction. Indeed, this sort of provocation is the stock-in-trade of moral entrepreneurs.[45] In their efforts to precipitate a particular outcome, they eagerly roil the waters, oblivious to any damage done the truth.

Bill Clinton, for instance, when launching his race initiative, publicized a spate of Southern church burnings. Indignant that white racists so viciously sought to destroy black houses of worship, he demanded immediate legislation to punish their depravity. Only later, when reporters uncovered the fact that white churches had been torched as often as black, and that the North was almost as susceptible as the South, did the furor subside. There was even evidence that most arsonists were not acting from racial motives. In the end, with the atmosphere of crisis diminished, the proposed legislation faded into oblivion. The same course was followed in the Tawana Brawley affair. In the immediate aftermath of her accusation that white police officers had abducted, violated, and abandoned her, there was momentum for a public apology and a legal remedy. Al Sharpeton,[46] and her other lawyers, brandished the image of her lying in an alley, smeared with feces and covered with racial epithets, to effectively orchestrate an outcry that for awhile made their demands seem irresistible. Once it was disclosed, however, that her charges had been manufactured for private purposes, the tempo slowed and the consensus in her favor melted away.

These fiascoes have nevertheless failed to discourage racial agitators from continuing to stir the pot. Crisis creation is so potent a tool that its occasional miscarriages serve only to whet their appetites. They have learned, among other things, that charges of police brutality can put whole cities on the defensive and that large corporations such as Texaco can be induced to fork over tens of millions of dollars even after allegations of racism prove groundless. Martin Luther King himself was expert in manipulating opponents into providing object lessons in racism that could then be publicized to excite the sympathies of potential supporters. Had he not possessed this skill, the moral consensus regarding equal access to public facilities would probably not have developed.

The Thernstroms[47] graphically relate how King acquired this lesson. Following an ignominious defeat in Albany, Georgia in the fall of 1961, he determined not to repeat this error in Birmingham, Alabama. In Albany, an attempt to desegregate public facilities through a campaign of sit-ins and prayer meetings fizzled when the authorities remained "firm and polite," thereby ensuring that there were "no televised pictures...of Albany police bashing protesters with their nightsticks." Without these provocations, the moment was lost. In Birmingham, the idea was to be more "confrontational." Intentionally seeking to bait the notoriously hot-headed police chief, Bull Connor, they marched and sang until he obliged them by calling out the fire trucks and police dogs. Though subsequently only three young people received bites serious enough to merit medical attention, the sight of German Shepherds straining on their leashes to tear into human flesh, and of burly police officers menacing children with their batons, was incendiary. The television scenes produced were so riveting that "The spectacle transfixed the nation."

"Here," conclude the Thernstroms, "was precisely the 'crisis' that the planners of the campaign had sought. Most Americans were revolted. President Kennedy expressed the common sentiment when he said that the sight of the pictures from Birmingham had 'made him sick,' and that he well understood 'why the Negroes of Birmingham are tired of being asked to be patient.'" The nation at large was so "disgusted" that the electorate was primed for quick and drastic change. And it was not to be disappointed. Within a few short years, sweeping Civil Rights legislation made its way through Congress, and, as importantly, the moral tenor of the white community was transformed. In due course, even the South responded to this pressure, with Jim Crow legislation falling to the reformers' ax. Absent this state of crisis such alterations could not, and would not, have occurred.

To sum up, again in the words of the Thernstroms, it has been "in the interests of the Civil Rights lobby to maintain the illusion of moral simplicity. As long as race remains a problem of the heart, they own the high moral ground." The question is, however, is this in the interests of the rest of us? More pertinent still, is it in the interests of truth and morality?

Chapter 3

"Died of a Theory"

"I waited and waited and waited. After the ninth taxi refused me, my blood began to boil. The tenth taxi refused me and stopped for a kind, well-dressed, smiling female fellow citizen of European descent. As she stepped in the cab she said, 'This is really ridiculous, is it not?'" Cornel West, *Race Matters*

TAXI DRIVER

It was the 1970s and I was completing my doctoral studies at the City University of New York. Being without private funds, like many other poverty stricken graduate students, I took a job to meet my expenses. In my case, this entailed driving a taxi. The garage that employed me was located in Brooklyn, but as we cabbies understood, the majority of the work lay on the other side of the East River. The first thing we did each morning therefore was to cross the Manhattan Bridge. Once beyond this span, we would cruise up and down the island, transporting passengers on short, lucrative hauls along well-worn tracks. To recross the river was an act of folly that placed one in an area with fewer fares and where one was in jeopardy of getting lost.

Early one spring morning, at about 5, I followed my customary route toward downtown. It was pitch dark, but even at this hour I knew there would be partygoers making their way home from the nightclubs at the lower end of the island. After conveying them uptown, I could retrace my route and begin the process again. It consequently came as a surprise when I spotted a man on a corner of Canal Street several blocks from the nearest bar. Nevertheless, because his arm was held out to flag me, I headed in his direction. As I approached, it became plain that he was black. This did not faze me because I had earlier decided I was not going to be the stereotypical

49

cabby who refused to accept customers merely on account of race. As a sociologist in training, I had been sensitized to such iniquities and determined not to participate in them.

Yet the closer I drew to this silhouetted figure, the more uneasy I grew. Not only was this a black man; he was evidently a pimp. After years of working in Harlem, I instantly recognized the implications of his broad-brimmed, red satin hat. Still, I stopped because he was a person and a potential fare. When, however, he got in and I asked where he wanted to go, I was jolted by the Brooklyn address he volunteered. Not only was it in Brooklyn; it was in Bedford-Stuyvesant. As I knew from having worked there, Bed-Stuy was one of the more dangerous neighborhoods in the city and the intersection he designated was one of its worst. Immediately the muscles at the back of my neck grew tense. What was I getting into? What might be awaiting me when we arrived?

For fifteen terrifying minutes, scenes of having my throat slit flashed before my mind. Would this man who was bigger, stronger, and meaner than I do something untoward once we were alone together on a dark street in a deserted area? In my frenzied imagination I speculated that, given his occupation, he would not be averse to engaging in another illegal activity, namely robbery. He might even have an accomplice who would join in ripping me from my seat. Since this was early in my shift, they would quickly discover that I had little money and in revenge beat me senseless. From the statistics with which I was familiar, I knew these sorts of things happened and I was worried that my turn had come.

Much to my relief, upon arriving at our destination, my passenger unceremoniously handed me the money I was due, plus a decent tip. He then exited the back seat and disappeared into the night. As soon as he was gone, I headed for Manhattan, but made sure to turn on my off-duty sign lest someone hail me before I got there. My heart was still pounding and my forehead damp as I pledged never to repeat this folly. I may have survived this time, but there was no point in tempting fate again. The more I thought about the matter, the more I was reminded of something Jefferson Davis[1] had said. As the confederacy was crumbling, and he found himself unable to stem the tide of destruction, he remarked that his infant nation could fairly be described as having "died of a theory." The theory to which he alluded was, of course, "state's rights." Years of functioning as the South's chief executive convinced him that the sentiments that persuaded eleven states to secede from the union also prevented them from submitting to the central authority needed to preserve their independence. Now it occurred to me that the policy of being "color-blind" when picking up fares was equally myopic. In allowing myself to be persuaded that race was irrelevant to accepting passengers, I was risking my physical well-being in order to comply with someone else's ideology. Yet, as my recent apprehension counseled, some people were less safe than others. To ignore this because it unfairly compelled innocent bystanders such as Cornel West[2] to stand nonplused on a rainy street-corner was not sensible. He might resent the treatment, yet why should I be asked to pay the price?

Still, I felt guilty. I knew I was engaged in stereotyping and that stereotyping was wicked. Had I been aware of D'Souza's[3] argument that stereotypes are often rational, I might have been easier on myself, but this lay years in the future. Instead, I found myself a victim of my own moral blindness. While an instinct for self-preservation pushed me to make distinctions, a desire to be a good person made me feel shabby for doing so. What I did not then suspect is that powerful moral commitments can be self-defeating. They can literally prevent the apprehension of important facts, while making chimeras seem real. This characteristically turns out to be true with stereotypes, where excessive moralizing regularly distorts what is happening.

A central error perpetuated in this domain is blaming stereotypes for racism. Jane Elliott is not alone in attributing prejudice and discrimination to these archetypes. Nor is she unique in suggesting that eliminating them would obviate the resultant injustices. Many sociologists and social activists are also convinced of the connection. Indeed, rather than examine this nexus, they treat stereotypes as a moral trump card. Whenever someone makes a distasteful judgment about members of a defended group, they hasten to condemn it as illicit. The person who has made the observation is then asked to recant and accept his status as a moral inferior.

In sociology a consensus has developed that stereotyping is more than a sloppy way of thinking. Most practitioners agree that it inevitably reflects an inaccurate representation of the world and hence ought be eschewed. Virtually all introductory texts are dominated by authoritative explanations of why these mental images are invalid. Representative is the work of Brinkerhoff[4] et al. which reports that "The foundation of prejudice is **stereotyping**, a belief that people who belong to the same category share common characteristics—for example, that athletes are dumb or that African Americans are naturally good dancers." Like prejudice itself, this sort of stereotyping is said to be "irrational." A somewhat more sophisticated account is found in Appelbaum and Chambliss,[5] which notes that "One form that prejudice takes is **stereotyping**, that is, *generalizing a set of characteristics to all members of a group.*" It continues that "Negative stereotypes serve to justify prejudice and discrimination" and that even positive generalizations, such as the "model minority"[6] designation often affixed to Asian-Americans, "may sometimes prove damaging."

As might be expected, texts intended for Race and Ethnicity courses are somewhat more sophisticated. They usually attempt an explanation of the concept's origin and present qualifications regarding its usage. Thus, John Farley[7] observes that while "various definitions of a *stereotype* are possible...Allport's (1954)[8] will do quite well [i.e.]: A **stereotype** is an exaggerated belief associated with a category [of people]." Marger[9] goes beyond this. He begins by reporting that stereotypes "were first suggested in 1922 by [the columnist] Walter Lippman, who described them as 'pictures in our heads' that we do not acquire through personal experience." Said by Shibutani and Kwan[10] to be "shorthand depictions" of an out-group and by Erlich as "a special language" that functions to "reinforce the beliefs and disbeliefs of its users," Marger too affirms their role in maintaining prejudice. He is scrupulous, however, in including studies that suggest that over time their specifics can be modified. Nevertheless, one is left with the distinct impression that they are invariably illegitimate.[11]

More simplistic are works intended to disabuse students of particular stereotypes. One example is Devon Mihesuah's[12] *American Indians: Stereotypes and Realities.* Mihesuah, herself a member of the Choctaw Nation, laments the poor quality of texts that discuss American Indians. She then presents a catalog of some twenty-four alleged stereotypes, together with advise on how to counteract them. Listed as number eighteen is the belief that "Indians have a tendency towards alcoholism." To this is opposed the "reality" that "Indians are no more predisposed to alcoholism than any other ethnic group."[13] In the body of her work this author admits that some Indians use alcohol for escapist purposes, but she insists this propensity is exaggerated by the greater visibility of Indian drunkenness. She also insists that it is a stereotype to believe Indians arrived on this continent over a land bridge from Siberia; the truth being that they originated in this hemisphere.

Even the American Sociological Association has lent its prestige to eradicating stereotypes. In the third edition of one of its handbooks on teaching techniques,[14] one contributor offers a method for dealing with them. Though his stated objective is "to stimulate a frank, meaningful discussion of stereotyping," he advises his readers that before students toss a bean bag from one to another to designate who will answer questions about a specific racial or ethnic group, the teacher should start the proceedings by interjecting a "few outlandish remarks that he has heard." Once additional examples are presented by the students, their "limitations and biases...are [to be] emphasized." The point of the exercise is to demonstrate why and how stereotypes are wrong, not how, or why, they occur.

It is also useful to observe the fate of dissenters. Those who express reservations regarding this received orthodoxy are generally chastised by their peers. In our age of "political correctness," they are often disparaged for a presumed ignorance. John Leo,[15] one of our more prolific chroniclers of political correctness, quotes Bill Bradley to the effect that when he says something deemed insulting to a particular constituency, for example, explicitly noting the self-destructive behavior of some minorities, "a cloak of silence and denial" descends to choke off the discussion. Those with a good word to say about stereotypes uniformly receive this treatment. Like those who during the sesquicentennial of Christopher Columbus' "discovery" of America denied that Europeans deliberately gave smallpox infected blankets to Indians, they may be shouted down as apologists for "genocide." From all this it becomes apparent that authoritative dismissals of stereotypes are not scientific judgments, but moral ones. They reflect the ethical commitments of social scientists, not disinterested observations of human behavior.

STEREOTYPES EXPOSED

Were their moralism at less of a fever pitch, advocates of the theory linking stereotypes to prejudice would recognize its error. As with most social issues, what is characterized as uncomplicated is actually a complex phenomenon that possesses both positive and negative aspects. Far from being the answer to why some groups are treated unfairly, it distorts a conflict-riven reality. Sad to say, stereotypes have become a politicized football and a caricature of themselves. Regardless of what the partisans maintain, all of us indulge in stereotyping, mostly without ill effects. In consequence, there must be more going on than they allow.

When Walter Lippmann introduced the idea that people categorize others through simplified generalizations, he did so in an avowedly political context. As a nationally known media pundit, he was not introducing a technical concept, but one intended to aid in debate with his opponents. Those operating in the same arena understood this. Robert Park,[16] for instance, although also active in attacking discrimination, took this coinage in stride.

He knew full well that Lippmann had said "The public thinks only in stereotypes," but observed that "There is, in fact, no other way in which the public can think." Succeeding sociologists seem to have forgotten this and imagine themselves elaborating upon a precisely defined activity. Yet in doing so, they indulge in an ideological tautology. Enmeshed in moral struggles, they do not recognize that many of their assertions are true by definition.

To be concrete, Aguirre and Turner,[17] in their recent text on race relations, unabashedly promote a stereotype theory that presupposes its own validity. They hypothesize that "When dominant ethnic groups feel threatened, they develop prejudices and portray those who threaten them in a negative light. If the sense of threat is severe, these negative portrayals are codified in a series of beliefs and stereotypes about the perceived undesirable characteristics of [the] subordinate ethnic population." These "codified beliefs and stereotypes not only escalate the sense of threat, which then ratchets up the level of discrimination, but also legitimate [the] discrimination." At first blush, this sounds like a scientific report about what people do, why they do it, and with what consequences. It has, however, nonempirical dimensions. Specifically, the thesis is so constructed that stereotyping *must* be wrong. Because their alleged negativity is tied to a presumed function—namely the defense of a dominant group's privileges—and, because they are thought to be transmitted intact from one generation to the next, these generalizations cannot help but be unfair. Moreover, the very formulations employed to characterize them, for example, "negative portrayals," ensure that their presumed adverse affects are accepted without challenge. In addition, the pernicious consequences of stereotyping are said to be so devastating that unless they are completely reversed, intolerable injuries must follow. Without proof of these outcomes, the overall utility of abstaining from stereotypes is assumed. Absent even an iota of evidence, what amounts to an ideology, rather than a theory, insists that people must identify stereotypes whenever they arise and eschew them at all costs. The young, in particular, are instructed to avoid them in their every guise.

The argument that stereotypes perpetuate discrimination has been made so persistently that it seems banal. Constant exposure has desensitized most of us to its faulty logic and obscured the fact that it begs the question. The fact is that stereotypes are unavoidable, often correct, and frequently useful. Although they are regularly misappropriated in exactly the manner Aguirre and Turner indicate, and can function as rationalizations for repression, this is far from the entire story. When we take off our moral blinders, it becomes evident that these generalizations are employed by everyone and often with positive effects. Rather than being pivotal in causing social disparities, they are more a consequence.

For the past several years, I have sought to introduce my students to some of these complexities through a procedure that seems to work fairly well. It is as follows. I begin by asking for the characteristics of several designated groups. Starting with the less controversial, I invite them to say whatever comes to mind. The first category is always "college professors." After some initial reticence, the more intrepid commence with observations such as "read books," "live in an ivory tower," "are impractical," and so forth. Next I ask about Jews. Since by now they are aware of my Jewish heritage, there is again some reticence. After further urging, however, they typically volunteer an abundance of suggestions such as: rich, intelligent, clannish, lawyers, cheap, etc. Next I turn to Italians and this time proposals such as "in the Mafia," "Italian stallions," and "loud" come flooding in. At this point, I move closer to the lives of my students and ask, What about Wasps? Once more there is a pause, but soon phrases such as "white bread" and "uptight" are bandied about. Since I teach in northern Georgia, I next mention "Rednecks." Thanks to the comedian Jeff Foxworthy, there ensues a barrage of answers and the laughter becomes pronounced. Students compete to give responses such as: "They have rifle racks on the back of their pick-up trucks," "There are cars up on blocks in their front yards," and "They go to family reunions to pick up dates." If someone interjects "Rednecks are stupid," no one is irritated and there is merely a nod of savvy approval.[18]

Finally I enter what I know to be hazardous waters. What about blacks?, I ask next. The response to this is predictable. Where there was a delighted boisterousness, an abashed silence suddenly appears interspersed with nervous laughter. Finally one of the students, generally a black, chirps up "on welfare," "dishonest," or "lazy." Only then do the white students join in with "athletic," "have rhythm," or "are dumb." The unease, however, does not fade. Once these proposals subside, I ask the class to look back upon what has just transpired. Several things immediately become evident. The first is that the silence that has overtaken the room betrays a critical discomfort. The second is that almost everyone is familiar with the basic stereotypes. Black or white, ethnic or Wasp, all share a common repertoire of group images. Whatever else may be true, it is clear that these portrayals are not the exclusive property of the bigots. Virtually everyone harbors them. The students then realize that stereotypes per se cannot be a sufficient cause of prejudice. If everyone entertains them, and only some are prejudiced, it logically follows that some other mechanism must intervene.

My next line of investigation concerns the accuracy of stereotypes. Having been loosened up, it does not take long for the class to conclude that they are partly true and partly false. Generalizations, they quickly recognize, are never completely right and rarely totally wrong. Because they attempt to cover more ground than any concise facsimile can accurately reflect, some distortion is inevitable. Even the legitimate synopsis that "Men are taller than women," if taken as absolute, is contradicted by the reality of millions of tall women. Only when the original statement is understood as probabilistic, and not applying to every case, is it valid. Were total accuracy required, no linguistic formula could ever do justice to the myriad of conflicting details of the real world. To state, for instance, that black males are disproportionately involved in crime is to assert something that is true. Even though our outlook on street crime may be skewed by media coverage, the image is not without foundation. Nor is it incorrect to conclude that Jews are disproportionately doctors and lawyers. Obviously most Jewish-Americans occupy other professions, but a statistically higher proportion are concentrated in these vocations.

D'Souza[19] summarizes the situation by noting that the "premise that all group perceptions are misconceptions: that every negative generalization about blacks is automatically false and the product of distorted projections" is itself false. Most blacks are in fact aware that young black males are disproportionately violent. As has been cited many times, including by D'Souza, Jesse Jackson has admitted that "There is nothing more painful to me than to walk down the street and hear footsteps and start to think about robbery and then see it's somebody white and be relieved." In the privacy of their own living rooms, most African-Americans agree with William Oliver's[20] observation that their communities are infested with violence and danger. As an employee of New York City's Department of Welfare, I heard as much when my black colleagues told endless war stories over lunch.

When I follow this up by asking my class where stereotypes come from, the conventional answer is that they are learned. Bigoted parents are said to teach their children beliefs that induce them to become bigots. In Rogers and Hammerstein's[21] musical *South Pacific* there is a song which proclaims that "You've got to be taught to hate all the people your relatives hate; you've got to be carefully taught." This neatly encapsulates the socialization theory. When I then ask whether this is so, it becomes evident that my students' responses were themselves learned. If pressed, they come up with no evidence to back up their socialization claims. The reason for this, once it is sought, is easy to perceive. As Dennis Wrong[22] cautioned decades ago, there is a tendency to overstate the efficacy of socialization. Though it makes a difference, other factors do as well—often decisively. The historian Thomas West[23] inadvertently highlights the nature of this problem when he quotes Thomas Pettigrew to the effect that a stereotype is by definition "acquired culturally rather than through personal experience." West, in consequence, mistakenly assumes that since another historian's characterization of the French was drawn from his personal experience, it cannot be a stereotype. This, however, naively implies that when determining whether a particular generalization is a stereotype an effort is made to determine its provenance. This almost never happens. What actually decides whether a characterization is regarded as a stereotype is not its provenance, but whether it is approved by those who have so designated it. Consider for a moment how difficult it would be, in any given case, to discover the extent to which earlier socialization was operative. As a practical matter, this is not possible and not even attempted. Instead, a predisposition against a particular generalization intervenes to invent its presumed history.

Stereotypes, in fact, are not merely the result of childhood socialization. While they are part of our communal heritage, they are also the joint result of having grown up in a common society and been subjected to similar experiences. A belief in black violence derives not only from parental stories about African-American brutality, but also from our having been exposed to black violence, either in the media or more immediate encounters. If this is so, then stereotypes are inherently more open-ended than most of their critics allow. Rather than being transmitted in an undiluted fashion, they are susceptible to revision by unfolding events. This, of course, would make them more difficult to eradicate. Without a restricted point of intervention at which to correct them (for example, grade school), the efforts of particular change-agents can always be undone by subsequent occurrences.

The simple, if unpalatable, truth is that stereotypes are cognitively normal. As psychologists[24] have been discovering, they are natural, automatic, and unconscious. Their universality does not flow from a reversible social defect, but from the way ordinary people think. No amount of hand wringing or concentrated efforts to reform socialization can alter this propensity. When people are confronted with large quantities of data, their minds simply summarize them in the form of stereotypes. Alfred Schutz[25] called these "typifications" and cognitive psychologists designate them "schemata."[26] In any event, with complex phenomena, human beings need clarity and will impose it, even by means of a Procrustean bed. Two generations ago Karl Mannheim[27] observed that to understand complex political phenomena people resort to ideological explanations, while more recently Alvin Gouldner[28] has argued that we are all prone to "basic assumptions" which both simplify and inject values into our world views. Attribution theory too has confirmed these tendencies. As Massimo Piattelli-Palmarini[29] and Stuart Sutherland[30] point out, research indicates that, especially regarding moral issues and matters of causation, observers are prone to a variety of nonscientific mechanisms whereby they project mental images onto what they see. To illustrate, one "inevitable illusion" prompts them, when asked in what direction one should fly to travel from Los Angeles, California to Reno, Nevada, to say "northeast" rather than "northwest," because they idealistically conceive of the West Coast as parallel to the continent.

The psychologist Elizabeth Parks[31] summarizes the matter as follows: "Stereotypes are a cognitive adaptation to the highly complex social world in which human beings function and are probably a necessity for survival." In this she is of one mind with Alexis de Tocqueville,[32] who more than a century earlier indicated that people think in terms of categories because "If a human intelligence tried to examine and judge all the particular cases that came his way individually, he would be lost in a wilderness of detail." It therefore seems fair to say that a cognitive predisposition, combined with the predictable circumstances of growing up in a convoluted society, generate the specific stereotypes that children acquire. Lawrence Hirschfeld[33] argues that racial categories are among the easiest of these to develop. He believes that just as an ability to learn language is built into our mental equipment, so a tendency to construct human categories is innate. In the cultural context of contemporary America, this means that attention is inevitably drawn to what become the commonplace racial categories. Paradoxically, the very conflicts that the civil rights reformers want to eradicate provide the raw materials for incipient stereotypes. Their emotional content makes them salient and therefore influential.

If we human beings do learn to generalize in this way, then it follows that racial stereotypes are preordained. Trying to outlaw them would have as much chance of success as legislating against gravity. It does not, however, follow that any specific stereotype is true.[34] What counts as a misleading *over*-generalization, as opposed to a normal and acceptable one, is an empirical question. Yet the fact is there is no agreed standard for determining when a generalization as wandered too far from its sources. In practice, this is a judgment call—often made in accord with the values of the judge. An "over" generalization thus tends to be one regarded as "bad," that is, as one a person "should *not*" make.[35] In essence, the labeling of a generalization as a stereotype is a disguised form of moral exhortation. It is to state that, by definition, a particular conceptualization is ethically inadmissible. Evidence of its having gone too far is not adduced, but implied, and the conversation ended by fiat. Who indeed would want to defend an immoral assertion, much less explore its empirical roots?

Likewise, to assert that a generalization is "too simplified" is to engage in an evaluation. With no objective criteria for determining when a descriptive image has been insufficiently qualified, people tend to extol those judgments with which they agree and dismiss those to which they object. Truth value rarely determines which generalizations are labeled genuine. An especially vivid example of this is provided by the moral chagrin entailed in acknowledging that black crime rates are extremely high. This embarrassment continues to prompt many people to deny their validity and to censure those who stress them as being engaged in stereotyping.

STREET-LEVEL STEREOTYPES

If stereotypes are cognitively normal, and blanket rejections of them morally inspired, they may still be dysfunctional. Because that which is true can nevertheless be harmful, to assert that stereotyping is socially necessary demands additional evidence. But such evidence is readily available. To begin with, ours is a Gesellschaft society and stereotypes are especially advantageous in navigating within such an environment. More than a century ago Ferdinand Toennies[36] pointed out that the modern world was being converted by mass market industrialism into a civilization in which most people were strangers to one another. Even though they were dependent— for their very survival—on people they did not know, there was no hope of becoming familiar with these others on a personal level. When they met on the street, they did not even recognize one another as producers or consumers operating within the same chain of economic transactions. Instead they relied on shorthand calling cards to suggest how they should treat one another.

This then is one of the major functions of stereotypes. In public places, on the job, and even at social gatherings, they provide information about strangers. As generalizations about the group to which an exotic face may belong, they suggest what to expect and how to orient oneself. Is this a friend or a foe, a superior or an inferior, a sales clerk or a fellow customer? Should we approach closer, or move away? In this way, they help organize society and make what would be an overwhelming pastiche of indecipherable events psychologically manageable.

But let me be more precise. Some decades ago, when I was a counselor at a summer camp, one of my assistants was from Denmark. Night upon night, after the campers were asleep, he would proclaim that his fondest wish before returning home was to visit Harlem. Since I had worked there, I volunteered to take him at the season's close. And this is what we did. He was delighted, as we sauntered down 125th Street, passing scores of diligent black faces. As one point, however, we noticed, about a block and a half away, a group of males, ranging in age from their late teens to mid-twenties, standing on a corner and apparently handing things to each other. It was difficult to make out what they were holding, but whatever it was, it was modest in size. At this, my companion grabbed for his camera and raised it to take a picture. With a broad smile, he remarked at the romantic character of the scene before us.

When I share this vignette with my students, the narrative is usually interrupted at this point. Several coeds invariably gasp, What happened? They realize—as did I—based upon our shared understandings, that my companion and I had probably stumbled onto a drug deal. When I assure them that I instructed him to put his camera away, there is a sigh of relief. Even though we could not make out the bags of heroin, and my students obviously had no way of doing so, we are all sufficiently confident in our knowledge of the drug trade to believe that my action prevented a painful confrontation. Ironically, when I told the same story at Lake Lanier Islands, my GSA colleagues fell silent. Ten minutes later one piped up to suggest that I was projecting my own fears onto a situation that was in all likelihood innocent. Had my KSU students been present, they would have been incredulous.

The politically correct may be appalled by this turn of events, but ordinary people know it makes sense. When their nontheoretical, nonmoralistic selves are appealed to, they understand that they would have behaved just as I had in Harlem or as a taxi driver. Indeed, one of the reasons Jesse Jackson's remarks are so often repeated is that they strike most people as honest. His admission that he too uses generalizations to guard against street crime sounds normal. A majority of blacks, when not in a moralistic mode, would agree. They too know that such simplifications are essential to survival. Elijah Anderson,[37] in explicating how blacks and whites interact in public, cites Erving Goffman[38] as his authority for declaring that "In negotiating public spaces, people receive and display a wide range of behavioral cues and signs that make up the vocabulary of public interaction. Skin color, gender, age, companions, clothing, jewelry, and the objects people carry help identify them, so that assumptions are formed and communication can occur." In other words, simplified symbols are the currency of our everyday transactions.

Writing about interracial encounters in an integrated neighborhood, Anderson describes the sorts of indicators to which people resort. As he tells it, distrustful of blacks, "White newcomers continue to view the ghetto as a mysterious and unfathomable place that breeds drugs, crime, prostitution, unwed mothers, ignorance, and mental illness. It symbolizes persistent poverty and imminent danger, personified in the young black men who walk [its] streets." For them "Common racist stereotypes persist, and black men who successfully make such disavowals are often seen not as the norm but as the exception—as 'different from the rest'—thereby confirming the status of the 'rest.'" Needless to say, blacks resent these pigeonholes, but for whites they are the stuff of everyday experience. Anderson relates the following case:

> On a Wednesday afternoon in June at about 2:00, Sandra Norris pushed her nine-month-old daughter down Cherry Street. The gray stone facades of the Victorian buildings sparkled in the sun. The streets seemed deserted, as the Village usually is at this time. Suddenly, three black youths appeared. They looked in their late teens. As they approached her, one of the young men yelled to the others, "Let's get her!" Making sexual gestures, two of the youths reached for her menacingly. She cringed and pulled the stroller toward her. At that, the boys laughed loudly. They were playing with her, but the feigned attack was no fun for Mrs. Norris. It left her shaking.

Most observers would regard Mrs. Norris' response as neither irrational nor prejudiced. The potential for harm was so great that refusing to take its signs seriously would have been illogical. As significantly, the perpetrators knew this and reveled in the distress they aroused. Anger and a sense of powerlessness may have driven them to exploit what they recognized as the likely response, but they would not have chosen this avenue of attack had they not shared the same vocabulary of threat as she. As Anderson reports, "In some cases black males capitalize on the fear they know they can evoke. They may 'put on a swagger' and intimidate those who must momentarily share a small space on the sidewalk." They may also "confront others with behavior they refer to as 'gritting,' 'looking mean,' 'looking hard,' and 'bumping.'" As he explains, "Out of a sense of frustration, [they] mock or otherwise insult the whites they see in public places, trying to 'get even' with them for being part of the 'monolithic' group of whites."

This confirms that both blacks and whites are aware of black stereotypes and that both may manipulate or be manipulated by them. What may not be as apparent is that were there no underlying basis for their conceptions, whites would not be as vulnerable to intimidation, nor blacks as attracted to public displays of coercion. Less obvious still is that blacks utilize stereotypes in assessing other blacks. Because they too operate in an environment of uncertainty, in which most "soul-brothers" are actually strangers, they have no choice. Again, to quote Anderson, "blacks tend to relate cautiously to unknown black youths, [and] are inclined to look at them longer, inspecting them and noting their business to see whether they deserve to be trusted." Whites, it must be admitted, because they have less personal exposure to blacks, tend toward cruder stereotypes, but then too, black stereotypes of whites are coarse instruments.[39] As Anderson puts it, "whites...are anything but a monolithic group....But it is convenient for certain blacks to see things this way, placing all whites, whom they see as the source of their troubles, into an easily manageable bag." Anderson has doubts about the validity of the procedure, noting that "In this way, blacks as well as whites become victims of simplistic thinking," yet its universality suggests that it provides a crucial service. Though a little knowledge may be a dangerous thing, it supplies more protection than none at all.

This is not to say that stereotypes are an unalloyed good. Their ability to furnish direction in moments of ignorance is offset by a tendency to point the wrong way. Another of my colleagues, Nurudeem Akenymi, a political scientist originally from Nigeria, has more than once expressed annoyance at being warily scrutinized when shopping at the local department stores. A college professor with the income and inclination to pay for his purchases, he resents being associated with other blacks merely because of his skin color. What, he wonders, is the point of achieving success if you get no credit for it? The same sentiments are often expressed by other prosperous blacks upon being pulled over by the police for such infractions as driving an expensive automobile through an upscale neighborhood.[40] Yet what are the police or commercial security guards to do? The profiles[41] they use work precisely because they are drawn from reality. Skin color is, in fact, correlated with shoplifting, drug-dealing, and auto theft. Taking it into account does, therefore, improve the odds of uncovering illegal activity. As unsatisfying as this may be to acknowledge, it is a case where no one is in the wrong. Those mistakenly accused of a crime because of a misapplied stereotype certainly have the right to resent it, but just as certainly those charged with controlling legal infractions have a duty to utilize whatever information increases their ability to apprehend the bad guys.

Historically, of course, the descendants of African slaves have been subject to more than their quota of unflattering labels. Originally considered "happy, but irresponsible children" whose limitations destined them for indentured servitude, both before and after the Civil War, their supposed shortcomings were employed to justify the worst sorts of cruelty. More recently, these libels have become a self-enforced trap. Claude Steele,[42] the brother of Shelby Steele, has made us aware of the pitfalls of "stereotype vulnerability." His investigations into how people react to being characterized as inept provide evidence that simplified group identifiers have unintended side effects. If people give credence to an image of themselves, their subsequent behaviors can be shaped by it. When such representations are positive, there is no difficulty, but when they are negative, the implications can be devastating. Among blacks this propensity can be seen in teenagers, who, because they believe—not unlike others physically similar to themselves—they can be gifted basketball players, practice the sport until they become proficient, yet who, because they doubt their intellectual capacities, do not put as much effort into preparing for IQ tests.

But there is another connection here, one that is fundamental to the practice of social ranking. As Claude Steele's researches demonstrate, minorities can succumb to "stereotype threats."[43] Convinced by their own faith in the conventional stereotypes, when reminded of them, they tend to do less well than they are able. As we shall later see, this vulnerability to a tainted social reputation is one of the ways in which status hierarchies are maintained. No doubt some may conclude that this is an argument for dismantling such hierarchies, but if, as seems likely, we human beings are naturally hierarchical, the real challenge is to learn how to use these mechanisms for one's own benefit. Rather than be intimidated by one's perceived weaknesses, one can instead discover how to generate a reputation for being a winner.

WHOSE OX?

With the balance between utility and dis-utility as precarious as it is, deciding whether a particular stereotype falls within allowable limits can be a matter of whose ox is gored. When on the receiving end of an insulting characterization, a person may become indignant whether or not it is accurate. By the same token, when on the transmitting end, even the most dire consequences can seem trivial. Most of us do not consider ourselves bigots, hence we choose to believe in the validity of assessments consistent with our biases. Paradoxically, although she would bridle at the suggestion, Jane Elliott reveled in stereotyping. Her characterizations of Southerners, Baptists, and heterosexuals, despite their gross naiveté, were excused by her, and her audience, as justified by these other's moral failings. If told that her raillery offended those at whom it was aimed, she would have smiled and asserted that it was appropriate in light of their villainy. She would not have agreed that it was too simplistic.

With stereotypes, mistakes are notoriously easy to make. In addition to our proclivity to credit only what is favorable to us, generalizations, in general, are sloppy instruments whose exaggerated reach habitually exposes them to error. So does their propensity to build on conspicuous social indicators. Derived as they invariably are from limited information, the differing salience of various pieces of data become critical to their construction. Not surprisingly, that which is dramatic and emotionally gripping tends to monopolize our attention and, therefore, to dominate our imaginations. Since it fills our cognitive space, it appears more representative than it actually is.[44] This is not a personal flaw, but a universal human inclination. It is why when my classes are asked about Jewish stereotypes, someone usually says "religious." Typically the students who do so come from a rural area where there are few Jews. They seldom have an opportunity to discover that Jews are among the least religious Americans. What intervenes in their imaginations are media images of identifiable members of the group, for example, the Hasidim. This minority's long beards, dark clothing, and ubiquitous yarmulkes constitute an arresting ensemble that makes them seem more prevalent than they are. For similar reasons the large number of blacks nowadays appearing on our television screens leads many people to overestimate their proportion of the total population.

Moral salience has similar effects. Crime, for example, commands our attention. The threat it represents causes people to note its presence, even when it is atypical. Whether we like it or not, immoral behavior is often dangerous and, therefore, fear provoking. As a result, moral prominence can distort what is perceived; ergo the white conviction that most blacks are criminals. Yet the same mechanism applies to blacks. When they discern a CIA plot behind the crack epidemic, or speculate that AIDS was introduced into their communities for genocidal reasons, or argue that the Tuskegee studies wherein black subjects suffering from syphilis were denied suitable drug treatments were intended to wipe out African-Americans,[45] more neutral observers perceive a black paranoia. They recognize, in each of these cases, a white indifference to black suffering, rather than a homicidal conspiracy. In this instance blacks are assuredly wrong, but only on a factual, not a moral, plane. The indignities to which they have been subject understandably convince them that the abominations are deeper and more widespread than they in fact are.

To this must be added the effects of luminosity blindness.[46] Hopes, as well as fears, can deform our judgment. When people become transfixed by an ideal, it can take on a glowing reality that prevents an accurate assessment of what is at issue. The vision of a more perfect world becomes so radiant that its devotees fail to perceive its blemishes. This penchant for error does not, however, demand that stereotypes be extirpated. Although their employment may be at odds with our view of how the world should work, to eliminate them would be a classic illustration of throwing the baby out with the bath water. Besides being impossible to achieve, the resultant lack of discrimination would be as egregious as the errors thereby rejected. First, as psychologists have demonstrated, exhorting people not to stereotype can actually make such generalizations more salient.[47] It is like asking them to stop thinking of an elephant. Second, many stereotypes are reasonably accurate and hence their summary rejection would further remove us from reality.[48] What is necessary instead is to utilize them with care. That which is dangerous need not be excluded, merely handled with discretion.

Since a tendency to error is present on all sides, mutual tolerance is in order. Those transgressed upon by a damaging overgeneralization must be aware not only of having been libeled, but of why. When a mistake has been made by someone who has reason to make it, this ought to be taken into consideration. Years ago, when I was a college undergraduate, I had a summer job selling encyclopedias. Going door to door in the Bronx, I recited a prepackaged sales pitch that ended in asking for a return appointment if I discovered that the man of the house was not present. The purpose of this was to reassure a lone female that I did not intend her harm. Nevertheless, when I came back to one apartment house, there in the lobby was a police officer who was looking for a young man with a beard who had been terrorizing the building. I was apparently that young man. At first, I was incredulous. As a gentle soul who meant no one any ill, I could not understand the consternation. But the more I reflected upon the matter, the more clearly I realized that the ladies who found me threatening did not know me. They regarded my newly sprouted goatee as the emblem of a social misfit whose motives were questionable. Since this was the beginning of the 1960s, they associated it with beatniks and street-level thugs. Upon reflection, I understood why and was less affronted. Might not the average black come to a similar conclusion when his appearance and location are such that a white female stranger questions his trustworthiness? Isn't it true that an unknown African-American male represents a legitimate cause for concern?

Fortunately we human beings can learn from experience. When grievously wrong, stereotypes can be corrected.[49] They may seem eternal, but have a way of fading into obscurity when the ground-level facts change. It is these, and often these alone, that provide the occasion for people to revise their generalizations. Contrary to the socialization thesis, the salience of new information, rather than moralistic injunctions, is what is most likely to modify our opinions. Thus, the danger that men with beards were thought to represent declined once beards came into fashion. Another graphic example of the connection between facts and images is the case of black quarterbacks. In the 1950s, the conventional wisdom was that "Negroes" were not intelligent enough to run a football team.[50] In recent decades, however, the success of figures such as Warren Moon and Randall Cunningham has been such that one almost never hears the claim today. Had these athletes been "tokens" who could not perform, the outcome would have been the different. A time-worn estimate would have been confirmed and the public persuaded that blacks were not up to the task. A related alchemy awaits appraisals of black criminality. When black crime rates decline, when young black men no longer commit several times more robberies and murders than young white men, the judgment made of ordinary blacks will also be transformed. As significantly, when more blacks are economically successful, estimates of their social class status will rise accordingly. Ordinary people will perceive unknown blacks as more substantial figures who will then receive greater respect.

Nonetheless, the impulse to engage in race-based propaganda can be overwhelming. Unacceptable images are banned and more edifying ones promulgated in their place. The enemies of stereotyping may be scandalized by the suggestion, but they often engage in nothing less than reverse stereotyping. Just as Adolf Hitler and his minions sought to enhance images of noble, blond-haired German supermen, so contemporary Civil Rights moralists sponsor Black History months to celebrate black achievements. As long as such simplifications are used for educational purposes, they are a benign form of political theater. Still, the line into coercive manipulation is easy to cross. People with good intentions may not imagine themselves going too far, but this is because they are oblivious to their excesses. Illustrative of such overindulgence is a policy advocated by Mark Willes,[51] publisher of *The Los Angeles Times*. In 1998, he told *The Wall Street Journal* that he intended to set goals for the number of women and minorities quoted in his newspaper. Because he wished to encourage the perception that these groups are as knowledgeable as others, he would require his reporters to select experts by their affiliations. To their credit, most of his staff found this proposal chilling. They believed experts should be chosen for their expertise. As frighteningly, this sort of unenlightened do-goodism is not an aberration. John Leo writes that "One such checklist that has been making the rounds at various newspapers asks, 'Am I furthering stereotypes as I seek diversity?' and 'Am I battling stereotypes?'" "Both," he rightly interjects, "are very peculiar questions implying that reporters are properly engaged in social engineering, not just newsgathering." To euphemize this procedure by calling it "mainstreaming" or "diversity friendly," as is sometimes done, does not obscure the grim implications. One need only imagine the tactic in the hands of the Nazis. For them the quotas imposed would be in terms of Aryan descent and the stereotype suppressed that of the "good Jew."

On a more reassuring note, a complete denial of the facts upon which stereotypes rest is nigh on impossible. However extensive the propaganda, it cannot alter the realities. "Facts are stubborn things," John Adams once declared, and that has not changed in more than two centuries. What is, is, and pretending that it is not, cannot alter this, although it can interfere with a rational response. People can be coerced into presenting their opinions in a specified manner and acting as if falsehoods were true. Happily, our private convictions are not so easily governed. Readily cloaked from prying eyes, they can be sustained in secret. Contemporary attitudes toward black crime confirm this. It used to be routine for media outlets to state the race of an alleged perpetrator but, because the preponderance of black culprits was said to be biasing the public against the innocent, the practice was discontinued. This has not, however, persuaded people that fewer blacks are committing crimes. More subtle cues, such as names and the locations of events, combined with information passed through informal channels, perpetuate what is ironically a more accurate appraisal than the reformers prefer. These idealists find themselves in the position of Communist Party commissars who after almost a century of robust propaganda could not convince the Russian people that they were more prosperous than Westerners.

A more promising approach to containing the harmful effects of stereotypes lies in how they are applied. The primary problem is not that people harbor them, or even that they use them to judge others, but that they do so in an inflexible manner. Mistakes, for the most part, become mistakes only when they are not corrected. Once adjustments have been made, initial mis-steps can be converted into stepping-stones to greater awareness. Thus, when stereotypes are employed as first approximations in situations in which little other information is available, they can be functional even when they are wrong. If they operate, as it were, like hypotheses intended to direct one's attention toward some areas rather than others, they can be illuminating. It is when they cease being regarded as postulates and are treated as immutable facts that the trouble arises. They may then be upheld in the face of contradictory data. Rather than guide people in discovering relevant information about an unknown person, they now erect barriers that make fictions seem real.

In other words, it is when stereotypes interfere with particularizing[52] the given case that they cause problems. If, for instance, one assumes that Colin Powell[53] must be a good dancer because all blacks have rhythm, by his own testimony, one would be wrong. While the original assumption is excusable, retaining it after learning this fact is not. Competent adults have to be flexible enough to adjust to changing information. They must individuate their responses rather than be trapped by appearances derived from other circumstances. The latter strategy is problematic because it regards a three-dimensional human being as a symbol even when his flesh and blood self is available for examination.

Given the way the world works, it takes emotional courage to deal with it on its own terms. But doing so is imperative. People can be disappointing and even depraved, but, to repeat, what is, is. If one's friends are capable of shallow self-interest and one's enemies of magnanimous profundity, this may be difficult to accept, yet the alternative is worse, for it entails ratifying a fantasy. This is why it makes more sense to develop the fortitude to handle reality in its raw form, rather than to sugar-coat it with wrappings that may dissolve in a heavy rain.

Perhaps the most difficult to remedy of the negative effects of stereotyping are those that flow from a damaged self-image. Many who seek to eliminate stereotyping hope that its absence will stimulate positive socialization in vulnerable minorities. They assume that if the young are not told that people like them have limitations, they will not impute these to themselves. The strategy is, however, nullified by the fact that minorities are already familiar with these stereotypes. They acquire them, not merely from members of the larger society, but from their own experience. African-American boys, for instance, do not have to be told that they are "athletic." They come to this conclusion from what they witness on the street and on TV.

The bottom line is that the most reliable strategy for altering stereotypes is to change the realities sustaining them. The case of black quarterbacks speaks eloquently to this point. Other adjustments, however, may be more difficult to achieve. A particularly troublesome area is school performance. It has not responded to demands for improvement, nor to truckloads of money squandered in search of amelioration. But even here the direct approach may be the most feasible. Minority academic achievement can be promoted, not by blinding ourselves to the weaknesses of a generation of children, but by holding them to the same standards as others. Only then will their self-images be improved, for only then will they be based on real accomplishments. In the words of George Will,[54] "What works is discipline, mutual respect, moral seriousness, high standards and not condescension dressed up as compassion."

Chapter 4

The American Creed

From the point of view of the American Creed the status accorded the Negro in America represents nothing more and nothing less than a century-long lag of public morals. In principle the Negro problem was settled long ago; in practice the solution is not effectuated.   Gunnar Myrdal, *An American Dilemma* (1944)

VALUES UNDER ASSAULT

A moral unease has crept into the American psyche. Political speeches, earnest books, and even fireside conversations are laced with speculation that our moral standards are in a state of decay. A nostalgia for the "good old days," when it was possible to leave one's front door unlocked, is contrasted with a rise in drive-by shootings and "gangsta" rap. Comparisons with the decline of the Roman Empire spring to mind and we wonder if we too are experiencing the sort of decadence Edward Gibbon[1] so richly recorded. Has the pre-eminence of being the world's only remaining superpower allowed us to lose our bearings and encouraged us to devote ourselves to profligate pleasures—the equivalent, as it were, of dining on peacock tongues and quail eggs?

Some, such as Robert Samuelson,[2] believe that this portrait is overdrawn. They blame it on a rampant historical ignorance and a self-pity born of prosperity. Our complaints, they say, are on a par with those of a hypochondriac who has the opportunity to pretend they are real precisely because the good life he is living frees him from more legitimate concerns. Others, like Francis Fukuyama,[3] are genuinely disturbed. They contemplate the rising incidence of crime and the soaring rates of family dissolution, and perceive a moral disruption of historic proportions. These, they insist, are not figments of our collective imagination. As a result, they search for explanations. What has led to this coarsening of our civic institutions, and, just as importantly, what can be done to salvage them?

Among the more pessimistic observers is the historian Gertrude Himmelfarb.[4] Her studies of Victorian England convinced her that comparisons between then and now reveal a precipitous decline in social standards. Citing ballooning levels of crime and illegitimacy, she frets that the fabric of today's society is unraveling at a dizzying pace. Himmelfarb begins by noting that "In nineteenth century England, the illegitimacy ratio—the proportion of out-of-wedlock births to the total births—rose from a little over 5 percent at the beginning of the century to a peak of 7 percent in 1845. It then fell steadily until it was less than 4 percent at the turn of the century." Strongly proscribed by middle-class opinion leaders, pregnancies among the unmarried fell below their previous average even in the country's poorest sections (e.g., East London). In the United States, where similar attitudes prevailed, the trends were comparable. Though precise nineteenth century figures are not available, a tendency toward sexual continence predominated well into the twentieth century. As she remarks, "Starting at 3 percent in 1920 (the first year for which there are national statistics), the illegitimacy ration rose gradually to slightly over 5 percent by 1960...." As late as the 1950s, it was still regarded as scandalous for an unmarried woman to become pregnant and she might be sent out of town to avoid the damage that would otherwise be done to her, and her family's, reputation. The disgrace was potentially so severe that when Ricky Nelson, 50s teenage icon, and scion of the nation's poster family for traditional values, fathered a child born only seven months after he and his wife wed, the hospital records were altered to indicate that the birth was premature.

A dramatic shift occurred sometime after 1960. Statistics disclose the rate of illegitimacy grew abruptly "to almost 11 percent in 1970, over 18 percent in 1980, and 30 percent by 1991—a tenfold increase from 1920 and a six fold increase from 1960...." Though these figures surged in virtually every segment of society, they grew most starkly among the poor, where now more than one child in three can claim to be born of an unwed mother. In the black community, things are worse—with more the two out of three children suffering this fate. Apparently, where once the stigma attached to unmarried parenthood was a potent source of social control, ordinary people have today become more concerned about the devastation inflicted upon the teenage mother and her child. Why, they reason, should one mistake cause a vulnerable girl and her still more vulnerable infant to be ostracized and their entire futures put in jeopardy? It is much better to be broad-minded and assist them in overcoming whatever human frailty led to this pass. The consequence, of course, is a tolerance of casual sexuality.

Another dramatic shift lamented by Himmelfarb is crime levels. Despite a dearth of accurate nineteenth century data it is evident that until very recently an astonishing escalation of serious law-breaking has occurred. Best documented are homicide frequencies—at the beginning of the century "The national rate was 1.2 per 100,000 population. That figure skyrocketed during prohibition, reaching as high as 9.7 by one account (6.7 by another) in 1933, when prohibition was repealed. The rate dropped to between five and six during the 1940s and to under five in the fifties and early sixties. In the mid-sixties, it started to climb rapidly, more than doubling between 1965 and 1980...." This means that by the 1980s people were killing each other with more abandon than in the heyday of Al Capone and the Tommy gun. Incredibly, the homocide rate was more than ten times higher than when the frontier was closing and cowboy gunfighters roamed the countryside.

The question thus becomes: Why has this happened? Why have so many people become so apparently blasé about what would seem to be a legitimate cause of alarm? Himmelfarb attributes much of this transformation to a decline in our moral standards. Deliberately entitling her book *The De-Moralization of Society: From Victorian Virtues to Modern Values,* she believes that we are, in a real sense, less moral. Where once our ancestors were preoccupied with making moral choices, today we are less concerned with doing so. Certainly we discuss moral rules less often, are less bothered by nagging consciences, and are more tolerant of egregious violations. In Himmelfarb's view, we have been "defining deviance down." Citing Senator Daniel Patrick Moynihan's[5] seminal article of the same name, she writes that "What was once regarded as deviant behavior is no longer so regarded: what was once deemed abnormal has been normalized." To be specific, a gradually increasing exposure to drive-by shootings, unwed pregnancies, and mental patients sprawled on heating grates has prompted many of us to reconceptualize these as "random violence," "single parenthood," and "homelessness." Unflappable even in the face of accumulating outrages, like the man whose hand is immersed in a tub of imperceptibly warming water, our flesh may be parboiled, but we fail to notice.

Amazingly, this state of affairs is not only accepted, but excused. Stephanie Coontz,[6] for one, has denounced Victorian families as both an aberration and a myth. She claims that their emphasis on stable nuclear attachments was belied by the many families torn asunder by premature death. In a society swept by crippling epidemics and dependent on medical care that killed millions of mothers from septicemia during childbirth, the notion that a husband and wife must collaborate in lovingly raising their children was more a hope than a reality. As dangerously, its glorification in modern times reflects a desire to denigrate non-Western traditions and to seduce women into renouncing their right to success outside the home. What Coontz recommends instead is a "multicultural" standard that respects diversity and that refuses to impose a debilitating fantasy on the unsuspecting.

Both David Popenoe[7] and James Q. Wilson[8] would disagree. Popenoe presents a strong case for the nuclear family. After assembling massive amounts of evidence, he concludes that absent a father and a mother who are committed to each other and to their children, the latter suffer. They grow up less confident, more poorly prepared for academic and social success, and handicapped in their quest for a secure relationship with a devoted spouse. This leads him to argue that we should not reject the value placed on loving families, nor cease enforcing it. Wilson would second this motion, but he expands on it by pointing to the necessity of enforcing rules in general. He has observed that when a society allows small transgressions to pass unnoticed, larger ones multiply. If, for example, the citizens of a city, let us say New York, rationalize subway graffiti as "street art," they not only find their public transport encased in spray paint; they also get a higher murder rate.

The fraying of our social fabric may thus be explained partly by a loss of important rules and partly by the less energetic enforcement of those we retain. This view emphasizes both the damage done by lowering the social bar and a decline in our capacity to make anything stick. It argues that as ours has become a Gesellschaft society, that is, a large, impersonal, and market-oriented one, the bonds that once linked us together have loosened, thereby depriving us of the power of a united community.[9] Where our ancestors lived in villages and neighborhoods in which they freely interacted with one another, we now pass each other on the street without recognition or shared commitment. This lack of solidarity prevents us from joining together to sanction wrong-doers or to revere heroes. Instead, we agree only to leave each other alone.[10] Thus, when a U.S. President engages in what in years past would have been regarded as an illicit sexual act, the first reaction is that it is no one's business but his and his wife's.[11] The exquisite irony here is, of course, that not long before she[12] had touted the notion that "it takes a village" to raise a child.

The sociologist Amatai Etzioni[13] surveying this situation has diagnosed the problem as a need to reaffirm our sense of community. The guiding spirit of the Communitarian movement, he envisions this as a revived commitment to traditional values and to time-tested institutions. He would like to restore law and order, family authority, and quality schools, and implores his readers to create "a new moral, social, and public order, based on restored communities." After enumerating our shared values, he invites people to participate in reinstating their prominence. Instead of submitting to a world of too many rights and too few responsibilities, we must not be ashamed to become "each other's keepers." After all, "Neither human existence nor individual liberty can be sustained for long outside the interdependent and overlapping communities to which we all belong."

Others too have been persuaded of the urgency of reanimating civil society. As one of these, Wolfe[14] contrasts the limitations of governmental and economic institutions with the promise of civic ones. A vibrant morality, he insists, cannot be entrusted to rigid political structures or rapacious market processes, but depends on the day-to-day activities of private persons acting from their personal convictions. Only these offer the prospect of sensitive human concern and true helpfulness. Frank Hearn[15] likewise endorses the virtue of strengthened civil institutions. He fears that, unless we develop what he calls "social capital," people will be bad parents and bad neighbors. Harking back to Durkheim's[16] notion that society, by affirming its allegiance to particular standards, creates sacredness, and hence morality, he advocates a greater attention to things that count. Along with Wolfe and Etzioni, he supports social control through community interdependencies.

More specific still is Putnam.[17] He worries about what he terms "the strange disappearance of social capital and civic engagement in America." History, he argues, demonstrates that a vibrant democracy is contingent on a socially active citizenry. When "social networks, norms and trust" fall into disrepair, so does representative government. Putnam claims that people learn the skills necessary to participate in administering their fate—including upholding social rules—by doing so. He is thus alarmed by evidence of a decline in popular associations, and fears that signs of people more inclined to "bowl alone" or to engage in isolated television watching, portend a citizenry without the connections to defend their rights.

Relatively overlooked in these analyses is the changing nature of our social standards. Instead of blaming a lack of rules or a dearth in competent enforcement, this third interpretation ascribes most of the problem to a change in their content. In other words, it does not emphasize a loss of rules, or a diminution in their effectiveness, but rather a shift in their focus. Its claim is that fundamental standards have not so much disappeared as been replaced. Victorians may have believed that violent crime and casual infidelity are utterly unacceptable, but today these are considered lesser offenses. In short, it is our priorities that have changed. Society has not become immoral, amoral, or impotent, so much as it has reoriented its belief systems.

To be blunt, the content of a society's values do matter. When these shift, the consequences can be momentous. Who would deny the impact of Nazi standards of racial purity, Pol Pot's ideal of agrarian self-sufficiency, or the Afghani Taliban's bloodthirsty version of Islamic fundamentalism? The same considerations apply to the United States. Its adoption of a radical Civil Rights agenda has had moral implications that may not at first be obvious. Almost unobserved has been a cataclysmic shift in fundamental values, a shift pregnant with negative repercussions. To be more exact, as the nation's political leadership has become transfixed with instituting racial justice, the importance of *equality* has been drastically elevated, whereas that of *freedom* has been correspondingly reduced. Almost unseen, because it is obscured by the blindness endemic to intense moralism, the former has become our "master value." Others now languish in its shadow, invisible and unenforced, not because they are insignificant, but because their worth tends to go unrecognized. Old institutions remain as potent as ever, but their services are no longer used to support standards no longer perceived as salient.

During the 1963 March on Washington, Martin Luther King exulted "Free at last! Free at last! Thank God Almighty, we are free at last!," but it was not long before his disciples shifted gears. Jesse Jackson[18] has not shied away from asserting the primacy of equality. Arguing in defense of the poor and disenfranchised, by the 1980s he had come to believe that the Civil Rights movement needed to change its emphasis. With Jim Crow having been vanquished and voting rights established, economic security and business development assumed greater importance. Even King, before he was assassinated, became consumed with achieving economic parity. It need to be remembered that he was in Memphis to lend his prestige to a sanitation strike.

What must concern us here is that, in the name of morality, social reforms now encourage a myriad of evils.[19] Those pushing these forward notice only the virtues of equality and none of its liabilities. On the mistaken assumption that virtue is absolute and self-correcting, they promote alarming goals. In fact, an hierarchical society cannot be understood purely in terms of equity. Not only is this objective incapable of transforming the world as desired, but when employed exclusive of freedom, makes things much worse. Social responsibility, truth, and personal merit are thrown into decline, and a bogus Jeffersonian democracy is in danger of causing more suffering than it prevents.

EQUALITY FOR ALL

Absolute equality is a false God. As odd as it may seem, an excessive dedication to social balance can undermine personal happiness. When conceived in simplistic terms, as Myrdal[20] and many of his followers have done, it appears to have magical properties. They do not consider the possibility that total equality is impossible or, if achieved, might have negative ramifications. Indeed they seem not to have analyzed what "equality" means, assuming that once extended to former slaves, America's inherent contradictions would automatically be remedied. It is, therefore, essential to examine the significance of the concept, and, as importantly, its implications.

Central to Myrdal's version of the American Creed are the opening lines from the Declaration of Independence. As all American schoolchildren learn, they contain Jefferson's immortal words: *We hold these truths to be self-evident; that all men are created equal; that they are endowed by their creator with certain unalienable rights; that among these are life, liberty, and the pursuit of happiness.* Having attained the status of secular scripture, these are now infused with nearly sacred powers. Precisely what they imply may not be agreed upon, but evidently decreed by a divine source, they seem impossible to refute.

When Americans discuss "civil rights," those enumerated by Jefferson immediately spring to mind. Equality, life, liberty, and the pursuit of happiness are assumed to be everyone's birthright. Only the privileges conferred by the Bill of Rights rival them in our national pantheon, but, as derivative rights, are less compelling. It is further assumed that these warranties are mutually reinforcing, that the package is literally indivisible. But is this so? Are liberty and equality always mutually compatible? The place to begin answering this question is with an inquest into the meaning of "equality."

First, it is clear that no two people are exactly the same. Some are tall, some short; some smart, some dull. When defined as equivalence in all dimensions, equality is inarguably a fantasy. Certainly, in my sociology classes, not a single student has ever endorsed this sort of radical symmetry. Nor has anyone willingly defended the proposition that ours is a classless society. All acknowledge that some people have greater status, wealth, and power than others. So what can it mean to assert *that all men are created equal?* Back at Abraham Lincoln High School we were told that what the Declaration of Independence promised was equality of opportunity. Although, in a democracy, people might begin their journeys from different stations, all had the prospect of going as far as their talents would allow.

At Brooklyn College, however, this "truth" was called into question. As my political science professor assured us, opportunity was unequally distributed. Since those born into wealthier families received better educations, superior credit references, and access to more lucrative social networks, they started with advantages that improved their life chances. Given all this, equality was redefined as equal protection under the laws. Democracy, it was now declared, encompasses a legal system that makes no distinctions between persons, with everyone subject to the same public ordinances administered by the same legal machinery. Later on, of course, this thesis too was challenged. In graduate school we were informed that there was in fact a lack of uniform treatment in the courts and by police departments. Those born to privilege were shown to have the means of bending the law to their own purposes. They could afford the attorneys, the political influence, and even the time to take advantage of its loopholes and technicalities.

But if these formulations were not satisfactory, is there one that is? It may help to consider what Jefferson meant. His stirring words have proven a rhetorical treasure, yet on a material level, what do they imply? The less than gratifying answer seems to be that as abstractions, they are insubstantial. Political language is often designed to obscure difficulties and this, above all, is what Jefferson accomplished. The document that so many of us regard as an inspired recipe for democracy was from its beginnings a piece of civic propaganda. Although Jefferson was sincere, the proclamation's goal was to persuade people of the legitimacy of a war for independence that had already commenced. It was not, as some have read it, a detailed political treatise. Moreover, Jefferson's by now well documented capacity for self-deception render his later statements about its meaning unreliable. In the words of the historian Joseph Ellis,[21] Jefferson had an "affinity for idealized or idyllic visions, and the parallel capacity to deny evidence that exposed them as illusory." More a thinker than a doer, he could be astonishingly impractical. We, who are his political progeny, have thus been bequeathed a standard that is inherently imprecise. As a consequence, when we try to iron out its contradictions, we fail not from a want of effort, but from a want of an empirical referent.

One thing is clear: the equality to which Jefferson alluded was a moral equality.[22] An examination of the language of the Declaration reveals that the respect in which men were said to be the same was in the inalienable "rights" with which they were endowed. Rights, if they are anything, are moral entities. They are not empirical facts. Were they such, it would make no sense to insist they are "self-evident." In this Jefferson was following the natural law tradition. As a patrician trained in the theories of John Locke and the French philosophes, he believed, as per Locke's social compact assumptions, that in order to secure natural rights "governments are instituted among men, deriving their just powers from the consent of the governed." In other words, everyone was born with identical claims to freedom and happiness.

Still, the problem remains in translating this moral equivalence into a civic reality. It is one thing to assert an identical entitlement to happiness, but quite another to convert this into hard facts. The lack of a universal assembly in which everyone has an equal voice or an agreed upon mode of calculating just deserts ensure widespread social wrangling and a host of nagging inequities. Jefferson's response to this predicament is discernible in a statement he sent to a ceremony honoring the fiftieth anniversary of Independence. In it he observed that "The mass of mankind has not been born with saddles on their backs, nor a favored few, booted and spurred, ready to ride them legitimately, by the grace of God." This arresting image suggests nothing less than a maternity ward crowded with innocent babies, unclothed and indistinguishable in terms of relative power. It is not, however, descriptive of the material world.

Jefferson seems to have imagined that with everyone starting at the same point, we would all arrive at the same destination, that is, if the government did not intervene by favoring some over others. His ideal was of an agrarian nation composed of independent yeoman farmers, sovereign on their own plots of land and secure from a federal establishment too weak to make its writ felt in their neighborhoods. Today this vision creaks from an outdated romanticism. Almost no one imagines that it might literally apply to an urbanized, industrialized society with a polyglot population and multicultural roots. But it was mythological even in Jefferson's time. As a scion of Virginia's tidewater aristocracy, he should have been aware that some people have advantages that are convertible into disparities of power. More genuinely democratic onlookers, such as John Adams,[23] knew this, but Jefferson rationalized his naiveté by placing his faith in an "aristocracy of talent." If some obtained greater respect because of their accomplishments, this was fair and not to be confused with unearned forms of social priority.

Contemporary equality theorists have likewise had difficulty reconciling an abstract moral equivalence with undeniable differences in social status. Possessed of a Rousseau-like faith in the elemental goodness of human beings that implies that when left on their own people will automatically respect the rights of others, they nevertheless seek a more substantial expression of equality than universal good will. This they often find in economics. One of the more poignant incarnations of this notion is the so-called "American Dream." In its simplest manifestation this is the belief that everyone in America has the right to get rich. Presumably why millions of immigrants crossed broad oceans, Jennifer Hochschild[24] has analyzed the dream as comprised of four premises, to wit: (1) success is open to everyone; (2) significant accomplishments, though not guaranteed, can be reasonably anticipated; (3) the individual holds the keys to these in his or her own hands; and finally (4) the pursuit of economic success is a virtuous endeavor. Added together these suggest that financial advancement awaits every decent human being. If he or she does not attain it, this reflects badly on him. The person is thus assumed to bear the moral responsibility for failure. But, muses Hochschild, this is unfair to members of minority groups. African-Americans, in particular, confront obstacles that have nothing to do with their individual efforts.

Considerations such as this have led to a redefinition of equality intended to ground it in tangible indicators of economic or political advancement. Equality is now said to be absent unless people have demonstrably equivalent achievements. As early as the 1960s social activists lobbied to have schools reorganized on the basis of "equal results."[25] Asymmetrical educational treatment was allegedly confirmed by differences in achievement tests and college admission rates. These, however, were impossible to compare on an individual level. Inserted in their stead therefore were group results. Thus, if a particular racial, ethnic, or gender cohort did not exhibit the same proportion of success, inequality was declared to be manifest. Herein lay the seeds of social quotas and group-oriented affirmative action. By assuming that only equal percentages of group participation affirmed genuinely equal opportunities, the die was cast for the government to redistribute social rewards coercively.

The inadvertent result has been to transform a vague Jeffersonian imperative into a neo-Marxist one. In its classic formulation Marxism[26] insists that the world is destined for a communist utopia in which there will be no governments and where everyone is to become so selfless that each voluntarily gives to each according to his needs and takes from each according to his abilities. The image promulgated is of a proletariat resplendently free of capitalist chains, clasping hands in a universal brotherhood of dignity and enlightenment, and singing in one grand, unified chorus. Thomas Sowell has highlighted the extremism of this vision by labeling it a quest for "cosmic justice."[27] The goal here has evidently drifted away from comparable political and economic rights to total parity in all measurable dimensions. As Sowell asserts, however, this is a daydream. The real world is such that it is impossible for all goods to be equally divided all of the time.

As one might suspect, a devotion to such cosmic justice casts capitalism, with its emphasis on selfishness and private property, in the role of villain. According to the radical egalitarians, were its ruling cabal of self-interested business-types overthrown, and thereby prevented from submerging those they exploit, the causes of conflict and self-aggrandizement would disappear. If this seems overdrawn, and not applicable to black-white relations, the writings of Harold Cruse[28] demonstrate that a significant proportion of black intellectuals have been deeply influenced by collectivist theories that they perceive as fulfilling their longing for a world from which all hierarchical distinctions are banished.

Perhaps the gentlest interpretation of the equality ideal is that of Paul Sniderman.[29] He harks back to a concept associated with Talcott Parsons,[30] that is, *universalism*. Most Americans want a world in which the same rules apply to all. Obviously related to the notion of equality under the law, universalism is broader in that it refers to social norms of all sorts. The idea is that distinctions such as race, gender, and wealth are irrelevant to the operation of these standards. Although perfection in this is unattainable, it is an endpoint for which we must strive. Equality, in this sense, is an asymptotic aspiration never fully realized. Given the imperfections inherent in human ranking systems, gaping injustices never fully disappear. The best that is possible is to guard against the more egregious violations of equal treatment. Historically this has meant a rough equality before the common law, one man-one vote in general elections, and a public etiquette that discourages displays of social deference.

Before concluding our survey of the meaning of equality, it is essential to consider two of its corollaries. The first is *"niceness."* Many of those who insist on total equality also assume that all human beings are basically the same. The only reason they behave differently is that they have been treated differently, that is, if environmental disparities were eliminated, all residual distinctions would evaporate. In psychological and educational circles this has led to a faith in the value of rewards.[31] Punishment is said to bring out the worst in people. The basic assumption, though it is rarely formulated as such, is that if one is nice to other people, they will be nice in return. This supposedly applies to everyone, including criminals, for we are all theoretically blameless at birth.

A second corollary of radical equality is *"tolerance."* We are told that even though people have divergent beliefs and customs, all are deserving of dignity. Instead of condemning that which is strange, it ought to be revered, with the resultant diversity recognized as a good in itself. All of us are thus supposed to tend to our own knitting and allow others to do the same. To fail to do so is condemned as a form of discrimination. It is to make the mistake of being ethnocentric. Rather, one must be nonjudgmental[32] and allow those with different visions to pursue them unmolested. Those familiar with the anthropological literature will recognize this as a version of cultural relativism.[33] Most scholars make a distinction between the teachings of Franz Boas[34] and Edvard Westermarck.[35] Boas taught that cultures can be understood only in their own context, whereas Westermarck wrote that the ethical beliefs of every society are equally valid when judged on their own terms. In practice, however, the two tend to blend, with the advocates of both asserting that no one has the right to condemn another's commitments. There is even a tendency to glorify that which was once dismissed as "primitive." Its simplicity is lauded as "pure" in a way that modern mass societies presumably are not.

In his book on racism D'Souza[36] roundly denounced this disposition as transforming all negative judgments of African-American culture into forms of prejudice. Rather than consider the possibility that some behavioral patterns are dysfunctional, it automatically assumes that those doing the judging have nefarious motives. In this case, extreme tolerance is stubbornly intolerant of those who frown on it. Loury,[37] for instance, has attacked D'Souza for presenting a weak anthropological argument that he claims makes "a horrific error by suggesting that blacks in an urban ghetto are part of a culture separate from the rest of America." To imply that blacks are more like Australian aborigines than their white peers is, to his mind, insulting.

The real pathology found in inner-city America is the pathology of white racism. Its viciousness has only called forth a reasonable defensive strategy. What the champions of relativism neglect to acknowledge is that theirs is an elitist stance. Though promulgating what they perceive as a form of egalitarianism, they claim the right to determine what is acceptable. Paradoxically, as earlier discussed, despite their assertions of being nonjudgmental, they consider black behavioral patterns normal and white ones destructive.

LIBERTY FOR ALL

Lost in the confusion about the meaning of equality is the desirability of freedom. The Jeffersonian formulation regarding our equal right to liberty is taken as foreclosing conflicts between the two. It is even assumed that they mean the same. Yet the truth is otherwise. Liberty has a different referent and different implications. Its significance is, however, often as misunderstood as that of equality. In consequence, its definition too must be investigated. Only then may its benefits and prerequisites be recognized for what they are.

Ironically, although every school child is familiar with the chant that "This is a free country," those who take this too literally with respect to race relations are likely to be reproached as fascists. If they are business-types, they are accused of rationalizing their greed; if religiously oriented, of being retrograde fanatics; if political, as using code words to promote invidious distinctions. Far from commended as defenders of the American Dream, they are reproached for undermining it. Hochschild[38] would have us believe that the essence of this dream is an opportunity to get rich, but others perceive it as an opportunity to live in peace, undisturbed by those who would force them to be what they were not. They would also argue that America's historic commitment to freedom is responsible for the blessings of democracy and prosperity.

The fact is that without free choice, democracy is an empty phrase. By the same token, without an ability to make personal decisions, market economics is a charade. A government based on majority rule and an economy grounded on individual initiative are impossible in the absence of an unfettered citizenry. As the course of the twentieth century has proven, systems dependent upon centralized decision making are vulnerable to the good will of those doing the deciding.[39] No matter how unsullied their intentions, as Lord Acton[40] warned, power corrupts and absolute power corrupts absolutely. Worse still, no centralized authority can understand the wants and needs of all those it attempts to direct. These are always too complex and too fluid to be fully comprehended. Liberal philosophers such as John Rawls[41] may speculate about decisions made in accord with the dictates of an objective observer, but in the real world, no one has the ability to stand apart and dispassionately judge a society in its entirety. The result, in the worst cases, is nothing short of the totalitarianism of which Friedrich von Hayek[42] warned.

Fortunately, many of the founders of the American Republic recognized these dangers.[43] In their efforts to guard against tyranny, they assumed that an absolute monarch and an absolute public would be equally unsafe. The one might arbitrarily impose his will, but so might the other if a single faction became dominant. John Adams[44] wrote that "My opinion is, and always has been, that absolute power intoxicates alike despots, monarchs, aristocrats, and democrats, and jacobins, and sans culottes." The solution was the "checks and balances" system so effectively incorporated into the Constitution by James Madison.[45] Because the founders believed that selfishness was an ineluctable fact of human nature, they sought to limit the potential mischief by controlling one set of ambitions by pitting it against another. It was not imagined that everyone was equally good, or that talents were equally distributed, but that in the process of competing with each other all would emerge with a degree of self-determination. Freedom, in short, was to be built into the system by dividing responsibilities between an executive, a bicameral legislature, and an independent judiciary. In time, this came to be supplemented by a two-party system that arrayed shifting alliances against each other in elections held often enough, and local enough, to "throw the rascals out."

Adams, as has increasingly been recognized by scholars, was emphatic in his belief that teaching "All men are born with equal powers and faculties, [and] to equal influence in society...is a gross fraud." Contrary to Jefferson, he did not blame civilization for introducing distinctions between people, but placed the responsibility on the aspirations of people themselves. "In all government," he declared, "in every individual, there is an eternal struggle to rise above somebody or other, or to depress somebody or other who is above him..." People, in consequence, use all sorts of devices to gain an advantage, some fair and some foul. "By his virtues, his talents, his learning, his loquacity, his taciturnity, his frankness, his reserve...his face, figure, eloquence, air, attitude, movements, wealth, birth, art, address, intrigue, good fellowship," even his "drunkenness, debauchery, fraud, perjury, violence, treachery, pyrrhonism, deism, or atheism" is priority attained. To assume, therefore (in the words of Joseph Ellis),[46] that freedom and equality were always compatible was "a lullaby disguised as a set of political principles." Adams considered the proper role of government "not to pretend that such forces did not exist, but rather to assure they were 'directed to virtue.'" Governments, in short, were charged with restraining immoderate appetites and harnessing them to socially productive goals.

On the economic front, unequal abilities and achievements are also the rule and must likewise be restrained to produce social benefits. But without the freedom of individuals to operate autonomously, capitalism cannot function. Fortunately, when people apply their personal ambitions, talents, and insights to becoming successful, markets tend to flourish. It is then that entrepreneurs invent new modes of production and consumers explore their unfulfilled needs. This process may seem chaotic, but imperceptible laws guide it toward ever more effective modes of exchange. Much in the manner of Adam Smith's[47] "invisible hand," a myriad of barely discernible forces interact to keep things on track.

Just as importantly, capitalism provides the underpinnings for both democracy and freedom. Its left wing critics often accuse the free market of being the enemy of freedom; they say that its greed is so extravagant it undermines the liberty of others. Indeed, capitalists are regularly portrayed as manipulating others to their own advantage, as creating monopolies, as corrupting governments, and as promoting restraints of trade. But this overlooks a larger pattern. The economist Milton Friedman[48] has eloquently argued that, however imperfectly, market forces also militate toward unobstructed institutions; that while individual entrepreneurs may gain a short-term advantage in controlling the market, in the long term a community of producers and customers are better served by liquid and impartial forms of exchange. When there is no dominant player with the clout to impose his will, all can contribute to determining their comparative preeminence. The players may not relish the uncertainties entailed, but a critical mass will perceive an interest in safeguarding the emancipation of even their most serious competitors.

Putnam goes even further. He asserts that freedom is also essential for democratic institutions. His work in Italy makes it plain that in communities in which people associate with each other on the basis of mutual trust, that is, communities in which they are not obliged to submit to the power of authoritarian patrons, they are at liberty to work together toward their joint interests. Just as Alexis de Tocqueville[49] found when he toured a nascent America, an independent citizenry holds the potential to ensure its own autonomy by participating in freely initiated associations. Absent this unfettered inclination toward self-help, autocratic institutions can prevail. In Putnam's words, "Voluntary cooperation is easier in a community that has inherited a substantial stock of social capital, in the form of norms of reciprocity and networks of civic engagement."[50]

The problem, of course, is that perfect freedom is no more possible than is total equality. If hierarchy is inevitable, so is cheating and incomplete knowledge. There is always someone prepared to exploit a privileged position or a vulnerable associate. This has impelled Friedman to invoke the need for neutral umpires. They are to be the guardians of an infrastructure of rules that prevent exploitation. In practice, this function tends to be entrusted to none other than the government. Its court systems, regulatory agencies, and constabularies are mandated to keep the economic playing field reasonably even. Indeed, de Tocqueville[51] cites self-administered law as one of the principal linch pins of democracy. In a similar manner, the state is required to control what Friedman calls "neighborhood effects." There are some evils that no individual has the capacity to manage alone. Pollution, for instance, may impact people so far from its source that they have no way of identifying, never mind disciplining, the perpetrator. Only a civic leviathan has the knowledge, and the reach, to impose rules from which the community may benefit. Not incidentally, the community effects of racial discrimination fall under this rubric. Only formal laws against this custom may be able to prevent its more pernicious effects.

Ironically, the abolition of slavery was itself made possible by the triumph of capitalism. In one of those odd quirks of history, as European-centered market economies became more efficient, they at first revived what had been a dying institution. Commercial forays down the African coast, combined with the emergence of Caribbean sugar plantations, raised the demand for ultracheap labor, especially after the native American labor pool succumbed to unfamiliar European diseases. In the United States it was the tobacco and then the cotton trade that produced the desire for indentured workers. Nevertheless, the very prosperity this fostered was to generate the conditions for its demise. With this newfound wealth came a passion for material possessions, as well as the capital to finance their production. The subsequent industrialization so altered the relationship between buyers and sellers, and between owners and workers, that slavery became untenable. Despite its detractors, the norms, values, and beliefs cultivated by a victorious capitalism were antithetical to the plantation mentality of the old South. In an open marketplace, slave labor represents intolerable competition to free workers. Because it undercuts their wages, those who sell their labor (and these constitute a progressively larger proportion of the population) agitate against it, and eventually prevail. Likewise the rigidities of a conservative slave-owning class discourage the innovation so characteristic of free exchange. Because these aristocrats fear their bondsmen, they devote their energies to maintaining stability, that is, to resisting change. It was thus no accident that abolitionists in the northeastern United States, and the factory workers in midland Britain, were in the forefront of combating slavery.

As significantly, and intimately related to the decline of slavery, was the rise of a social class system. Prior to this modern form of social stratification, caste and estate systems were dominant.[52] In places such as India, people were born into a social position from which escape was impossible. In Europe, there was less ossification, but the boundaries between serfs, merchants, and nobles were relatively firm. It was not until capitalists became immensely successful that wealth alone, as opposed to land ownership, military prominence, or religious standing, became the acknowledged measure of status. But this transformation contained the seeds of what amounted to a revolution. It made it possible for people to move from one social position to another more easily than previously. Because money is fungible, and economic success unpredictable, the lucky and talented might find themselves employing their one-time superiors. Today we take this social mobility for granted, but it was a hard won victory that was contingent on the prior emergence of a free marketplace.

Moreover, without the ascendancy of a mobile social class system, democracy would have been unlikely. Rule by the people, in which ordinary citizens influence governmental decisions, presupposes that they are sufficiently respected to be trusted with power.[53] This respect, however, emerges, in large part, from their possibility of being successful in the economic sphere. When there is no chance of individuals coming to prominence, their wishes need not be taken into account. Slaves and serfs can usually be overpowered, whereas competitors who might someday be prosperous, and workmen who can sell their services elsewhere, need to be placated. Their loyalty is conditional and often available only at the cost of including them within the tent.

In America, as de Tocqueville[54] speculates, freedom seems to have preceded equality. If freedom is roughly defined as an ability to exercise free movement, to change jobs and/or to start one's own business, to say what one thinks, even when this is unpopular, to participate in self-government, and to call on protection of the common law, then the trans-Atlantic passage from England to a relatively unpopulated continent clearly had a liberating effect. In voluntarily removing tens of thousands of persons from the direct supervision of their sovereign to a land in which abundant resources were cheaply available, and in which these could be freely traded within a sophisticated marketplace, all under the guardianship of respected laws, both the idea and the habits of freedom took form.

Contemporary Americans tend to take their liberties for granted. Yet for freedom to work, a variety of conditions must be sustained. Among these is a widespread internalization of personal *responsibility*. If decision making is to be broadly delegated, a citizenry must be prepared to shoulder the burden of making good choices. People must be able to select between a plethora of options, and, if proven wrong, to recognize their role in this debacle. But unless individuals perceive themselves as capable of making choices, they are apt to abdicate the function to others. Without sufficient knowledge and self-discipline to weigh the alternatives before them and ample confidence and self-awareness to be able to hold up under the criticism that inevitably accompanies authority, they might easily collapse.

A second prerequisite of freedom is *individualism*. A free people need a sufficient sense of self to hold themselves apart from the crowd.[55] If they perceive themselves only as members of a group, they are vulnerable to manipulation by those who represent themselves as their legitimate leaders. Fortunately, Americans have historically celebrated the rugged individualist.[56] The frontiersman who went out to brave the dangers of the wilderness, and the inventors who dared to actualize dreams others could barely imagine, have been our heroes. They represent the independence, the know-how, and the courage most of us cherish. Even today, when the schools and media extol the virtues of cooperation and group identification, as the work of Robert Bellah[57] and his colleagues has shown, most Americans retain a streak of stubborn pride in their personal autonomy.

A third requirement of freedom is *universalism*. A bridge concept between liberty and equality, this commitment to applying the same rules to everyone enables people to treat each other with respect and as ends in themselves. Its widespread acceptance provides the warranty of a fair marketplace and an impartial polity, for unless the same standards are prescribed for all, cheating can run rampant and the whole idea of personal independence break down. Universalism is also the necessary yardstick of the relatively neutral umpire Friedman has recommended. It is the carpenter's level that keeps the playing field even.

All of this brings us to a paradox that sometimes befuddles public discussions of freedom and equality. Nowadays most people identify themselves as either liberal or conservative, with liberals more committed to defending social equity and conservatives leaning toward individual liberty. Generally, liberals favor collective social policies to redistribute social goods, whereas conservatives prefer a hands-off policy that trusts people to sort things out without government intervention. Yet, the left would like niceness, tolerance, and social-mindedness to prevail, whereas the right insists that hierarchy, selfishness, and inequality are irrevocable facts of life. The implicit irony comes into focus when one notices that each faction often advocates the opposite of what it seems to believe. Perhaps the easiest way to explain the disparity is to describe liberals as *sour optimists* and conservatives as *sunny pessimists*. Liberals, for instance, tell us how nice people are, then insist on governmental interventions to coerce them into doing the right thing. They claim to love tolerance, but obviously not for the enemies of the downtrodden. Almost as a mirror image, conservatives bemoan the potential for human evil, then turn around and assume social relations to be self-correcting (as per Smith's invisible hand). They may want the government to monitor their beloved marketplace, but only to the minimum degree necessary. The left, in its turn, imagines that the constraints it promotes can bring out the good in the worst miscreants. The ultimate irony is that egalitarian liberals frequently set themselves up as elitists whose mission is to instruct people on correct behavior, whereas economically successful conservatives hire indigent minorities when they perceive a profit in it.

AN OVERDOSE OF EGALITARIANISM

Assuming for the moment that there has been a tilt in American values away from freedom and toward equality, what consequences flow from this? Implausible as it may seem, an emphasis on racial equity has contributed to the erosion of standards most Americans once considered dear. Where once a respect for personal responsibility, social rules, truth, individual merit, and family values held sway, today these are in relative eclipse. They may still be honored, but more in the breach than previously. The result has been detrimental to our individual and collective well-being. Many of the democratic institutions upon which we depend and the economic arrangements from which we benefit have been compromised. Moreover, as individuals, people have been steered away from values that would assist them in attaining personal success. Both blacks and whites, but more particularly blacks, have been persuaded to eschew standards that would facilitate their rise in a social class system.

What many reformers miss is that in raising the profile of some goals, they unconsciously dismiss others. People are urged to be nonjudgmental and to exhibit unconditional positive regard[58] rather than enforce more demanding standards. As is the case with many social revolutions, a moralistic excess blinds these partisans to the negative implications of their refurbished ideals. Specifically, instead of eradicating racism and social injustice as is their intent, they undermine the very practices necessary for giving everyone a fair shake.

Personal Responsibility

Even though personal responsibility is critically important in our modern Gesellschaft universe, there has emerged a crusade to abolish it. "Excuse abuse"[59] has become rampant as experts and laymen alike earnestly compete to explain why people should not be held liable for what they do. The exceptions to personal accountability are typically described as "victims" who did not create the circumstances in which they operate. For many, the African-American experience has become the paradigm of this condition. When members of the underclass assert "I'm poor and black, and therefore it is not my fault," they nod in assent. Whatever wrongs are thereby perpetrated are palmed off as of someone else's manufacture.

Myron Magnet[60] has argued that this is a legacy of the 1960s. In those heady days of civil rights, feminism, and antiwar activism, many middle-class Americans became convinced that equality must be taken literally. As a Beatle's song proclaimed, love was all you needed. On a more concrete level, this was translated into urging the poor that welfare was their right and that street crime and graffiti were valid forms of protest. Timothy Leary's siren call to "Turn on, tune in, and drop out" was believed to be a profound insight and it was assumed that someday the world would be converted into one huge hippie commune. Such flower-power blandishments were especially attractive to the young, who, lest one forget, have grown into today's adults. Despite now having families and running corporations, many retain a warm spot for the dreams of their youth.

The resultant elevation of irresponsibility is especially puzzling given the middle-class reliance on responsibility. Members of this strata, more than any other, make the decisions that keep society going. On the job and at home, they are leaders and planners, who, to be effective, must be competent thinkers and administrators. This, however, entails an ability to be self-directed and the courage to stand up under pressure. It also entails a lofty estimation of the need for personal accountability. In his survey of middle-class values, Wolfe[61] found that this is the case. Time and again his respondents proclaimed their desire to be reasonable, restrained, and dependable. Convinced that individuals are responsible for their own fate, "They reserve the seventh circle of their moral hell for people like the Menendez brothers who kill their parents but claim it was because of abuse...."

And yet they also want to be "nice." In Wolfe's words, "reluctant to pass judgment, they are tolerant to a fault...." In particular, those who are poor, entangled in the criminal justice system, or victims of social prejudice are treated as if they have a special claim on their sympathy. Many in the middle class, despite their social position, have been influenced by the liberal ideals of their salad days and speak "the language of a cultural elite committed to tolerance, relativism, and personal and group identity, [thereby separating] themselves off from the traditional moral views of hardworking middle-class Americans, [and] becoming, in the process, a 'new class' committed to an 'adversary culture' of collectivist values, therapeutic remedies, hostility to corporations, and even anti-Americanism." Most would deny these proclivities, but the split between the standards to which they hold themselves, and the "compassionate" expectations they direct toward those less well off, belies their protestations. Marvin Olasky[62] has characterized this disposition as an American "tragedy" and blamed the resultant permissiveness for trapping the poor in their misery. He contends that a failure to distinguish between the deserving and undeserving poor has robbed the latter of the motivation to extricate themselves from their dilemma; that letting them off the hook, rather than being an act of kindness, underestimates their potential and provides a pretext for their not doing what they can to help themselves.

Respect for Rules

Another value in precipitous decline is the respect for rules. Many Americans pride themselves in living under "a rule of law rather than of men" and count themselves fortunate that the nation has a constitution that is taken seriously.[63] And yet here too an excessive dedication to absolute equality has had deleterious effects. It has convinced many citizens that because all rules are not enforced with complete equity, few are legitimate. Both formal standards, as embodied in legal statutes, and informal rules, as exemplified by codes of etiquette, are derided as insincere and therefore not worthy of respect.

When the criminal justice system tries and convicts more African-Americans than European-Americans—as it does—this is attributed to an unacknowledged bias. The result is that laws and court procedures are condemned as arbitrary and discriminatory. Yet no well thought out substitute waits in the wings. New rules are proposed, but they are not based on universalism. Designed specifically to even out the numbers of identified groups who end up incarcerated,[64] justice is relegated to second place. If a disproportionate number of blacks are punished for dealing in crack cocaine, then the penalties for so doing must be lowered. If more blacks are executed for homicide, then the death penalty must be repealed. The consequence of such modifications would seem to be a markedly greater tolerance of crime and violence. With the emphasis shifted from apprehending and convicting malefactors to finding reasons for releasing them, those who break the law are less in awe of it. This has converted many of them into jailhouse lawyers, concerned not with obeying the law but with finding ways to assert their personal rights.[65]

On a less weighty plane has been the deterioration of interpersonal civility. A veritable epidemic of vulgarity has infected our schools, politics, music, and television shows. Language and behavior once considered emblematic of the low-born has become evidence of sophistication and open-mindedness. From the White House to the family living room, jargon associated with the uneducated is now defended as "authentic." Although defenders of more refined standards, such as Yale legal scholar Stephen Carter,[66] appeal for a return to more genteel practices, their arguments have so far gone unheeded. Nor are Putnam and Fukuyama[67] heeded when they report that civic trust is the glue that holds successful, democratic societies together.

Much of this plague of cursing, insults, and sexual references can be traced to black street culture. Interpreted by relativists as a cultural style equal to any other, it has been emulated at all levels of society. Illustrative of this trend was the career of Muhammad Ali. An extraordinarily gifted boxer, he flouted earlier expectations of what a champion was supposed to be.

Previously those who achieved uncommon success in the arena could be counted upon to serve as role models for the young. Ali, however, shattered this tradition. Against the desires of the public, he changed his religion, altered his name, and refused to be drafted into the military. Worst of all, he declined to be modest. Instead of attributing his achievements to hard work or the luck of the genetic draw, he loudly and repeatedly proclaimed that he was "the Greatest." Faster, smarter, and "prettier" than others, he alone could "float like a butterfly and sting like a bee." Given this barrage of braggadocio, what was the public response? After an initial period of rejection, he was embraced by ordinary people and the media alike. Howard Cossell, the most prominent sportscaster of the time, lionized him, commending him for "telling it like it is." Far from being condemned as a braggart, he was praised as an innovative showman and a courageous defender of the dispossessed. What many failed to appreciate is that Ali's style was a variation on the "cool pose." His poetry, boastfulness, and disdain for others were very much of a piece with the raunchiness of black teenagers playing the dozens.

Individual Merit

A further casualty of the drive for equalization has been standards of merit. Jefferson may have assumed that an aristocracy of talent would emerge from an unfettered democracy,[68] but contemporary egalitarians tend to be suspicious of talent. They suppose, a la Stalinist communism, that all human beings are born with the same competencies and whatever differences develop are the result of unfair patterns of socialization and wealth. If someone does better than someone else, he can only have benefited from going to better schools,[69] having better connected parents, and so forth. Their recommendation is thus that opportunities be equaled out, or failing that, that social positions be randomly distributed by group membership. Competent performances, they insist, spring into existence in response to the demands made of the individual. In other words, all people can learn by doing.

Given this bent, when Robert Herrnstein and Charles Murray[70] suggested that IQ was related to social success, a hue and cry arose among the academic elite. They were offended that fellow intellectuals could seriously argue that intelligence determined how well one would do on the job or in one's personal life. They were further affronted by the proposition that educational attainments made a huge difference in later achievements. But what really got their dander up was the idea that there might be race-related differences in measured intelligence and therefore in correlated vocational/personal success. This seemed nothing short of a brief in favor of biological disparities. Although Herrnstein and Murray tried to stake out an agnostic position, this was castigated as a smokescreen. The only allowable conclusion was that IQ was of trivial importance and that it was distributed randomly.

Representative of this mainstream attitude is Mary Guy,[71] a former president of the American Society of Public Administration. In response to an article on affirmative action by conservative activist Christina Jeffrey, she wrote "I believe that *merit* is a subjective term that must be redefined for each context in which it is applied." For Guy, the notion that some people are inherently more competent than others is a fraud. Dismissing "workplace competition" as a "clever means of motivating employees," she complains that it is a subterfuge for the Caucasian "proclivity to hire and promote those who are like [them]selves." In the same vein, Duke University English professor Stanley Fish[72] derides the entire notion of merit as only a "political viewpoint claiming for itself the mantle of objectivity." Although conservatives say that success is determined by performance and that performance is enhanced by ability, for these critics the truth is that favoritisms based on race, gender, or ethnic identity dominate the marketplace.[73] How much more fair it is to eliminate the charade and hire people according to social categories. Only this can ensure that those previously mired in servitude receive a fighting chance.

Writing largely about recent developments in the nation's law schools, Daniel Farber and Suzanna Sherry[74] flesh out these opinions. They quote such legal scholars as Derrick Bell[75] and Richard Delgado to the effect that "standards of merit are socially constructed to favor the powerful."[76] Delgado, in particular, is cited as observing that "Enlightenment-style Western Democracy is...the source of black people's subordination" and that "Racism and enlightenment are the same thing." Delgado also suggests that "Merit is that which I...use to judge you, the Other. The criteria I use sound suspiciously like a description of me and the place where I stand...."[77] Even more damningly, "Like white people's affirmative action....[it is] a way of keeping their own deficiencies neatly hidden while assuring only people like them get in." What could be less legitimate?

Wolfe,[78] in his survey of middle-class values, found a sharp division between whites and blacks on this issue. All "indicated a strong disagreement with the statement that African-Americans should have priority in jobs or college admission because of their past experiences with slavery and discrimination," but "The most common response among whites was one of puzzlement [over how the goal of fairness can] be served by classifying and counting by race." They believed in the sort of universalism Sniderman advocates and assumed that people should be judged according to their personal achievements. Blacks, however, concluded that the system is skewed against them and that they are permanently deprived of the credit they deserve. As one of Wolfe's subjects expressed it, "My skin tone automatically subtracts ten percent from my merits." If this is true, then ignoring measured merit or adjusting for it through affirmative action is no more than a reasonable means of restoring equity. The problem is that such adjustments are often arbitrary. Instead of seeking more accurate ways of determining achievement, the entire notion of merit is scrapped and new forms of social advantage substituted in their stead. Some even defend these, despite their unfairness, submitting that they are just an updated version of what others have always done. They are, as it were, a "good old boy" network for the underrepresented.

Truth/Knowledge

Also a victim of the stampede toward social equivalence has been knowledge. An adherence to truth has always been a fragile commodity. The partisanship that pervades most social venues has a way of justifying the manipulation of facts to serve the interests of those doing the manipulation. Individually and collectively people, with a clear conscience, engage in impression management[79] and outright lies to promote that to which they are devoted. If this is so, the passion behind their commitment to equality may provide its partisans the license to see only what they prefer to see.[80]

As an academic, I have been impressed by the depredations of multiculturalism.[81] Primarily in the humanities and social sciences,[82] in disciplines as diverse as psychology, sociology, anthropology, English literature, history, and philosophy, but also in areas as far afield as law and business, a large proportion of my colleagues presuppose that the truth is found on the liberal side of the political divide.[83] Confusing their own values with empirical evidence, they assume that only politically correct conclusions are intellectually valid. Because so many academics enter their careers hoping to make the world a better place, and because they then lead an ivory tower existence, they are able to convince themselves that their ideals, and only their ideals, are true. Academic freedom, though theoretically favored by most, is often reserved for the politically dominant faction.[84] This group changes with historical regularity, sometimes benefiting liberals, sometimes conservatives, but whichever camp is ascendant imagines its motives pure and its perspective objective. Nowadays with egalitarian-loving multiculturalists calling the tune, they are the ones determining which courses are taught, what books published, and which scholars promoted. Though not many years ago C. Wright Mills[85] complained that the roles were reversed, with memories short and ambitions large, this does not temper their fanaticism.

Among legal scholars, for instance, traditional standards of knowledge are in decay at present. Instead of seeking objectively confirmed facts, these are eschewed as seductive fantasies. As Farber and Sherry[86] put it, "For the radical multiculturalists, knowledge is communicated not so much by dispassionate reasoning as by telling stories that inspire faith." This encourages many to be careless with the truth. Because they believe reality is socially constructed, they are untroubled when their parables stray from the data. Thus when they assert that there are hiring biases for minorities at elite universities, and there are not; that Beethoven was a mulatto, when there is no evidence he was; that single-parent homes are as beneficial to children as any other, in the teeth of mountains of contradictory information, they are undeterred by an exposure of error. In their heart of hearts, it is the spirit of their stories that matters. As long as these promote the appropriate interests, they are as good as truth, and maybe better.

Family Values

It has become a cliché, but family values too have gone into eclipse. At least since the Murphy Brown incident, wherein then Vice President Dan Quayle criticized the sitcom for extolling unwed motherhood, Americans have been aware that a significant proportion of their number are unhappy with what they perceive to be an onslaught against the traditional family. Having been raised to treat the nuclear family of Mom, Dad, and the kids as nearly sacred, these conventionalists are scandalized when it is denigrated as no better than what was once condemned as "illegitimacy." This outlook has been building for some time. One of its watersheds was the Moynihan Report.[87] Back in the 1960s, beginning with the Johnson administration, Moynihan—at the time a politically active sociologist—warned that the black family was in danger of disintegration. Unless something was done to stem a tide of teenage pregnancies and single-parent households, he feared that African-American children would suffer egregious harm.

The reaction to this alarm was contrary to what Moynihan had hoped. In its aftermath, instead of leading a concerted effort to rectify the problem, he found himself assailed for slandering the black family. What was needed, he was told, was a celebration of its strengths, not censure for its deficiencies. The private lives of African-Americans might be different from those of others, but they were no less satisfactory. The fact that blacks had survived centuries of oppression was proof of this. The same theme has since been picked up by the likes of Coontz.[88] Her argument that the traditional nuclear family was a myth invented in the 1950s and that a variety of other family arrangements are equally authentic has had enormous resonance. Under the banner of multiculturalism, her accusation is that those who look longingly toward the past are ethnocentric. A convinced relativist, she would allow everyone to decide their own family preferences without carping from outsiders.

Though most laypersons would be surprised to learn it, radical family egalitarianism has become the conventional wisdom among social scientists. For these experts, family values mean whatever family you happen to value. This approach has proceeded so far that when, under the auspices of the Institute for American Values, Norval Glenn[89] authored a report entitled "Closed Hearts, Closed Minds: The Textbook Story of Marriage," he was roundly denounced. At professional meetings, and in the newsletter of the American Sociological Association,[90] an almost unbroken front of sociologists virulently accused him of glaring errors for having unfavorably reviewed most of the textbooks currently in vogue to teach the sociology of families. Glenn complained of their antifamily bias, but this was rejected as arrogant. Those who have read these works will discover that most are unabashedly feminist and relativist, but having the audacity to say so apparently violated new-age sensibilities.

Faring little better was the sociologist David Popenoe.[91] Hitherto respected by his peers, when he wrote a book advocating a renewed emphasis on fatherhood, its intellectual credentials were challenged in *Contemporary Sociology*. The reviewer Scott Coltrane,[92] himself the author of a postmodernist work on the family, castigated Popenoe for presenting a fricassee of half-truths. Complaining of strained rhetoric and flawed logic, he predicted that most sociologists would reject the work outright. In fact, Popenoe was reprimanded for trying to "sound scientific," while a rival was commended for making sardonic postmodern comments.[93] In other words, traditional family values contained only a pretense of validity, whereas radically egalitarianism was the wave of the future.

In sum, when absolute equality becomes the ultimate arbiter of right and wrong, other values suffer. In area upon area, its devotees abandon standards previously thought compelling. In return for this article of faith, they promise a brave new world of fairness. The evidence for this is slight, however. Indeed, there is reason to believe they leave vital factors out of their calculations. As we shall soon see, with regard to race, their proposals fail to account for the cultural and structural liabilities dogging many African-Americans. Despite Myrdal's authority, America has endured more than a lag in applying its implicit values.

Chapter 5

The Culture of Slavery: Origins

Africans were drawn into the vortex of the Altantic slave trade and funnelled into the sugar fields, the swampy rice lands, or the cotton and tobbaco plantations of the new world. The process of enslavement was almost unbelievably painful and bewlidering.... Completely cut off from their native land, they were frightened by the artifacts of the white man's civilization and terrified by his cruelty until they learned that they were... expected to work for him.... John W. Blassingame, *The Slave Community*

MORALITY AND CULTURE

Excessive moralism can distort our perceptions in a variety of ways. Besides rearranging our priorities, it can misrepresent the world and how it works. Without so much as pausing to observe the collateral damage, a newly energized master value can shoulder equally significant objectives off-stage. In the case of race relations, when freedom is declared expendable, whites can be identified as the source of all difficulties, and stereotypes condemned as the central mechanism of racial oppression. As materially, the role culture plays in maintaining caste-based relationships can be totally rejected. The fact is that liberty and equality occur within a social context. We human beings are not isolated creatures whose choice of values takes place in a vacuum. Both the social structure in which we are embedded and the culture operative within this structure determine what we will demand and ultimately what is possible. We must therefore turn our attention to examining the cultural factors molding race relations.

It should be obvious, but evidently is not, that the customs and values of today's African-Americans were not developed *in* freedom. It should likewise be manifest that they were not developed *for* freedom.[1] Slavery was slavery. Its aim was to keep people in submission.[2] Those in its thrall, though they might yearn for liberty, had to cope with its absence. Their immediate concern was surviving days and years of bondage, degradation, and terror. If they developed an idiosyncratic viewpoint or an impenetrable emotional armor, what was the alternative? Similarly, given that their masters had no interest in preparing them for release, how were they to develop the skills free citizens need for success in a class-based society? Sometimes we imagine that all it takes to prosper in a market economy is to join the competition. But much more is involved. A basketful of affirmative competencies and a dearth of debilitating obstructions are also essential.

Cultural disabilities are, of course, largely invisible. Unlike broken legs or whip-scarred backs, they are intangible. An amalgam of predominantly unremarked feelings, beliefs, and behaviors, the incapacities a culture imposes can be as immaterial as a failure to recognize one's options or as interminable as a refusal to relinquish festering resentments. These may be undeniably real, and frequently decisive, but are nevertheless easy to neglect. Yet the penalty for doing so can be stiff. The immediate victims of an unrecognized cultural liability tend to be stymied in their hopes, cheated in their achievements, and consigned to social ignominy. Furthermore, many of those who are most handicapped never suspect what is holding them back. Looking outward at what they do not possess, or inward at aches that will not subside, they are transfixed by the consequences, rather than the causes, of their plight. They are thus victimized a second time by an impatience so persistent it pushes them to adopt change strategies that are only marginally effective.

Some have labeled the cultural legacy of slavery as "pathological." Like D'Souza,[3] they implicitly compare it with a disease and assume it must be cured. The roots of this habit extend back at least to Myrdal[4] and it has been ratified by Civil Rights activists with credentials as impeccable as Kenneth Clark's.[5] The characterization is nonetheless rejected by most contemporary blacks. They understand full well that it connotes being "sick," "crazy," "immoral," or "inferior." Although the underlying medical analogy was intended to be neutral, the repellent nature of mental illness has undermined the original objective. Because the strange behaviors of schizophrenics, obsessive compulsives, and sexual predators are identified with mental disorder, anything described as pathological acquires a corresponding disrepute. To subsequently insist that a particular behavior is normal does nothing to remove this stigma.

This makes it advantageous to portray cultural disabilities as "dysfunctional" rather than pathological, as bothersome rather than disordered. Most people recognize that patterns of behavior that emerge in one social environment may later prove costly when repeated under different circumstances. In particular, the attitudes toward authority, education, and personal relationships that made slavery bearable can subsequently interfere with attempts to integrate into a more kindly society. Socially transmitted patterns literally cease to "function" as effective barriers against oppression and instead impose a drag on those trying to get ahead. Although the term dysfunctional too has sometimes degraded into psycho-babble, its underlying meaning more closely reflects the ineffectiveness of culturally reproduced forms of conduct.

The ravages a dysfunctional culture can visit on its primary carriers are relatively easy to discern. The squalor of inner-city neighborhoods, the emotional devastation wrought by fragile families, and the anguish of unfulfilled dreams are unarguable signs that something is amiss in the lives of many African-Americans. Yet there are also more remote casualties of a culture of slavery who may not consider themselves victims. To be blunt, whites, as well as blacks, have been betrayed by customs that originated in the ante-bellum South. Ironically, when whites adopt these, they too become entangled in dysfunction. Violence is rationalized, educational standards are undermined, and family stability impaired. Ignorance of the culture of slavery is decidedly not bliss. Far from it; it is a poison coursing through the body politic.

As previously indicated, Myron Magnet[6] makes a potent case against the cultural excesses of the 1960s. The simpering self-indulgence of unemployed middle-class radicals determined to trash the work ethic and to obtain reparations for poor blacks was an abysmal failure. Rather than encourage efforts to develop commercial competence, their crusades promoted bigger welfare checks, defaced subway cars, and the right of the mentally ill to defecate in public. These would-be social saviors may have sung songs about love, but they simultaneously petitioned the government to redistribute the wealth in their favor. Such proclivities, Magnet argues, weakened the cultural forces essential for fighting poverty. Instead of providing succor to the underclasses, they were lulled into a false sense of entitlement. Thus, if Korean grocers were making money, it was not because of their personal efforts, but because they received unfair subsidies. Never mind that this was a vicious canard, it was believed and justified a passive anticipation of imminent rescue. As disastrously, it laid the groundwork for a "me-generation" in which almost everyone claimed victimization. No longer were private failures a personal responsibility; they were an indicator of social injustice. As a result, the entire nation, not just the least fortunate, could, and did, demand recompense.

What Magnet left out of his account was that the 60s assault on middle-class virtues had precursors, and one of these was the culture of slavery. Values and beliefs forged in the crucible of plantation life rang, like the plaintive melody of an old Negro spiritual, in the ears of millions who never themselves experienced the hardships of bondage. Other pressures, such as those emanating from a more bureaucratic workplace and more isolated heterosexual relationships, doubtlessly played a role, but the notion that universal civil rights could reinvent humankind was intimately connected with the then expanding hopes of African-Americans. So too did an almost magical faith in the ability of the central government to dictate moral behavior. Once middle-class college students came to identify themselves with the deprivations of the slave quarters, they could eagerly look forward to a new—albeit bloodless—civil war that would overturn the existing order and present everyone with the equivalent of twenty acres and a mule. Angry at their parents for not bestowing the success they believed their due, they attempted to employ the moral standing of the dispossessed as a tool to extract a personal advantage.

Many contemporary observers would, of course, disagree with this characterization. They downplay the role of culture, and specifically of black culture, in shaping recent trends.[7] For what they perceive as valid scientific and moral reasons, they prefer to stress economic and political factors. Some go so far as to deny that there is an identifiable black culture. The idea that slavery could produce a host of debilitating adaptations strikes them as both blasphemous and demeaning. The view is exemplified by Loury[8] who believes that blacks are defamed by insinuating that they are different from other Americans. As he remarks, this places "poor urban blacks outside the orbit of American civilization, [intimating that] their lives are governed by barbarism; [and that] they are the enemy within." Marger,[9] in his text on race relations, seconds Loury's interpretation. In a table on American ethnic assimilation, he lists Southern Europeans and Jews as having achieved only moderate cultural assimilation, whereas blacks are credited with attaining much higher levels. Presumably because they speak English and aspire to own large houses and fast cars, they are fully Americanized. Hochschild[10] implies the same in contending that blacks subscribe to the same American Dream as Anglo-Americans.

Loury cites the ethnographies of Elijah Anderson[11] to support his contentions. Anderson's investigations of inner-city neighborhoods found a host of hardworking and ethical blacks.[12] Living and laboring much like their neighbors, their humanity, when described in detail, could hardly be denied. But Anderson also elaborated upon a unique set of gang behaviors and linguistic disparities. In the end, he presents a universe of similarities, but also of differences. Loury, however, insists that "The youth movement of the 1960s, with its celebration of drugs and sex, and its cult of irresponsibility, was no invention of black culture." In this he is only partially correct. Blacks did not "invent" drugs or sex; nevertheless values emanating from slavery did facilitate their diffusion. Nor is it accurate to repudiate a uniquely black subculture.[13] The way some African-Americans talk, the jokes they tell, the manner in which they walk, the music they prefer, the heroes they emulate, the attitudes toward crime they espouse, the child-rearing techniques they perpetuate, the ways they dress, and the jobs they hold are sufficiently different to merit notice. This does not place them outside the ambit of American civilization, but does reveal an exotic variation upon it.

A more sophisticated critique of the role of black culture is found in the works of William Julius Wilson.[14] He does not deny that there is an inner-city black culture, but attributes it primarily to concurrent structural causes. Christopher Jencks,[15] himself a liberal, praises Wilson for courageously admitting the problems inherent in ghetto culture. But he also alleges that Wilson believes "historic discrimination is more important than contemporary discrimination in understanding the plight of the black underclass," which is not quite accurate. Jencks further stresses that "Wilson's greatest contribution may be his discussion of how liberals' reluctance to blame blacks for anything happening in their communities has clouded both black and white thinking about how to improve those communities."

In fact, Wilson places more emphasis on the ravages of contemporaneous social arrangements than on historically determined factors. As he somewhat ambiguously puts its, "cultural factors do play a role, but any adequate explanation of inner-city joblessness and poverty should take other variables into account."[16] Wilson expressly assigns a lack economic opportunities and the flight of middle-class black role models to the suburbs for keeping people down.[17] Indeed, the cultural explanations he finds most persuasive are grounded in an evolving response to poverty. He writes, "Cultural values emerge from specific circumstances and life chances and reflect an individual's position in the class structure." Arguing that social class has become as important as race, he recommends, not cultural change, but government sponsored efforts to provide jobs that channel blacks into positions of higher status.

Be that as it may, a culture of slavery, initiated centuries ago, reverberates as we speak. Robert Park,[18] a leader of the Chicago School that dominated academic sociology in the 1920s, was convinced of this. Active in efforts to improve race relations, and an intimate of Booker T. Washington,[19] he observed that "Customs persist and preserve their external forms after they have lost their original meaning and functions." By this he meant that patterns of behavior traceable to slavery could be detected in black communities almost a hundred years later. Park's contemporary, William Ogburn,[20] popularized this insight as the phenomenon of "cultural lag." Referring principally to the slowness with which culture adapts to technological and institutional advances, he maintained that these hinderances must be addressed if progress is to be achieved. Although modern social engineers seem to have forgotten this, Ogburn documented his thesis with evidence of how fertility does not decline immediately upon medical discoveries that ensure the survival of more children. He noted that it takes more than a generation before parents react to this and decide to have smaller families. In the United States in his era, and Mexico in ours, it has been the progeny of the immediately affected generation, and not themselves, who adopt the goal of having two to three offspring. By the same token, Weimar Germany's approval of a democratic constitution did not instantaneously convert the German people into ardent democrats. Their previous experience of coming of age under an autocratic Kaiser primed them to accept Hitler's totalitarian promises of protection from the vagaries of the ballot box.[21] It took another social cohort and a catastrophic war to convince their descendants that democracy deserved a chance.

Long-term historical changes are nonetheless difficult to grasp. Besides the fact that most Americans are unfamiliar with anything that happened more than a decade ago, dynamic explanations are inherently less precise than well-defined contemporary ones. This makes something like *Strain Theory*, with its unambiguous causal explanations, socially appealing. Associated with the work of Robert Merton,[22] its hypothesis is that a disconnect between the aspirations of individuals and the social resources available to them is responsible for their decision to reject the larger society, either by breaking its rules, withdrawing from it, or attempting to transform it. Doubtless, if the dispossessed have neither the money, the social networks, nor the information necessary to get good jobs or social respect—but they continue to strive for these goals—in their discomfort, they may reject the entire system.

Hochschild[23] certainly fears such an outcome. As noted previously, she points out that African-Americans, like most other Americans, embrace the "American Dream." They assume that if they work hard enough, they too can reap substantial rewards. The trouble is that often, through no fault of their own, they do not. But because, again like others, they have been taught that such failures indicate personal deficiencies, they tend to blame themselves. Hochschild suspects this self-incrimination is wearing thin. She believes that, despite the Civil Rights revolution, as evidence mounts of persistent discrimination, blacks will be in a less forgiving frame of mind. What, she wonders, will be the result when the strain becomes too great? Will dislocations precipitated by those who can no longer contain their rage threaten the entire edifice? She is not sure, but implores her fellow whites to live up to their own aspirations.

For many reasons then, cultural explanations of race problems are not attractive. Less visible and less apparently invidious, they are not the first that come to mind. This is unfortunate, for they should. Culture is a powerful determinant of who we are and what we are destined to become.[24] It surrounds us, engulfs us, and permeates us all. Yet often it is so familiar that we do not see it. Culture is virtually in our bones. It shapes the lenses through which we see, stokes the flames of our passions, and guides our fingers as we reach toward the future. Though not per se a disability, it is an integral part of being human, and thus, when it goes wrong, the implications can be devastating.

A CONCEPTUAL INTERLUDE

Before going on, we must pause to clarify a few critical points. Some of the concepts we have been using require a more precise definition. The first of these is, not surprisingly, "culture." A normal part of our contemporary lexicon, its technical meaning is not universally appreciated. For sociologists and anthropologists, *culture* refers to a learned and shared form of life. Often conceived of as a comprehensive whole, it is typically composed of many subfeatures. For our purposes the most important of these are "beliefs," "norms," and "values." What we *believe*, including ideas derived from religion and science, is generally not of our own invention, but the result of instruction from others. Nearly always, we fail to investigate what people tell us is true.[25] Instead, when these tellers are credible, we adopt their teachings in toto and employ them as a guide in making sense of an otherwise complex cosmos. The *norms* we live by, including how we talk and comport ourselves, are likewise a consequence of demands to behave in particular ways. Although we may quibble over their details, years of indoctrination in these rules make them seem the only reasonable modes of conduct. Finally, the *values* we hold dear are not merely an outgrowth of personal tastes, but are derived from examples presented as worthy of pursuit. If norms dictate what means we should utilize in doing things, values point toward socially sanctioned endpoints. Without such shared goals, we might not even know where to hunt for personal satisfactions.

Contrasted with culture, but not in opposition to it, is *social structure*. If a culture, in effect, tells us how to behave, a structure tells us with whom to behave. It is, at its core, a web of enduring interpersonal relationships. Among the most important of these are our intimate attachments, individual roles, and hierarchical associations. Each of these bonds almost surely has biological precursors, but the specific shapes they take emerge only through a concrete series of social interactions. All of us are born into societies that expose us to particular persons who themselves have particular connections with other persons. First among these acquaintances are usually our parents. They are not merely there for us, but are the objects of strong emotional linkages. If we are lucky, we later form other loving relationships, the most meaningful heterosexual varieties of which are cemented in courtship processes. We also develop social roles that are coordinated with the roles of those with whom we interact. Roles[26] are, as it were, designated clusters of enduring social tasks, often identified by labels such as *mother, daughter, teacher, student, banker* and *pedestrian*. Many of these are quite personal, for example, *caretaker, family genius*, or *alcoholic*, in which case they become central features of our personal identities. Lastly, we human beings are an *hierarchical species*. When in groups, we tend to rank ourselves in terms of power and respect. Those at the top of this social ladder frequently obtain greater benefits, including food, houses, and mates, whereas those at the bottom must content themselves with the leftovers. Persons in the superior positions also acquire a disproportionate say in organizing joint activities, in which case they are typically labeled *bosses*.

Far from being alternatives, culture and structure are in constant contact. Each tends to mold the other and be molded in its turn. Thus, a particular culture will direct people toward those with whom they are supposed to communicate. Roles, for instance, are almost always enacted in conjunction with role partners who, in turn, instruct one another on how to fulfill them. To be a teacher is virtually impossible without having students to teach. But students, for their part, influence how they are taught. Particular social structures thus expose people to demands with which they must cope. In addition, individual responses, for example, toward particular authority figures, may later be solidified into norms that reduce interpersonal frictions. In essence, culture and structure together participate in an unending dance in which they both modify and sustain each other.

With respect to race relations, this long-term dependence has significant yet unanticipated consequences. Indeed, this interaction constitutes the substrate of how blacks and whites relate to one another. More particularly, the interaction of culture and structure places limitations on how either race will behave and how their relative statuses will evolve. Reformers concerned only with rational plans for improving society delude themselves if they believe they possess a unilateral ability to make either culture or structure conform to preselected ideals. Human societies are too intractable for that. Just as would-be economic reformers cannot ignore the laws of economics, so would-be social innovators cannot safely disregard social facts.

But let me be more specific. The conjunction between structure and culture often takes a form that hampers social change. To wit, social structures frequently prompt cultural responses that subsequently recapitulate, and thus perpetuate, the initial structure (this relationship may be conveniently summarized as S-C-S, i.e., as structure-culture-structure). Though time has passed, and circumstances have altered, a world much like the antecedent one is reconstructed by people who have internalized beliefs, norms, and values initially fabricated to meet the exigencies of the former circumstance. Those reproducing these past relationships may be oblivious to what they are doing, but their actions can prevent progress just as surely as would an anchor. Consciously, they strive to develop new ways of interacting, but what they think and feel push them toward patterns they had intended to reject. A simple example is provided by one aspect of Soviet life under Joseph Stalin. Determined to eradicate the last vestiges of Romanov feudalism, he sought to reorganize peasant villages along communitarian lines.[27] But what emerged? The notorious Communal Farms, which if inspected without benefit of ideological spectacles, resembled nothing so much as the huge aristocratic estates of pre-Revolutionary Russia. Another example is provided by soul food. In the old South, bondsmen were typically relegated leftovers. Foods that their masters did not savor (e.g, pig intestines) found their way onto their tables. Slaves consequently developed a taste for chitlines and sweet potato pie, which, in time, came to be relished as "home cooking."

Slavery, lest it not be apparent, is a social structure. It is a social system in which one group of people own and extract labor from another against the latter's will. A caste system is likewise a social structure—one in which the social positions are not easily exchanged. In a caste society, a designated group is, by force and common convention, prevented from improving its lot. Should its members decide to marry or seek employment outside the allowable range, they may literally be killed. The S-C-S pattern predicts that both of these structures will produce cultural artifacts that tend to perpetuate themselves; that both at their top and bottom the players will acquire internalized beliefs, norms, and values that recapitulate their relative ranks. Ironically, even when it is agreed that the original arrangement is immoral, the participants unconsciously conspire to retain their familiar places.

It must, however, be admitted that this simplifies an immensely convoluted reality. The world does not stand still for any particular structure or culture. As a case in point, intervening between pre-Civil War slavery and our postmodern society have been many structural developments, among which have been industrialization, urbanization, and multicultural immigration. Each of these has had a colossal impact that should not be underestimated. Likewise, fresh cultural alternatives always present themselves for emulation. Whether these are derived from immigrant groups, international trading partners, or cultural innovators, they divert people from time-worn paths. Nonetheless, the S-C-S prototype provides a useful model that is best conceived of as a ligature, that is, as a core around which additions accrete. Max Weber[28] described the central feature of this way of theorizing as an "ideal type." The sort of image involved may not be found in nature, but rather cleans up nature's details and straightens its lines, thereby making the actual connections easier to comprehend.

Central to the S-C-S model in the *conservatism* of culture.[29] At the nexus between structure at time 1 and structure at time 2, were cultures subject to effortless change, they would be ineffective in transferring the features of one to the other. Ordinarily, a style of life is thought to be extremely malleable. It component beliefs, norms, and values seem insubstantial and therefore ripe for modification merely by changing individual minds. The truth, however, is quite different. Culture can be very persistent. Its elements are built into people and communities in ways that are difficult to expunge. Consider for a moment what the world would be like if patterns of personal or interpersonal behavior transmuted at the whim of any and every participant.[30] Life would be utterly unpredictable and no one could reliably coordinate his efforts with any others. Children could not count on their parents being there to feed them, commuters would not know when the trains might run, and nations could not rely on armies sent out to defend them to hang together as they approached the front lines.

Fundamental to maintaining the integrity of specific cultures are the role scripts of those who adhere to them.[31] As a basic constituent of social structures, roles require blueprints to stabilize the conduct associated with them. Without some form of guidance, people would simply not know what was expected of them. Yet role scripts are cultural elements, and as such, created and transmitted between role players. Learned and shared, they make up the common currency of most social exchanges. Moreover, in its parsimony, nature seems to utilize the elements found in role scripts to shore up other social structures such as hierarchies and personal attachments. A natural economy thus recycles a limited vocabulary for a variety of purposes. It therefore becomes doubly important to recognize that key to role scripts are four elements: (1) cognitions, (2) emotions, (3) volitions, and (4) social demands. Each of these, save for the last, is incorporated into every individual. As a result, behavior patterns are less susceptible to manipulation than might be imagined.

Each of these elements deserves some explication. Let us begin with cognitions. These are the thought processes through which we understand the world. Beliefs are an example of cognitions—as are those linguistic symbols that enable us to communicate and cogitate. But the cognitive domain is larger than this. To navigate our social and physical environments, we spend years developing integrated, if sometimes inconsistent, worldviews. Analogous to detailed maps, these tell us who we are, who other people are, and what kinds of consequences we can expect from specific actions. They also tell us where the demons lie in wait and where treasure troves can be unearthed. As such, they are vital to our welfare and not lightly dispensed with. People are especially wary of removing foundation stones, put together brick by brick, lest the whole pile crumble. This means that settled opinions tend to stay settled and are not jettisoned merely because someone challenges them.

Our emotions, the second element of our role scripts, are, if anything, more conservative than cognitions.[32] Despite being thought of as ephemeral, feelings are remarkably tenacious, particularly when intense. Although their general outlines are part of our biological equipment, individual emotional experiences are shaped by our biographies and temperaments. What we fear, why we feel angry, and whom we love are not inherited in our genes, but developed in response to the specific dangers we encounter, the frustrations we endure, and the persons to whom we acquire attachments. Once in place, however, they tend to persist, even in the face of altered circumstances. Thus, having learned that fire burns, a terror arises that steers us away from what looks like fire and will not abate simply because someone tells us that an apparent flame is harmless.[33] Strong emotions are also important in fixing memories in our psyches. That from our past to which we presently react tends to be what we experienced in moments of emotional stress. For this reason too, intense feelings make some events more salient than others. Emotions literally determine what we will pay attention to and what not. As a result, they motivate us to do some things and to avoid others and will do so despite our conscious efforts to act otherwise. Lastly, when it comes to hierarchies, emotions are crucial to determining who wins "tests of strength," to instilling respect for the winners, and to stabilizing relative rank over time. Though we may be loath to acknowledge it, social standing is not so much an intellectual achievement as an emotional outcome.

"Volitions" may at first seem an odd phenomenon to discuss.[34] The term is certainly not in everyday currency. A moment's reflection, however, should make it plain that what we think and feel must be converted into action to be effective. It is not enough to know where the furniture of our universe is located or to develop a preference for a particular easy chair; we must also decide to sit somewhere before doing so. A *volition* thus refers to an act of will or a behavioral inclination. Returning to terms with which we are better acquainted, "norms" and "values" are forms of volition.[35] They are mechanisms that guide our action decisions. As with cognitions and emotions, they evolve over the course of a lifetime. From our earliest childhoods, we are directed toward some patterns of behavior and away from others. Our parents, friends, and even strangers exert pressures to which we respond by incorporating some, rejecting others, and modifying still others. Because it is impossible for us, every time we are confronted with a new situation, to work out an entirely novel response, we embrace habits and routines that go on automatic pilot. In the end, these deeply worn channels limit the options available to us. Theoretically we can decide to do whatever we wish, but as a practical matter, we tend to reiterate customary choices.

Lastly, our role behaviors are responsive to demands made by contemporary role partners. The other three components of our role scripts are internalized, often from previous social demands, but external influences never cease entirely. We are always surrounded by people who want us to think, feel, and decide in ways congenial to themselves. None of us, as John Donne cautioned, is an island. Because we are inherently social creatures, we are always embedded in a matrix of social pressures. To complicate things further, the persons applying these pressures have thoughts, feelings, and volitions of their own that determine what they will require of us. And since these too are conservative, their demands are not random. Their role-related requirements flow along well-known channels and therefore tend to keep us within familiar cultural pathways. What is more, our role partners have role partners of their own who demand loyalty to what in the aggregate amount to community standards.

The sum total of all of these mechanisms is what makes culture conservative. Their outlines may change, but they do so slowly. Indeed, it may take millennia before the central elements of culture are relinquished. Contrary to the rational image of ourselves we prefer, when it comes to important attitudes and beliefs, conscious logic plays little part. Thus, rarely do people coolly decide to take up a new way of life because their calculations indicate it will pay off. More often they are the pawns of prior socialization and of dramatic contemporary events. This means that even when they honestly decide to move from a caste to an open class society, it is not within their power to do so. As human beings, we are trapped by our humanity and sociability in lattices of constraint we barely recognize, and, in any event, scarcely have the capacity to impact. Strong emotions, in particular, are not subject to direct manipulation. Like firestorms in the soul, they command us more than we command them.

If all this sounds pessimistic, we should remind ourselves that cultural conservatism has its benefits. A world pliant enough to yield to momentary impulses would also expose us to impetuous transformations, most of which would be ill considered.[36] Since even our fondest projections are based on fragmentary information, it is just as well that cultural commitments slow us down. It is also crucial that the world not shift with kaleidoscopic rapidity. Besides throwing us dizzyingly off-keel, this would make it virtually impossible to coordinate complex activities. While flexibility in making plans can permit us to adjust to unexpected contingencies, too much flexibility makes for unreliability. It is disconcerting and socially unworkable. What is best is thus a combination of conservatism and innovation. The degree to which is exercised, however, depends on the individual circumstance.

CULTURAL CONSERVATISM IN ACTION

In *The Future of the Race*, Henry Louis Gates,[37] the current chair of the Department of Afro-American Studies at Harvard University, recounts a painful memory. He recalls that "Not long after I arrived at Yale [as an undergraduate], some of the brothers who came from private schools in New Orleans held a 'bag party.' As a classmate explained it to me, a bag party was a New Orleans custom wherein a brown paper bag was stuck on the door and anyone darker than it was denied entrance." Gates hastens to add "That was one cultural legacy that would be put to rest in a hurry—we made sure of that. But in a manner of speaking it was replaced by an opposite test whereby those who were deemed 'not black enough,' ideologically, were to be shunned."

Most whites are surprised to hear that there is such a thing as "bag parties." They are also amazed to discover that many blacks categorize and discriminate against one another as "high-yellow," "blue-black," or "purple." Nevertheless, in *School Daze*, his chronicle of social life at an historically black college, the movie-maker Spike Lee[38] vividly delineates the persistence of color-based distinctions. What he and Gates make clear is that these are not impositions maintained by the contemporary white community, but are a black cultural inheritance. Obviously derived from a plantation system in which white was better than black, and light superior to dark, it is blacks who themselves have sustained these patterns. In essence, they have been reproducing a system in which house servants, often allied to their masters by blood ties, set an example to which few, if any, field hands could aspire. Their straighter hair, less broad noses, and sepia complexions acquired the cachet of being good, attractive, and high tone. Although their owners would obviously agree with such assessments, it was the slaves and their descendants who fashioned them. These beliefs and values then became part of a worldview that has lasted for more than a century. Gates boasts that he and his classmates put an end to them at Yale, but, as he surely knows, they survive in the heads and hearts of millions of African-Americans.

Similar cultural patterns can be found to have endured in ethnic group after ethnic group—often for millennia. Jews, for instance, are celebrated for having been able to maintain a religious tradition that goes back a thousand years before Christ.[39] Occupying a stretch of territory astride the land bridge between Asia and Africa, they were in an unfortunate position in that any Mesopotamian power intent on annexing Egypt and any Egyptian Pharaoh interested in expanding into the fertile crescent needed to conquer them first.

Their constant military inferiority to these potential aggressors, a structural arrangement they were impotent to alter, called forth a cultural response based upon religion. To maintain their integrity, they emphasized a solidarity derived from a common belief system. An innovation that enabled their convictions to remain consistent, and therefore to impose effective internal discipline, was nothing less than the Bible. This written account of their spiritual history formed the kernel around which they could rally and one they could pass on to their progeny. For this mechanism to operate, however, a literate community was essential. Such an ability was eventually enforced through the ritual of the Bar Mitzvah in which every Jewish boy, upon approaching adulthood, was required to prove his literacy by reading a passage of the Torah before the congregation. The result was that education became a central feature of Jewish society. It was highly regarded and carried forward even during periods of external oppression. Up to this very day, this cultural peculiarity has encouraged those who identify themselves as Jewish to seek and honor scholarship. In the United States this reveals itself in the fact that the ethnic group with the highest individual academic attainments is none other than the Jews.

A different pattern, but one consistent with the S-C-S paradigm, can be found among Italian-Americans. Sicily, the ancestral homeland of many of the Italians who emigrated to America, like Israel, has a record of invasion and foreign domination.[40] Located in the middle of the Mediterranean Sea, it has proven vulnerable to virtually any rapacious power with access to a navy. Unlike the Jews, however, Sicilians chose the family as their primary refuge. Its honor became the touchstone of their existence and they poured their energies into the personal loyalties and vendettas that sustained their kinfolk. When transplanted across the ocean, the offspring of this community sent their children forth, not to get a better education, but to obtain jobs that would enable them to enrich the family coffers. As former farmers and fishermen, they could also be distinguished by the resources they dedicated to buying houses and to tending gardens. Almost amusingly, their Jewish neighbors, as befitted long-term merchants and urbanites, favored apartment living.

Thomas Sowell,[41] in *Migrations and Cultures,* a detailed survey of six European and Asian groups, confirms this impression. Whether discussing Germans, Japanese, or Indians, he documents cultural patterns that remain surprisingly consistent even when peoples migrate across oceans. The famous German penchant for discipline, for example, survived along the Volga River, in the jungles of Brazil, and on the prosperous farmsteads of the Pennsylvania Dutch country. Although their contemporaries might be living a disorganized, hardscrabble existence, the Germans beginning with little more than their own ferocious desire to prevail time and again recreated the solid homes, barns, and well-tended fields from whence they came.

In America, these traditions contrasted starkly with those of the Scotch-Irish.[42] Although both groups immigrated contemporaneously, and occupied adjoining valleys, the latter became renowned for being unruly and impetuous. Habits of independence and disorder cultivated in the turmoil of the Scottish lowlands—where centuries of warfare between the English and Scotch made it irrational to invest too much energy in establishing farmsteads that could be swept away in the next battle—were announced in a less substantial building style, a tendency to squat on unoccupied territories, and a constant movement over the horizon. They even chose to settle on different sorts of land than their German compatriots, preferring less fertile slate hills similar to those of Scotland rather that more productive limestone valleys.

That there should be a specific African-American culture with a similar proclivity to endure should not shock. Loury may find the prospect offensive and indicative of a belief that blacks are outside the orbit of American civilization, but this is a normal human propensity. What would be disrespectful would be to contend that blacks are so unique that they do not respond to external stimuli the way other human beings do. It would imply the very sort of biological idiosyncrasy Loury is at pains to deny. That said, since all human groups develop cultural adjustments, the question should not be whether blacks have these, but rather what sorts they have created.

If I may be forgiven for driving the point home one more time, yet another example of a culture associated with a social structure, a culture that also results in the perpetuation of its point of origin, is the so-called "culture of poverty."[43] Not linked with a single ethnic or racial population, this design for living has been blamed for binding the underclass to its squalid roots. Although some sociologists deny its existence,[44] or that if it exists, it has an impact, the real issue seems to be a matter of degree. Many poor people, as a consequence of being poor, live disorganized lives devoid of routine, planning, or foresight. Without a dependable job to set boundaries to their behavior, they tend to drift from one incident to another, taking advantage of whatever boon may present itself. Convinced by years of desolate experience that nothing ever works out, they don't count on their world getting better. This makes them haphazard in the extreme, coming late for jobs when these are offered, failing to take advantage of medical treatment when it is available, and descending into intoxication in woeful numbers. No wonder they squander opportunities that could improve their lot. No wonder too that few others, including employers, are prepared to entrust them with responsibility.[45]

Of more relevance to us, of course, are the slave cultures that have developed in conditions other than the American South.[46] In ancient Rome, in India, and in China, slavery seems to have had a demeaning effect on those thrust into it. Forced to live in misery, disrespected by their masters, and unable to escape, regardless of their race or ethnicity, their styles of life underwent remarkably parallel transformations. A particularly revealing case is that of Europeans abducted on the high seas and forced into servitude in Moslem North Africa. As John Blassingame[47] explains, "Within a few years of their capture, the world the white bondsmen had known began to recede from their minds, and the degradation of slavery forced them to adopt new behavioral patterns. In the bagnios and slave quarters, strength and guile replaced rank and wealth as the keys to status and survival." Alcoholism became rampant, as did a resort to theft to compensate for insufficient rations. Constantly told by their Arab masters that they were naturally inferior and dishonest, this became a self-fulfilling prophesy. Even violence became an accepted aspect of their lives. Blassingame, for instance, reproduces a report of slaves "driven by oppression almost to madness, [who] wreak their vengeance on the old men, spitting in their faces, striking them, and pelting them with stones." One is reminded of Zimbarbo's[48] experiment with student-prisoners in which, when punishment was permitted as a means of maintaining discipline, things quickly got out of hand. Viciousness erupted among guards and prisoners alike, even though all knew they were participating in a charade.

To summarize, slavery would seem to be an ideal breeding ground for the emergence of both distinctive and long-lasting cultural adjustments.[49] Its combination of painful confinement and personal degradation appears almost purpose-built to arouse intense emotional responses. The sheer desperation inflicted fosters a situation in which anger and fear sit side by side with depression and hunger. A profound hostility, a deep demoralization, and a desperate recklessness may then turn inward, there to conspire in inventing ways to survive, but not necessarily to prosper. Other more gentle styles of life become so remote that they are driven out of mind and become almost impossible to access, even when slavery has been officially abolished. The lash of the overseer, the bemused sneer of a master's daughter, and the impossibility of social mobility are captured within and convert a self-imposed captivity into a permanent feature of an ex-slave's existence.

Nor were slaveowners immune to the pressures of a slave-based society. They too are molded by its internal imperatives. If their bondsman had to cope with the brutality of enforced servitude, they had to deal with the brutality of their own excesses. To inflict pain on others, to look them in the eye—at least occasionally—before or after the deed, and to benefit from their involuntary exertions, takes an inner hardness that does not come naturally to most people. Heinrich Himmler is infamous for praising his SS troops for retaining their humanity even as they shot and gassed millions of Jews, Poles, and Russians. That they could remain sensitive and refined human beings as they executed such repellent functions struck him as evidence of superior moral fiber. In the American South, the slave aristocracy had to struggle with similar burdens and they too found ways to rationalize their cruelties. But just as with their victims, these found their way into a culture with the power to persist.

THE ORIGINS OF SLAVE CULTURE

Turning specifically to the antebellum South, we must look toward the structural precursors of its culture of slavery. What was it about chattel slavery that made whites and blacks alike adopt beliefs, norms, and values that would generations later linger to haunt their descendants in their search for a better, fairer, and more successful society? In its broad outlines, most Americans are acquainted with the basic features of slavery. They know about the African slave trade, the plantation system, and the runaway slave laws. It is the connection between these and the culture they spawned that they fail to appreciate. It is, therefore, with these we must begin, and it is the white half of the equation that must come first.

White Structural Precursors

Imagine being a slaveowner. Imagine living in a large house surrounded by bondsmen bowing and scraping as they did your bidding. Imagine too that some of these slept under your roof or in Spartan cabins within easy walking distance from your bedroom. That you dressed better than they, ate better than they, and had more freedom of movement than they could hardly escape your notice. Nor, if you allowed yourself to look, could you miss the fact that your subordinates aspired to the advantages you possessed. Many of these pathetic figures might honestly proclaim their joy at the benefits you bestowed upon them, but if you listened carefully to the hymns they sang on

Sunday morning, you heard them plaintively vocalize about being bound across the river to a better land over Jordan. "Swing low sweet chariot," was their incantation, with death preferable to the toils under which they labored.

Remember too that these were estates where farm implements and hunting weapons were readily available and that, for the most part, they were isolated from other white slaveowners who lived some distance away. Under these circumstances, how could slave masters not have feared for their safety? Knowing, as they must, of slave resentments, aware that knives capable of cutting their throats were close at hand, and cognizant that they were badly outnumbered, how could they have rested easily? In point of fact, they did not. Beneficent as many masters were, and loved as some were, an undercurrent of apprehension ran through the entire white ruling class. Before Nat Turner's rampage, but surely after it, they understood the need to guard themselves against slave insurrections.[50] They recognized that a confluence of "motive, means, and opportunity" might result in their demise as surely as in any contemporary murder mystery.

Then too, people become accustomed to their advantages. They enjoy the power and perquisites thus bestowed. When one grows up habituated to having one's commands instantaneously honored, to dining in genteel comfort at a large table, and to engaging in stimulating conversation with other well-educated planters, these begin to seem the normal order of events. Thomas Jefferson,[51] prophet of egalitarianism though he was, could not conceive of life without a large and varied library. Even as his farm revenues were in decline, it seemed to him only fitting that he build, then rebuild, then rebuild again, his fine mansion of Monticello. Yet, as he walked past the slave quarters on his estate, it is barely conceivable that he felt guilty because of the disparity. Ethnocentrism did not originate in our modern era. Derived from a familiarity with the world immediately surrounding us, everyone is susceptible to it.

Black Structural Precursors

If residing at the top of a seriously skewed hierarchy has cultural implications, being trapped at its bottom has many more. The fears and selfish complacency of a ruling gentry are as nothing compared with the fears and furies of a violently submerged social caste. The deprivations, indignities, and hopelessness visited hourly, daily, and yearly upon these reluctant bondsmen accumulated and festered, and were bound to have consequences. To be deprived of power, prestige, and basic foodstuffs, and to see one's wife and children bereft of comfort, security, and a promising future must rankle. These situations inevitably aroused emotions so intense that they possessed the capacity to reshape the psyches of those experiencing them.[52]

The impact of such indignities was so extensive that to gain an accurate overview of their implications, we must divide them into several categories. Separating them along lines similar to those employed in discussing the casualties caused by a radical egalitarianism will enable us to draw the connections between the value shifts portrayed in the last chapter and identifiable aspects of slavery. It will be recalled that the categories discussed earlier included: personal responsibility, respect for rules, individual merit, truth/honesty, and family values. These will now be recast as: responsibility/self-discipline, violence/rule breaking, merit/work ethic, honesty/education, and family values/sexuality. For the sake of clarity, a slight shift in their order, with violence and rule breaking taking precedence, will also be effected.

Violence/Rule Breaking

Slavery was an inherently violent institution. As long ago as the eighteenth century, John Locke[53] concluded that anyone who "attempts to get another Man into his Absolute Power, does thereby put himself into a State of War with him." Thrusting people to the bottom of a radically imbalanced hierarchy required force. The victims had to be emotionally threatened and physically compelled to accede to subjugation. Beginning with their kidnapping in West Africa,[54] their transport in shackles in horrifically overcrowded slave ships, and their sale as human animals in the slave markets of the Caribbean and tidewater South, terror, pain, isolation, and degradation were employed to intimidate them into docility. Moving thence to the plantations where they worked for the benefit of others, they labored under the lash, the casual insult, and an atmosphere of uncertain retribution. Any white person, even a child, could call down a vindictive punishment that the slave was powerless to resist. Although members of the master class varied in their malice, the potential for a grisly whipping was ever present. White owners might not monitor every aspect of a slave's life, but an intermittent and unpredictable capacity to vigorously, and arbitrarily, intervene in their lives was unsettling. So was the possibility of a slave being murdered for a trivial affront. Frederick Douglass[55] relates how he witnessed a fellow worker being shot by an over-seer who interpreted his slowness to respond as a personal insult. Both the victims and the perpetrators of such atrocities knew that because bondsmen were property, killing them was not legally considered murder and would not be punished as such. They also knew that if a slave resisted by running away, a society-wide net would be spread to ensnare and bring him back. An example might then be made by chopping off a foot or selling him down the river (that is, the Mississippi).

In this environment of apprehension and dread, slaves had little recourse. Better than anyone else, they realized that honest efforts at protest were unacceptable and might provide the pretext for further punishment. Trapped by their very powerlessness, they had few outlets for venting their frustrations. The most obvious was inter-slave violence.[56] To cut, to insult, or to beat a fellow slave might be frowned upon by masters who did not want to see their property devalued, but it was less risky than attacking a white. The upshot was that to be a slave was to live in a world imbued with violence.

Given this ambiance, and the concurrent inability of slaves to control the resources they craved, crime was endemic among them. That which one could take, and get away with, from scraps of food to moments of leisure, was considered fair game. As significantly, disobedience and successful thievery became marks of distinction within a community where the longing to rebel was more common than an ability to carry it off. The rules to which they were subject, it must be understood, were not of their making. These regulations were enacted without their input and in contravention of their interests. As such, they might be obeyed, but not with unalloyed glee. In the slaves' eyes, laws imposed by their masters were illegitimate, so to violate them did not constitute a crime. Whatever arguments might be mustered to convince them to conform seemed no more than rationalizations. Even the informal rules of the masters, such as those entailed by etiquette, were spurned. Fancy language and manners were for his house and his benefit; they did not apply to squabbles with other slaves.

Responsibility/Self-Discipline

On the plantation there was no question of who was in charge. Its organization, from the largest policies to the smallest details, was the responsibility of the master, his wife, and those to whom they delegated authority—most notably their white over-seers and black slave-drivers. As owners of the land, all the improvements thereon, and most of those who labored to tend these, they decided what crops would be grown, what foods were served for dinner, and who was invited to next month's soiree. Whether these were good choices, and concluded with a profitable harvest and/or community admiration, depended solely upon them. They were of little concern, save as a point of abstract identification, to those who executed them.

The slaves, in contrast, had few responsibilities and those that they did possess might be transferred elsewhere at the whim of another. Though they might be blamed for a failure to carry out orders, they were not charged with deciding the shape of these commands. The particulars of shoeing a horse or plowing a piece of land might be entrusted to them, but not what that night's menu would be or which crop should be sown on what acres. With so little control, the benefits that came a slave's way depended mostly on the good will of others. If the master paternalistically chose to bestow a choice work assignment, a well built cabin, or an extra food and clothing ration, it was an occasion for rejoicing. The slave might be able to manipulate his master, and do so with considerable ingenuity, but he had little direct impact on events. Given his inability to issue commands, or make them stick, it did not make sense to think things through too far in advance. The probability that his desires would come to fruition was much too low to invest an abundance of mental or emotional energy. More rational was to react spontaneously, and agilely, to the initiatives of others. Tactical, not strategic, skill was his forte.

With this sort of division of responsibility, discipline was, from a slave's perspective, an external phenomenon. He or she was much more likely to be told what to do rather than be asked for a preference. Likewise, if a task was improperly performed, the sanctions for incompetence came primarily from the outside. Why would a slave force himself to do what others wanted, especially when these things were not in his interest? Rather than internalize self-discipline, he or she was much more apt to rely on being vigilant. Because rules of behavior and plans of action were the domain of his tormentor, they were not something to be imported within, much less enforced by means of internal coercion. The circumstance of being a slave aroused not guilt or personal responsibility, but a sensitivity to the demands, the favors, and the momentary dispositions of those towering over him. The plausible excuse, not voluntary obedience, was what saved him.

Merit/Work Ethic

A large amount of research has been devoted to determining if slavery was profitable. Despite the fact that overall it was, considerable evidence exists to suggest that on an individual level, slaves tended to be inefficient. Not working at their own behest or for their own advantage, there was little incentive to work hard or intelligently. Quite the contrary, it was in their interest to produce the minimum possible. If they could escape scrutiny, they thereby gained some measure of personal autonomy and maybe a modicum of revenge. The slave system was, therefore, efficient as a whole, but not in detail. The masters did indeed benefit, as witness their lavish lifestyles, but the per capita production was not impressive. In the end, of course, it was spectacularly surpassed by the industrial, free-labor North.

Merit, as it existed on the plantation, was, in consequence, a standard that applied primarily to its self-appointed aristocrats. Intellectual pursuits, fashionable elegance, and economic success were their prerogative, and only a parody of them was allowed their chattel. If they could, the masters would have implanted a strong work ethic—to do so would have been profitable— but the resistance to this was too persistent and too strong. Some slave craftsmen and house servants might take pride in their expertise, but on the whole a Calvinistic attitude toward life was absent from the slave mentality. They neither demanded of themselves, nor their children, conformity with objectives not of their own devising.

Honesty/Education

A slave system is clearly not conducive to honesty or trust. With exploitation as its central feature, there was simply no basis for mutual positive regard or a shared frankness. First, it was in the interest of the masters to tell slaves only what they wanted them to know. Excessive information was a distraction that might enable their property to resist control. As authority figures the world over have discovered, knowledge is power.[57] To maintain an advantage, it is frequently necessary to deceive one's subordinates or, at least, to keep secrets from them.[58] If they understand what is going on, they might object, or, even worse, devise effective means to intervene. There is thus a proclivity to limit information that evinces itself most obviously in the area of education. Slave owners rightly feared overeducated slaves and vigorously sought to deny them formal learning. Reading, writing, and academic study were reserved for those in charge of organizing the system, not those who were at its base.

From a slave's standpoint, it was equally sensible to limit the flow of information. There were things the master did not need to know, things that might result in brutal punishments or unwelcome speed-ups. Especially when slaves broke the rules, they needed to keep this to themselves. Misleading an overseer or appropriating an extra portion of food must be concealed as cleverly and inconspicuously as possible. Dishonesty, particularly when directed toward the master, was therefore likely to be protected by all. The entire group would thus close ranks to confirm alibis they knew to be bogus.

Family Values/Sexuality

Africa has extensive, complex, and strictly enforced patterns of family life. Be they Muslims or animists, in their homelands Africans demonstrate an abiding respect for family authority, tribal traditions, and separate gender roles. When they were removed to the New World and plunged into bondage, all this was disrupted. Although there are unresolved controversies regarding whether black families survived on Southern plantations, the traditional arrangements were clearly interrupted. Research also seems to show inconsistencies between what happened in different regions and with different masters. In some cases family stability was encouraged; in others it was a matter of indifference; in still others it was actively discouraged. Religion, housing arrangements, and child-rearing concerns might militate toward keeping nuclear families intact, but economic profits, personal lust, and individual jealousies could dictate otherwise. What is unequivocal is that the maintenance of family life was not an imperative of the system and, given the property status of the slave, could be unilaterally revoked. Even when heterosexual fidelity was espoused, for example to promote slave fertility, all concerned understood that it could be violated whenever a white desired.

A primary cause of family vulnerability was the sexual appetites of white males.[59] They might appropriate the services of a female slave any time they liked. Regardless of her preferences or those of her mate, she would have to accede to whatever was demanded. Another cause of vulnerability was economic necessity. A gambling debt, a failed crop, or the decision to open a nail factory might dictate the sale of one or more slaves and the purchase of others regardless of any prior relationships between them. Despite pledges that family integrity would be maintained, the need to make money took precedence. The conclusion was that if one were a slave, one never knew when trouble was brewing, with the resultant tensions making personal commitments a challenge. A realization that one's family might be broken up to preserve group discipline, to get revenge for a perceived slight, or to honor a promise to a fellow planter made secure bonds a virtual impossibility.

Between parents and children, a similar vulnerability was manifest. Because they were the property of their owners, not their parents, slave children could at any moment be wrenched from their families and directed to perform chores wherever the master wished. As painfully, they were most likely to be raised not by their mothers, but by their grandmothers.[60] Since women of childbearing age were at their economically productive height, their efforts were typically required in the fields or the kitchen. It was the older, less physically able women, that is, the grandmothers, who remained behind to supervise the young. Then too children might be sold just as were their parents and for reasons as arbitrary and egoistic.

Of enormous importance, although usually overlooked, was, in the words of Blassingame,[61] that "As slaves...black men could no longer exercise the same power over their families as they had in Africa." "First, and most important of all, his authority was restricted by his master. Any decision of his regarding his family could be countermanded by his master. The master determined when both he and his wife would go to work, when or whether his wife cooked his meals, and was often the final arbiter in family disputes." Moreover, "The most serious impediment to a man's acquisition of status in his family was his inability to protect his wife from the sexual advances of whites and the physical abuse of his master." Unable to protect even himself, he could not visibly demonstrate the sort of power that has universally won men the respect and loyalty of their loved ones.

Not fully appreciated either, because it is such a delicate subject, was the salience of sex. In a climate in which family satisfactions are beyond the control of the participants, they may turn to that which is within their power, and which, not incidentally, seems to be valued by those with more clout than themselves, namely their sexuality. Even under conditions of slavery people have dominion over their bodies. Furthermore, an ability to arouse lust in another is a remarkable confirmation of one's worth and potency. For those with few other outlets, sexual power can seem like magic. The pleasures it makes available are undeniable, as is its ability to motivate others with a simple touch or look. Unfortunately, when sexuality takes primacy over personal commitment, the cement that holds families together is further eroded.

Chapter 6

The Culture of Slavery: Outcomes

Facts are stubborn things; and whatever may be our wishes, or inclinations, or the dictates of our passions, they cannot alter the state of facts and evidence.
John Adams, *Defense of British Soldiers in the Boston Massacre Trial*

TRANSITIONS

How can it be? How can a pattern established hundreds of years ago, under conditions that would be barely recognizable today, have the power to bind people to a cheerless style of life? Are not those in its grip smart enough to see what is happening and just change? These are questions my students ask all the time. Utterly uninterested in history, they can scarcely imagine what sorts of mechanism might keep the past alive. Indeed, most doubt that it happens. But they are wrong. The past does operate in the present, and it does so with a vengeance. They have nevertheless stumbled upon a legitimate problem. If the S-C-S model is valid, there remains the question of how transitions from one time period to another are effected. How do particular social structures become frozen into distinct sets of cultural features that manage to persist over decades or centuries? More than this, having succeeded in enduring, how are these characteristics converted back into structural elements? Just as geologists had difficulty accepting the theory of continental drift before plate tectonics provided a reasonable mechanism for rafting the continents apart, so a culture of slavery theory requires a plausible method of getting from then to now.

First, how can a structure create a culture? By what means do particular relationships, hierarchies, and roles produce a coherent collection

125

of beliefs, norms, and values? The answer is simpler than might be supposed. Social structures, by confronting people with a host of demands, influence the way they think, feel, and decide to act. The attachments, unequal ranks, and role partners to which they are exposed literally alter their cognitions, emotions, and volitions. To give a humble, but pregnant example, a social structure that lays people open to intense, omnipresent, and unequal violence necessitates a response. Without some way of defending themselves from what is happening, people would flounder. They might actually lose their will to live and thrash about until something disastrous occurred. What is needed is a cognitive map of their environment, an emotional adaptation to its threats, and a set of activities that provide safety amidst the chaos.

On the cognitive level, in the case of slavery-induced violence, a slave's tormentors will appear very powerful and very vindictive. By contrast, the victim will be perceived as lacking the capacity to resist this threat. As a result, the master will seem more intelligent, less compassionate, and infinitely more deceitful than his prey. Although they would abhor the thought, and verbally dispute it, in their own view, blacks would emerge as relatively inept. Moreover, because of their proclivity for violence, they might even come to accept themselves as dangerous.

Turning to the emotional level, in the slave's world fear, rage, and sorrow would be the predominant responses. Both individually and as a group, the possibility of injury would be so strong and the prospect of frustration so pervasive, that dread and a desire for revenge would be almost universal. Yet because slaves remained social creatures, these reactions would be conducted along communally favored pathways. The targets of their anger, and the forms this anger took, would not be purely private, but interpersonally orchestrated. Thus the victims might reinforce each other's negative reactions and encourage specific forms of emotional retaliation.

Finally, on the volitional level the slave response to violence would entail the creation of norms and values designed to mount an effective defense and/or to create compensatory pleasures. Although not consciously planned, trial and error would produce a varied toolkit of shared behaviors. Techniques for answering the master with a smile on one's face and hostility in one's heart would become second nature, as might procedures for sabotaging his possessions without getting caught. The values slaves adopted could thus include an admiration of physical strength, as well as a grudging respect for white dominance. Together these would provide a plan for living, which, although not enviable, would be workable. Because humans are goal-oriented, we require something to aspire to even under the worst structural conditions and this is what such attitudes provide.

A specific illustration of how structure can produce culture is provided by skin color. The fact that, under American chattel slavery, the masters were white and the slaves black was a visible difference that none could cognitively escape. To look at someone was simultaneously to classify him. Even if a first impression turned out to be wrong, and a black person was not a slave, he would still be accounted as slave material. On an emotional level, brown skin would, therefore, be associated with either fear or disgust, depending upon the circumstances under which it was noticed. The result was that for the master, and by extension, the slave, a black servant was lowly, nasty, and repugnant when engaged in a servile occupation, but might be an object of alarm when stumbled upon unexpectedly on a dark night. For better or worse, the way we feel about people is often a reflection of their relative power. So, in fact, is the value we assign them. Unfair as it may be, the powerful are perceived as more beautiful, intelligent, and moral.[1] For example, in ancient Rome, the most elegant form of nose was the regal Roman nose. Its aquiline shape, that is, its eagle-like profile, was deemed noble. Only the later ascendancy of straighter nosed northern Europeans altered this standard of attractiveness. In the American South, for similar reasons, light skin, straight hair, and thin lips came to be regarded as "best." They literally looked more attractive to whites and blacks alike. The result was that a fair-skinned child might be treated more generously than his darker skinned sibling.[2] Likewise, slave children, to the degree that they were able, were encouraged to seek light-skinned mates.

Turning now to how cultures are maintained, it is at first necessary to observe that this is an enormously complex process. In sociology, there is a tendency to collapse a variety of mechanisms into one by referring to them all as "socialization." Socialization[3] literally means the process of learning to become social and the image transmitted is that of a parent consciously teaching a child what he or she needs to know. It is as if the parent's accumulated wisdom is poured unaltered into the empty vessel of the child. As every parent must realize, however, children are not so cooperative. Nor are they themselves so well organized or self aware. Actual learning is a much more complicated affair in which everybody puts in their two cents, often for reasons that have nothing to do with passing along culture. This informal pushing and pulling, with influence being exerted in unrecorded ways between multiple participants, may seen wasteful and irrational, but it is a potent instrument, and, in any event, the way things work.

Yet formal cultural transmission also occurs. Parents do inculcate intentional lessons, and schools and churches are mandated to teach a myriad of specific skills and beliefs. The previously noted Jewish penchant for literacy is, in part, maintained by parents who send their offspring to Synagogue to acquire the rudiments of the Hebrew language. Religious beliefs in general tend to be deliberately inculcated, both at home and in specialized institutions. As was alluded to earlier, on the cusp between formalized and informal education is the sort of transaction described by Rogers and Hammerstein[4] in *South Pacific*. The musical's major plot features the imperiled World War II love affair of nurse Nellie Forbush and island planter Emile de Becque. All goes well between the two until the Little Rock born Nellie discovers that Emile has mixed-race children by his deceased Polynesian wife. She is horrified and immediately breaks off all communication. Emile is confused and goes to Lt. Cable, who is himself ambivalent about his relationship with a local girl, for an explanation. "What makes her talk like that? Why do you have this feeling, you and she?" Emile asks. "I do not believe it is born in you. I do not believe it." This is when Cable replies in song:

You've got to be taught to hate and fear,
You've got to be taught from year to year,
It's got to be drummed into your dear little ear—
You've got to be carefully taught!

I know of no finer synopsis of the socialization theory. Prejudice, in this case, is assumed to result from direct inculcation. The child is presumably instructed to hate particular people for identified reasons. It all sounds so simple. Nevertheless, this is rarely how things happen. The intended lessons may be impossible to miss, but they are hardly ever presented as a lessons. Much more prevalent is the fit of passion with crude declarations such as: "Them God Damn niggers! You can never trust any of them!" The hate here is palpable, and the target unmistakable, but there is no explicit instruction to detest anyone. The learning is by example, not overt pedagogy. Perhaps unexpectedly, this sort of transmission is common within the black community too. Now that the term "nigger" is so taboo it is referred to as the "N-word," it is invoked far more frequently among blacks than whites. To do so is a sign of contempt that implies another person is coarse, violent, and uneducated. Yet here too the lesson is implicit. The judgment may be dramatic, but conscious instruction is absent.

Informal socialization takes place in a variety of ways. During the course of ordinary living people engage in a multitude of behaviors that result in the transmission of beliefs, norms, and values. The process can be so subtle that information is passed along by gossip, a raised eyebrow, or a sardonic grin.[5] People are able to see what others think, and hence believe, merely by hearing their explanations of a particular act. They likewise determine what others truly feel by gauging the intensity of their reactions. A sudden flicker across someone's face will send a very different message than a violent tantrum. People also glean values and norms from actual behaviors. Because so much learning is accomplished through imitation and modeling, they simply appropriate patterns witnessed in others.

Informal learning also occurs within social negotiations. Humans perpetually try to influence each other and in the process arrive at mutually honored arrangements regarding norms and values. These transactions can be very diverse. Sometimes we attempt to manipulate the way others think and feel; sometimes we force them to act along a preferred direction. Among the techniques employed are: (1) telling others only that which we expect to have a particular effect, (2) engaging in outright deceptions, and (3) regulating our feelings so they elicit a desired emotional response. We also resort to rewards and punishments to get our way. Creative to the core, we entice our associates with flattery and/or promises of economic benefit. Conversely, we can intimidate them with threats of physical harm or damage to their business.[6]

This ability to teach through interpersonal influence is enhanced by our aptitude for recruiting one another into specific structural positions. As role partners, members of the same hierarchies, and personal intimates, we reciprocally assign each other circumscribed roles, statuses and social positions. In the process, we also instruct one another in the conduct associated with these positions. When engaged in the interactions mandated by these structures, we let each other know which behaviors are legitimate and guide one another in acting accordingly. Thus, a parent will tell a two-year-old that he is no longer a "baby" and hence must not cry, or a boss will demand correct behavior by monitoring when his employees go for lunch, or a white person will visibly expect deferential behavior from a black stranger encountered on a train.

On the cognitive plane, informal socialization can perpetuate ancient stereotypes. Because in conversation people are liable to swap what they think they know, the notion that blacks are uniquely violent can become stabilized in feedback loops that roll along of their own accord. What seems true will be repeated so often that it sounds natural. But this is not the whole story. Structured social experiences can also result in standardized perceptions. Since the extraordinary violence of the black community is itself culturally perpetuated, conventionalized beliefs about black violence are sustained by what people actually see. Were there fewer black murderers, the lack of confirmation would change many minds. As it is, individuals encounter what they expect more often than the laws of probability would predict. Reality and stereotypes are therefore juxtaposed in an uneasy, self-perpetuating alliance.

On the emotional plane, anger has a knack of generating further violent anger. In recent times, and with good reason, it has become a cliché that abused children grow up to become abusive adults.[7] This connection is painful, but real, in large part because those who suffer unjust punishments rarely do so passively. A rage builds in their breasts, even if it has no immediate outlet. Should striking back at their tormentors prove impractical, an alternative target will be appropriated, preferably someone with less strength. In the black community these scapegoats generally have been other blacks, especially wives and children.[8] They bear the brunt of furies that do not abate until they inflict aches that themselves require retaliation. These second-level grievances may in turn generate what Anna Freud[9] labeled "identifying with the aggressor." The secondary victim now expresses anger in a manner similar to what he previously witnessed. Rather than lash out this way, some persons, to be sure, engage in "reaction formation" or in self-abuse. They are so distressed by the rage they encounter that they vow never to repeat it. The problem here is that when rage becomes prevalent within a community, it tends to monopolize center stage and to set the cultural standard. As it were, it draws all the oxygen out of the atmosphere and forces everyone to react to it.

Turning to the volitional plane, and more particularly to its value dimension, cultural imperatives are sustained by an assortment of mechanisms dedicated to promoting social standards. That which individuals determine to have worth is not confined to solipsistic judgments. It is also manifest in shared judgments. People tend to act on their values and to encourage their role partners to do the same. These endpoints are sought and enforced, not merely held. This means that violence may be admired and praised. If this is the case, it may then be inflicted with pride. A person will feel justified in beating up another and openly communicate his sense of righteousness to his peers. Should they challenge him, he will passionately insist that the victim had it coming. When a sufficient number of consequential persons partake of such attitudes, they become dominant. The building of such a consensus can also be very subtle. Lee Rainwater[10] describes an incident in which a mother encouraged her ghetto-born son to lie about a school-related matter. When he was caught in an earlier falsehood, she rebuked him sharply, but when he later told an equally untrue story, but more boldly, she not only failed to become upset, she also exhibited unmistakable satisfaction. In her eyes, he was now being clever. Norms too are upheld through social interactions. People habitually instruct one another on the correct way to behave. Whether it concerns the clothes one should wear, the food one should eat, or the proper way to hold a spoon, their targets respond with discomfort when a rule is broken. They know that if the violation is serious, the offender may be ostracized. Most of the time, however, people do not need to be reminded to stay within bounds. The behaviors they see a majority of others performing appear "normal." That there might be other ways of acting will not occur to them, even though this standard of conduct may unimaginable to outsiders. Because this is so, when violence pervades a community, fighting may seem both sensible and unavoidable.

Also an aspect of cultural socialization are what might be called intermediary social structures. In the S-C-S model, it must not be assumed that structure is absent in the middle of the sandwich. People always operate within some structural arrangement. The demands they make of one another are always patterned in recognizable ways and the relationships they enter always hang together in identifiable segments that have predictable consequences. One way to describe these patterns is as *institutions*. Gangs, for instance, can sustain culture by perpetuating violence and anger. The peer pressures they engender encourage predatory behaviors directed against other gangs, thereby ensuring that their enemies will launch reprisals against them. Another institution, but one with more benign repercussions, is the church. The fellowship, beliefs, and values incorporated into its structure invite loving relationships. Likewise, the bag parties to which Gates alludes are a mechanism for perpetuating color-based divisions. They provide locations where people can gather to reinforce a shared worldview. In the instance of the bag party, its association with New Orleans can be traced to a Creole culture wherein light-skinned blacks, for centuries, supported a highly organized, and well-respected, social and commercial community.

The last step in all this is, of course, the recapitulation of the initial structure. Since S-C-S is a dynamic arrangement, the flow of culture into structure is a continuous one. Any boundaries imposed are artificial and a concession to our need for concreteness. They provide only a frame around a snapshot that would differ were it taken at some other moment. By the same token, the structure at time 2 will not be identical with that at time 1. The claim that it represents a recapitulation of the former does not imply total congruence. Life's details are willy-nilly always too innumerable to be replicated exactly. What is the same is the general outline. To illustrate, when talking about the Jews, it is their long-term emphasis on education and not instruction in the original materials that is repeated. Similarly, for African-Americans, it is a milieu of violence and color-based stratification that are reconstructed, not slavery per se. In any event, the resultant structure is sustained by the sum total of cognitions, emotions, volitions, and institutions that precede it. These shape the relationships and behavior patterns of people who, were they asked, would consider themselves independent agents. Although they make choices, and these choices make a difference, the overall picture has a consistency beyond their ability to manipulate.   Humans are social creatures, often at the mercy of unrecognized social forces. Our hubris may convince us that our capacity to command fate is boundless, but the world has a way of teaching us there are limitations we cannot eliminate.

A PAINFUL STORY

All of us, even the pessimists, like a happy ending. We may scoff at a performance that contains too much treacle, but we secretly long for hope and justice to triumph. In my race and ethnicity classes, this propensity manifests itself in a student desire for a positive spin on the cultures of various groups. Saying too many negative things is regarded as depressing and unjustified. My black students, in particular, become distressed if I say too many disturbing things about their heritage. They may acknowledge the truth of what is alleged, but request that this be counterbalanced with a more upbeat assessment. That which is unflattering to their ancestors strikes them as reflecting upon themselves, and they become discouraged about overcoming these liabilities. Only when I point to their higher than average levels of religiosity, or their unparalleled achievements in the arts, are they somewhat mollified.

The problem, as this relates to the culture of slavery, is that it embodies a gigantic tangle of dysfunction. Slavery was an appalling institution[11]— which few today deny. But neither do people enjoy lingering over its more atrocious aspects. Still, it is slavery's present-day consequences that are most often disowned. They are simply too distressing and too extensive to be comfortably endured. Because chattel slavery is safely in the past, its excesses can sometimes be conceded with frankness. The details may be jarring, but they can be coped with much as one deals with a frightening movie, that is, by keeping them at an emotional distance. Its cultural legacies are, however, another matter. Their ravages can be as close as one's front parlor and as personal as one's fantasy life. Tangible, tenacious, and debilitating, they retain the power to ruin lives.

Given this unease, a social science analysis the culture of slavery can be a challenge. A combination of personal disabilities and moral commitments prime a great many observers to dispute whatever is asserted. Rather than contemplate the validity of a proposition, they pick at its particulars, looking for a discrepancy that might discredit the whole. Theirs is not a search for truth, but a last ditch stand to ward off the barbarians. Guarding—as they see it—the future of an entire race, in their own minds, they are Leonidas at Thermopylae or Horatio at the bridge, hence the determination to change the subject, or, failing that, to undermine it.

And yet the culture of slavery deserves to be examined. To the degree that it reflects reality, it must be comprehended and its implications appreciated. For this to occur, however, the pattern needs to be discerned as a whole. Because its many facets are interlocked in a self-sustaining entirety, the relationship of each part to the others illuminates the meaning of all. Anthropologists who follow the Boasian[12] tradition point out that a culture can be understood only on its own terms; that when its pieces are wrenched out of context, they may seem senseless and trivial. One must instead recognize its idiosyncratic history, the resources available to it, and the knowledge at its disposal. Seen in this light, peculiar clusters of folkways blend together into seamless tapestries that conform with their own environments. The same is true of the culture of slavery. From the perspective of those reenacting it, its components mesh in a manner that makes sense. Even if the assemblage is ultimately dysfunctional, it is not irrational. Within the world from which it arose, it was a reasonable rejoinder.

As a theory, the culture of slavery must also be assessed as a whole. The evidence supporting its individual components may, or may not, be compelling, but their number and cohesion provide impressive testimony to the validity of the overall hypothesis. The situation is comparable to that of the theory of evolution.[13] Both have called forth a myriad of critics who want to extirpate them root and branch; nevertheless they rely on a mass of consistent facts that are difficult to deny. In the case of evolution, the weight of evidence is so great that continuing to call it a theory is more a tribute to the tenacity of its detractors than to any lack of confirmation. Indeed, the proofs of evolution are almost too abundant to enumerate. Geology with its worldwide panoply of fossil-rich layers of rock; plate tectonics with its account of how continental drift has both separated and reunited populations; anatomy with its manifold correlations between the bones of related species; embryology with its surprisingly uniform recapitulations of past evolutionary trends; genetics with its evidence that some populations are more closely allied than others; and artificial breeding techniques with their ability to develop new varieties of horses, dogs, and pigeons, all point in the same direction.

The culture of slavery likewise draws many threads together to fashion a sturdy rope from a skein of slender strands. The myriad kinds of evidence upon which it depends come from the present and past and from the black and white experience. Patterns of racism, violence, crime, etiquette, discipline, child-rearing, personal values, religiosity, attractiveness, employment, recreation, and family relationships all contribute to the final picture. As with evolution, however, each of these has been attacked. Separately plausible arguments are, for instance, made that contemporary black violence is a response to present-day discrimination or that slave families were more stable than was once believed.[14] Nevertheless it is difficult to discount the sum total of factors upholding the hypothesis. Our understanding of these may need to be modified by future scholarship, but this no more refutes their overall integrity than the discovery of a carnosaur larger than *Tyrannosaurus rex* would obviate evolution.

Nor should the discomfort caused by the individual facts disqualify them from consideration. Facts, as John Adams[15] insisted, are stubborn things. They will not go away no matter how much they displease us.[16] Though a grand political consensus may be reached by white and black, liberal and conservative, this unanimity can no more repeal a social truth than legislatures can invalidate the law of gravity. Race relations may have a moral dimension that elicits moral responses, yet they remain a legitimate focus of social science.[17] Because what is happening is a matter of fact, not merely value, some assertions are true and others false. Objectivity may be difficult to sustain when passions are inflamed, but our well-being is contingent on aiming for it. Only then can we make informed judgments; only then can we avoid the pitfalls of an uncritical idealism.[18]

In the account that follows, a mountain of details will be adduced to demonstrate the impact of the culture of slavery. More of these will concern blacks than whites, not because what occurred to them was more real, but because African-Americans have encountered greater difficulty in extricating themselves from its clutches. They have also had a greater tendency to deny its effects. Though some disagree, slavery was more destructive to its victims than to its beneficiaries. For them, its heat was so caustic it reconfigured the deepest recesses of their souls. Whites, by comparison, had other areas of success available. Giving up their unearned advantages may have been done with reluctance, nevertheless, as society's leaders, they had broader opportunities to restructure events.[19]

The dishonor inherent in slavery and its aftermath similarly invite denial. No one likes to be reminded of their weaknesses. If a cultural inventory reveals that one group far outstrips another, the impetus to revise history can be overpowering.[20] Accurate social science, however, requires that this impulse be resisted. In any event, the white and black cultural responses to slavery are mirror images of each other. One is the yin to the other's yang, the key to the other's lock. Neither can be correctly apprehended without an appreciation of how they complement each other.

WHITE CULTURE

White Racism

That European-Americans have been racist, and that this racism continues to infect race relations, should not come as news. Whites, in general, not merely Southern whites, are prone to considering themselves superior to nonwhites. Even my grandparents, who were immigrants to this country, adopted the prevailing racial attitudes. They might verbally attest to universal brotherhood, but knew that if there was a dirty, backbreaking job to do, you got a "schwatza" to do it. Day-laborer and domestic positions seemed their natural turf and it never occurred to my relatives that this was demeaning. Racism, therefore—defined as a combination of prejudice and discrimination directed toward an identified racial group—is a pervasive white cultural legacy. The belief that blacks are not as "good," as proficient, or as entitled to the same benefits as others, persists to excuse unequal treatment.[21]

Racism may have originated as a justification for oppression, but it has survived as a rationalization for asymmetrical standards. In colonial American, African slaves were considered childlike primitives incapable of organizing their own lives. Their servitude was considered inevitable— explicitly decreed by God. As the descendants of Ham, they required Christianizing by altruistic Europeans. After the Civil War, this assessment was updated in the scientific guise of Social Darwinism.[22] Alleged not to have evolved to the same level as whites, their apelike qualities consigned them to fail in competition with more fully human beings. Today this appraisal has transmuted into a more diffuse form; it is widely believed, if not loudly enunciated, that blacks are not as intelligent as whites.[23] If they flounder at academic pursuits, they cannot help it. The consequence is that fewer academic demands are made of them and fewer intellectual tasks are assigned them in the marketplace.

On a lighter, and less negative note, antebellum Southern attitudes endure in the concept of Southern Hospitality. Back on the old-time plantation, the patrician class lived a comfortable, if relatively isolated, existence. Surrounded by family and servants, they hungered for social stimulation. This was often provided by visitors who were encouraged to tarry by being lavishly put up. Jefferson,[24] for example, almost always had company at Monticello. In the modern South, this tradition finds expression in the politeness with which strangers are greeted. Even Northerners are given the benefit of the doubt and to their faces greeted with a smile. Blacks too are treated cordially, but in line with a lingering racism this is more grudging and not as uniform.

Violence

Nor has the violence attendant to slavery completely subsided. In the old days, the coercive control of blacks was considered imperative. The master class, of necessity, became inured to inflicting pain. This insensitivity, however, did not disappear with manumission.[25] One of its most notorious manifestations came shortly thereafter. Returning confederate veterans discovered almost by accident that they could terrorize their former slaves by riding around in bed sheets and burning crosses in the town square.[26] From its modest beginnings as a fraternal organization created by a handful of Tennesseans, the Ku Klux Klan exploded in popularity among a white population comfortable with visiting casual brutality on blacks. Even murder was condoned, that is, if their former slaves could not otherwise be intimidated. Ultimately, even after the KKK was repressed, a penchant for lynching became a hallmark of the South. For frequently trivial offenses—such as looking too directly at a white woman— hundreds, and perhaps thousands, of black men became "strange fruit" dangling from trees as warnings not to transgress.[27]

Another manifestation of this white proclivity toward racial violence has been on display in the courts. With the criminal justice system under their control, they could arrange for summary decisions and brutal sentences. An emotionally gripping narrative of this capacity to railroad innocent African-Americans is presented in Harper Lee's[28] Pulitzer Prize winning novel *To Kill a Mockingbird*. Its lawyer hero, Atticus Finch, must contend with a community prepared to convict a black man on the uncorroborated testimony of an odious redneck who is lying to conceal his cruelty toward his daughter. Sharing in this same tendency have been police brutality and the uneven application of the death penalty. Further evidence of institutionalized violence is available in the history of eugenics. Ostensibly a scientific movement intended to elevate the biological endowment of humanity, in practice eugenics was applied almost exclusively toward defenseless blacks.[29] States as broadly separated as Virginia and California compelled thousands of their welfare clients to be forcibly sterilized on the pretext that they were mentally retarded. Only the eugenic excesses of Nazi Germany made this procedure repellent to a vast majority of Americans.

Also tinged with violence has been the attitude of labor unions. Frederick Douglass[30] and W.E.B. DuBois[31] recounted flagrant cases of physical intimidation visited by working men against potential black co-workers. Douglass describes how he was personally attacked by whites who could not abide his laboring at their side in a Baltimore shipyard. When he later escaped bondage and attempted to ply his trade in a presumably more tolerant New England, he was again threatened. DuBois, for his part, explains that the Philadelphia Negroes he studied were denied equal industrial employment by rioters determined to consign them to laborer positions. Race riots were at the time a white custom, not a black one.

More broadly, and particularly in the South, white violence found an outlet in military careers. Illustrative of this was General George Patton, who gloried in deeds of his confederate ancestors. Skill in riding horses and using guns continued to be a matter of pride, despite the fact that the rural character of the South was fading. Now urban cowboys pretend, on weekends, to be free spirits by wearing tooled Western boots and broad-brimmed hats, while redneck wannabes laugh at jokes about owning pickup trucks with rifle racks in the back.

Rule-Breaking

On Sundays in church, and on business days when in a moralistic mood, Southern whites insist on the primacy of law. They vigorously profess themselves to be scandalized by violations of the Ten Commandments and of family values. And yet their attitude toward rules can be remarkably flexible. Among themselves the earlier turbulence of a free-wheeling plantation society is evident in a continuing admiration of people who stand up to the authorities. In the not too distant past, taking the law into one's own hands was even considered the manly thing to do. Although the extreme version of this, as manifested by the legendary

Hatfields and McCoys, was rare, feuding and "bad blood" were not. Fox Butterfield[32] concludes that in places such as Edgefield County, South Carolina the white residents were renowned for being "pugnacious, reckless and prone to shed blood"—not only of blacks, but of themselves.

With specific reference to blacks, a cavalier attitude to rules was rampant. Each white man was, in essence, a legislature and court system unto himself. Under slavery, master's promulgated and enforced private standards of behavior. State-sponsored slave codes certainly existed, but their interpretation and imposition often relied on the judgment of those on the spot. Later on, decisions about whether to hold an individual black accountable for violating the honor of a white woman depended on the whim of white crowds. The determination to lynch was itself outside official legal purview.[33] More recently the level of government financing directed toward segregated black schools was within the arbitrary domain of local white politicians. They might proclaim themselves to be guided by legislation, but exercised a pliant discretion which waxed and waned with the state of their own interests.[34]

Responsibility/Self-Discipline

With the defeat of the Confederacy, the South's slave-based economy lay in ruins. A Northern imposed reconstruction promised to wash away old institutions and to raise former slaves to freedom and prosperity. But this did not happen. "Forty acres and a mule" proved an impossible chimera, as did assurances of a sustained black presence in Southern legislatures. Instead the ex-slaves found themselves without employment and their former masters discovered themselves with cotton lands that needed tilling. The solution that emerged was the sharecropping system.[35] This was essentially a deal in which white property owners allowed black peasants to work tracts of land in exchange for a portion of the crop—usually a small proportion.

Under this new arrangement the responsibility for keeping records and for disbursing the proceeds of a season's work lay firmly in white hands. Very much as they did when they administered the plantations, whites organized what would be grown, distributed the requisite supplies, and decided how much their workers should receive. The creation of a pattern of systematic loans further encumbered blacks with debts that enabled the land barons to perpetuate what was essentially a market-based slavery. This left whites very much in charge and blacks with few options. Although a sense of entitlement condoned this exploitation, it was counterbalanced by a *paternalistic* outlook toward those perceived as "inferior."[36] Many in the reworked master class continued to believe they were doing their minions a favor. Regarding themselves as more sober, hard-working, and dependable than those who cultivated their fields, a sense of noblesse oblige impelled them to disburse beneficences among those considered incapable of caring for themselves.

In the North, responsibility was likewise regarded a white perquisite. Its burgeoning community of capitalist businessmen virtually cornered the market on economic and political power. Some of this bounty was shared with free white workmen in the form of higher wages and democratic reforms, but no one seriously contemplated extending these privileges to blacks. As they migrated northward (initially in small numbers) to fill freshly minted industrial jobs, the former slaves were shunted into segregated neighborhoods and demeaning work assignments. Consultations to determine their needs, if these occurred, were likely to be with a tiny clique of black "leaders" who served more as intermediaries than power brokers in their own right.[37]

Merit/Work Ethic

Ironically, in view of the intellectual supremacy of its pre-Revolutionary tidewater aristocracy, white Southern culture placed a limited cachet on individual merit and achievement. Status was highly regarded, but visibly expended effort was not. Those at the top of its pyramid supposedly deserved to be there on the basis of blood and talent.[38] Even though many who succeeded were clever businessmen and adroit politicians, they were encouraged to effect of an appearance of facile elegance. Such merit as they possessed was thought inherent and therefore impossible for blacks to emulate.

Furthermore, the market economy, which so transformed the North, was slow in coming to the South. As a provider of agricultural staples, it possessed an active commercial life, but not an innovative industrial one. Whereas a work-oriented go-getter mentality served the interests of the Yankee entrepreneurial class, a more laid-back style seemed appropriate to Dixie's conservative economy. Boosterism set the mid- and far-West alight with boom-towns and restless migrations, but the old Confederacy, for the better part of a century, was a "sleepy" backwater. Even its writers, who inspired by the likes of a Faulkner, McCuller, and Cather, were later to lead to a literary preeminence, until the twentieth century, lay dormant.

Honesty/Education

Among the legacies of the old South are the tall tale and the grand self-deception. Those who could spin a sprightly yarn were admired and those who could gallantly uphold regional myths were lauded. Primary among these myths was that of the "lost cause." The Civil War may have ended in tragedy, but it was hailed as a noble effort to preserve an honorable way of life. A chivalrous master class, a contented servant class, and an abundance of yeoman farmers had been more than justified in defending states rights and in execrating boorish Yankee oppressors. Despite the sometime misery of their condition, Southerners convinced themselves that the truth was as they wished. In particular, they denied that whites had in any way been cruel to blacks or that blacks had any desire for freedom.[39] Nor were there communal pressures to be honest when dealing with blacks. Whatever rationalizations achieved a desired outcome were deemed legitimate.

In terms of education, the Southern states also lagged behind. Outside of colonial Virginia, with its College of William and Mary and Jefferson's University of Virginia, there were few institutions of higher learning. The eminence of Duke, Rice, Vanderbilt, or the University of North Carolina were all in the future. The scions of a landed aristocracy might be provided with tutors and an opportunity to enroll in Northern schools, but for ordinary whites instruction was at a low ebb. For years, Mississippi's dismal school system was emblematic of a disinclination to foster quality learning. The image of the "dumb" Southerner thus became the object of national jokes and was confirmed whenever state achievement tests were compared. An earlier denial of education to blacks seems to have spilled over to a reluctance to fund schools for lower class whites (so-called "white trash"), whose disenfranchisement was facilitated by keeping them in ignorance.

Family Values/Sexuality

Turning now to the effects on the family, slavery had an unexpected but profound impact on whites. Their culture was enduringly altered by submerging the black family. To the extent that the latter were torn asunder, whites had to expend extra efforts to see that their own were not. Central to this strategy was placing white womanhood on a pedestal. Noble and pure, her beauty and chastity became renowned. The Southern belle, with her demure, feminine smile, her gracious manners, and her desire to please, was an object of pride among Southerners and of envy among non-Southerners. Warm, yet aloof, when beauty contests became a national craze, she became the sweetheart of millions of her countrymen. To achieve this, of course, another reality had to be denied. That white women might have sexual longings for black men was impossible to contemplate. That they might have sexual commerce with, or marry, them was inconceivable. To ensure this, interracial sex was made illegal through miscegenation laws. More recently, the impetus to protect the family by protecting its sexual integrity has been manifest in the "family values" movement. It is no mere happenstance that the conservative South, and its even more conservative churches, has been in the vanguard of fighting against sexual liberation. Although divorce and promiscuity are common features of the New South, they have yet to be accepted into its panoply of values.

This is not to say that white culture has not featured a double standard. Women may have been closely guarded at home, but men were granted unconstrained liberty to indulge their lust with African-American females. In most Southern towns, and many Northern ones, an underbelly of vice flourished in the black sections. When a young white man came prowling in these neighborhoods, it was generally understood what he wanted. What is more, among his peers, such conquests were a mark of respect. Bragging about them was allowed, as was mythologizing the sexual talents of his dusky paramours. If his wife (or girlfriend) discovered these philanderings, she was expected to look the other way. Today, the more noxious aspects of this tradition are on the decline, but teenagers are still allowed to gawk at black sexuality in rap videos.

BLACK CULTURE

Black Racism[40]

Despite a multitude of vociferous denials, the evidence that slavery produced a virulent black racism is ubiquitous. If racism is understood as a combination of prejudice and discrimination directed against a particular racial stock, it is difficult to see how this does not apply to black attitudes toward whites. A profound distrust, and dare one say it, a profound dislike, is clearly harbored in the breasts of a large proportion of African-Americans. Having been on the receiving end of so many grievous wrongs, that they should resent and wish to retaliate against those deemed responsible is utterly reasonable.[41] What would be miraculous would be a forgiveness so total it perceived whites as blameless.

One of today's sturdiest myths is that most African-Americans do not wish to treat European-Americans the way they were themselves treated; that having been victimized, they are determined not to become victimizers. This, however, naively ignores their humanity. Virtually every abused human being resents it and projects this resentment on those responsible. Slavery, and its aftermath, did not confer sainthood on anyone. To suppose that it did for blacks is a moralistic ploy largely designed to relieve them of the stigma of their bitterness. If they are accepted as especially "good" people who are prepared to pardon every transgression committed against them, then whites have no recourse but to overlook their animosities. Indeed, their good intentions, and purported powerlessness, entitle them to moral leadership. This is the essence of the white guilt strategy so elegantly delineated by Steele.[42]

Yet many whites, when they deal with blacks, privately complain that they have a "chip on their shoulder."[43] Black radicals, in particular, seem prepared to blame whites for all their troubles. Long before anything unpleasant has happened, they grouse about what they expect to happen. Persistent cries of racism, an ability to detect evil motives even in the most benign situations, and a conviction that only they understand the truth about racial matters, stand between them and candid communications with whites. The latter, rather than being met on the terrain of a shared humanity, face the perpetual prospect of being trumped by the race card.[44] Should they attempt to explain themselves, this becomes further proof of perfidy and a reason to continue regarding them negatively.

This proclivity to believe the worst of whites has sometimes been described as paranoia and sometimes as whining. Roy Innis, the former head of the Congress of Racial Equality (CORE), has estimated that between 80% and 85% of blacks are paranoid. He describes them as ultra-sensitive to slights and perpetually fearful of being betrayed. Indeed, many blacks seem to believe that most whites are complicit in a series of conspiracies directed against them. Even well educated African-Americans will, with a straight face, accuse whites of genocide. They will allege, for instance, a huge CIA plot to distribute crack cocaine in their neighborhoods and will give credence to tales that the Centers for Disease Control developed AIDS as a means of exterminating inner-city blacks. When no reliable evidence emerges to support these contentions, this very absence is touted as confirmation of an expert cover-up. In cases where whites have actually been responsible for the deaths of innocent blacks, as in the Tuskegee syphilis study, the injury is made to seem more terrible than it was by imputing the worst possible motives to those involved. Thus, the doctors who ran the Tuskegee experiment are charged with deliberately infecting their subjects so as to disseminate wholesale death. In fact, the African-American men chosen were already tainted by disease.[45] The sin of those manipulating them was not intentional murder, but a callous indifference to their fate. By denying their subjects newly available medical treatments, they allowed, rather than forced, them to die. This was bad enough, but to those who identify with the victims, it can seem too mild.

When it is pointed out that despite white cruelty, the African-American population continues to rise, the genocide hypothesis is transmuted into a charge of "cultural" genocide. The white objective is now interpreted as a desire to destroy black integrity by obliterating the black "soul." Flaunting an unconscious ethnocentrism they would decry in others, black spokesmen routinely assert that they possess a distinctive humanity that Caucasians envy, and wish to bleach out, by forcing blacks to talk, think, and feel as they do. In this scenario, to be an "oreo," that is, black on the outside and white on the inside, is to be a traitor to one's race. Even when whites offer to adopt otherwise unadoptable black children, this is perceived as an attempt to abduct them from their own people.[46] The possibility that they might grow up feeling unsympathetic toward black culture is interpreted as a scheme to undermine, and ultimately eliminate, black lifestyles.

Black racism is not only manifest in an ethnocentric preference for black styles of life, but in a willingness to visit negative consequences upon whites. It not only condones prejudice, but also promotes discrimination when it can. While it may be true that African-Americans do not control the executive suites of large corporations or the inner sanctums of political parties, they are not without influence. The policies and rewards these power centers make available are different than they would have been had blacks not lobbied to change them. But what is wrong with this? All Americans surely have a right to seek benefits for themselves and their kin. Whites have done so for centuries. Why then should blacks not be allowed to do the same? How, indeed, can equity be achieved if there is no opportunity to correct past disparities?

As reasonable as the preceeding sounds, realistically the only way to accomplish this agenda is through reverse discrimination. Only by taking from Peter to compensate Paul, that is by denying whites who have committed no wrongs advantageous jobs, college admissions, and government contracts, can the balance be rectified. Instead of universal standards, inclusively administered, preferences are offered to some and excuses to others. Although a cry goes up that these are not really preferences, they unequivocally are. The fact is that some people are benefited and others not. Were this untrue, why would anyone invest the effort in fighting for them? The sad fact is that the indifference many blacks feel toward white interests testifies to a willingness to discriminate. Though their passionate denials of inflicting injury are every bit as emphatic as were those of white racists who insisted that slavery caused slaves no harm, they are as superficial.

The upshot is that whereas white racism prevented black upward mobility by actively keeping blacks down, black racism achieves the same outcome by keeping them separate. Its rejection of whites, and its spirit of reverse punishment, may not be calculated to be off-putting, but they are. Blacks may, for instance, be wary of interacting with whites because they expect non-acceptance, yet preemptory decisions to sit only with other blacks in college classrooms or to invite only fellow blacks to parties send the message that they are not fond of whites. This, in turn, makes it less likely that blacks will develop useful connections within the socioeconomically more successful white community.

Violence

I have been mugged twice in my life, both times on my way to work at the Harlem Welfare Center. Although my vigilance probably saved me from other hostile encounters, violent crime was endemic to the streets I traversed. Actually, I was lucky. One of my colleagues, a black man in his early forties, was beaten to within a hair's breadth of death. My attackers had threatened me with fists and lead pipes, but desisted when I meekly gave them my money. His used knives and bats to break his bones and give him a concussion, apparently because he was not sufficiently servile. It took weeks before he emerged from the hospital, but even then he was thoroughly traumatized and emotionally unable to return to work.

Years later, my clients at a methadone clinic had sufficient confidence in me to implore me to safeguard their weapons. When they suspected they might be searched by a law enforcement officer, they would quietly press a gun or a knife into my hand. But if a fight broke out, suddenly razor blades would appear in the hands of the combatants. Part of my job was to get between the parties to effect a peaceful settlement. From this vantage point, it was impossible to miss the hatred in their eyes. In one memorable skirmish, a young black man with a reputation for being a pretty boy had his cheek sliced open from temple to jaw. The ghastliness of the wound nauseated me, but even more abhorrent was the joy with which the assailant greeted this disfigurement. It was clear that in his world physical violence was not only customary, it was a source of respect.

These snapshots of black violence are confirmed in a cornucopia of statistics that reveal its extent. Murders are so much more prevalent in the black community that they are the leading cause of death among young black men. Robberies are so much more common that an absolute majority of those in prison are now African-American even though they constitute 13% of the population. Drug use too had become so widespread that few black teenagers escape exposure to heroin or cocaine. It is therefore with good reason that Himmelfarb and others have raised an alarm. Their opponents, the apologists for this tidal wave of violence, attribute it to biased police reporting, but independent victim surveys corroborate its dimensions.[47] The fact is that, as when I was mugged, there is a greater probability of people saying nothing to the authorities than of the authorities manufacturing imaginary incidents.

William Oliver,[48] in his *The Violent Social World of Black Men*, explores possible reasons for this concentration of bile. One of the factors he finds most persuasive is the "compulsive masculinity" of black men who have few other outlets through which to demonstrate their importance. Submerged in a world of poverty, social disorganization, and the displaced aggression of others, their self-regard is continuously under siege; hence they resort to an exaggerated toughness to prove that they are real men who merit the admiration of others. If the larger world shuns them, if they are economically, politically, and socially impotent, they are at least physically impressive. With tough talk if they can, but violent deeds if they must, they certify that they are persons to be reckoned with. Who, when he is on the receiving end of a violent assault, would deny that such an attacker is powerful? And who would confront him knowing that he is consumed with an explosive sense of inadequacy, one that, with its centuries-old lineage, refuses to disappear.

Janet Mancini Billson[49] takes this analysis a step further. Having ventured into the childhoods of boys who grow up to be violent adults, she notes that many become troublemakers who incite violence for no apparent reason. As one of her respondents reported, "I get all mad...and wanna fight." Unable to exercise self-control, these man-children act "mean" and launch into preemptory strikes before others detect their weaknesses. Unwilling to allow parents, siblings, or friends to push them around, they push first. This pushing, of course, can be quite energetic. Although it is essentially defensive, it sometimes inflicts ruinous harm in order to be taken seriously.

The extent to which this reactive violence can be taken is startling. Indeed, an extensive literary genre now chronicles its range. In confessionals such as Sanyika Shakur's[50] *Monster: The Autobiography of an L.A. Gang Member* and Nathan McCall's[51] *Makes Me Want to Holler*, the perpetrators recount the viciousness of their early careers. Shakur, for instance, revels in the title "monster." Awarded for such achievements as "pumping eight blasts from a sawed-off shotgun at a group of rival gang members" when he was only eleven years old, it set him apart as more brutal than his peers. In the world of the Crips and Bloods, with its random drive-by shootings, this was no mean feat. McCall, in contrast, experienced an almost placid childhood. Growing up in a working class neighborhood, it was not until he was fifteen that he began carrying a gun and participating in criminal activities. Five years later he was imprisoned, not for murder, but for armed robbery.[52]

Others, such as Butterfield,[53] have reported on the savagery of black street life. A journalist, he tracked the violence in the Bosket family to its roots in South Carolina. Beginning with Willie, an unrepentant multiple murderer who at fifteen claimed to have committed two thousand crimes, continuing with his murderous father Butch and abusive grandfather James, he journeyed back to the poisonous plantation system from which their tendency toward intrafamilial aggression emerged. Willie, the star of the drama, became a celebrity when he shot two men to death on the New York subway and then, after his incarceration, plunged a homemade stiletto into a prison guard's chest. At his trial, he defiantly admitted his guilt, but excused it on the grounds that he was "only a monster created by the system."

Similarly, Leon Dash,[54] also a journalist, entered the lives of a Washington, D.C. mother and her family to try to figure out why they were so self-destructive. In his account of the life and times of Rosa Lee Cunningham, he recapitulates the drug abuse, prostitution, and crime that were bequeathed from one generation to the next. Going back to Rosa Lee's poverty-stricken sharecropper roots, her conflicts with her mother Rosetta, and her struggles to survive in a world that offered few avenues of success, he makes it clear that misery and self-hatred can be inherited. In one particularly poignant episode, Dash recounts how Rosa Lee cajoled her adolescent daughter into having sex with an older man in exchange for drugs for herself.

Television too provides a window into the horrors of inner-city street violence. For decades it has not only graphically broadcast its petty mayhem, but has also periodically displayed those exhibitions of brutality we call race riots. Millions became voyeurs watching downtown Detroit go up in flames or L.A. looters scurrying out of storefronts clutching television sets. From Watts to Miami, we have been treated to visions of angry black faces shaking their fists at police, throwing stones at camera men, and promising that the next time it will be worse. We have also heard Stokely Charmichael lead chants of black power, watched Huey Newton of Black Panther fame strutting the streets with an automatic weapon,[55] and stood by as Malcolm X was assassinated by his ex-religionists. We have even sat impotently before our screens as a young black man threw an almost lethal brick at Reginald Denny's head, then did a victory dance for the benefit of his buddies.

At the bottom of this procession of infamy, we are told, lies black rage. A stubborn fury born of slavery and discrimination, the strength of this anger is allegedly so great that it cannot be constrained; so great, that it is self-justifying. Figures such as Frantz Fanon,[56] bell hooks,[57] and Ellis Cose[58] assure us that it is found at all levels of African-American society. The street punk, the political radical, and the middle-class executive are all described as harboring a resentment so immense that at times they would like to kill. Reasonableness may be appropriate for those in control of their destinies, but for them—society's perpetual victims—it is a crippling luxury.

Drug abuse too is attributed to this pervasive fury. Its slow-motion violence is directed primarily at its users, who, even more than those they plunder, suffer its ill effects. The long-term, and frequently fatal, ravages of cocaine and heroin betray a self-hatred so intense that death seems preferable to an ordinary existence. They betray a self-loathing so extreme that choking on one's own vomit or being stepped over like a piece of trash seem condign punishments for worthlessness.[59] Prostitution too is often an indicator of a violent self-enmity. Women (and men) who rent their bodies to strangers generally have little regard for their own safety or social standing. They willingly subject themselves to pain and disgrace for short-term gains.

Less obviously a form of violence is the verbal abuse to which many African-Americans voluntarily submit. Young black men, in particular, take delight in participating in what are essentially carnivals of insult. In playing the "dozens," they ritually slander each other and their relatives—especially their mothers—for the fun of it. Those who devise the most ingeniously poetic put-downs are extolled for their skill and daring. Yet most of these verses are extraordinarily vulgar. The images employed are so defamatory and tasteless that outsiders can scarcely imagine themselves uttering them. Lee Rainwater[60] reports that inner-city St. Louis youngsters engaged in the following exchange:

Albert:

Well I fucked your mamma in a barrel of flour.
She shit tea cakes for half an hour.

Malcolm:

I fucked your mamma between two splinters.
I hung my dick and it stayed all winter.

John:

I saw your mammie run across the field.
I shot her in the ass with a chesterfield.

The connections between this tradition and the recently popular gangsta rap are transparent. Both rely on a chanting quality for effect and both trade on the gratuitous slur. Furthermore, threats of violence run lyrically through each, as does a casual disrespect for women. In a culture in which interpersonal cruelty is an ordinary occurrence, promising to kill the police or to rape one's girlfriend do not seem objectionable. Moralists such as William Bennett[61] may crusade to prevent record companies from purveying what they regard as filth, but rap "artists" defend the same material as an accurate rendition of street life. The connections between this latter approach and social incivility are also apparent. When a linguistic coarseness that is more expletive than substance is portrayed as a species of entertainment, the bar of public decency is obviously being lowered for all.

The bottom line seems to be that violence breeds violence. Brutality literally causes emotional and cognitive reactions that perpetuate itself. In families, gangs, and the media, the toxin flows from one person to the next, provoking an energetic response and modifying their role scripts to make violence more likely. The counter-rage incited in those attacked, combined with norms directing others to "mind your own business," escalate the chances that they too will inflict injury. Ultimately, a community of internalized wrath re-creates an atmosphere of pervasive violence that appears inescapable to those trapped in it.[62]

Rule-Breaking

When I worked as a methadone counselor, one of my colleagues came from the rural South. He was a dapper man, who was good at his job, and a reliable friend. Most importantly, his clients liked him because they knew he cared about them and because they could trust him to tell the truth. One day we learned that one of his charges had been arrested for robbery. This came as a jolt since the young man had apparently been doing well. The response from my colleague was immediate and emphatic. "How could he be so stupid!" He reiterated this several times, each time vigorously shaking his head from side to side. Later, after he had calmed down, he looked at me through squinted eyes and declared, "You know what he did wrong, don't you? He got caught! He was stupid and he got caught!"

At first I thought my colleague was joking, and my face evidently revealed as much, for he quickly interjected, "You think I'm fooling, don't you? But I'm serious. I'm serious man!" And he was. Later that day, and for several weeks thereafter, we discussed the matter. I insisted that the client's crime had been robbery, but again and again he maintained that it was getting caught. Whenever I suggested that he was putting me on, he returned to his mantra about being serious. As he patiently tried to explain, getting caught really was criminally stupid. It was worse than being a thief, for it was being caught that would ruin your life. The opinions of others who joined our conversation divided on strictly racial grounds. The whites agreed with me that theft was wrong, but the blacks insisted that being an incompetent thief was worse.

This was my first introduction to a united black justification of what I regarded as immoral behavior. Never before had I met anyone who genuinely thought of law breaking as a second-level problem. Yet my colleague was more concerned that his client be clever enough to get away with his offense. Most Americans were alerted to this same attitude in the O.J. Simpson affair. Shortly after his acquittal, they watched in shocked disbelief at the gulf it revealed between whites and blacks. The sight of black audiences cheering wildly caught them off guard. They could scarcely imagine that, given the weight of evidence, O.J. would get off, never mind that he would be regarded as a hero. After many whites rushed to express their dismay, a black lawyer on the John McLaughlin's *One on One* complained that they did not have the grace to allow African-Americans "to win one." Why, he wondered, couldn't they just accept this newfound power?[63] More recently Robert Johnson, the president of Black Entertainment Television (BET), defended the suitability of broadcasting

O.J.'s self-serving apologia on the grounds that whites had no right to determine what blacks should do. Neither gentleman seemed troubled by the fact that, even if one concluded there was reasonable doubt of O.J.'s guilt, there was more than ample reason to question his innocence. To cheer him on was thus equivalent to proclaiming that murder did not count.

Earlier on, in his charge to the jury, Johnnie Cochran had implored blacks to send a message to the police by acquitting his client. His tone was very much apiece with the McLaughlin guest in that both believed victory mattered most. Neither was particularly concerned with the integrity of the legal system. What is ironic is that for the past several decades, the black community, more than any other, has been dependent upon the legal system to uphold its integrity.[64] The Civil Rights movement from its inception was primarily about obtaining equality before the law. When members of the black community subsequently assure an O.J. that he is one of them and that their first priority is to protect him from white vengeance, they implicitly proclaim a disrespect for the rules. They also send a message to the next generation of black children that in refusing to condemn criminality, they excuse it; that no matter how vile the conduct, a black rule breaker can expect acceptance from his friends and relatives.

This same indifference to maintaining the law is on exhibition in the almost universal scorn heaped on the police.[65] Part of the attitude that D'Souza[66] and Douglas Massey[67] called "oppositional" and Anderson[68] characterizes as opposed to white rules, peace officers are perceived as the enemy. Complaints of police brutality are nowadays more numerous than are black expressions of solidarity with the law. Most African-Americans, having personally been subjected to rough treatment by the police, are disturbed by their mere presence and would rather deride them than cooperate in any way. Few, however, take the next step and correlate police distrust of them with their own dismissive demeanor or with soaring black crime rates. Even the advent of a black constabulary has not changed this.

By the same token, crime itself is an indicator of a disposition to break the law. The official records are spotty, but ever since Reconstruction both white and black observers have remarked at the greater propensity of blacks to engage in crime. Even DuBois[69] acknowledged it. In his study of Philadelphia Negroes, he documented the much higher rates at which blacks were incarcerated. In the 1840s the high point of this phenomenon, 44.29% of those in prison, out of a population in which they constituted 7.39%, were black. More apt to commit violent crimes, such as homicide, and property crimes, such as theft, they were less apt to commit white collar crimes, such as forgery. DuBois went on to explain this criminality in terms of their submerged condition. Sadly, an' examination of the contemporary scene discloses a continuation of this pattern. In inner-city neighborhoods across the country street crime is rife. Parents are constantly on guard to protect their vulnerable young, but these same children look admiringly upon the drug dealers, numbers runners, and pimps among them.[70] Their evident prosperity is a mark of achievement and a signpost to potential avenues of success. It is not uncommon for youngsters to speak knowingly about the "hustles" of their elders. In their short lives they have learned that almost everyone has an "angle" which is not only tolerated, but applauded. Many of these same children come to regard going to prison as a rite of passage. Far from being a stigma, it is looked upon as a mark of manhood that one must endure without complaint.

Even a decline in sportsmanship can be correlated with this disregard for rules. When Terence Sprewell choked his coach for "dissing" him, he was surprised that others were outraged. As he later explained to a press conference, he thought he was defending his honor. Commentators nationwide wrote that he was lucky to escape with a fine and suspension rather than a jail term, but he felt justified in suing his team for revoking his contract. In his eyes, he was one of the good guys who was inexplicably persecuted by the white establishment. Another multimillionaire sports victim, Mike Tyson, admitted that he had gone too far in biting off a section of Evander Holyfield's ear, but excused this as a natural reaction to the heat of battle. If this was to be punished, it should only be for a short period—a year at most. In the same vein, if less seriously, a generation of football stars has reveled in performing vulgar end-zone victory dances. Where once it was considered in bad taste to rub an opponent's nose in his failures, they adhered to an "If you've got, it flaunt it" philosophy. It took the NFL's enactment, and enforcement, of severe penalties against excessive celebrations to control their exuberance.

Responsibility/Self-Discipline

A veritable mirror image of this tendency toward rule-breaking is the lack of responsibility and self-discipline. Millions of African-Americans still view themselves as helpless pawns of fate. Because they regard the world as intrinsically unfair, it seems ridiculous that they should be held liable for their own troubles. Anyone who expects a downtrodden people to take charge of their destinies is obviously expecting the impossible. The "man," having stacked the deck, and too powerful to defy, must be deferred to. Unless he can be overthrown—a situation that does not seem promising—he remains in control. This converts social rules into external affairs, into standards created and imposed for the benefit of others. To internalize them would be equivalent to conspiring in one's own downfall. Once this interpretation is accepted, there thus arises both a need to cajole "the man" and to evade his impositions.

Oddly, because whites have historically been paternalistic, many blacks take advantage of this. They respond to promises of care by demanding that these be honored. Indeed, they exploit them by insisting on additional benefits. In other words, white society continues to be perceived as the font of all good things, which, though no longer sought through supplication, can be accessed via an aggressive sense of entitlement. The trouble with this strategy is that in maintaining a donor-donee relationship, it preserves African-American's lower status. This revised paternalism may be less virulent than its predecessor,[71] but it too depends on the recipient possessing less power. The bowing and scraping may be gone, but a demand for protection, which acknowledges white superiority, reveals what some of my black students describe as a "plantation mentality."

Today the donor in these arrangements is likely to be the federal government. Its plantation, and hence the goodies at its disposal, are far more extensive than anything a slaveowner might muster. Civil Rights leaders, who once petitioned for relief from invidious laws, now lobby for civil benefits. Whether the goal is affirmative action, redrawing legislative districts, or increasing welfare allowances, they ask to be given advantages, not to be protected from external threats. Activists may bridle at describing these as preferences, but what else are they? To be given something that others are not, whether these are slots at a prestigious college or a percentage of government contracts, is to be given special treatment. Whether or not this is good social policy, it allows some to go to the head of the line. The boundaries of this sense of entitlement can go quite far. Lani Guanier, President Clinton's original choice for Civil Rights Commissioner, proposed altering the constitution so as to confer a race-specific right of veto on blacks. She reasoned that a perpetually oppressed minority could preserve its security only by being granted political control over its fate.

More common are demands for jobs—now often conceived of as a "right." It is assumed that the federal government has the power, and duty, to create and disperse employment.[72] Just as plantation owners once assigned servants any task they chose, it is now imagined that legislators can perform the same alchemy by passing a law. That the United States in not a proprietary estate, but a market economy, is lost sight of. In the eyes of those clamoring for jobs, the man is the man, even when he protests that his authority is limited. They are convinced that with sufficient ingenuity a means of directing occupations their way can be devised, perhaps via tax credits, training programs, or mandated quotas. All that is lacking is the political will.

In any event, a large proportion of American blacks are currently employed by government agencies. Be it as teachers, social workers, soldiers, or clerical workers, they have flocked to the security and standardization of civil service positions.[73] The private sector, in marked distinction, has been shunned. This tends to be attributed to the discrimination practiced by private employers—a fact that cannot be denied—but it also stems from a flight from uncertainty. The marketplace— the bedrock of our social class system—makes few guarantees. It demands sustained performance to continue bestowing its rewards. Money, as has often been noted, is neither black nor white, but green. To accumulate it as profits depends on being efficient, innovative, and persistent. If others are more so, they can spurt ahead.[74] This means that what any particular individual or group can control is inherently restricted. They may yearn for monopolies, but as long as the system is free, these are denied them.

At the center of this swirl of uncertainty are the capitalists, and more particularly the entrepreneurs. As self-motivated risk-takers who invest their energy, ingenuity, and financial resources in new ventures, they expose themselves to wild success or abysmal failure. In assuming responsibility for what happens to their businesses, their decisions can be ratified by making money or vetoed by losing it. But statistical evidence discloses that African-Americans have been loath to accept such hazards.[75] As a group, they have not assumed the burdens of business ownership or of capital accumulation. Korean immigrants are much more likely than they to pool their resources and buy a storefront in black neighborhoods. Admittedly, black poverty has been a handicap in amassing the required funds, but a greater impediment has been a disinclination to organize commercial enterprises. Community leaders may agitate for buying from other blacks, but, unless their compatriots exercise the self-discipline to establish efficient retail outlets, this must remain vacuous rhetoric.

A very different sort of irresponsibility and lack of discipline is on display in the impulsivity exhibited by many African-Americans. This is a delicate topic; nevertheless it is widely remarked upon—at least in private.[76] Whites are sometimes in awe of the apparent ease with which some blacks express controversial opinions or the flamboyance with which they enter a dance floor. Whites envy what seem to be a spontaneity, a joie de vivre, and a willingness to expose one's inner feelings. Yet these qualities, which makes entertainers vibrant and student protesters compelling, can be a bane to long-term planning. Those easily diverted by a rousing party or a gospel-style emotion can have difficulty holding themselves back to think through a complex decision. Self-control may be boring, but it is an essential aspect of responsibility.

The opposite of impulsivity is retreatism.[77] It too is a legacy of the culture of slavery, but retreatists, rather than confront a hostile world, withdraw from it. Far from being exhibitionists, they demonstrate a refusal to take responsibility by being uncooperative loners. Where once their ancestors avoided the master's wrath with incessant "yassus'," they become passive and uninvolved. Billson[78] has documented this propensity among young black men. "Ensconced in a familial setting that is at once hostile and confusing" and a school system where others "are always fighting," these adolescents feel simultaneously rejected and assaulted. The result is that they stop trying and surrender to the flow around them. Some retreatists find comfort in drug addiction. Alcohol, heroin, or cocaine provide a cocoon of indifference and a "barrier that mitigate[s] the impact of interpersonal relationships." In the end, they take responsibility for nothing, including themselves.

Merit/Work Ethic

Also a delicate topic is black attitudes toward merit and work. Some of these are so antithetical to what had been assumed to be our national consensus that shining a spotlight on them can be embarrassing. The political scientists Donald Kinder and Lynn Sanders[79] assert that merely to question the black work ethic is tantamount to being a racist. They consider it a slur against an entire people's biological makeup. When surveys suggest, as they do, that most whites make a distinction between IQ and motivation, Kinder and Sanders harrumph and attribute this to a desire to say the socially correct thing. Their hackles are especially aroused if anyone suggests that blacks are "lazy" and do not take advantage of the opportunities open them.

Certainly there can be no doubt that in some areas African-Americans are as achievement-oriented as any others. When it comes to sports and entertainment, intense efforts are obviously applied to achieving success. Indeed, the essence of competitive sports is victory based on competence. Basketball games are not won through special dispensations, but by extraordinary skills brought to bear with incredible intensity. Michael Jordan is a nationally acknowledged wonder. As importantly, he is a wonder who is dedicated to being the best. Some athletes may occasionally "dog it," but to become a professional in any sport requires years of practice and commitment. The object is to win legitimately. Anything less would rob the participants of the accolades they crave.

The same, unfortunately, is not true in all areas of endeavor. Mary Guy,[80] as we have seen, has argued that merit is a fraud. Having risen to the presidency of a professional organization, on a personal level she clearly has high aspirations, but she nevertheless presents an impassioned justification of the worst caricature of public service. "Close enough for government work," as the saying goes, and we contrast the Post Office with Wal-Mart, not to the benefit of the former. Are there any standards, we wonder, besides job security, to which government workers aspire? This may be unfair, but it expresses a broad-based perception. When one realizes that African-Americans disproportionately choose government jobs, the implications are chilling. Entrepreneurship is particularly sensitive to merit and effort, but it is not a black specialty.

Recall too that Wolfe's[81] research uncovered middle-class blacks who pleaded for a system skewed in their favor. Convinced that their merits would not be recognized, they sought fairness by rigging the outcome in their direction. Although they describe this as recognizing merit, by making benefits contingent on group membership, they remove excellence from the equation. Affirmative action programs, in general, do the same. Whether they are based on preferences, quotas, or goals, something other than excellence motivates the final selection. Often they create a two-tiered system, with different standards applying to specific races. For instance, if tests are required for college entrance, the minimum scores required of blacks may be lower than for others. A "race-norming" occurs wherein black answers are compared only with those of other blacks.[82] But the implications of tying success to race are appalling. What is being suggested is that blacks are incapable of performing at the same level as whites or Asians. Some, such as Carter,[83] bemoan the assumption that because they are black they are automatically less qualified. He is rightly proud of having earned his way into Yale University first as a student and later a law professor. Nevertheless, many others seem content to accept whatever advantages come their way. Cynically presuming that this is the best they can do, they cease holding themselves to standards expected of others.

Deplorably, many blacks stop trying.[84] Convinced that nothing they do will make a difference, they blame others for their plight. Rather than look for a job or conscientiously train for a promising occupation, they drift from chance event to unplanned happenstance. Kinder and Sanders[85] may be horrified that this pattern is equated with laziness, but how else would one characterize hanging around on street corners or surviving on a girlfriend's welfare check? Blacks themselves arrive at this conclusion. DuBois[86] and Dollard,[87] report that this was a widespread belief at the beginning and midpoints of this century, while Wilson[88] and Sniderman[89] cite current survey data to reach the same conclusion. To be sure, many unemployed blacks put significant amounts of effort into their street hustles, but others retreat into the listlessness of watching television or getting drunk on malt liquor. Especially melancholy is the plight of the working poor. They are so denigrated and abused by their unemployed peers that they must rationalize working at McDonald's.[90]

When I was employed by New York City's Welfare department in the 1960s and a New York State Vocational Rehabilitation agency in the 1980s, my colleagues and I had to contend with clients who voiced a desire to work, but found excuses for not reporting to particular jobs. In moments of candor, they would admit that welfare was a right they did not intend to relinquish. It might provide a poor living, but it was the life they knew. Besides, as Jencks[91] has shown, most had a source of income in addition to their welfare checks. In any event, there was no dishonor in using the system to extract unearned dollars. If "the man," in the guise of a government caseworker, required work, evading this was a source of pride. The welfare department had no more claim to one's labor than the white slave master did. Indeed, the act of being defiant brought a gratifying sense of independence, and perhaps a measure of payback.

Honesty/Education

When, in 1946, Horace Cayton and St. Clair Drake[92] published *Black Metropolis*, their massive chronicle of the history of blacks in Chicago, they included many observations that might today be considered impolitic. Among the patterns of African-American behavior cited was something they called *The Cult of Race*. According to them "Negroes feel impelled to prove to themselves continually that they are not the inferior creatures their minority status implies." The objective was to be a *Race Man* who was proud of his origins and ready to defend them at a moments notice. Working at about the same period, Frazier[93] wrote that members of the black middle class were prone to boasting about minuscule accomplishments. He observed that the Negro press was "the chief medium...which creates and perpetuates the work of make-believe of the black bourgeoisie." In his view, it sought to compensate for injured self-esteem by "exaggerating the economic well-being and cultural achievements of Negroes." "Police magistrates become judges....[and a] Negro student who makes a good record in a northern university is reported to be a genius." Not unlike their slave progenitors, who put on airs in their own quarters, these middle-class blacks sported fancy clothes and spoke in terms thought sophisticated.

For many blacks, the truth has become a casualty of pride. Misinformation is accepted as fact without undergoing a critical examination, and fantasy is elevated to actuality without stopping at the ground floor. If hyperbole can bolster one's self-image, or disingenuous denials ward off insults, these are embraced. For instance, Innis has asserted that a majority of blacks believe O.J. guilty, but continue to deny this in public because they do not want to give credit to the proposition that all blacks are criminals. Similarly, when Keith Richburg[94] wrote, after serving as a journalist in Africa, that he was glad to be American, he was attacked for denigrating his African heritage. Only the good of being black was to be acknowledged; the less admirable was to be passed over in silence. The goal of accentuating the positive is partly to correct the egregious lies of the past, but also to compensate for perceived inadequacies. Slavery, having denied people the glorious history of which others brag, and discrimination keeping them from a superlative present, they use words to erect what reality has not.

In the present climate, this disposition has culminated in a wholesale historical revisionism. Frazier noted that in his day "Even obscure and relatively unknown persons of Negro descent are represented to the Negro public as persons who have played important roles in history." This has recently escalated into claims that civilization itself is an African accomplishment. The Afro-centrists and the multiculturalists assure us that science, mathematics, and literature all have their origins in sub-Sahara Africa.[95] The assertion is even put forward that America was discovered by intrepid African explorers.[96] Though not backed by credible evidence, these allegations are presented as confirmed truths, if through nothing else than their emphatic and repeated recitation. Should scholars challenge them, their own credibility is questioned. A Mary Lefkowitz will be chided for never having visited Africa and a Dinesh D'Souza for disavowing the existence of racism.

One of the reasons for this disregard of truth is the disconnect that has occurred between black Americans and their African roots. Slavery created a fissure that has been filled by myth and by what Frazier characterized as "wish fulfillment." The depth of this chasm is manifest in the mutations of African-American names. Forced by their masters to adopt English sobriquets, contemporary blacks have sought to declare their autonomy by creating names of their own. The result has been an epidemic of neologisms.[97] Young black mothers literally make up names that sound African. Not having been exposed to actual African names and not having done research to discover these, they make do with ersatz substitutes. Where once their masters assigned them unusual Romanesque names such as Cato, Pompey, and Jupiter, they now adopt coinages like Calendula, Olithyn, and Zikkiyyia.

Nor is honesty held in high repute. In the antebellum South, whites were told what it made sense to tell them. In contemporary America this tradition has been upheld. If whites ask blacks what they really think, they are apt to respond that "It's a black thing; you wouldn't understand." One of the patterns that struck me when I worked in a majority black environment was how I was included in conversations that would never be shared with white strangers. These others always heard the cleaned up version. The word "nigger," for instance, was never used in front of them, but in private it was the coin of the realm. Other whites in similar situations have told me they have experienced the same phenomenon. By the same token, African-Americans are frequently dishonest among themselves. The habit of distorting the truth to gain a manipulative advantage has apparently transferred to their private relationships. Oliver,[98] in his study of black violence, remarks at how common it was for his subjects to misrepresent their circumstances. A man might talk tougher than he was to give the impression that he should not be messed with, or sweet talk a woman into surrendering to him sexually, or tell tall tales to inflate his achievements and reduce those of his rivals. The "cleverness" Rainwater[99] found among ghetto children, when detected among themselves, was revered, with ingenious lies celebrated for their cunning, rather than condemned for their deceit.[100]

Turning to education and its formalized transmission of truth, a huge gap appears. Ever since Reconstruction, efforts to elevate the condition of black education have been made, resisted, and made again. Yet the results continue to be disappointing.[101] Enormous improvements have occurred, with most black children now graduating from high school, but their levels of achievement remain consistently below those of whites or Asians. Test scores in language and mathematics have gone up, but, for inexplicable reasons, have recently plateaued. Even at the college level, dropout rates, save at the most prestigious universities, are much higher than for others. Nor have the same proportions of blacks majored in the more difficult fields such as engineering.

It has become almost de rigeuer among blacks to acknowledge the importance of education, yet this is not universally translated into action.

The anti-intellectual habits inculcated during slavery seem to have persisted in homes where parents tell their children it is essential to learn, then fail to buy or read books. When these youngsters later venture to school, they are apt to be told by their peers that learning is "a white thing" they can safely ignore. Should they resist these blandishments and do well in their studies, they are likely to be ostracized by the in-crowd. Add to this the distractions inherent in living in a violent community and it can take superhuman strength to remain focused on one's studies.[102] It is much easier to accept the notion that true merit is found in sports and being anti-white. No wonder that to be considered an "authentic" black, it is often necessary to exhibit the ignorance and vulgarity of a street thug.

Family Values/Sexuality

A startling circumstance unfolded shortly after it was revealed that President Clinton had lied under oath about his relationship with Monica Lewinsky. It quickly became apparent that African-Americans were among the president's most loyal and vociferous defenders. Night after night, the television talk shows focused on ordinary men and women deemed typical of the black community. With angry passion glinting in their eyes, most asserted that "Everybody does it;" that is, everyone lies and cheats. What, they uniformly inquired, was the big deal? How did this rise to the level of an impeachable offense? At one point I witnessed a black minister preaching forgiveness of the president. Sexual infidelity, he declared, was nobody's business except his and his wife's. He then began a chant that was quickly taken up by his congregation. "I don't need to know, what goes on behind closed doors. I don't need to know, I don't need to know, what goes on behind closed doors." Sitting at home, I was thunderstruck. Was I hearing correctly? Was a minister of the gospel actually urging that one of the Ten Commandments, the one against adultery, be disregarded?

Something similar occurred several decades earlier. In the late 1960s, when the Moynihan Report[103] first became public, its warning that the black family was in danger of disintegration brought howls of protest. Instead of reacting in horror to the news that the illegitimacy rate among blacks had risen from the single digits to the mid-twenties, most black spokespersons denounced what they regarded as a slur against their community. Moynihan, they declared, should not be blaming blacks for their deficiencies, but highlighting their resiliency. The danger, they insisted, was not some defect in their families,[104] but the disrespect to which they were subjected. Only decades later, when the black illegitimacy rate had soared to over two out of three, did some black leaders acknowledge that something had to be done.[105]

In both of these cases, the concern has been with self-protection—in the one of black reputations and in the other the reputation of an ally. Yet to do so, people have exhibited an appalling view of marriage and the family.[106] They have said, in effect, that illegitimacy is normal and so is cheating on a spouse and lying about it. Everybody, they proclaim, fools around and everybody is unconcerned about the consequences.[107] Stable marriages, however, require stable commitments. Spouses need to trust one another and to be dependably there for one another. They also need to be there for their children. That so many blacks take a jaundiced view of this possibility speaks volumes about their personal experience. Like everyone else in America, they know the ideal is fidelity, but from where they sit, it is another fraud.[108]

Whatever else may be true, events of the last several decades have revealed the fragility of the black family. Although divorce and illegitimacy have gone up across the board, nowhere else have they risen as fast or gone as far. Virtually every inner city black is familiar with multi-child families in which every child has a different father, with women who toss their dead-beat partners out of their apartments for carousing too openly, and teenage girls who become pregnant so that they can have a baby to love and a welfare check to make them independent of their mothers. African-Americans, like all Americans, want to be loved, but find personal betrayal an ineluctable fact of life. The irony is that so many of them have been so deprived for so long that, in their neediness, and consequent demands of each other, they jeopardize the love that might help heal their wounds.

Abiding academic disputes make it impossible to be sure about the exact configuration of black families in history, but the institution's frailty does seem to be an enduring theme.[109] A vulnerability to white manipulation, so characteristic of the plantation, was subsequently replaced by the vulnerability of the sharecropper's cabin. The precarious economic situation of blacks, in tandem with continuing social indignities, placed strains on marital relationships that resulted in the establishment of a serial monogamy. People married, then separated, then married again, often without benefit of clergy or a marriage license. With record keeping almost nonexistent, we have not been able to quantify this process; nonetheless first-hand observers, including DuBois, have testified to its prevalence. As Donna Franklin has noted in her survey of the black family, this trend was exacerbated by moves into town, where it was easier for women to find jobs as domestics than men to find openings as laborers. This was further aggravated by the trek north.[110]   Jobs became more plentiful, but the trauma of migration separated men and women who independently made their way to its teaming cities.   Critics such as Herbert Guttman[111] claim to find evidence for family integrity, but there are also indications of violence, jealousy, and spontaneous amalgamations.   Patterson[112] and Waller,[113] for instance, cite the remarkable lack of trust between black men and women.

Sadly, with the twentieth century advent of public welfare,[114] it became easier for people to act out their passions.   It is often alleged that few women have children in order to get welfare, but a large number did come to regard public financing as a safety net that allowed them to escape unsatisfactory relationships.   From the male point of view, this was equally liberating. There was no need to be concerned that the children they produced would starve as long as a government check was available.   Nor need young women find their social lives cramped by the burden of child care.   With so many becoming pregnant so early, battalions of youngish grandmothers interceded to raise their grandchildren.[115]   The white world might be taken aback, but this did not seem strange in a community where grandmothers had long been crucial to family continuity.

Another heart-wrenching irony of this situation has been the emphasis on predatory sex.[116]   People raised in an emotional cauldron, subject to unpredictable, and uncontrollable, separations, and tutored in a deep pessimism regarding the authenticity of love, found in their sexuality an undeniable reality.   Desperate to fill an inner void, they cleaved to what was tangible and at least momentarily gratifying.   An offhand perusal of cable television demonstrates what happened.   The popularity of gangsta rap wherein the central event is "doin it" confirms the victory of the sex act over the personal relationship.   A comparison between the programming of BET (Black Entertainment Television) and CMT (Country Music Television) exposes a breathtaking cleft between the white and black worlds.   Where CMT is overstocked with sentimental love songs and odes to morality and patriotism, BET is awash in vulgar sexuality and elegies to personal pleasure.   Particularly enlightening is a hit song by the female rap group Salt n' Peppa.   Its theme, "none o' yo business," warns anyone tempted to interfere with the heroine's trysts that she has a right to have sex with anyone she wishes, anytime she wishes.   Those who moralize about this are derided as doing so from jealousy.   They are clearly uptight prudes with no sex appeal of their own.   BET also specializes in crude comedy.   Its stand-up reviews feature comedians who invariably delight their audiences with lascivious sexual jokes and sarcasm about individual frailties.   Body parts are ridiculed, four-letter words pepper their commentaries, and getting even with one's sex partners is converted into an indoor sport.

This coarse humor finds its antecedents in the dozens. The following illustration of its mean-spirited sexuality is provided by Majors and Billson.[117]

I was walking through the jungle
With my dick in my hand
I was the baddest mother-fucker in
The jungle land.
I looked up in the tree
And what did I see?
Your little black mama
Trying to piss on me.
I picked up a rock
And hit her in the cock
And knocked that bitch
A half a block.
I hate to talk about you mama
She's a sweet old soul
She's got a rap-pa-tap-pa tap dick
And a pussy hole.
Listen mother fucker
You a two-timing bitch
You got a ring around your pussy
Make an old man rich.

This obsession with indiscriminate sexuality is corroborated by a multitude of sources, some quite unlikely. Thus, Gates,[118] in his memoir of growing up in a small West Virginia town, informs us that sex was the universal topic of discussion among the adults he knew. They regularly and authoritatively swapped stories of who was cheating on whom, and, who, based on appearances, seemed the likely father of whose child. According to Gates, sex was virtually the neighborhood hobby. People assumed that it was everyone's favorite recreation and that others were engaged in it where and when they could. Oliver,[119] observing a much rougher urban crowd, found a similar obsession. He wrote that his male subjects believed in a "Sexual Conquest Norm" and reveled in being "players." Their objective was to dress, groom, and talk in ways that would induce women to submit sexually. Females were not considered human beings to be understood or loved, but victories to be counted and trophies to be shown off. The player with the most seductive "rap" was the winner and hence the most masculine. He was the one who gained respect and the one who was emulated.

It must not, however, be supposed that this sort of exploitive sex is the monopoly of African-Americans. Howard Stern and MTV amply demonstrate that vulgarity comes in many shades. Nevertheless, the culture of slavery cast blacks in the role of sex object that many continue to play with gusto.[120] For some black men in particular, there is no greater success than being a "stud" who can have his way with white women. To possess that, which under slavery might end in death, is the best possible proof of one's power. The price of this triumph may be to divorce sex from love and family, but it is one they cheerfully pay.

Chapter 7

Racial "Empowerment"

> *All our power lies in both mind and body; we employ the mind to rule, the body rather to serve; the one we have in common with the Gods, the other with the brutes.* Sallust, *The War with Cataline*

THE MYTH OF EMPOWERMENT

Few concepts are more encrusted with myth than is power. Most of us crave it; some of us are its captive; but all of us are, at some point or other, at its mercy. In its complete absence, life is hollow. At such moments, we may try to control our environments, but, as in a bad dream, our muscles freeze and we find ourselves running in place. Love, beauty, safety, and success fade into nothingness and we cower under the bedsheets expecting little—and getting less. Is it any wonder that many of us adopt substitute visions of glory? We literally find it preferable to pretend that we have been touched by greatness than admit our all too ample weaknesses. In our imaginations, at least, we brush our enemies aside and appropriate their possessions for ourselves. Such daydreams can be comforting, that is, while they are in progress. They become a problem, however, when they reach into our waking lives and deceive us about what is feasible.

How then can genuine power be obtained? How, despite our personal limitations, can we obtain the control we covet? For those who have been less than fortunate—those whom fate has dealt a losing hand—these are not academic questions. They are enigmas that demand answers on pain of impotence. Unfortunately, a lack of experience may leave the dispossessed unequipped to find a way out. They fantasize about acquiring power, but are unable to make tangible improvements. Slaves, their children, and their great-

great-great-grandchildren are singularly handicapped in evaluating how authority works. Centuries of bearing the brunt of other people's domination have left them with a distorted impression of what is involved. Back on the plantation, absolute command was the prerogative of the master. If a bondsman was to procure advancement, it was almost always by way of delegation. The master, or his overseer, would tell him what was expected and then provide the clout to do it. In the most conspicuous case, a slave might be appointed a "slave-driver" with the right to whip other slaves. He could not, however, make an independent determination of where to apply this power.

This pattern has convinced many African-Americans that authority is achieved almost exclusively through transmission from one person to another. They, in essence, subscribe to the rich "father-in-law" theory of power. In their imaginations, an ability to command is conferred from one person to the next, for example, by parents who impart it to their children or bosses who grant it to favored employees. More particularly, in the father-in-law scenario, an impecunious, but deserving, young man woos and weds the boss's daughter. The older man is then so taken with this new addition to his family that he designates him the manager of his company and heir to his holdings. The young man then slides effortlessly into this role. He outfits himself in the appropriate clothing, buys a suitable house, and, most significantly, assumes an unmistakable mantle of command. An invigorating aura of power now exudes from his pores. When he gives orders to his subordinates, they instantly comply.

When this story line is transferred into the domain of race relations, the boss is transmuted into an uncle, that is, a rich Uncle Sam. In top hat and white beard, he presides over an entire nation and, at long last, having noticed that his step-nieces and -nephews have suffered innumerable unjustified indignities, decides to set things right by raising them to the status they deserve. He gets them jobs, sees that they are elected to office, and ensures that they acquire the resources to live decently. In this fable, once these poor relations obtain their due, everyone forthwith recognizes their worth and pays them the appropriate homage. Relatives, neighbors, and complete strangers begin to take their words seriously and allow their affairs to be directed by their one-time subordinates.

One of the most candid expressions of this vision comes from Harvard sociologist Orlando Patterson.[1] A strong advocate of affirmative action, he argues that America can become democratic only if it engages in a form of "state-sponsored mobility." Instead of a redistribution of wealth, he envisions "formerly excluded groups" shepherded into elite positions from whence they can acquire the social capital to pass on to their descendants. Having learned the "language and culture of power" from being allowed to occupy spaces in which it is present, they will now possess its reality and become full-fledged players in the social stratification game.

Like most fantasies, however, this one is more hope than fact. Power, unfortunately, does not lie within anyone's domain to confer as an unencumbered gift. On the contrary, it is a capacity that must be achieved and exercised. Today, with politicians of both parties promising to "empower" the disenfranchised, it may seem that they have the ability to confer this sort of strength, but they do not. Despite claims that legislation can create domination-free zones in which the downtrodden can blossom, this is not so. In fact, once power has been delegated, it must be defended. The one to whom it is granted must make it work. Although a doting father-in-law can appoint a callow stripling to run his company, he cannot guarantee his competence. Once the son-in-law appears in the office, he is on his own. If he does not know what to do, if he does not possess the gravitas of a leader, he will be found out. Sooner or later someone will challenge his authority and he will have to make it stick. If his actions produce disasters, insurrections are inevitable, and he will probably lose. His sponsor can, of course, return to back him up, but this is a stopgap measure. In the end, the personally weak forfeit what they are given.

A classic illustration of this sequence has been provided by Alvin Gouldner.[2] In a study of a mining and manufacturing complex, he observed a boss who had been appointed to replace one who recently died. The older man, "old Doug," was well loved, but from the point of view of his superiors too indulgent. The new man Peele was therefore mandated to shape things up. As an outsider, however, he was resented. Without experience in his new position, or allies on the local scene, he floundered. His underlings refused to accept his authority and attempted to go about their business as they always had. Since they outnumbered him, they could cover for each other, and did. Peele was beside himself with dismay and scrambled for a way to assert himself. One technique he employed was coercion. He engaged in close and intimidating supervision by appearing unexpectedly to catch people unaware. Not surprisingly, they resented this and in his absence derided him as a mouse popping up from a hole. Rather than induce compliance, he thereby incited efforts at sabotage. Another method Peele tried was "strategic replacements." He brought in outsiders who were already his friends to take over jobs from others deemed too independent. These interlopers became his allies and loyally supported him where others would not. A third tactic was to appeal to his superiors for support by asking them to threaten the jobs of those subordinates who balked at particular policies. Yet after awhile, they too resented Peele's impositions. These executives had expected him to be strong enough to impose his will on his own and when he turned out not to be, wondered if they had made the right choice. To sum up, Peele's power was tested by all those around him and he was found wanting.

Similar tests occur on most jobs. They are certainly seen in teaching. In my first stint in a college classroom, one of my students took out a newspaper and ostentatiously opened it in front of me. Had I not found a way to get him to put it down, my control of the situation would have evaporated. Later, when I began to teach at Kennesaw State, I was confronted with pupils who resented my being a Northerner and a sociologist. Having grown accustomed to my Southern social worker predecessor, they disputed every measure I tried to impose. Only after I stuck to my guns—and some time had passed— did they relent and accept me for whom I was. This pattern is not, however, universally understood. One of my African-American colleagues assumed that difficulties identical to these that she had to endure were unique to her race. Having been asked to explain to a gaggle of white professors what it was like being black, she began by bemoaning the fact that she continuously needed to prove herself to her white students. In her view, they presupposed a lack of competence that she was forced to demonstrate was absent. Caucasian professors, she was convinced, escaped this sort of harassment. Yet the truth was otherwise. All of my colleagues, of whatever background, told stories of arrogant students who put them through a wringer. The social reality is that virtually anyone who claims authority will be examined; they are merely tested in different areas. The same is true regarding social status. Those who aspire to a higher social class can count on being disrespected by those who have not yet accepted them in this station. They may be ridiculed or disobeyed, but will, in some fashion, be required to confirm their new rank.

Sustainable power turns out to require palpable strengths. In mano-a-mano contests, a person must be able to establish that he or she is no weakling. In fact, most people who obtain power demonstrate their strength on the way up. Relying on a combination of innate abilities, hard won experience, and trustworthy allies, they stave off a myriad of competitors who themselves covet a slot at the top. Like it or not, we humans are hierarchical in nature. Despite the obeisances we make to equality or brotherhood, we all want to win and to control our destinies. Lamentably, pecking orders have both a top and a bottom. This means that those who intend to succeed must do so by surpassing others. Some individuals invariably lose and when they do, surrender a portion of mastery over their lives. Since few of us volunteer to sink to the bottom, the competition can become fierce. Although luck can play a part in determining how one will fare, our deficiencies tend to be ferreted out by rivals who are motivated to exploit them. Because it is in their interest to recognize our vulnerabilities, they can be very determined in locating them.

To reiterate, social stratification, and more particularly social class, are hierarchical phenomena. They may be generalized forms of social ranking, but are not on that account ceded without a fight. Because to be a member of the upper classes is to lead an infinitely more comfortable life than one in the lower orders, it is highly desired. Those already in the ascendancy, therefore, find it in their interest to close off pathways of social mobility. If they can institute, and maintain, social arrangements that prevent people from challenging them, their positions will be more secure. This is what caste systems are about. They fix people in the stations they already inhabit, thereby reducing potential conflicts. Those who hope to unfreeze these patterns undertake an arduous task. If they are to gain upward mobility, they need to hold their own against an army of others determined to keep them back. Social status, like power, must consequently—within a free society— be achieved and defended.[3] This is often unfair, and depends on partially inherited capacities, but, in an open system, is not assured. People move up, and down, often depending on personal merit.

Relative power in a class system is likely to be decided, in part, by the social demands to which an individual is subject. In other words, the nature of the competition that one faces matters. If it is weak, it will be easier to speed ahead; if it is brutal, it will not. Likewise, when others are prepared to lend a hand, they can be helpful; if not, they can be a hinderance. Where one enters a stratification system thus makes a difference. Lucky people, for example, those born into a higher rank, have a head start. Through no effort of their own, they have access to resources and associates that ease their way. Others are disadvantaged. How they look, the jobs their parents hold, and the neighborhoods in which they grow up set obstacles in their path. As a result, if they are to prevail, they will have to do more than their contemporaries.

Some of the impediments to moving up come from the culture in which one is raised. These ways of living can provide tools for competing or infirmities that slow one down. The beliefs, norms and values they impart may point either toward winning or losing strategies. Since some cultures are honed in environments of success, they tend to incorporate useful patterns.

Others, fashioned in more dire circumstances, can be more concerned with survival than supremacy. Like the culture of slavery, they transmit cognitive, emotional, and volitional legacies that hinder positive change. The images one develops of one's self or others, the values placed on responsibility or merit, and the availability of family supports, if embittered by years of suppression, rather than lend strength, undermine hope. They can convince a person that success is not possible, not valuable, and not even endurable.

TESTS OF STRENGTH

In the animal kingdom, aspiring to hierarchical dominance can be a straightforward affair.[4] The pecking orders among chickens are usually determined by which bird is the most physically powerful. Even among baboons, the alpha animal must prove his mettle by besting his rivals in sometimes bloody battles. Yet as primates, baboons have social skills that are more complex than birds, hence they can improve their chances of winning by developing coalitions with other animals. Nonetheless, the options open to them are insignificant compared with those available to human beings.[5] With our big, imaginative brains, we excel in inventing novel means of proving our superiority. The tests of strength[6] wherein we defeat our opponents are enormously varied. They measure power on so many potential dimensions that these are impossible to enumerate fully.

And yet, as with lower animals, the fundamentals of interpersonal power between people are humble. William Foote Whyte[7] captured their essence among the members of an Italian street gang in pre-World War II Boston. Operating as a participant observer, he joined in their activities and developed warm relationships with them. After awhile he became so esteemed that he could ask the sensitive questions. One of these was how their leader Doc came to occupy his position of dominance. Eventually he was told that Doc had entered the group in a subordinate role, then challenged the previous leader for preeminence. They literally engaged in a fist fight to determine who was best, and when Doc won, he took over. The old leader quietly departed and Doc solidified his victory by cementing his relationships with those who became his loyal lieutenants. After this he faced few serious threats, the assumption made by the gang members being that he was too powerful to overthrow.

This reputation for being the toughest and most astute paid unexpected dividends. Not only was it presumed that Doc's ideas were better than other's, in head to head competitions with them, he gained an unconscious advantage. In a classic section of his book, Whyte explains what happened when the group went bowling. Doc was a better than average bowler, but the results he achieved were enhanced by an intimidation factor. Because success in bowling depends not only on physical prowess but also on "steady nerves," those who "tighten up" are at a disadvantage. One of the gang who did was Frank. "On his athletic ability alone, Frank should have been an excellent bowler. His ball-playing had won him positions on semiprofessional teams and a promise—though unfulfilled—of a job on a minor-league team." Nevertheless, when pitted against Doc, Frank panicked. Not only did he do less well, but his score was one of the lowest. Nowadays such losses are often attributed to one's being "psyched out." In essence, Doc's dominance was confirmed by the anxiety generated in a subordinate who "knew" ahead of time that he was destined to fail. Ultimately Frank was defeated by an image in his head, by an idea that had been implanted through his earlier experiences is social competition.

Another of Doc's rivals, Chick, challenged him at a different level. He too aspired to a leadership position, but understood that physically, and even socially, he was no match for Doc. Instead he sought to alter the criteria for success. Whyte summarizes their difference by noting that they had "conflicting attitudes toward social mobility. Chick judged men according to their capacity for advancing themselves. Doc judged them according to their loyalty toward their friends and their behavior in their personal relations." In the end, Chick unilaterally shifted the locale of their competition. He decided to go to college and pursue dominance outside the gang. Doc, more firmly committed to the street corner crowd, made no similar transition, and ultimately became Chick's economic inferior.

More recently, Elijah Anderson[8] has found inner-city blacks engaged in similar machinations. He describes how street kids are forced to test "each other's mettle, discern...important limits, and gain...an abiding sense of what each one will 'take' from the other." Since each "is confronted with the local hierarchy based on toughness...the premium is placed on being a good fighter." Moreover, "people understand that you are not always tested, but you have to be ready when the test comes." In Anderson's world, his "good kid" hero Tyree had to campaign for respect by demonstrating his willingness to fight a gang member who was physically larger than he.

A number of lessons about human hierarchies become clear from Whyte's and Anderson's accounts. First among these is that human power can be based on multiple criteria. The most basic standard is a physical competence akin to that found among other species, but this is supplemented by many other forms of competence. When people compare who is best, the measures they adopt vary with the hierarchy in which they compete. Those inhabiting Doc's territory valued, above all, a pugnacious spirit backed by an iron fist. Those in Chick's favored educational credentials and a superior job performance. Complicating this malleability is the fact that a variety of bases for determining strength can be simultaneously operative. Doc was clearly proud of both his fighting skill and his capacity for personal loyalty. When his primacy was calibrated, he intended to come out ahead on each. Also muddying the waters is the phenomenon of overlapping hierarchies. Chick was both a college boy and a gang-banger. Which of these would take precedence was not always apparent.[9] Nor was it certain, even when operating within the gang, whether he was trying to prove himself according to its standards or those imported from the outside. The same phenomenon was found in Anderson's neighborhood, where "decent kids learned to code switch."[10]

An enumeration of the most effective tools for establishing dominance would take some time. It would, however, include at minimum: coercion, rewards, "rational/legal" status, expertise, and alliances.[11] While not all authorities on organizational development subscribe to the same factors— indeed, the number of categories recognized varies dramatically—most would agree that these entail an ability to get others to do one's bidding even when they prefer not to.[12] Whether through force or persuasion, these objects of power act in ways decided for them by a more potent other. Coercion, the first of these sources, involves duress. Its targets may be physically compelled to act in a certain way, yet are more likely to be frightened into acting as if they had been compelled. Rather than actual harm, they respond to threats of harm. It is the gun pointing at them and not the bullet tearing through their flesh that induces them to submit.

The use of rewards is obviously a more gentle method of gaining compliance. When people are offered inducements—either material or social—to cooperate, they willingly go along with what they had not previously considered. In tests of strength, the person with more valuable goods to proffer will usually prevail. In modern human societies, this is generally the one who is richer or more highly placed on the corporate ladder. Rational/legal status, a third source of power, is connected with both coercion and rewards. The term derives form Max Weber[13] and refers to the power obtained from one's position in a bureaucracy. Those who occupy legitimate offices within these structures are authorized to issue instructions within a circumscribed area of competence. Their subordinates are required to obey them as long as their prescriptions remain within their mandated responsibilities. If they do, they will be backed by the clout of the entire organization. Those who defy such persons can then be punished, for example, by being fired, whereas those who collaborate are rewarded with raises and promotions.

Expertise too incorporates aspects of both coercion and rewards. The person who is skilled at a particular task can assert his priority over those who are less skilled, in part because he can intimidate them, and in part because he can assist them in achieving significant goals. Consider what it is like to play tennis with someone who is much more competent at the game than oneself. Her ability to smash a stinging serve past one's ear is not only awe inspiring, it is daunting. Having too many of these experiences makes one look bad and shakes one's confidence. Superior competence can, therefore, force a person into submission. Similarly, a certified expert can be the ideal leader. If the task at hand is complex, and the prospect of success uncertain, a guide who knows the way comes in handy. If she can demonstrate a better understanding of what is at stake, others will voluntarily defer to her opinion. Their desire to obtain the rewards of mastery makes deference in their interest.

Lastly, alliances can amplify one's personal strength. One's ability to impose coercion or to offer rewards is enhanced by compatriots who are able to make one's threats more intimidating or one's promises more attractive. As Anderson[14] puts it, "Part of what protects a person is...how many people can be counted on to avenge his honor...." The homely truth is that no one, no matter how physically strong or mentally agile, is as potentially powerful as a group of others. Bullies, who think they can overwhelm anyone they encounter, sooner or later run into a more vigorous collective, for example, a constabulary potent enough to put them in jail. Skills in coalition building are, therefore, among the most effective avenues to power. They are, for instance, at the heart of a politician's skills—politics essentially being the art of coalition building. But politics must not be assumed to be limited to winning elections. Virtually every human organization, and every human hierarchy, is rife with them. People seek to rise to the top by persuading others to join them in pursuing particular goals. They demonstrate their superior strength by assembling combinations of individuals who are better placed and stronger than rival assemblages.

Doc understood most of this. Thus he intentionally proved his coercive proficiency by defeating an hierarchical superior; he demonstrated an ability to reward others by planning gratifying expeditions (for example, bowling); and he constructed stable alliances by soliciting loyalty from his subordinates. Chick too had a grasp of power. He knew that economic success provided the money to reward others (for example, by purchasing a house for a future wife); that going to college could provide the expertise to get a satisfying job as an engineer; and that, if he were ever to supplant Doc, he must first woo his lieutenants away from him. Tyree too had a grasp of the rudiments of power, understanding full well the need to prove himself on the street, regardless of his family's disapproval.

But this is not all. Those who would win tests of strength must not only have the power to win, they must also be willing to expose themselves to defeat. If they want to succeed, they have to risk losing. If they always hold back, attempting to protect their resources from dissipation, they become irrelevant. Power is proved in action, not fantasy. People who hide in the corner can be safely ignored, whatever their potential. This means that those who would rise up must have the confidence to dare sinking down. Once others begin exerting counterpressure, they must be able to stay the course. If they cut and run at the slightest show of resistance, they have already lost.

Superior power, in fact, is not merely a matter of superior strength, but of perceived strength. It is when others are convinced that someone is stronger than they that they back off. Power is to a great extent a matter of reputation.[15] It is a matter of "respect," or what on Anderson's streets was called "juice." People may even seek a reputation for being "quick-tempered" if this will discourage others from testing them. In the real world, were tests of strength constant, the wear and tear would be unbearable. Because no one is strong enough to win every contest, those denied an interval in which to recover sooner or later succumb. In consequence, a single decisive victory often has long lasting repercussions. Others who witness it decide that it is not worth their while to risk a similar defeat. Instead, they react as Frank did. Despite a desire for personal advancement, they become anxious and fumble their chances.

This unwillingness to engage in an actual contest has further implications. It means that people often decide who is strongest based on appearances. Reputations for power are often earned on the basis of physical size or bodily carriage. But looks can be deceiving. We humans can cleverly devise a myriad of techniques for appearing "larger" than we are. Lions may be limited by the manes with which they are born and male deer by the antlers they can grow, but we human beings can change our clothing, buy larger houses, drive faster cars, or speak in a more sophisticated accent. We can also be boastful, hang around with the right crowd, or obtain academic credentials. These then substitute for a powerful right cross or a devastating first serve. So, unfortunately, can *stereotypes*. In essence reputations assigned entire groups on the basis of perceived achievements, they can indicate that a particular individual is less powerful than he is. This is the function of what Claude Steele[16] called stereotype threats. When individuals can be made to identify with the failures of those like them, they can be intimidated into backing down. They literally give up without trying. This turns out to be one of the major mechanisms through which groups sort out, and maintain, their relative priority. The generalizations we call stereotypes are part and parcel of the reputation for toughness that both individuals and groups accumulate. The trouble is that if these learned images perpetuate a misrepresentation of one's competence, a person may be relegated to a lower status than otherwise possible.[17]

All of us, including those who begin at the bottom of the pack, resort to a combination of the above when we pursue power. Not all of us, however, are equally adept at employing them. In this regard most African-Americans find themselves at a disadvantage. Having been deprived by slavery and its epilogue of an opportunity to learn the finer points of competing for priority, they begin several notches down. Slavery taught them only part of what they needed to know. In particular, it taught them the importance of coercion, rewards, and rational/legal positions, but not of expertise, and alliances. By the same token, it emphasized the virtues of appearances, but not of risk taking. Being on the bottom of the pile thus inculcated habits of mind and body that limited their options and converted them into victims.

The impact of coercion was obviously visible to slaves. Those on the wrong end of the lash were intimately aware of how intimidating it could be. They were also privy to the enticements of the well-timed reward. The paternalism of the plantation made it clear that an ability to provide benefits also made it possible to manipulate others. Similarly the hierarchical nature of their environment revealed the potency of rational/legal status. Antebellum plantations were not bureaucracies; they were, however, dependent on delegated authority. African-Americans were therefore able to fathom the value of being appointed to a position of power wherein others backed them up. Translated into the modern world, these three lessons made it attractive to try to intimidate others, as in urban riots, to seek the money with which to buy people off, as from a lucrative hustle, and to petition for organizational preferment, as in an affirmative action program.

Less apparent from a bondsman's point of view were the power of expertise or alliances. Expertise was denied most slaves.[18] Save for a few craftsmen, most of their jobs required a strong back and instant obedience. They were not even privy to the master's expertise. Because they were denied responsibility and an education, the white man's administrative skills and scientific attainments remained a mystery. Much as the Pope's relationship with God once seemed unattainable to the ordinary Catholic, they could not imagine understanding that which they were not allowed to witness. Updated into today's world, this places less of a premium on obtaining academic skills. For many blacks, the objective in going to school is to earn a credential rather than to gain insights into how things work—hence the phenomenon of degrees in African-American studies outpacing those in engineering. As regards alliances, the objective of many slaveowners was to divide and conquer. While slaves often stuck together in self-defense, there was also a proclivity to betray others in exchange for personal benefits. What was almost impossible was a stable coalition between whites and blacks. Whatever promises a master might make were not legally or morally binding. This condemned the slave to eternal inferiority compared with an adversary who could reliably call upon a host of powerful supporters. Again, updated into contemporary society, this phenomenon is converted into the show of kinship effected by many blacks. There nevertheless exists an underlying reality of betrayal and undependability.[19] Political solidarity may be rigorously enforced among people who call each other "brother," but on a personal level promises and relationships are routinely broken. Nor are whites perceived as reliable confederates. A lingering distrust often interferes with the development of enduring coalitions. Despite the emergence of political voting blocks, whites are generally perceived as potential enemies. Their words may sound encouraging, but even these are interpreted as efforts at domination. Thus, when whites assert that they want to be color-blind, this is construed a cover story for continued superiority.

Nor are many contemporary African-Americans comfortable taking social risks. In the caste society from whence they came, a black person who was too assertive could pay with his life. Certainly competence did not guarantee success, since whites might at any time band together to teach an "uppity" black a lesson. Testing one's strength against those in power could, therefore, result, not in rising up, but in falling off the ladder. Nor were such uncertainties conducive to confidence-building. Too broad an experience of losing is excellent preparation for continued losses. Even when opportunities for achievement become available, they are surrounded by an aura of defeat.

This, according to Shelby Steele,[20] is exactly what has happened in the wake of the Civil Rights movement. Because it was successful beyond the ability of many blacks to cope, instead of grasping the openings made available, they manufactured a plethora of excuses for holding back. In their inexperience, they blamed others for an inhospitable welcome, rather than recognize the consequences of their own apprehensions. A fear of failure, born of centuries of failure, convinced them to not seize the moment, but to renew their demands for additional protections.

What was visible, however, was the value of appearing powerful. For relatively little personal investment, one could claim all sorts of strengths. Small triumphs could be trumpeted as huge accomplishments and modest capacities magnified into prodigious aptitudes. But more than this, they could become expert in manipulating symbols. In their book on organizations, Lee Bolman and Terrence Deal emphasize the importance of symbols in influencing others within a business setting. They point, in particular, to rituals and myths as mechanisms for shaping interpersonal decisions. Drawing on the dramaturgical model of Erving Goffman,[21] they compare saying the right thing at the right moment with theatrical performances. If, therefore, at a meeting, an individual affirms his belief in an historically grounded guiding principle, he can steer others into acknowledging their fidelity to it. This agreement may then be used to manipulate these others into expressing their commitment to a course of action ostensibly in accord with that principle, even if they initially preferred another. The same is true on a larger plane. Societies have their rituals and myths, which, when invoked, can determine the way they do business. Those who wield such symbols thereby gain a measure of social hegemony, and African-Americans have become adept at doing so. Today iconic concepts such as "inclusion," "diversity," and "multiculturalism" are invoked at the drop of the proverbial hat to gain assent for desired policies. Permitted even under slavery, significant expressive latitude, for example, as grateful lackeys who praised the wisdom of their masters, they have grasped the importance of defining the public agenda by sculpting the ethos upon which it is based. If, for instance, blacks can persuade whites to acknowledge that racism is the sole cause of our dilemmas, they may thereby promote policies from which blacks can derive an advantage. What is advocated need not be correct, as long as others believe it is.

A FLOATING CEILING

The United States has a long history of racial discrimination. It also has a long history of increasing the power accorded to its former slaves. No matter how vociferous the complaints lodged against it, there has been unflagging movement from a closed caste to an open class society. Then too, no matter how ample the praise, the nation has a long way to go before total equality becomes an actuality.[22] Besides laboring under the handicap of a pervasively dysfunctional culture of slavery, black Americans have had to endure an ongoing structural inferiority. Not only did the hobnailed boot of bondage grind them into submission, but subsequent structural arrangements forced them to acquiesce in a subservient status. Put another way, their lack of relative power was due not simply to culturally transmitted deficits, but to the tenacious opposition of an entrenched elite. Those in power not only forced them to continue losing, but induced them to maintain defensive strategies developed decades and centuries earlier.

Still, there has been progress.[23] One might say that African-Americans have been held down by a floating ceiling. The weight of those above them has borne down on their heads, but not with a uniform pressure. Though always heavy, and at times debilitating, the burdens imposed have lessened as the years have passed. The fact is that American blacks have lifted themselves a long way off the bottom.[24] If they remain relatively deprived, they are not as powerless as they once were. It is also a fact that white Americans are not as repressive as they once were.[25] More are prepared to stand aside and yield the right of way to qualified blacks. Where once it was unthinkable to work for a black boss, live next to an African-American family, or choose a black spouse, these things are now done, not merely contemplated.

A cursory look at history reveals just how much the balance of power has shifted. Chattel slavery took some time to reach its full repressive potential, but once King Cotton became the South's primary cash crop the intensive cultivation it required reinforced the demand for super-cheap labor. During the American Revolution, many of the founding fathers, from both North and South, considered ending slavery.[26] Their calls for freedom from British tyranny seemed incompatible with depriving Africans of their liberty. In the northern states this freedom was granted, but Eli Whitney's Cotton Gin ended all hopes of manumission in Dixie. The subsequent prosperity brought by cotton agriculture seduced most southern whites into defending the extreme measures needed to keep their "peculiar institution"[27] going.

After the Civil War made emancipation a legal reality, expectations ran high for its becoming a social one, but these were frustrated.[28] Reconstruction began explosively, but ended when Northern politicians quietly capitulated to a South intent on governing its own affairs. Share-cropping and white terrorism succeeded in keeping blacks "in their place." Besides, it was expensive to maintain troops amidst a population that would not tolerate them. In the end, the old order was to reassert itself in a modified form. Blacks remained a prominent feature of the landscape, but economically and socially were virtually invisible. They might themselves long to alter this condition, yet they had little recourse. Still, their mere presence constituted an unresolved threat. Northern efforts to improve their lot, for example, through education, were made, but had little impact. Nevertheless the former masters were uneasy. From their perspective, stability had to be reimposed.

Eventually Southern whites resorted to Jim Crow legislation to institutionalize their dominance. Blacks were thenceforth prevented from voting or mingling with whites. The Supreme Court even declared it legal to maintain separate racial facilities as long as these were comparable—which, of course, they were not. Black leaders such as Booker T. Washington[29] and Alexander Crummell pressed ahead, but their options were limited. It was not until the advent of the twentieth century that a significant northward migration changed this.[30] Until then, blacks were at the mercy of whites who continued to treat them as if they were property. The former slaves might exercise an unacknowledged cultural influence, as was evident in the prevalence of minstrel shows and emotionally animated white churches, but they could not openly assert their personal desires without an accompanying show of deference.

It was probably the Harlem Renaissance that enabled African-Americans to raise their first significant emblems of cultural independence.[31] Ragtime music had long since entered the national consciousness, but when jazz arrived in places like New York City, it did so with an unabashed "Negro" cachet. Eubie Blake and the Cotton Club did what spokespersons such as W.E.B. DuBois could not. DuBois, first through the Niagara Movement and later through the National Association for the Advancement of Colored People (NAACP), had proclaimed that personal ability, no matter what one's color, must not be denied, but it was via the performing arts that black talent was permitted to flower. Riding on the coattails of this efflorescence was Marcus Garvey,[32] who announced the birth of Black Pride. Parading through the streets of Harlem in his quasi-military finery, he offered the prospect of genuine autonomy from whites. Blacks could now, on their own, plan a return to Africa, whatever a resurgent KKK thought of the project.

Yet until deep into the 1920s, and the invention of the cotton picking machine, the northbound exodus was only a trickle. Just as it was about to become a flood, the Great Depression intervened and a last-hired first-fired ethos took hold. Without the machinery of public assistance, a grinding poverty kept blacks almost as impotent as slavery and Jim Crow had previously. Almost, but not quite, for Franklin Roosevelt and his wife Eleanor were about to help out. Despite the objections of his Southern Democratic allies, he launched the Social Security Act and Aid to Dependent Children to provide a safety net that extended even to blacks. More than this, Eleanor, without official government portfolio, weighed in with symbolic sustenance. In addition to hopeful words, she provided a platform from which the opera singer Marian Anderson could thumb her nose at the Daughters of the American Revolution, who, because of her color, had barred her from performing at Constitution Hall. At the same time, the NAACP began to make legal history. It was to sue for, and win, admission to college programs for blacks from Maryland to Texas.

During World War I, the Southern-born president Woodrow Wilson had applauded D.W. Griffith's racist epic *The Birth of a Nation* and insisted that black doughboys not fight side by side with their white peers. By the time the United States entered World War II; notwithstanding the misgivings of many Caucasians, African-Americans were allowed to prove their mettle as pilots and tank operators. After the conflict, Harry Truman even saw fit to desegregate the military. Officially, at least, blacks were no longer automatically second class soldiers. Yet the real progress was only about to begin. Once more the NAACP, and especially Thurgood Marshall,[33] were in the forefront with a Supreme Court victory in Brown v. School Board. Arguing that segregated schools were, in fact, inferior schools, it induced the court to rule that "separate was inherently unequal." This, in turn signaled the advent of the Civil Rights movement. Subsequent to President Eisenhower's use of the National Guard to enforce an integration order in Little Rock, Arkansas, blacks were emboldened to demand integration of other facilities as well. Ultimately led by Martin Luther King Jr., a whole generation of African-Americans boycotted for the right to stay at the front of the bus, sat-in for the opportunity to be served at whites-only lunch counters, and marched for a chance to vote in open elections.

Fueled by a growing black middle class[34]—whose aspirations rose even more precipitously than did their achievements—this Civil Rights crusade became a national obsession. Schools in both the North and South were integrated, drinking fountains desegregated, and black faces became more prominent in the media. Presidents Kennedy and Johnson made it their policy to promote Civil Rights legislation, even as inner-city neighborhoods burst into flame. Talk of black power became rife, as did a cadre of black elected officials. Nor did this trend end when a Republican reentered the White House. Nixon might have been perceived as an enemy of blacks, but he did more than his predecessors to establish affirmative action programs. And through this all, as the Thernstroms[35] have documented, the ranks of middle-class blacks kept swelling. In ever growing numbers, they went to college, got better jobs, and moved out into the suburbs. Complaints that whites were repressive continued to be heard, but the progress did not stop.

Viewed in its entirety, this has been a magnificent spectacle. Although not approaching the calls for instantaneous equality, the changes have been sweeping and deep. They have not, however, been consistent. There have been many more steps forward than back, but there have been many retrograde moves. Those intent on blacks obtaining legitimate power have pressed hard, but have been opposed by others to whom this represents a nightmare. A continuous push and pull has thus been evident amid the larger improvements. At any given moment, the players are transfixed by the tactical swings engulfing them, but the victories of those favoring an open society keep adding up. In the innumerable tests of strength that form the scaffolding of our social structure, African-Americans, and their allies, have demonstrated greater and greater muscle.

Let me repeat—African-Americans and their allies. There has not been an exclusive division between blacks and whites. The increasing power that blacks have been able to garner is attributable in no small measure to the millions of whites who have joined in demanding a truly open system. Far from being enemies, these whites have been reliable friends. They may not always agree with what blacks ask, but they have been consistent well-wishers. The reason there has been a floating ceiling is that they have helped brace it up. Although their motives have often been selfish and their help not always constructive, without them to share the burden, it would have been unbearable. The Roosevelts, Trumans, and Johnsons of this world, along with the Washingtons, Marshalls, and Kings, deserve some credit.

SITUATIONAL IMMATURITY

As African-Americans have acquired power, their ability to exert themselves has developed apace. Beginning in the structural sub-basement, and hobbled by a set of beliefs, values, and norms that subverted their efforts, they have gradually clawed their way to a position of respectability. Fortunately, as time has passed, the strengths they have been able to muster have multiplied. Their personal resources, including their emotional strengths and social understandings, have expanded, as have their interpersonal resources, including their wealth and social connections. Nevertheless these accretions have come with agonizing slowness. More in evidence has been what can only be called a "situational immaturity."[36] Both cultural and structural factors have conspired to deprive blacks of many of the skills that might have eased their path.

To assert that African-Americans have acted immaturely in their quest for social power may have the ring of a racist slur. It certainly appears to imply that individual blacks have been childish, and worse than this, that their immaturity is due to a personal fault. On the surface it may even seem to be on a par with the sorts of slander plantation owners once lodged against their slaves. The classic rationale for maintaining absolute control was, after all, that Africans were inherently too childlike to be entrusted with the direction of their own lives.[37] And yet there is a difference. Antebellum Southerners were convinced that their bondsmen were biologically deficient. They believed that they must guide them because they were intellectually incapable of guiding themselves.[38] The suggestion that blacks have been immature power-seekers should, however, have no such implications. Instead of blaming their genetics, it points toward the ravages of structural suppression and the encumbrances of cultural dysfunction, neither of which is per se race-based. Many whites too have labored under such handicaps. Joseph Howell,[39] for one, has demonstrated how Appalachian refugees in inner-city Washington, D.C., subverted their economic prospects with a juvenile toughness and a romantic restlessness. Unfamiliar with the big city or its bureaucratic ways, they lived hard, unstable, socially alienated lives, that drew on patterns forged in the impoverished hollows of West Virginia. Nor does an hierarchical immaturity imply that any particular black is immature. Individuals such as Frederick Douglass,[40] Booker T. Washington,[41] and Martin Luther King, Jr. have surely been far from this. No, the implication is that, at given moments in history, the most prevalent communal techniques through which blacks have asserted power have not been as sophisticated as they might have been were these acquired in circumstances that allowed for greater savoir faire. To be concrete, a community that initially learned that power grew out of the business end of a whip quite naturally assumed that coercion, rewards, and delegated power were the surest means of achieving superiority. They could not, at first, appreciate that expertise and alliances might provide a more adequate route to power.

In comparing the development of African-American strengths to a progression through childhood, adolescent, and adult stages, as I am about to do, the objective is to explore how a people came to cope with their relative powerlessness. It was not an accident that slaves were likened to children, for both confronted overwhelming arrays of force they were unprepared to match. The latter are held to be inferior because their biological capacities have not yet matured, while the former were compelled to act like children lest they seemed too formidable as adversaries. Sadly, in acting immature, some aptitudes, specifically those associated with responsible adulthood, became atrophied. Decision-making, like many other skills, is perfected only in the doing. But more than this, when trying to prove one's mettle to others who are intent on denying it, people can behave like teenagers. They become rambunctious and imprudent. In short, when it comes to asserting hierarchical muscle, a submerged people can operate immaturely even though they personally are not. Their situation, and the responses it produces, give the impression that they are less able than they really are.

The positive side of this predicament is that as blacks have risen in the social hierarchy, their capacities for self-assertion have grown accordingly. Improved circumstances have fostered their personal development and a higher status has opened a host of learning opportunities. The result has been an unmistakable progression in the refinement of their skills. This sequence can be characterized as a movement from dependence, through an exaggerated independence, into a mature interdependence. The Psychiatrist Karen Horney[42] divided neurotic coping strategies into *moving toward, moving away from,* and *moving against people.* The analogy may be somewhat strained, but slaves and their descendants have also been forced to move through periods of excessive reliance on others, excessive separation from them, and excessive reaction against them. Beginning with a stage of imploring others for help, they eventually came to demand assistance, and then adamantly to reject it. If Horney's analysis is correct, the ultimate destination of such a series is a problem-solving stance in which one works with others to solve mutual dilemmas. In this view, adult powers are contingent on cooperating with other adults. As this applies to African-

Americans, it means working together with whites to maintain a truly open society. The enlightened self-interests of both dictate an adherence to uniform standards, uniformly administered. Both must recognize that an open class system, in which merit is free to seek its own level, enables everyone to pursue a Jeffersonian happiness unencumbered by the weight of a caste-oriented past.

Childhood

When Sherman's armies were marching triumphantly through Georgia, they cast their eyes backward toward a rag-tag throng of newly liberated slaves who dogged their every step. Fearful of being slowed down by this emaciated mob, and unprepared to feed it, the Yankees sought to leave it behind by failing to help people cross the rivers in their path. The ex-slaves themselves did not know where else to go. They were exhilarated to be free, but had no idea of how to take advantage of this condition. As a result, they became the equivalent of mendicants. From the federal government, they hoped to receive forty acres and a mule and from their former owners the respect due fellow citizens. Instead they found themselves adrift, dependent on antagonistic whites for their very subsistence. The bargain later offered them as sharecroppers was seriously flawed, but what was the alternative?

It may, therefore, justly be said that for African-Americans, the journey toward equal status began with a passive subordination. As much as they might have wished it otherwise, they were not active players who set their own agendas. Others, be they former masters or Northern philanthropists, initiated their conditions of work, education, and political participation. Because they knew they did not have the resources to confront the overwhelming odds arrayed against them, publicly at least, they were deferential. Polite and appreciative, on the surface, in private they might be bitter and scornful. In any event, they found it necessary to be reactive, rather than proactive. It did not even occur to most that they could move out of the South.

By the end of the nineteenth century, Booker T. Washington[43] became the poster boy for this strategy. In numerous speeches, such as the one that became known as the Atlanta Compromise, he told blacks that they must learn to crawl before the walked, and whites that blacks had no intention of challenging their hegemony. In his Tuskegee Institute, he concentrated on teaching practical skills, such as brick-laying. His students also learned the rudiments of literacy so that they could pass these along to other blacks, but a college education was not to be within their reach. Nor were they to seek social parity. In particular, whites were assured that blacks had no desire to intermarry or live in communal intimacy with them.

Since black resources were limited, Washington toured the country soliciting funds from sympathetic whites. In meeting after meeting, he told them uplifting stories of nonthreatening blacks who only sought a separate and innocuous position in society. What he did not relate was that he was also financing lawsuits to challenge segregation and initiating real estate deals to make blacks property owners in places such as Harlem. His specialty, to put it baldly, was *indirection*. Personally ambitious, like many of his fellow blacks, he found it prudent to be circumspect. Though his goal was to increase the competence, economic resources, and individual confidence of African-Americans, he did not want to alarm those he expected to supplant. Much as a child must carefully measure how far he can go in resisting a parent, and even then has to do so behind her back, he sought to lay the groundwork for future advances.

Adolescence

To hear the advocates of Black Power tell it, by the middle of the twentieth century nothing had changed. No longer content to be passive, polite, or indirect, like teenagers unwilling to tolerate parental domination, they impatiently demanded Freedom Now![44] Huey Newton, head of the Black Panthers, sat like a king on a throne; Stokley Carmicheal, leader of the Student Non-Violent Coordinating Committee (SNCC) spoke of "offing the pigs"; and rioters in Watts flagrantly looted shops in the name of personal liberation. From their rhetoric, one might never suspect that black incomes were rising, that lynchings had become a thing of the past, or that the government had recently launched a war on poverty whose prime beneficiaries were to be African-American. Quite the reverse. Where not long before Martin Luther King had cautiously confronted Bull Conner's police dogs in Birmingham Alabama, they now recklessly incited violent conflicts in Northern cities which ironically had track records of greater toleration.

A respectful way of describing this eruption is as a display of *assertiveness*. Adolescents, it must be recognized, specialize in assertiveness. Having endured years of deprivation attributed by their elders to their inability to handle independence, they no longer brook constraints. Now grown as tall as their parents, with brains as biologically mature as theirs and with a sexuality more pressing than theirs, they stop asking permission and insist on it. When frustrated, they not only get angry; they allow their rage to spew forth in every direction. The parallels between this and the long hot summers of the 1960s should be obvious. Many African-Americans had reached a point in their development in which they were eager to shoulder their way to the front of the line. Unwilling to bow and scrape as their ancestors had, they were certain that an exhibition of muscle flexing would provide them the power to reorganize society.

The number of resemblances between the excesses of the black power movement and those of adolescents is instructive. Teenagers are *brash* and *passionate*. They wear their emotions on their sleeves. When enraged by what seem to be social injustices, they pour out their vitriol in torrents. Conversely, when enraptured by visions of a glorious future, they wax poetic. Unsure of what is actually possible, they call for the maximum imaginable and then demand it immediately. Impulse control is not one of their virtues. Thus, if they encounter resistance, their tone is one of defiance. In the manner of teenage soldiers, who are at once convinced of their immortality and terrified by the possibility of appearing cowardly, they rashly charge directly into the machine gun nests. Likewise, if faced with social machinery not of their own devising, they become modern-day Luddites. They would rather tear down an obstacle that gets in their path than find a way of accommodating it. Compare this with the rhetoric of the Civil Rights movement. Even after the worst excesses of the 1960s, black politicians continued to make "non-negotiable" demands. In the language they employed—if not always their actions—they were prepared to fall on their swords rather than relinquish a tiny piece of their legislative programs. Brash and passionate, the fire of liberation flashed as hotly from their eyes as from any high-schooler's.

Nevertheless, teenagers are *insecure*. Their uncertainties about themselves and their futures breed a sensitivity and a defensiveness that border on the obdurate. In their view, they are never wrong and are always being put upon. When told that they are making progress, they bridle at what they interpret as an insult. Why, they demand to know, is it being suggested that they need to make progress? Nor are their mistakes admitted. Instead they are denied in a barrage of excuses. If challenged, they put on a show of bravado. Whatever doubts they may have are submerged in a sea of exaggerations or in a vigorous assault on potential adversaries. The object is to obscure their weaknesses by changing the subject or by making their deficiencies less visible. In terms of the quest for black power, this tactic is revealed in a chip on the shoulder attitude and an inability to accept responsibility for failures. It is whites who are wrong; whites are always wrong. If these oppressors would only take the time to understand why blacks act as they do, they would realize that what seems to be erroneous is, in fact, morally necessary.

Since the power of adolescents is more limited than they would like, they often rely on the appearance of power. When asserting themselves, they tend toward the *dramatic*. Hyperbole is their normal mode of expression and the flamboyant gesture their habitual form of action. The way they dress, play, and talk are all designed to generate attention. They will simply not allow themselves to be overlooked the way a child might. Nor will they allow themselves to appear nonplused, hence the theatrical shows of being in control. Observant adults may suspect them of having been thrown off stride, but whatever embarrassing mistake they are discovered to have committed, they insist was intended. African-Americans too, during the height of the Civil Rights era, doted on the grand gesture. Freedom rides, boycotts, and Marches on Washington were their stock-in-trade. "What do we want? Freedom! When do we want it? Now!" Such were their incantations. On an interpersonal level, there also evolved a stylized technique for flamboyantly demonstrating power. Because a show of anxiety might betray weakness, a display of being "cool" became de rigeuer. This mask of imperturbability made it clear that one was in control, and, as it were, a man among men. Cool clothes, cool wheels, a cool walk, and a cool way with women left no doubt as to one's dominance.[45] Even very successful African-Americans succumbed to the temptation to show off. Sammy Davis Jr.[46] admitted as much in his autobiography, in which he detailed the over-the-top shopping sprees in which he engaged after attaining financial success. More surprisingly, so did Thurgood Marshall,[47] who told his biographer that upon being selected for the Supreme Court he immediately went out and bought two cream-colored Cadillacs, one for himself and one for his wife. Somewhat abashedly, he described this as the "nigger" in him coming out.

Another mark of adolescence is *egocentricity*. Self-involved to the point of arrogance, their world begins with themselves and only grudgingly moves outward. A combination of weakness and inexperience forces their attention inward on whom they are and what they want. In Eric Erikson's[48] pregnant phrase, they undergo an "identity crisis." Though they seem selfish, they are really consumed with an awareness of how little they have. Their "me, me, mine, mine" litany is a way of testing out what works in a world that still has the power to deny them the respect for which they yearn. On the racial front, a comparably self-involved quest for identity has similar functions. A people who have been defined as second-class citizens have a need to develop a more potent image. If they interpret everything in racial terms, it is because they are consumed with desire to move forward. Hence it is that we see so many conspiracy theories. From the point of view of those have not yet reached the place they want to be, others must be holding them back, others who are as focused on them as they are on themselves. Only people so self-consumed could give credit to a theory such as Louis Farrakhan's that the Lewinski affair was a Zionist plot to embarrass a president who was too favorably disposed toward blacks.

Egocentricity, it must be recognized, is antithetical to forging mutually beneficial alliances. Stable coalitions are generally contingent on a balance of rewards and this usually depends on the partners who are aware of each other's needs. Teenagers, however, are notorious for ignoring others' points of view. Whereas their parents are likely to be tolerant of this self-involvement—although this patience can be tested—strangers are less apt to be forgiving. Fortunately adolescents customarily outgrow this phase without too much damage. In the political arena, however, a similar stance can be debilitating. To be successful, politicians must be able to make bargains, that is, to be flexible and to compromise. If they cannot, they become isolated pariahs devoid of influence. Another aspect of the egocentricity of the young is their rigid conformity. Despite their insistence on doing things their own way, the manner in which their immediate friends do them is often deemed the only acceptable one. In racial terms, this tendency can appear as group solidarity. Unless a person acquiesces in the political line of his peers, he is considered a traitor to the cause—an Uncle Tom, a conservative hypocrite, and an ignorant "N-word." This, of course, hinders the development of alliances within, and across, group boundaries. So does an intolerance of the strength of one's allies. If a potential friend possesses a higher status than one's own, this may be resented. Regardless of how fair he is behaving, a potential for invidious comparisons makes working with him uncomfortable. Fragile egos do not relish being in the shadow of a "big brother." Such has been the situation between blacks and Jews.[49] Although many Jews have identified with blacks and sought to be helpful, their skills have been interpreted as pretentious. In the process of discovering their own powers of influence, many African-Americans seem not to have been prepared to see them usurped, even if this cost them support.

Also associated with adolescence is a tendency to be *antagonistic*. Teenagers look for fights. They are not only sensitive, but on a short fuse.

The culprit in this is again personal weakness. Strengths, to be acknowledged, need to be proven. It is not sufficient for others to be deferential; they must defer because they have no choice. If power is accorded as a personal favor, it is not really power and can easily be withdrawn. The object then is to make certain that others perceive one's ascendancy. Since the tests of strength in which this can be illustrated do not always obligingly appear on cue, it may be necessary to arrange them. Thus the artificial fight, the I-dare-you attitude, and the disposition toward overkill. Paradoxically, the less sure a person is of his status, the greater the need to keep demonstrating it. This may explain, in part, why some African-Americans have gone out of their way to defy whites. Whether they have publicly toted firearms, engaged in jury nullification, or demanded special preferences, the apoplectic impotence this generates in put-upon whites is not an irrelevant by-product. The very inability of whites to thwart what they dislike confirms their provocateur's relative potency.

Lastly, adolescents are notorious *idealists*. They want things to be perfect. Having recently discovered parental blemishes, they are determined to avoid these. Yet theirs are aspirations steeped in ignorance. In their efforts to understand a world they have not yet entered, they resort to glowing simplifications.[50] Their elders may warn them that life is complex, but if they are to have an independent fix on where they are headed, it must seem uncomplicated. Anything less would, for them, be both unintelligible and uncompelling. In their own eyes, at least, they have to be heroes who are capable of staking out a separate existence.

The Civil Rights agenda, it must be admitted, is likewise unmistakably idealistic.[51] Its call for a moral crusade to instill complete equality and its reliance on government programs to effect this outcome are visionary expressions of hope. The touching confidence in human nature, the wholesale innocence of market economics, and the complete disregard of the nuances of social stratification evinced bespeak a callowness in figuring out how to overcome past injustices. But idealism must not be disparaged. Its luminosity is an essential spur to necessary improvements. This, however, does not diminish the potential for mischief. As Thomas West[52] warns, "The job of the prudent [person] is to determine the right course in a world in which the immoderate pursuit of moral perfection will more often lead to misery and terror than to justice and happiness." Whatever its intentions, an uncritical idealism can go dreadfully astray.

Adulthood

Adults, in contrast to those younger than themselves, have less to prove. With many more resources at their disposal and a longer history of having asserted their power in many more venues, they are more apt to possess a hard-won *self-assurance*. Less in need of a passive withdrawal, or active belligerence, they possess a better sense of who they are, who others are, and what they can expect to achieve. This means they have less of a tendency to overdo. Just as when learning to drive, there is a proclivity to oversteer that is rectified with practice, so they have overcome the need to prove more than needs to be proved. Because many of their strengths have already been acknowledged by others, they do not have to be shrill to be noticed.

Their greater confidence also enables adults to be more *flexible* in demonstrating their power. Instead of rushing forward to demand their due, they can hold back to assess a situation before acting. Even then, they have more options from which to choose. Having long since learned that not every tactic works in every circumstance, they husband their energies to apply them with just the right force at just the right moment. And because they are likely to be experts in some areas of endeavor, they can turn to competencies they know to be superior. They can even settle for half a loaf in the full expectation that one hardly ever gets the whole.

Adults are similarly liable to be *better informed* and *better connected*. Their experience helps them decide what is likely to work and what not. Years of accumulated facts illuminate their judgments and improve their quality. Similarly, they are apt to be better evaluators of other people. Previous events have taught them who is likely to be the more reliable ally. They know, for instance, that some people do not honor their pledges. Likewise, they better understand who will capitulate to their demands and who will fight with the intensity of a berserker. What is more, in tests of strength, because bluff is often a factor, and bluff is better assessed by those who have endured the discomfort of having previously been fooled, they are less apt to be misled.

Adding these factors together, social maturity can be decisive in determining who has the most power. This is no less true in the racial arena than any other. Only when people have had the opportunity to gain self-assurance, to learn how to be flexible, and to connect with networks of dependable allies, can they rise from the lowest stratas of society. Their greater expertise, superior ability to discern fact from fiction, and cooler heads in a crisis, make it possible to survive the challenges that are sure to arise. They attain power, not because someone has granted it to them, but because they can defend it in a crunch. Those African-Americans for whom this is true—and today there are millions of them—are most likely to be from the middle classes. As we shall later see, they are the best situated to have learned the lessons of power. They are also the ones best able to overcome the dysfunctions of a culture of slavery and the liabilities of structural disadvantage. As significantly, they are the ones least likely to be trapped by caste and the ones best equipped to take advantage of social class mobility.

Chapter 8

Change Strategies

> *You say you want a revolution*
> *Well you know*
> *we all want to change the world...*
> *But when you talk about destruction*
> *Don't you know you can count me out.*
> Paul McCartney, *Revolution* (1968)

FOUR APPROACHES TO CHANGE

The denouement came with the proverbial whimper. After having been inaugurated with much fanfare in the spring of 1997, by September of 1998 President Clinton's Race Advisory Board presented him with a 121-page report on the state of race relations in America. Amidst the brouhaha caused by the Lewinsky affair, a "national conversation" that was supposed to illuminate the reasons for our racial malaise ended in disappointment. Buried on the back pages of most newspapers, hardly anyone noticed that the panel's recommendations were neither new nor exciting. Mostly a rehash of its member's preexisting beliefs, what was advertised as a "study" of an important issue, rather than stimulating an in-depth communal examination, exposed its author's quasi-moralistic agendas.

Chaired by the noted historian John Hope Franklin,[1] the board reflected his belief that a corrosive racism continues to pervade America. On more than one occasion while presiding over its public sessions, he lectured his audience on the evils of institutionalized discrimination. The committee also reflected the philosophy of a president steeped in 1960s Civil Rights activism. Although a scion of the old Confederate state of Arkansas—or perhaps because of it—he had, throughout his career, demonstrated a passionate commitment to black causes.[2] Thus, when urged by his advisors to help Americans understand "the facts of racial domination," he was being implored to do what he was predisposed to do. Surely his advisors were aware of how enthusiastically he performed when delivering sermons before black audiences. Surely too they had witnessed him touch the hearts of millions of viewers as he, with conviction and eloquence, appealed to them to care about those whom history had wronged. Knowing all this, and that white attitudes had profoundly changed during the preceding decades, the panel still insisted that "We as a nation need to understand that whites tend to benefit, either knowingly or unconsciously, from this country's history of white privilege" and that the president must employ his rhetorical skills to exhort them to do better.

Allies of the president, as might be expected, reacted favorably to this summons.[3] The Reverend Joseph Lowery agreed that "There are a lot of [white] people in denial" and Georgia congressman John Lewis averred that the board did what it needed to when it "started people thinking and talking." The president's friends also agreed that racial stereotyping must end, that police misconduct must be suppressed, and that affirmative action must be "mended, not ended." It was only critics such as Phyllis Berry Meyers of the *Center for New Black Leadership* who intimated that "The real work of racial reconciliation will never happen in the offices of the federal government, but in the streets, in our schools and at our churches." Largely excluded from the panel's deliberations, these nay-sayers, most of whom identified themselves as conservative, chaffed in the knowledge that their disavowals of being racist were not heard. Nor was the country as a whole impressed by the board's efforts. An almost complete absence of notice bespoke its expectation that something more novel would emerge.

Exhortation, it develops, has its limitations. While it may send political rallies into paroxysms of joy, it is less able to influence the thoughts or behaviors of the uncommitted. Had the president's minions read Elliot Aronson's[4] primer on social psychology, they would have discovered an exposition on the difficulty of changing personal attitudes. A liberal by conviction, but a social scientist by trade, Aronson marshaled years of psychological research to demonstrate that individual opinions are not easily swayed. Anti-Semitism, for instance, is not dispelled merely by showing people movies favorable toward Jews. As Aronson explains, "Where important issues are involved information campaigns fail, because people are inclined not to sit still and take in information that is dissonant with their beliefs." He then describes a study by Paul Lazerfeld in which radio programs designed to reduce ethnic prejudice had, in fact, preached to the choir. "Who was listening?" he asks. "The major part of the audience for the program about Polish-Americans consisted of Polish-Americans. And guess who made up the major part of the audience for the program on Italian-Americans?"

Given this intransigence, Aronson suggests that another course is more advisable. He argues that instead of trying to alter behaviors by modifying attitudes,[5] behaviors should be addressed more straightforwardly. Because scientific evidence reveals that people are inclined to change their attitudes only after they have first shifted their actions, they can be manipulated by a "psychology of inevitability." If they are presented with a circumstance in which there is no choice but to engage in the desired behavior, they will do so, then invent rationalizations to explain why. Aronson contends that desegregation, for example, is best advanced by giving parents and children no option but to integrate. Citing the work of Thomas Pettigrew,[6] he concurs that in the wake of Brown v. School Board, disorder "generally resulted in localities where at least some of the authorities [gave] prior hints that they would gladly return to segregation if disturbances occurred."

The conclusion seems obvious to Aronson. What is needed is a consistent and muscular public policy. In a section entitled "Stateways Can Change Folkways," he contends that interracial communications can be improved by government interventions that compel people to interact with one another. If, for instance, individuals from different backgrounds find themselves living or working together, they will get to know each other and hence to like each other. Just as the residents of a Newark, New Jersey housing project studied by Martin Deutsch[7] came to have more favorable opinions of those from a different racial stock once they began living side by side, so will the nation as a whole when required to engage in social intercourse.

What Aronson left out of his analysis is that the psychology of inevitability is rarely as pain free as a laboratory experiment. Most people do not like being manipulated. If they can find a way to subvert what is being imposed on them, they will. This was forcibly brought to my attention while working at a psychiatric hospital. As a counselor, I was asked to participate in developing a treatment plan for a recalcitrant teenager. To break her of a habit of excessive independence, it was decided to reward her when she complied with the unit's rules. This was to be achieved by giving the staff the power to allow her to listen to her radio when she was submissive. She nonetheless refused to cooperate. Although it had been thought that she had no choice—listening to music had always been her favorite amusement—once she realized it was being used to control her, she refused to have anything to do with it. Her situation turned out to be quite different from that of people who voluntarily enter an environment, for example, who sign up to live in a public housing project. In cases such as hers, they tend to be less accommodating. Just as in the Soviet Union, where citizens for some seventy years acquiesced in a coercively imposed economic system, once an alternative becomes available, they take it.

For the most part, public discussions of how to improve race relations have been confined to the two strategies Aronson discusses. Either an energetic moralism or a social policy orientation are considered the only feasible options. Indeed, in the political arena, where much of this drama is played out, policies aimed at altering behaviors are habitually peddled as moral. No distinction is made between behaviors and attitudes, and sermons designed to gain support for specific programs are treated as corrective actions. A content analysis of the more than 4000 entries concerning race offered by the on-line book service *amazon.com* reveals the extent of this bias. To judge from what publishers believe commercial, the public operates primarily in moral terms. Books on "racism," "inequality," "intolerance," "civil rights," "prejudice," "segregation," and "justice" crowd the computer screen. Another set of works is more reconciliation oriented, typically asking questions such as: Why can't we get along? These take inter-racial conflict as their text and denounce the present disharmony. Still others offer their moral agenda wrapped in historical raiments. The topics they highlight are chosen with the object of exposing past injustices. Works about lynchings, the Ku Klux Klan, and eugenics fall within this domain. Frequently well executed, they arouse indignation through the graphic depiction of horrendous events.

The market for policy-oriented books, that is, works which advocate programs designed to alter interracial behaviors, is also immense. Multiculturalism, affirmative action, welfare reform, cultural diversity, urban development, poverty, interracial marriage, and education all attract considerable interest. Each of these problem areas is regarded either an avenue to a more equitable society or a seductive dead-end that must be warned against. In any event, the partisanship can become quite heated. Sometimes cloaked in technical dispassion, but often festooned in rank argumentation, the typical assumption is that conscious change is necessary. These volumes may disagree over which alternative is best, but they concur in the belief that an effective formula for governmental intervention must exist.

In general, there seem to be four major approaches to racial reform. These are: (1) the moral model, (2) the social engineering model, (3) the clinical/educational model, and (4) the cultural/structural model. Of these the first two are easily the most prevalent. The darlings of politicians, social activists, and the man on the street, their efficacy is taken for granted. Few observers inquire into how, or whether, they work, in large part, because they are themselves committed to them. With their careers, self-images, and institutions bound up in their perpetuation, they are given a free pass.

The moral model proceeds from a faith in an irrepressible human goodness. It assumes that when people are enlisted into doing the right thing, the progression toward a better world is unstoppable. Since a conversion into "good guy" status can supposedly imbue individuals with the strength of a righteous cause, they cannot be denied. With roots reaching back to antebellum abolitionists, the culmination of this perspective was Myrdal's[8] influential assessment of America's race problem. First published in 1944, in his Swedish eye-view, the dilemma was essentially due to America's failure to live up to its Creed of Equality, but could be resolved, and the nation saved, by doing so.[9] The social engineering model, in contrast, is less concerned with fervor than with control. It views the world as a great machine that is in need of tinkering. Once an appropriate plan is adopted, it is assumed that the laws of nature will take over to keep the system on course. Social scientists, in particular, are partial to this policy-oriented approach, which often employs them to do the planning and evaluating. When combined with the moral model, engineering blueprints are treated as if they had been validated by heaven. What indeed could be more elegant, or ineluctable, than a clever plan guided by a moral inevitability?

The clinical/educational model, though far less broadly accepted, also inspires real devotion. Clustered in areas such as psychology and academe, its adherents believe that successful change depends on modifying defective individuals. The vision they endorse is of interracial conflicts automatically dissolving into amicability once a handful of troublemakers are reformed. Those with personality difficulties are urged to undergo a therapeutic regimen, while those wallowing in ignorance are directed toward reeducation. Put another way, mental health and knowledge are assumed to be sovereign antidotes to racism. Because most clinicians and educators believe people are basically good, they imagine that once they are liberated from what is ailing them, they will do the right thing.

Of the four approaches, the cultural/structural model is the most comprehensive, but also the least accepted. Combining aspects of the other three, it places them in a larger sociohistorical context. While the others do not totally disregard history or social relationships, they tend to treat them as disjointed incidents. Instead of recognizing complex processes ceaselessly in motion, they focus on specific individuals at specific moments in time. They thus give a false sense of precision. Yet because culture evolves within a dynamic network of social roles and hierarchies, it is within no one's sphere to command. The truth is that we all participate in the creation and enforcement of social standards from a particular position in society. In most cases, therefore, moral conversions tend to be less sweeping than desired, social policies less adequate than planned, and personal growth more limited than imagined.

THE MORAL MODEL

As we have seen, excessive moralizing has a number of drawbacks. First, its tendency toward a good guy/bad guy division inclines those in its thrall to demonize particular groups, for example, white persons. Second, its emotional intensity creates a moral blindness in which people fail to perceive how the world operates—as was the situation with stereotyping. Third, morality, because it entails intense commitments, can distort our priorities, resulting in the canonization of equality at the expense of freedom. Still, morality is essential. One of its fundamental tasks is to stabilize society. When particular rules are widely received, they help maintain a community's integrity. People who uphold common standards have a better idea of what to expect from each other. They know that if others deviate from what is required, they will be held to account. Similarly, when people internalize the same rules, they are less apt to be dissatisfied. As long as they voluntarily accept prescriptions thought to have positive outcomes, they are disinclined to rebel. Although people have competing interests, not all of which can be reconciled, their shared allegiance to a conjoint social order can confine their conflicts to a tolerable minimum. In essence, a shared ethical code keeps the playing field relatively even and the players content to operate within its bounds.

On a less elevated plane, morality has the ability to enhance the power of those who invoke it.[10] If, for instance, someone can persuade his role partners to follow rules favorable to him, he thereby acquires leverage over them. A person can also augment her potency by being the one who sets the rules. As Shelby Steele[11] contends, African-Americans have found it possible to manipulate white guilt in ways that inflate their own status. By portraying themselves as innocents in need of protection, they thereby induce others to cease being judgmental. Likewise, setting a nation's moral agenda, as President Clinton attempted to do via his race initiative, can elevate one's political status. In politics, power often derives from having the largest and most reliable constituency. Such groupings can, however, be assembled by championing an attractive "issue." Few issues, of course, are more attractive than moral ones. In Clinton's case, the race card both helped him mobilize his African-American base and put critics of his affirmative action policies on the defensive. Then too, as we shall later see, both black and white "enablers" can derive power from being perceived as patrons of racial justice.

To return to the question of moral change, or should we say moral salvation, it is often an afterthought. As opposed to moral stasis or moral posturing, attempts at conversion have more limited effects. Although the notion that one should fight for the right is built into its meaning, this does not guarantee that moral exhortation will have the intended benefits. People are much more likely to rally to a standard they presently accept than to shift to one that is novel. By definition, if they are being asked to change, it is from something they have hitherto believed. If this is so, then why ought they convert? No matter how passionate the missionary, why risk the untested? In fact, people rarely do, and generally resent the implication that they should. This is especially so when they are asked to turn away from an objective as attractive as freedom.

To begin with, given the morality game's good guy/bad guy dichotomy, partisans on both sides tend to regard their own position as ideal. Far from being prepared to question it, they perceive skepticism as an attack to be repelled. Instead of the scales falling from their eyes when someone tries to persuade them to abandon a current stance, they may regard this other as an evil influence. The chances of his receiving a fair hearing are thus marginal. Paradoxically, the more credible this other, the more forcibly he may be rebuffed.

The results of this were in evidence when Jane Elliott gave her Chautauqua talk. She did so at the behest of students who believed that her dramatic style would advance the cause of harmonious race relations. Convinced she could shame the remnants of the Southern redneck establishment into renouncing their obtuseness, they imagined that her blue-eyed/brown-eyed exercise would be too heart rending for them to reject. This, of course, turned out not to be so. Elliott was a compelling figure, but only for the true believers. They were the ones who attended her presentation; they were the ones whose eyes glistened as they endured her assaults. The intended converts were nowhere in evidence. Having been subjected to this sort of onslaught before, they were not about to volunteer for another round.

Strangely, the assumption that moral conversion can pave the road to racial justice is shared by individuals one would think too sophisticated for it. Thus, at a panel sponsored by the Sociological Practice Association,[12] similar sentiments were expressed on all sides. Seated at the head table, the coordinator of the American Sociological Association's (ASA) participation in Clinton's race initiative began by explaining that his task was to help people "see the light." Sitting beside him, Felice Levine, the ASA's executive officer, barely took notice of the implications of this phrase as she chimed in to second his assertion. Both "knew" that racism was a calamity that had to be expunged. Despite claims that the ASA intended only to educate people, their moral commitments induced them to think like missionaries. This impetus to convert the heathens is also present in the written works of prominent sociologists. To illustrate, Robert Merton[13] the dean of structural/functional theorists, in describing the interaction of prejudice and discrimination, labels nonprejudiced, nondiscriminatory persons "all weather liberals," a none too subtle reference to his own political preferences, while Joe Feagin,[14] a recent president of the ASA, in his textbook on race relations is intent on exposing "racial oppression."

Yet moral change rarely works the way its adherents contemplate. Sometimes "improvements" accumulate slowly, as when people drift from one position to another, and sometimes quickly, as during revolutions, but hardly ever do they follow the conversion model. Slow developments, which are the most prevalent, tend to be ponderous and barely perceptible. Generally people make such adjustments without realizing it. This seems to be what happened with ethical relativism. As the United States became a multicultural society, the proclivity to allow others to lead lives of their own choosing grew apace.[15] This fidelity to a norm of nonjudgmentalism did not, however, emerge at an identifiable moment. The writings of Frans Boas[16] and Carl Rogers[17] contributed to its propagation, but did not, of themselves, persuade Americans to embrace a standard different from their Puritan forebearers. Rather, it was the experience of living in a society with ever greater value divisions that progressively convinced them it was wiser to be flexible.

Other moral changes have been more abrupt. Best designated as "punctuated change,"[18] they come into prominence during circumscribed temporal periods. Because morality is grounded in intense and inherently conservative emotions, the rules people live by must frequently be jarred loose by firestorms of counter-emotion. In ordinary times, interpersonal anger, in the guise of moral indignation, and intrapersonal emotion, in the form of guilt and shame, prevent change from occurring. These viscerally enforce compliance with existing patterns of behavior. For modifications to develop, social crises must intervene. Circumstances so unsettling that they demand attention intrude to alter the ways people see the world. The Great Depression was one such event.[19] Before it shattered America's complacent belief in the inevitability of progress, the nation basked in a consensus favoring rugged individualism. People firmly believed it their duty to help themselves. Nonetheless, after being rescued by Franklin Roosevelt's New Deal (or at least thinking they had been), millions switched to more collectivist values. It now appeared that government interventions were not only acceptable, but preferable. This dramatically transformed attitudes toward welfare, federal regulations, and presidential power. Today it seems bizarre, but Calvin Coolidge had only a short time earlier been praised by Will Rogers for having done nothing "because that's what we wanted done."

To understand how attitudes toward race are modified, it is necessary to recognize that punctuated change is more prevalent than supposed. While gradual change occurs—as the imperceptible acceptance of black quarterbacks testifies—the profound changes activists demand are largely confined to historical turning points. At least three are discernible in American history—with each tied to an identifiable sociopolitical crisis. The first pivot was associated with the American Revolution. As the colonists began to perceive a need for independence from Britain, the value of freedom increased in salience. "Give me liberty of give me death" thundered a choleric Patrick Henry as his countrymen cheered. This, however, aroused the sort of cognitive dissonance[20] to which Aronson alluded. People began to ask whether it was fair to impose a condition on African slaves they would not tolerate for themselves. The answer for many was: No! One consequence was that all of the Northern states abolished slavery shortly thereafter. They even insisted on a Constitutional clause to discontinue the slave trade. This process was, to be sure, incomplete, for despite the agitation of slaveholders such as Thomas Jefferson, an influential coterie of Southerners balked at eliminating so lucrative an institution. Still, the die was cast and was to provide a fulcrum for further change.

For decades after the American Revolution, the status of slavery remained in limbo. Conflicts between the North and South simmered, but were contained by compromises that prevented either side from becoming dominant. A second moral turning point was to develop in conjunction with the gathering momentum of the Industrial Revolution. As the North increased in population and wealth relative to a more bucolic South, the danger of imbalance grew acute. With its burgeoning cities filled with free laborers who resented what they perceived as the unfair competition of an unpaid slave population, the North became a hotbed of abolitionism. Meanwhile Southern slaveholders became alarmed at the prospect of an insurrection by bondsmen who longed for an alternative to servitude. In the end, the Civil War could not be averted. Millions of men clashed on fields of carnage so sanguine, they have yet to be equaled in American history. Although a majority denied that eradicating slavery was their intent, the logic of the situation prevailed. The Union was not only preserved, but chattel slavery was outlawed by Constitutional amendment. Moreover, even though the participants may not have understood what emancipation entailed, after the radicals had finished their work, it was impossible to return to legalized bondage. Even in the South, where the bitterness ran deep, it was understood that there had been a fundamental shift. People might try to circumvent it, but there was no way to rescind it.

The last great moral turning point in race relations is of more recent vintage. Generally subsumed under the rubric of the Civil Rights movement, it was precipitated by a prior middle-class revolution. Subsequent to World War II, the United States experienced an unprecedented reorganization of its social class structure. Throughout most of the world's history, the majority of every nation's citizens dwelled in poverty. Even though America had for more than a century been relatively free and prosperous, it was not until a burst of postwar economic growth propelled millions of its citizens onto a higher plane that this middling group became dominant.[21] Symbolic of this transition was the GI Bill which allowed returning soldiers to train for technically responsible occupations. Once in these jobs, they purchased automobiles, suburban tract houses, and college educations for their children.[22] They also became more politically astute. Where once their own parents had been content to entrust their fate to heroic leaders, they now wished to seize the reins themselves. This became evident during the 1960s when their children claimed the right to transform society according to their idealistic lights. Included in this idealism was none other than Civil Rights. We today think of these rights as a bundle of government programs designed to help blacks achieve success, but at the time they represented an attempt to bring everyone under the umbrella of a common legal system. This made moral sense in a society where merit-based mobility depended upon a uniform playing field. Once again cognitive dissonance extended the protection of common rules to a community that, despite being technically free, remained submerged by the legacy of slavery. Their continuing caste status was an affront to a new generation that perceived the entire world as open to anyone with the audacity to seize it.

Seen from this perspective, the glory days of the Civil Rights movement take on a different coloration. The changes that occurred, instead of being attributable to the eloquence of a small band of moral leaders, owe more to the receptivity of a broader audience. Larger numbers of people could begin to perceive blacks as human beings, not because some magically persuasive words had been spoken, but because they were emotionally ready to see what was there to be seen. Better informed, more ambitious, and above all more able to comprehend themselves as independent human beings operating in an environment chock-a-block with other independent human beings, a desire for consistency made it possible to recognize the legitimacy of black complaints. Where less than a century earlier, few Americans were mortified by the brutalities visited upon assertive "Negroes," the triumph of the market economy had inculcated personal strengths that made it possible to tolerate strength in others. What need had they, the standard-bearers of the mightiest nation of all time, to deny the equal worth of their darker-skinned neighbors?

The events that culminated in the Great Society were a high point for many of those who pushed them forward. Indeed, for them, they came to typify the substance of morality. But the times have changed. The unprecedented upheaval in social class arrangements then in progress has subsided. Aging activists such as Julian Bond, John Lewis, and Jesse Jackson[23] may wish to recapture the excitement of their youth, but cannot. Ordinary people will not be forced to return to a long gone starting point merely so others can reexperience the exhilaration of surging from behind. As a result, that which resonated with the masses in the 1960s cannot resonate with their heirs today. That which brought hundreds of thousands onto the streets, induced thousands more to dedicate their careers to reform, and made millions of others willing to reconsider their personal commitments is gone and cannot be revived. This is why exhortation that once moved multitudes now falls flat, why it no longer has the emotional voltage to change attitudes or to modify perceptions.

Exhortation, to repeat, has limitations. Besides being keyed to the opportunities of the moment, one of its flaws is that no one can sustain moral intensity indefinitely. The state of arousal needed to support an endless revolution is not humanly possible. Indeed, the past is replete with examples of crusades that ran out of steam. Despite heroic efforts, Mao Tse-tung[24] could not rekindle the spirit of the Long March in the Cultural Revolution. Nor could the Pilgrim Fathers imbue their descendants with the religious enthusiasm that prompted them to brave a pestilential voyage into the unknown. Even the medieval Crusades petered out. Eventually the opposition of the Saracens and the demands of ordinary living reduced the volume of recruits. The fact is that whether the faithful are motivated by a radiant ideal or a revulsion against an intolerable evil, eventually the fires die down. In almost every case of moral enthusiasm, when the predicted millennium fails to materialize, the exhilaration of being among the chosen becomes less compelling. A kind of guilt fatigue then induces them to be less distressed by visible failures. Although specific individuals can sustain extraordinary levels of hope or shame, it is impossible for large populations to do likewise.

Of even more moment, intense moralism has serious drawbacks. When it arouses an excessive idealism, it can become a fearsome juggernaut.[25] In such cases, it can impel people to act in unimaginably dangerous ways. Some reformers do not shrink from insisting that the government enforce moral conformity.[26] They are prepared to advocate draconian measures to eliminate any residual racial discrimination. Just as with prohibition, they welcome proposals to jail people even if this places democracy in jeopardy. For some of these zealots a moral blindness occasioned by their participation in a mass movement reinforces their own prejudices and prevents them from recognizing when they have crossed the line. Emotionally convinced of their righteousness, they detect enemies everywhere. In their good guy/bad guy mentality not only are the bad guys always bad, but an "If you're not with me, you must be against me" certitude leads them to condemn even the moderates. This, not surprisingly, elicits a countervailing intransigence. Once this occurs, efforts at beneficial change are obviated and a return to sanity indefinitely postponed.

Such hazards make it essential to emphasize the hygienic functions of morality. Whereas an excessive moralism can be profoundly counterproductive, in its less flamboyant incarnations the enterprise is essential for human survival. Yet the rules that allow a society to be orderly do not enforce themselves. People must agree on standards they are willing to abide by and, in concert, make work. Rather than craving dramatic transformations, they do better to partake in the more mundane business of keeping the system honest. There is less glory in forestalling cheaters than in constructing a heaven on earth, but it is ultimately more profitable.

THE SOCIAL ENGINEERING MODEL

Most Americans like to think of themselves as pragmatists. Ever since the frontier days, they have prided themselves on a can-do attitude. When confronted with a problem, rather than analyze it abstractly, they prefer to roll up their sleeves and tinker with the machinery. This has produced unparalleled levels of achievement and invention. Nowhere else did agriculture and industry become so prolific. Nowhere else have so many people been able to draw upon so sustained a bounty. Given these facts, why should not most Americans transfer this disposition to social problems? Hence when, after having committed themselves to a "war on poverty," they encountered unexpected obstacles, the response was "If we can send a man to the moon, why can't we do (fill-in-the-blank)?" It seemed unimaginable that a people capable of succeeding in so apparently impossible a task should not be able to do whatever they set their minds to.

This social engineering mentality[27] perceives the world as a chess board in which all the pieces are subject to physical manipulation. If one is clever enough, and persistent enough, all things are possible. Whether one's favored tools include social science or spiritualism, the desired endpoint is believed within grasp. And yet the inducements to misperceive when one has failed, that is, to not learn from unwelcome feedback, can be enormous. Paradoxically, although most Americans would be shocked were it pointed out, this engineering orientation has more in common with the principles of Soviet Communism than with those of a market-oriented system. In a command economy of the Russian sort, central planners determined what was needed, then endeavored to bring this about by requiring others to follow their dictates. Capitalist economies, however, are more decentralized. Their decision-making is spread out, with those delegated to carry out particular plans very often the same people who devised them. This enables these systems to be more flexible. Since the planners are closer to the action, they can factor in more variables and, when things go wrong—as they invariably do—can respond more expeditiously. Moreover, when bad decisions are made, the impetus to correct them is strong.

Frederich von Hayek,[28] one of capitalism's more vociferous defenders, has justly observed that "Because it was not dependent on [prior] organization but grew up as a spontaneous order that the structure of modern society has attained the degree of complexity which it possesses and which far exceeds any that could have been achieved by deliberate organization. In fact, of course, the rules which made the growth of this complex order possible were initially not designed in the expectation of that result: but those people who happened to adopt suitable rules developed a complex civilization which then often spread to others." Writing in a similar mode, albeit with regard to radical feminism, Carolyn Graglia[29] notes that "It is the conservative view that one should advocate change with humility; that it is dangerous to seek to destroy an edifice such as the traditional family which in Burke's words, 'has answered in any tolerable degree for ages the common purposes of society.'" She contends that "The best protection against making extreme reforms—all the outcomes of which can rarely be foreseen—is the humility to recognize how little we can ever know and how vulnerable we are to being swayed by passion and unreason." In the same vein, David Horowitz[30] writes that "Conservatives do not pretend to shape the future by bending it to their will. They do not offer plans to remake human beings by inducing them to act in ways that are dramatically different from how human beings have acted in the past." He continues, "The 'first principles' of conservatism, then, are propositions about the existing social contract, about the nature of human beings in a social context. They are propositions about limits, and what limits make possible." Finally, The political scientist James Q. Wilson[31] observes that "If there is any article of faith common to almost every [neo-conservative], it is the Law of Unintended Consequences. Things never work out quite as you hope; in particular, government programs do not achieve their objectives or do achieve them but with high or unexpected costs."

Major reforms, therefore, tend to be hazardous. They may be born of a desire to fix what is broken, but often go awry. Nor are many significant reforms instituted by conscious mandate—at least not the successful ones. No matter how desperately they seem needed, the world is too complicated and too intransigent, and we human beings too fragile and self-interested, for effective change to be the product of specific individuals implementing determinate plans. Elites of whatever stripe, be they religious, political or academic, are always products of a limited perspective. Though their goals may be noble, they are more apt to be self-deluded idealists than responsive pragmatists. Just as the U.S. Congress, because of its irredeemably parochial concerns, has proven inept at fine-tuning the economy, so too are political activists inept at adjusting social equities. The result is that they are likely to fail in these endeavors. In a sense, the behavioral modifications they advocate are a species of coercive moralism that suffer the defects of both moralism and coercion. Myopic, as such crusades usually are, they generally misinterpret the way things are and attempt to bully their way to success over the objections of individuals prepared to resist.

Purpose-built schemes for improving human society are almost inevitably too simple. So many factors are involved, and so many of these are inaccessible to the planners, that they resort to ideological shortcuts. Their fantasies rather than their understandings substitute for reality and they blunder ahead convinced they know where they are going. This dilemma is universal. The economist Herbert Simon[32] won a Nobel Prize for revealing its presence in business. As he demonstrated, because managers know only a fraction of the alternatives available to them, their decisions tend to "satisfice" rather than optimize. Unable to determine what is best, they settle for solutions that are "good enough." Social reformers may be loath to acknowledge it, but a limited rationality also applies to their decisions.[33] With a larger canvass to work with, and more players intervening in unregulated ways, they find it even more difficult to predict what will work. This is why their emotions tend to take over and persuade them that they are on track when they are not even sure where the tracks lead.

The Head Start program provides a cautionary tale. Begun with the best of intentions, its very name betrays idealistic roots. Based more on a metaphor than careful research, it proposed to rectify the education of African-American children by starting them in school early. If, as the evidence then indicated, these youngsters fell behind academically, they could be brought up to speed by letting them begin the race beforehand, that is, by designating nursery schools to teach them reading and math prior to elementary school. It all seemed so logical, there was no way it could not work. And yet it did not. Some prototype schools benefited their target populations, but the nationwide program proved a disappointment. Its backers might trumpet its accomplishments, but these were meager. Most distressingly, lasting intellectual benefits for inner-city children proved elusive. While IQ and achievement scores rose during the first few years of school, these eventually descended to the levels they would have reached absent any intervention. Ironically white students were helped more than were black, with impacts on physical health being greater than on academic indicators. Advocates of Headstart, such as Doris Entwisle,[34] continue to proclaim its virtues, but these often boil down to such lesser achievements as reducing the number of children shunted into classes for the retarded.

The social engineering model seems to depend on three tenets, each of which is accepted on faith. The first is that the problem under consideration is sufficiently understood, that is, that people know what is wrong and hence what needs to be fixed. The second is that a solution to this problem can always be found. The third is that this solution, whatever its shape, can readily be implemented. Not only is it certain to work, but it is capable of being put into effect with the resources at hand. In the case of homelessness, for instance, it is taken for granted that the problem is that some people are without homes, that the solution is getting them homes, and that these homes can be acquired by funding them through federal legislation.

In fact, in many, if not most, cases, none of these conditions hold. Contrary to what the central planners assert, the nature of a great many problems is misunderstood, no feasible solution is easily accessible, and implementation is a nightmare. This was certainly true vis-a-vis homelessness. When people began appearing sprawled out on heating grates and living in cardboard boxes, the presumption was they had no place to go. Evidently priced out of the housing market by their poverty, they were surviving as best they could. The natural solution was to build affordable housing. Once this was available, these unfortunate souls, who were basically the same as the rest of us—only economically less well off—would have somewhere to reside. The obvious way to provide this was to appeal to the source with the deepest pockets, namely the government.

All this, however, was vitiated by the facts.[35] The real reason for the explosion in homelessness was another government program. The grubby panhandlers who caught everyone's attention had essentially been kicked out onto the streets by the policy of deinstitutionalizing the mentally ill. Operating on the premise that mental illness could be treated more humanely outside of the hospitals, hundreds of thousands of patients were discharged without a dependable place to stay. Essentially unsupervised, they went off their medications, and since hospitalization was now voluntary, elected the independence of outdoor living. To provide such persons refurbished housing was largely irrelevant. Since their primary problem was medical, a residential solution was beside the point, and, in any event, likely to fail when they hastily exited from whatever domicile they were offered. Nor were government officials, who were still congratulating themselves over the money saved by emptying the hospitals, eager to spend the surplus on housing. They might deplore stepping over unkempt derelicts on their way to the supermarket, but kept the governmental coffers firmly closed nonetheless.

With respect to race relations an engineering model fares no better. A simple illustration is provided by the proposal to issue reparations to African-Americans. The problem in this case is defined in terms of an historical injustice. American prosperity, it is asserted, rests upon the uncompensated labor of antebellum slaves. Were these bondsmen given the forty acres and a mule they were promised, their descendants would by now have attained economic achievements comparable to those of whites. The solution to this inequity is thus to provide contemporary blacks with the previously denied resources. This can be achieved through the expedient of legislative appropriation. All that Congress has to do is authorize the appropriate checks. Or would it? First, there is the question of whether the problem is as represented. Certainly millions of slaves were robbed of the benefits of their labor. Certainly too compensatory goods never materialized. But how does this apply today? Is the central difficulty confronting contemporary African-Americans the absence of a legacy they were personally promised? Surely not. Unlike Japanese-Americans who received reparations for property stolen during World War II, present-day blacks were not alive during slavery or its immediate aftermath. What was lost could not possibly have been personally theirs. Nor was the forty acres and a mule a legislative mandate. Fundamentally an unadopted political proposal, it was never legally binding. Neither is it accurate to characterize the central problem confronting modern blacks as a lack of money. If any of our earlier observations regarding the culture of slavery or social "empowerment" are valid, other concerns are more weighty.

But supposing that the request for reparations was accepted as legitimate, what would be the solution? The easy answer is money—lots of money. But how much? A few thousand dollars would clearly make little difference. If people's lives are to be altered for the better, they would need sufficient capital to make substantial investments. But again, how much? One figure bandied about has been $100,000 per person. This may seem high, but given today's prices, would be about right to purchase the equivalent of forty acres and a pickup truck. Yet what would happen if these funds were dispersed in the form of cashier's checks? Would this potential principal be put to good use? For some middle-class persons the answer is yes. They would know how to spend it to obtain the best effect. For most blacks, however, the answer is probably no. The poorest of the poor would likely go on a spending spree. They would get drunk, go to the race track, and/or buy the fanciest automobile they could afford.[36] If this prediction sounds disrespectful, it is based on experience. We know this to be the fate of many lottery winners. We also know that a precipitous loss of resources was the destiny of Oklahoma Indians whose lands were distributed to them at the end of the last century.[37] Intended to give them a stake in their future, it actually enabled unscrupulous speculators to cheat them out of their birthright.

But even if reparations could bring prosperity, are they practical to deliver? Look at the consequences of the indemnities levied against Germany in the wake of World War I. Not only did they not repair the devastation wrought by the conflict, but they were impossible deliver without sending the German economy into a ruinous inflation. Could the United States escape such devastation? Some simple calculations indicate that the cost to the treasury of the $100,000 proposal would approach four trillion dollars. That is almost as large as the entire national debt—which no one seriously proposes to pay off in one fell swoop. It is a figure so high that if paid, it would destroy our economy; a figure so high, that no government would ever pay it; so high, that no electorate would ever approve it. Finally, it is alleged that if reparations were paid, whites would never again have to apologize to blacks for the depredations imposed on their ancestors. But this too is unlikely. What is more probable is that if the policy failed, as it almost certainly would, people would continue to be aggrieved.

A more complex example of social engineering that people have tried to implement, albeit with minor success, is school busing. In Brown v. School Board, the Supreme Court defined the problem as one of separate schools. Separate, it rather magisterially decreed, is inherently unequal. The victorious argument was that even if the same resources were funneled into black schools as into whites ones, the instructional results would remain inferior because the students' self-esteem would suffer from an awareness that they were being treated as second-class citizens. The court's majority cited Kenneth Clark's[38] research which asked black and white children which doll, a black or a white one, they considered more attractive, intelligent, or a better potential friend, as verifying the damage done by segregation. Although no social psychologist since has suggested that Jewish or Chinese children are academically stunted by attending schools that are primarily Jewish or Chinese, it became a matter of social dogma that this is true for blacks. Without examination, it has been further alleged that lower self-esteem dictates a lowered intellectual performance. Recent research has, nonetheless, cast doubt on this linkage.[39] The lofty self-esteem contemporary psychological tests reveal is possessed by many blacks has not been translated into higher scores on achievement tests. Nor do the scruples

Chinese-American children express about their ability to handle numbers correlate with inferior test scores.

It seems to follow, however, that if separate schooling is the problem, integrated schooling is the solution. Physically moving children into the same buildings, by means of forced busing if necessary, would theoretically expose each race to the best qualities of the other. Whites would learn that blacks are human beings with feelings and brains, and blacks would acquire the academic orientation of whites. Almost by osmosis, a dedication to learning would filter from one group to the other. In the end, this would be confirmed in comparable test scores. Unfortunately, this too has turned out not to be true, at least not substantially so. Despite the commitment of generations of educators, the figures have been disappointing. While some claim that there have been demonstrable gains, these have been modest,[40] and in recent years not sustained.

But it is implementation that has been the real sticking point. Even if the problem and solution had been as advertised, converting them into facts on the ground proved more perplexing than the analysts allowed. Despite the ostensible rationality of their plans, the subjects of their ministrations were far from receptive. It was, the activists discovered, one thing to order a busing plan and quite another to have it honored. People resisted—by the millions. Whatever the courts might decide, ordinary parents reserved the option to picket, to elect sympathetic peers to school boards, and to withdraw their children from public schools and send them to private ones. Most importantly, as James Coleman[41] was to document, they engaged in white flight. They simply moved out of districts where busing was introduced into jurisdictions where it was not. Before long, in places such as New York City, the concentration of black students was so great there was no one left with whom to integrate. Nor was combining school districts an option, given that the time and expense in shipping pupils to the suburbs was prohibitive. Even when schools were formally integrated, the students spontaneously separated themselves. In the lower grades, play groups might assemble without regard to skin color, but by high school the players were more color conscious. They tended to concentrate in distinct classes, to sit at different cafeteria tables, and even to attend alternate proms.

Particularly instructive has been the experience of Kansas City,[42] where, in the 1980s, a Federal District Judge ruled that continued segregation must be relieved by totally reorganizing the affected districts. In taking over the authority to administer the metropolitan school systems, he forced them to adopt a $1.5 billion dollar plan designed to raise overall standards. Relying more on magnet schools than busing to accomplish this mission, buildings were erected, teachers hired, and curricula overhauled. In the end, the institutions were transformed, with many more students attending the same classes, but the achievement scores did not budge. Coleman's[43] decades old warning that facilities make little difference—that it is family values that matter most—was ignored with predictable consequences. What the judge and city were to learn was that they could compel actions, but not results.

Lastly, one of the more pervasive manifestations of the limits of racial engineering has been affirmative action.[44] A confusing tangle of set-asides, hiring preferences, and training programs that have sprouted at every level of government, education, and business, it was designed to increase the status of African-Americans by directly placing them in positions on a par with others. Impatient to achieve results, the goal of its sponsors is full and immediate equality.   Yet the potential outcomes of affirmative action were not researched before the policy was imposed. It sprang to life based on the gut-feelings of social reformers who were certain they understood all they needed to about the problem, its solution, and prospective implementation. Controversial, and surrounded by political turmoil ever since, the process has had a spotty record at best.[45] Contradictory claims continue to be put forth by advocates who seem more concerned with victory than social equity. Proponents, such as Patterson[46], assert that it is largely responsible for the demonstrable economic progress of African-Americans, while critics such as the Thernstroms[47] and Smith and O'Connell[48] dispute this. The Thernstroms, for instance, conclude that the largest African-American gains occurred before affirmative action was instituted and primarily in areas, like the South, where it was most weakly implemented.

What is beyond dispute is that these occupational and educational preferences have aroused white antipathy. As Sniderman[49] has documented, even whites unaffected by quotas resent them. They perceive these as an assault on universalistic principles and personal merit. If it is recalled that relative power is achieved through tests of strength, this testifies to the presence of a serious problem.   Even if blacks deserve preferences to eliminate the effects of past injustices—as most of them believe[50]—they wind up handicapping their pursuit of success. Because of affirmative action, whites are led to assume that blacks receive promotions not reflective of their abilities. They therefore adjudge their strengths to be less than they would otherwise.   In other words, power bestowed on the basis of race is not respected, even when it is deserved. It is power on loan, and that which is on loan can always be recalled. If this is true, then affirmative action poisons the well from which it drinks. Certainly observers such as Stephen Carter[51] and Shelby Steele[52] believe that it creates its own opposition. Carter, for instance, confesses that as an "affirmative action baby" he had to fight the presumption he was not qualified to be a Yale student or law professor.

The ideological nature of these disputes is ratified by those on one side who assert that whites will lose nothing by giving priority to blacks[53] and those on the other who claim that even if blacks gain little, whites remain in jeopardy. As Hochschild[54] puts it, "In the current American racial culture, affirmative action is more important to participants in the policy dispute as a weapon with which to attack enemies...." This may be why partisans such as Patterson[55] do not seem to recognize how drastic their proposals are. Characterizing them as "piecemeal" and modest in their impact, he nevertheless asserts that they are essential. Social activists on the left have long dreamt of redistributing wealth in order to make society more equal, but Patterson overtly advocates redistributing *power*. Even though he admits this would dramatically overhaul contemporary social standards, he is unperturbed. While acknowledging that "The covert agenda of the struggle for affirmative action is that it seeks to change the underlying rules of determination in our society" and that Tthis is clearly a power struggle," he is still prepared to defend the outcome on the basis of simple justice. Patterson further argues that "The struggle at this point is not about getting on the playing field or playing the game, but about the very rules of the game, about who sets the rules, and about the purpose and style of the game." This breathtaking confession acknowledges that the principles underlying our democratic and economic institutions are being challenged, but he sanguinely continues, "The rules by which we play in our social organizations are not like genetic codes. They can and do change."

With these innocent-sounding words, and without ever being precise about what the new rules might be, Patterson cavalierly dismisses the moral accomplishments of centuries of evolution in favor of an intellectual projection. Just how extreme he is prepared to be in reengineering society is revealed in the suggestions he makes with regard to promoting racial integration. Among other things, he recommends that the federal government provide incentives for people to move into multiracial suburban neighborhoods and that it likewise encourage them to enter into racially integrated marriages. Having cogently concluded that unless people interact as equals in all aspects of their lives, they cannot truly be equal, he wishes the government to manipulate them into doing so. That this is Big-Brotherism writ large—larger even than Soviet planners managed to dream—gives him little pause. Convinced his goal is just, he does not perceive these means as extreme.

Whether or not Patterson is excessive, what is clear is that affirmative action has instituted a form of "corporate pluralism." Corporate pluralism is a type of social organization in which strong intergroup boundaries are maintained and where the social rewards are distributed according to group membership. In dividing the country into categories with differential access to government services, it unintentionally ties the life chances of individuals to their racial or ethnic affiliation. Pessimists such as Arthur Schlesinger,[56] not unnaturally, fear that this will have balkanizing tendencies inimical to national stability. They contend that rather than create equality, these distinctions set people in competition with one another, and that this is likely to result in future iniquities. If so, then besides imperiling our personal freedoms, affirmative action would not even promote equality.[57]

With all of these confusions, failed assurances, and unplanned consequences, social engineering does not inspire confidence. Its blandishments may seem reasonable, but are fraught with gaps in their an ability to produce. The truth seems to be that the areas in which social engineering is most effective are fairly restricted. Oddly, with regard to race, the domains where it is most capable of effecting positive change are the "negative" instances. As may be recalled, the original demand for civil rights sought laws that were impartially administered. It soon became evident, however, that a major reason they were not was the presence of legislation specifically designed to handicap blacks. These Jim Crow statutes explicitly mandated segregation, a biased electoral process, and unequal prison sentences. Doing away with them—that is, a negative action—became the primary mission of the activists. This was an apt choice because it was doable, and ultimately was accomplished. The situation was such that a conscious, transformative intervention was feasible because what was to be modified was specifiable. Unlike more nebulous objectives, where the causes are uncertain, these were definable and within the realm of the actors to remove.

Other instances in which social engineering is feasible tend to those where the problem is simple and where a public consensus on correcting it exists. The decision made during the Eisenhower administration to build a national highway system was such a case. Though expensive and time consuming, the technology was well understood and the desire to improve roads widespread. But even here there were a multitude of unexpected consequences. Few planners recognized the enormous implications for suburban growth. Nor did they predict the enormous impetus given supermarkets or fast-food chains.[58] Not unexpectedly, with more complex objectives—such as racial justice—purposeful interventions enter upon a profoundly opaque territory with many more unanticipated detours.

THE CLINICAL/EDUCATIONAL MODEL

Clinical and educational change strategies also have drawbacks, but these are not always apparent. The darlings of academics and helping professionals, to their adherents they appear utterly unobjectionable. How, it is wondered, could anyone disagree with attempts to promote therapeutic growth or to combat ignorance? And how could these fail to ameliorate the human condition? Yet they too, upon closer examination, have limitations. To become a stronger and better informed person is almost always a benefit, but interventions aimed at achieving these have other implications as well. First, their premises are not self-evident. The causes they allege to be central often are not. Second, especially with regard to racial issues, the manner of their implementation may not be neutral. People can, and do, abuse what seem to be uncomplicated scientific operations.

One reason for distinguishing clinical and educational perspectives from social engineering and moral interventions is that their emphasis is on individual defects. By and large, social engineers wish to reconfigure entire systems to produce a desired result. They look to the big picture and propose maneuvers such as school busing and central city opportunity zones. Their favored tools are government programs and legalistic remedies. Morality, of course, seeks to convert individuals to favored positions. Its favorite tools are exhortation and intimidation. Clinicians and educators, in contrast, concentrate on eliminating personal limitations. They generally aim at hands-on manipulation that is intended, at a retail, not wholesale level, to reconstruct the behaviors and attitudes of target populations by altering the psyches of those involved. Either in classrooms or in therapy sessions, the object is to modify or eliminate those aspects of specific human beings that contribute to the perpetuation of social difficulties.

Clinical reformers tend to be "disorder" oriented.[59] They think in terms of diseases, pathologies, and personality dysfunctions. With professional roots in the treatment of mental illness, most assume that for biological and/or environmental reasons some people's brains are not functioning properly. Instead of coming to the right conclusions, or being motivated to engage in correct actions, these individuals are diverted down unacceptable channels. It, therefore, behooves competent professionals, equipped as they are, with suitable chemical and talk therapies, to attack their disordered conditions and assist them in becoming "normal." The expectation is that in a renewed state of rationality they will automatically choose the right course. With regard to racial matters, the assumption is generally made that an environmentally caused derangement is to blame. This suggests to clinicians that reversing the biasing effects of early childhood socialization will enable their clients will reenter the democratic mainstream.

One of the forebearers of this tradition was Theodore Adorno.[60] After World War II, he and his colleagues sought to discover how the entire German nation could have been seduced into cooperating with Hitler's barbarities. To this end, they tried to determine if personality factors accounted for their willingness to obey blatantly inhumane orders. A so-called f-scale (for fascist) was constructed to identify those individuals simultaneously inclined to slavish obedience and an overbearing insolence. They were labeled authoritarian personalities and it was hypothesized that German patterns of socialization produced dangerously large concentrations of them. If one hoped to obviate this threat, one had either to alter early family relationships or to induct those damaged by them into an appropriate therapeutic regimen.

The same reasoning has been applied to racists. If, as many assume, they have a personality defect, it too must either be prevented or cured. Some have conjectured that racial prejudice is at its heart attributable to an authoritarian streak. They opine that white bigots are rigid, closed-minded autocrats who enjoy imposing their will on subservient underlings. Others take a more direct route. They wish to establish the existence of an identifiably "racist" personality. Individuals with an inclination toward prejudice and/or discrimination ipso facto qualify for this designation. Their tendency to treat others shabbily merely because of observable physical traits is taken as a prima facie indicator of the condition and regarded as evidence of an underlying cognitive or emotional disturbance. Those who favor this diagnosis have actually sought to have it included in the American Psychiatric Association's Diagnostic and Statistical Manual of mental illnesses, the DSM-IV.[61] So far, they have been unsuccessful, but the effort continues.

The racism diagnosis is obviously intended to apply to the Caucasian persecutors of blacks, but clinical labeling and clinical interventions have also been recommended for African-Americans. Some people have taken the notion of black pathologies quite seriously and tried to codify them. They have argued that personal instabilities within the black community are responsible for much of their visible distress. Billson,[62] for one, has alleged that the deviant lifestyles thay develop in disorganized ghetto families have predictably deplorable consequences. When people grow up with their personalities contorted into such roles as that of the *conformist, retreatist, tough guy, actor,* or *cool guy,* their relationships with others, as well as their economic prospects, are undermined. Successful clinical interventions, she says, are therefore essential. These depend "first on an accurate analysis of style. Second [they depend] on designing balancing strategies.... *The key is that standard techniques are intentionally employed to help youths achieve greater balance between power and affiliation.*" (italics Billson's) The techniques she has in mind include sensitization, reframing, modeling, looping, and rehearsing and are to be used by youth workers to cultivate personal skills in damaged individuals who are desperately in need of them to fulfill their personal requirements. When successful, this program is expected to reconstruct their personality styles along more satisfying lines. Other clinicians, such as William Scott,[63] recommend the construction of shared meaning systems to build personal esteem. He endorses "therapeutic conversations," often in conjunction with family therapy, as a means to addressing racial dilemmas.

Herrnstein and Murray[64] have also been interpreted as locating black difficulties in black defects. Their tentative hypothesis in *The Bell Curve* that IQ scores are heritable and that therefore African-Americans may be condemned to lesser achievements would obviously be a biological account of failure. If true, it would imply that significant change is not possible. Similar implications are inherent in theories that proclaim that violence has a physiological footing and hence that the connection between race and crime is hard wired. If correct, this hypothesis throws cold water on hopes for learning-based improvements.

Even where personal change seems feasible, it is more difficult than usually imagined. For most therapists, it is a truism that significant growth is voluntary. Since nearly all of the work that must be done, must be done by the client, if he or she is unwilling to proceed, nothing happens. Thus the client who goes to a clinician and says, "Change me!" is in for a disappointment. So too is the jurist who remands a felon for enforced rehabilitation. Genuine therapy is an emotional experience that cannot occur without the emotional engagement of the subject.[65] While some behavioral modifications can be externally imposed, these are not as profound as the clinical model promises. Limited to surface features, they have little influence on the springs of an individual's motivation. More importantly, since neither white racists, nor black street people, are likely to present themselves for therapeutic treatment, diagnosing them with a psychiatric disorder makes little practical difference. Even if a particular form of intervention might work with a cooperative subject, their disposition to resist dooms the entire project.

Worse than this, clinical interventions often have nonclinical agendas. When someone is declared to be suffering from a disorder, the objective is often not to identify an observable mental condition, but to stigmatize the individual.[66] The diagnosis is, in essence, an ad hominem assault, with the labeled person effectively being told that science certifies him as in error and therefore in need of desisting from whatever he is doing. It is not merely that he is wrong; he is defective, and hence anything he says on his own behalf is irrelevant. This clinical maneuver is a powerful debating tool precisely because it short-circuits questions about who is right by bestowing the privilege of judgment exclusively on the one doing the judging. Because he is presumably nondefective, his verdict is certified as beyond discussion, whereas the objections of his target are automatically delegitimized. If the latter says, for instance, that he is not a racist, this becomes proof that he is. Likewise, if he asserts that his accuser is unfair, this is regarded as a sign of defensiveness.

With most clinical accusations at present leveled at whites, objecting to this procedure may seem like carping at a reasonable means of enforcing social fairness. Yet the potential for abuse is too great to go unremarked. Lest one forget, back in the antebellum South the same technique was brought to bear against blacks. When a slave ran away from a plantation he was often said to be suffering from draeptomania, that is, from an uncontrollable desire to run away.[67] Because he was presumed to be mentally deranged, he could be treated as in need of a painful cure rather than as a person who had justly sought his freedom. In other words, by applying a psychiatric label, the slaveowner could avoid having to consider the implications of slavery, while simultaneously justifying any barbarity he chose to impose.

Turning to the educational half of the clinical/educational model, one finds similar factors operative. Educators assume that the relevant defect inclining a person toward objectionable behavior is a lack of knowledge.[68] They are convinced that if he/she fully understood what was happening, prejudice and discrimination would be impossible. The goal, therefore, is to impart facts—lots of facts. The only question which must be asked is: Which facts?

Yet there is a difficulty in this. Before the query can be answered, several things must first be determined. To begin with, who is to decide upon the validity of particular facts? Second, how is it to be established which information is not known, that were it known, would make a difference? The central problem here is that those making these determinations may not be neutral. The conclusions they reach may have more to do with their own commitments than the state of the world. This leads to such additional quandaries as: Are there really people who are unaware of social inequalities? Are there, in fact, students wholly ignorant of the history of slavery? In this age of multiculturalism, it is hard to believe that there are individuals who have never been exposed to lessons on other cultures, never viewed movies about the pain of social rejection, and never participated in conversations about the evils of racism.

The truth is that even though ignorance is rampant, the primary reason for its continuing presence is not a dearth of information. Nor is it the case that only those on the wrong side of the moral divide are knowledge deficient. Human beings on both sides of every issue could benefit from more facts. No, the charge of ignorance is apt to rest on moral grounds. Like the accusation that someone suffers from a mental disorder, it relegates its object to a position of social inferiority. Ignorant people, like insane and immoral people, are not worthy of a hearing. Rather than being allowed to speak their minds, they must be forced to overcome their alleged difficulty, not through therapy, but via a training program that is only marginally different from its clinical counterpart. Totalitarians, it must be noted, are notorious for wanting to "reeducate" their opponents. Even in the United States, during the heart of the Vietnam War, academic dissenters were wont to engage in "teach-ins." They did not say to those who disagreed with them, "Come let us reason together," but rather, "You don't understand; let us tell you what you need to know." A similar sort of arrogance infects activists intent on reorganizing race relations. They too assume they have a monopoly on the truth.

What is more, genuine learning is as voluntary as is genuine therapy. If people don't want to learn, they won't. Either they will not attend the lessons, or having been forced to attend, won't listen, or having listened, won't believe what they are told. Their minds will either be so filled with anger that the message can't get through, or if their heads are clear, will be too occupied with counterarguments to consider contrary positions. To have any meaning, learning must generate mental connections with other things a person knows; otherwise it is rote and equivalent to a baby's prattle. This places strict limits on how much education can do to overcome the ignorance of those who truly are ignorant. Race relations might indeed benefit from improved intergroup knowledge, but this cannot be imposed coercively.

Nor is the kind of knowledge imparted in schools always suited to enhancing intergroup understanding. Clinicians make a distinction between cognitive and emotional understanding.[69] The latter, which is usually called empathy, entails being able to put oneself in another's shoes and feel what she might feel. It is a much more fine textured and motivating kind of knowledge than is an enumeration of facts. When in place, it helps a person figure out why another does as she does, and as importantly, fosters sympathy for her plight. This obviously comes in handy when interacting with people who are different from oneself and with whom one wants to deal fairly. It is not, however, conveyed in lectures about the importance of having empathy. Like any emotional capacity, it must be developed in emotionally laden relationships. People generally come to feel at one with others during interactions in which these others exhibit positive feelings toward them. In other words, honest emotions tend to generate reciprocal emotions. Furthermore, because empathic feelings are themselves feelings, they are inherently voluntary. Empathy called up on demand is a self-contradiction. It is a mere pretense of experiencing what it is expected one should feel.

THE CULTURAL/STRUCTURAL MODEL

History is a powerful force. Society is regularly swept by a myriad of unfathomed currents that are beyond the ability of those affected to divert. People may wish to change the direction of events, but repeatedly find themselves incapable of doing so. They are faced instead with something analogous to a river that can be temporarily deflected, but not indefinitely impounded. Whatever their initial success, sooner or later the flow surges forward to swamp their hopes of total control. This intractability is what the cultural/structural model strives to address. Whereas the moral, social engineering, and clinical/educational approaches all promise substantial mastery over events, it does not. Attuned to a larger picture than they, it attempts to place a variety of occurrences in context. Specifically, it aims to view history in long-term perspective and social processes in dynamic interaction. This means that morality is not rejected, but interpreted as part of greater whole; that social engineering is not ruled out, but understood as a modest adjunct; and that clinical/educational interventions are not vetoed, but treated with less arrogance. In the cultural/structural model, the change agent is neither an elitist who automatically knows best nor an omnipotent authority figure who unilaterally decides what needs to be done, but a meliorist who understands that as a small part of a larger melodrama in which many others also participate, he has neither a proprietary interest in what is happening nor an exclusive ability to intervene.

Less comforting than the other change models, the cultural/structural perspective attempts to come to grips with the limitations of human existence. Rather than conspire to strengthen the acts of denial that enable many people to cope with a burdensome reality, it attempts to do the doable. Scornful of imaginary remedies to fancifully understood problems, it recognizes that human efforts almost never terminate in complete resolutions. Those devoted to the perspective believe, however, that something is better than nothing; that although real improvements may be marginal, they are nevertheless superior to romantic fantasies.

Among those who have participated in establishing the cultural/structural model have been Robert E. Park,[70] E. Franklin Frazier,[71] Daniel Patrick Moynihan,[72] Thomas Sowell,[73] Alexander Smith and Lanahan O'Connell,[74] and Orlando Patterson.[75] Park clearly recognized that a culture created in one social structure can have unexpected impacts on a later structure. He was also one of the first process-oriented sociologists, and among the first to stress the importance of social change and intergroup conflict. Frazier, one of Park's students, made it transparent that these factors applied to the black family, many of whose failures could be traced back to slavery and subsequent collisions with white society. Moynihan elaborated upon this theme with specific reference to the disintegration of the black family during the 1960s, arguing that its observed instability had roots in interpersonal patterns prevalent on the plantation. Sowell, who has probably done more than any other to illuminate the role of culture in the ethnic experience, because he is an economist has highlighted the impact of economic structures on cultural developments and vice versa. Not content to deal exclusively with the American experience, he has extended his analysis to a worldwide stage. Less well known, Smith and O'Connell have been among the most explicit in attributing contemporary black difficulties to what they call "status frustrations." They, like Shelby Steele,[76] insist that it is a mistake to blame racism for impediments to black socioeconomic progress, which are actually due to difficulties in adjusting to increased opportunities. In essence, they argue that accommodating to an open class system can be bewildering to those not accustomed to it. But perhaps the most comprehensive, and curious of all, is Patterson. Despite his dalliance with draconian social engineering, he eloquently demonstrates that whatever the revisionists assert, slave culture did impact the family relationships of contemporary blacks, as it did their propensity for violence. To this he adds insights on how structural conditions, for example, employment opportunities, are in continuous interaction with culture.

The cultural/structural model understood in this way perceives shifts in social stratification as entangled in a web of almost impenetrable connections. It stresses the fact that so many individuals and cultural elements interact in a dynamic broth, that it is often difficult to establish exactly what is happening. Trends can be detected, but they are interwoven with countertrends and downright anomalies. Some years ago the science writer James Burke[77] developed an enormously successful television series called *Connections*. His thesis was that most people mistakenly attribute scientific advances to specific moments of creation, whereas they actually emanate from a succession of unplanned and loosely connected events. Instead of single persons cogitating until they deliver a full-blown discovery, many, often unrelated, persons contribute small pieces to a puzzle the outlines of which do not become recognizable until the whole has come together. The steam engine, for instance, was not the solitary brainchild of James Watt, but the consequence of many modest supplements by numerous, often anonymous, contributors—of whom he was the last. With regard to racial change, the cultural/structural model comes to a similar conclusion. It does not repose its confidence in moments of moral conversion, ingenious policy proposals, or sudden accumulations of insight. To the contrary, it attempts to comprehend a multitude of loosely associated causal components over which no one has complete command, but over which many exercise limited influence.

To reiterate, all of this adds up to an historical outlook. Change is perceived as marching to its own drummer; hence those who hope to effect it must get in step with its rhythm. If this sounds dangerously close to Karl Marx's[78] admonition that we must all fall in line with his theory of history because it was scientifically preordained, the hazard is real.[79] As most observers would today acknowledge, Marx's central predictions turned out to be wrong. As a consequence, those who sought to implement them have often been at odds with human happiness. Even more frightening is the realization that many ordinary people unreflectively subscribe to an historical determinacy. Lest it be forgotten, Ann Morrow Lindbergh[80] wrote a popular book in which she presented Hitler's fascism as "the wave of the future." At the time, even Cole Porter referred to Mussolini as "the top." If the cultural/ structural model makes comparable assessments, as it seems to, these too demand a dash of modesty. Yet the function of science is to make predictions. Should it prove correct that a culture of slavery has shaped the forms of mobility available to American blacks, ignoring it would condemn millions of people to wasting their time. It is, therefore, necessary to remain flexible and to modify one's judgment as events warrant.

Also possible is an attitude of alert responsiveness. When Darwin[81] was endeavoring to understand evolution, he found it useful to distinguish between natural and artificial selection. The latter included the sorts of breeding technique used by pigeon fanciers and horse owners. They intentionally paired animals to produce offspring with desirable characteristics. In natural selection, however, no one was in charge. An unplanned competition between individuals and populations resulted in the perpetuation of some characteristics, but not others. An equivalent distinction can be made between natural and artificial resocialization. Artificial resocialization,[82] that is, psychotherapy, is the process of consciously relinquishing dysfunctional behavior patterns so they can be replaced by more functional ones. It entails letting go of social roles that cause misery so a person can adopt more satisfying ones. In natural resocialization, a similar shift transpires, but no one intentionally orchestrates it. People simply go about their business in ways that result in moving from one form of life to another.

Assuming for the moment that moving up a social class ladder can be impeded by dysfunctional cultural factors, eliminating these might facilitate mobility. This could be accomplished consciously, as by going for therapy, but also in situ. A person, or group of persons, might come to behave in ways conducive to shedding unhelpful patterns without even realizing it. Indeed, given the fact that resocialization can be uncomfortable, relatively few persons consciously choose it. Assuming further that one might want to promote change, natural resocialization could be enhanced by an awareness of its existence. Unlike therapists who guide their clients in navigating the multiple steps of role change, those who promote this endeavor do not explicitly direct the actions of others. As opposed to the exhortations of moralists, the commands of social engineers, or the manipulations of clinicians, they merely bolster those beliefs, emotions, and relationships that make resocialization possible. While it is not within their province to direct people along unwanted vectors, by assisting them to do what they are intent on doing, they can enable them to arrive at positive endpoints more expeditiously.

Chapter 9

Natural Resocialization

In analyses it often becomes evident that first one, then another memory is activated and that the laments which are perpetually the same and wearisome in their monotony nevertheless each time take their rise in some different unconscious source. If the object had not this great significance, strengthened by a thousand links, to the ego, the loss of it would be no meet cause for either mourning or melancholia. Sigmund Freud, *Mourning and Melancholia*

CULTURAL CHANGE

It is doubtful that ordinary Aztecs loved the idea of human sacrifice. They might actively participate in intertribal warfare to capture the raw materials for these religious rituals, and even consume the sanctified flesh of their enemies, but on a certain level were probably horrified by the gore and misery. Certainly cannibalistic societies in the highlands of New Guinea, despite a proclaimed attachment to a life of raid and counterraid, when conquered by Europeans were only too glad to allow this custom to be suppressed. Nevertheless, both societies perpetuated their sanguinary rites for centuries before outsiders intervened. Their individual members might be distressed by the horrors of these dysfunctional practices, but singly were unable to abolish them. Whatever their reactions to seeing beating hearts torn from living bodies, they helped enforce what seemed the safest course. Indeed, had they done otherwise, their own bodies might have been rolled down the temple steps.

Cultures resist change. Whether functional or not, they reproduce the means of their own propagation. Beliefs and attitudes—often inculcated in early childhood—become self sustaining.[1] Because the very intensity with which they are held makes them inaccessible to rational review, they seem

226 _Chapter 9_

normal and therefore inevitable. In fact, they seem so normal they are usually invisible to those subscribing to them. Should an outsider try to modify these patterns, he would find himself denounced. Rather than allow an entrenched standard to be disturbed, people literally become homicidal—as Socrates found to his dismay.[2] Even on a personal level, violating the sanctity of a long held custom can be dangerous. Instead of feeling heroic, a would-be innovator typically finds himself assailed by guilt. Despite a desire to move boldly into new realms of activity, he continues to be influenced, and often tortured, by internalized commitments whose provenance is unrecognized.

Cultural change is thus not automatic. This is as true of the "culture of slavery" as it was for human sacrifice. The remnants of a way of life that was generated in the antebellum South may not be in the same dysfunctional league as the Aztec ceremonies, but the impediments it places in the way of social mobility are very real. To perpetuate them because they represent an "authentic" blackness is therefore self defeating. One must thus ask: How do people move on? How do they change their approach to life so as to facilitate the progress for which they yearn?

If we step back and inquire into how cultural change occurs, several possibilities present themselves. Roughly speaking the available alternatives are: (1) intrapersonal change, (2) interpersonal change, and (3) intergenerational change. Culture, it must be borne in mind, is a shared phenomenon. The attitudes and beliefs of which it is composed draw their strength from a collection of individuals. This means that what each personally thinks, feels, and pursues is shaped by what others in their community think, feel, and pursue. Change, should it occur, must do so on both an intra- and interpersonal level.

Of the three sorts of change, the first, intrapersonal change, occurs within individuals. When each separately undergoes a transformation, the sum total can amount to a cultural transformation. Since culture is a learned and shared way of life entailing a multitude of beliefs, values, and norms, those held by an association of individuals contribute to their common social legacy. In such a case, a modification to the whole will depend upon modifications occurring within multiple individuals. Yet because personal change can be enormously difficult, changes in the larger milieu are also difficult.

The second sort of change, interpersonal change, depends on between-person influences. Since those participating in a culture are part of a larger community, for it to undergo change, its members may need to encourage each other to shift their behaviors. Because we human beings are social creatures, individual modifications rarely develop in complete seclusion. How others feel, and what they demand, often determine the directions we pursue, and vice versa. Indeed, this is what it means to say that culture is learned and shared. Yet cultural influences are not consistent. Most people are more malleable in some areas than others. The result is that specific individuals may be more susceptible to being shaped by particular outside forces than their peers.

Lastly, the third sort of cultural change, intergenerational change, occurs not from peer to peer, or even contemporary to contemporary, but across the space of many years. In this case, modifications take place, not within individuals, or from one individual to another, but between people who may have no direct contact with each other. A society's culture may thus differ at two historical moments because its members have undergone differing experiences. The stresses to which each cohort has been exposed are so divergent that they do not react the same way. Whether these circumstances derive from newly injected cultural possibilities or structural transformations, the members of the second cohort find themselves adjusting to a world remarkably unlike that of their parents. Their shared beliefs, values, and norms are dissimilar, not because they have individually endured a shift in perspective, but because they did not develop the same attitudes in the first place. Indeed, from their point of view, the older generation may seem out of date.

All of these forms of cultural change, it should be noted, are fundamentally attitudinal. It is the internal perspectives and emotional reactions of a multitude of persons, not merely their external actions, that are modified. This does not imply, however, that these changes are due to moral exhortation. The circumstances and opportunities in which people find themselves enmeshed push or pull them in a variety of directions. Unlike the artificial interventions promoted by moralists, social engineers, and clinicians, natural processes induce them to make choices that result in change. Some of this will reflect a response to their fears, some to their hopes. Either way, most will occur subrosa. People generally act in momentous ways without being fully aware of where they are headed.

In any event, the key to why all forms of change can be difficult to effect is found primarily on the personal level. The various impediments to personal growth are more substantial than is usually realized. We human beings may conceive of ourselves as rational agents who are able to shift directions whenever our interests so dictate, but, more often than not, we are trapped by our own humanity.[3] The ways we think, feel, and respond to external demands limit our options. Indeed, how we think, feel, and respond often prevents us from recognizing what we are doing. From our point of view, we seem to be moving forward with all deliberate speed, but under the cloak of self-deception are the central agents of cultural conservatism.

The chief culprit in explaining why the moral, social engineering, and clinical/educational models do not work very well is none other than Sigmund Freud's[4] "repetition compulsion." It explains why beliefs and attitudes developed under intense emotional circumstances retain the power to influence people decades after they arise. Though this may sound counterintuitive to the uninitiated, Freud stumbled onto the fact that his patients routinely repeated patterns from their early childhood. Even though these made no sense in their adult lives, and they had vowed to alter them, they continued to reoccur, albeit in disguised forms.

Part of what Freud discovered is that what seem to be simple forms of conduct are connected by a myriad of emotions and cognitions to a person's history of development. It is therefore impossible to excise particular patterns without upsetting an elaborate network of associations and needs. In therapy one needed to "work through" these connections. Individually, and in combination, they had to be addressed and their impacts, including the unexpected ones, accounted for. This made for a lengthy process that often wandered down unanticipated pathways. The same, unfortunately, is true of cultural change. It too is subject to a kind of repetition compulsion in which individuals and groups inexplicably recapitulate scenarios that seem to have no place in the present. If anything, the hidden connections that exist on the social level are more complex and intractable than those on the personal level. With so many players, so many competing interests, and so many opportunities to engage in deception, it is more difficult for those involved to keep track of what is going on. As a consequence, cultures tend to feed upon themselves even as they proclaim that they are marching forward.

ROLE CHANGE

A fruitful prototype for grasping the personal aspects of cultural change is role change. Roles and cultures are related to one another. Besides sharing the same constituent elements, that is, their cognitive, emotional, volitional, and social features, roles are themselves part of culture. In addition to specific beliefs, norms, and values, individual cultures make repertoires of roles available to their adherents. People are taught not only the proper way to hold a knife and fork, but also that they may elect to become *doctors, lawyers,* and *Indian chiefs.*[5] More to the point, when considering race relations, blacks were traditionally limited to such options as *Mammies, Sambos,* and *Uncle Toms.* Nowadays among the roles disproportionally available to them are those of *scapegoat, mascot,* and *street thug.* Put another way, they are asymmetrically encouraged to fit into the larger culture by accepting the blame for others' prejudices.

Obviously some roles are more functional than others. That of *street thug* has limited viability. So does that of *scapegoat.* Both offer a virtual lock on unhappiness. When such roles go wrong, the agony they inflict can be heart rending. People in their grip methodically act in ways that keep them from meeting vital needs. The result is that instead of being loved and respected, they are picked on and rejected. This will make little sense, even to them, but they keep doing the same things anyway. Like the alcoholic who soon after drying out rushes to reactivate his habit, they return to their errant ways again and again.

Clearly, the life of a *scapegoat* can cause distress. A scapegoat must perpetually look over his shoulder in anticipation of the next criticism. Rather than pursue his own needs, he expends his energies in self-defense. What is worse, he is almost certainly complicit in his torment. Having many times been accused of treachery, he will probably believe in his own villainy. Indeed, when singled out, he is likely to partake in enforcing his own humiliation. As strange as it may seem to outsiders, scapegoats hold themselves responsible for their situation. One reason why they do is that they are aware, at least unconsciously, that their willingness to accept blame protects others from the consequences of their acts, and they accept this sacrifice as the price for remaining in their good graces.

Yet relinquishing a dysfunctional role can be an agony.[6] Although excruciating to maintain, letting it go entails releasing a part of one's self. This is why an unaccountable terror may sweep over a person whenever he contemplates acting differently.[7] As a consequence, he will recapitulate behaviors he sincerely hoped to leave behind. Much as painful memories are reactivated during periods of grief, his tendency toward self-punishment will return at the very moments he resolves to abandon his masochistic ways. Because these self-destructive impulses are attached by multiple cognitive and emotional links, they continue to surface even as he dedicates himself to their elimination. In essence, the manner he has learned to think and feel will continue to direct him along time-worn paths.

This sort of resistance to change is at the heart of psychotherapy.[8] If individuals did not prevent themselves from terminating their attachments to catastrophic relationships, professional helpers would have little to do.[9] Their primary responsibility turns out to be none other than guiding frightened and confused clients past the shoals of their own opposition to change. As experts in resocialization, therapists are trained to recognize the difficulties inherent in relinquishing dysfunctional ways of life and tutored on how to provide emotional support in surmounting these barriers. As practitioners of artificial resocialization, they are charged with encouraging, and accelerating, such changes.

But let us be more specific and examine an example of a dysfunctional role to see how it is maintained. A role familiar to many people, one whose repetitive character is well understood, is that of the *family caretaker*. A person, often a woman, will grow up being taught that her primary task is to care for others instead of seeking her own satisfactions. Perhaps her mother assumed the role of an *invalid* whose capricious whims had to be catered to. Or perhaps her father adopted the part of an overbearing *alcoholic*. Either way, she would acquire the habit of being sensitive to the requirements of these others. She would not, however, be sensitive to her own needs. When this girl grew to be a woman, the likelihood is that she would enter relationships that recapitulated this pattern. If she married, it would probably be to a man who demanded that she cater to him. If she had children, they would become the objects of her obsessive attention. Ironically, even should she decide that these asymmetrical associations are unfair, she would be apt to repeat them in the process of trying to change them. Thus, if she divorced, the chances are excellent that her next marital partner would also expect her to be superattentive.

This inability to behave differently may seem peculiar, but should not. In the process of growing up, all of us acquire role scripts that guide our interpersonal behavior. Many of these are quite helpful. The perceptions and the skills they inculcate prepare us for satisfying relationships. Some degree of caretaking, for instance, is quite useful to a woman who hopes to be a mother. If not implemented to the exclusion of her personal needs, being a loving mother can further her own happiness. It is when the caretaker role is overdone that it becomes a liability. It is when a person's sole purpose in life is sacrificing herself in the interests of others that she is in trouble.

When overblown, the *family caretaker's* role script will be such that she *cognitively* imagines herself too weak to do anything but care for others. After years of coaching, her self-image will be that of someone too fragile to exist outside the ambit of her family. Despite the fact that she does most of the work, she will be convinced that her accomplishments are due only to strengths borrowed from others. *Emotionally* such a person will feel bound to persevere in familiar vineyards. Too frightened to do otherwise, she will continue to respond to cues from her traumatic childhood. Perhaps when she balked at staying inside to tend her bedridden mother, she was accused of wishing her parent dead. Perhaps her mother's anger induced a counter-anger that was itself frightening. In any event, the consequence would be a galaxy of emotions best allayed by knuckling under to her parent's demands. Even as an adult these would have an effect. Rather than allow them to go out of control, a woman might try to placate others by activating the defenses she acquired early on. This, however, would encourage her to replicate the relationships in which they initially occurred.

On the *volitional* level, a caretaker would internalize reactions that supported an impulse toward repetition. In a sense, volitions are preset action plans. They guide a person's behaviors by providing ready-made blueprints. Instead of having to think through an entirely new strategy for each new situation, they furnish stereotyped goals and means—each of which may be on a hair trigger. Such goals, otherwise known as values, reflexively point toward certain endpoints, while the means, otherwise referred to as norms, insist upon particular courses of conduct to effect these goals. A caretaker might thus learn that protecting others is the highest calling to which she can aspire. Similarly, she might have it drummed into her head that only instant obedience brings love. These lessons would then prime her to be the instrument of those inclined to exploit her. Likewise, on the *social demand* level, the caretaker's role script can be a trap. Since it is probable that her current role partners were chosen because they reflect previous ones, that is, the partners whose demands contributed to her internalized beliefs, feelings, and values, these new ones can reinforce her old habits with their contemporary entreaties. They too will want to be catered to and will inform her in no uncertain terms that she is a weak person who has no choice but to do their bidding.

With all four aspects of her role script militating toward the same ends, it will be difficult for the caretaker to renounce her prior commitments. Whatever misery her subservience exacts will seem trivial compared with the dangers of independence. She will feel—to the marrow of her bones—that to be without a role script is to be rudderless; that it is to be small and weak, and buffeted by a myriad incomprehensible decrees.

Being trapped in a dysfunctional role is evidently no fun. It would therefore seem sensible to move on to something else. But that is not the way the world works. A person cannot simply substitute an alternate script for the one causing her trouble. Precisely because she is under the sway of the old role, she will be incapable of a detached analysis. As a consequence, before she can proceed she must relinquish the beliefs, feelings, and values holding her back. More than verbally denounced, these must be flushed from her system so that they do not inadvertently reappear. But, and herein lies the rub, this process of letting go, otherwise known as resocialization, is itself painful and protracted. Unlike turning the pages of a book, it is more akin to searing one's soul with fire. People who have not entered upon it may cavalierly underestimate the difficulty, but those immersed in it will know that the anxieties, rages, and despondency that accompany it can be debilitating.[10]

This resocialization procedure is closely related to mourning. As forms of relinquishing what is lost, both entail reorganizing a host of internal commitments. In the case of mourning, a person must pass through a series of stages before emerging in an unencumbered frame of mind.[11] If a man loses his wife of many years, he cannot merely shrug his shoulders and immediately enter a successful relationship with another woman. Under normal circumstances it takes at least a year before he is emotionally receptive. Along the way he will have to work through his impulse to deny that his mate has died, his anger that she has abandoned him when she was most needed, and his desire to make a deal with God so that she will return. But most of all, he will have to deal with his sadness. The central task of mourning is to undergo an intense period of depression in which one's ties with the past are severed.[12] One, as it were, withdraws from the world of the living to rethink and reexperience what was lost. In innumerable moments of reverie and intense anguish, a person comes to recognize that the past cannot be retrieved and hence that the part of himself attached to it must be disengaged. Only after this has occurred can he begin to look forward to other attachments. Only then will he be emotionally present to engage in the interpersonal negotiations through which new relationships develop.

But resocialization can be more challenging and more painful than simple grief. When someone dies, the fact of their loss is tangible. To be crude about the matter, there is a body in the coffin and an empty space in one's bed. When, however, it is a role that is lost, it is patterns of behavior that have gone bad. A caretaker role, for instance, does not vanish; nor do those who demand care. What is lost is the ability to meet one's needs. As long as a person is dedicated to placing other's interests before her own, it is her personal satisfactions that are sacrificed. But these are ephemeral. Possessing far less substance than a deceased person, they are easier to deny. Another way to think about this matter is that in the case of death, the person with whom one was having a satisfying relationship removes this possibility by disappearing from the scene, while in the case of a dysfunctional role, the possibility of a satisfying relationship is vitiated by the nature of the relationship. In any event, when a role cannot be fixed, the impossibility of its repair is less evident than is the demise of a living, breathing person.

Resocialization must thus begin with an awareness of what was lost. A person has to do more than intellectually realize a particular role is unsatisfying. He must feel it; he must experience it.[13] The ordinary tendency of people to deny their failures must be overcome and the unhappy truth entered into as one might a particularly gloomy room. One of the primary reasons why people avoid resocialization is that they are loath to endure such misery. Rather than reexperience how much they have been hurt, they prefer to act as if it never happened. Nevertheless, a role not experienced is a role that cannot be reconfigured. That which remains an intellectual exercise can be thought about in novel ways, but not transformed.

Once a dysfunctional role has been reactivated, it becomes accessible to modification. First it becomes possible to rework the emotions, volitions, and cognitions that have been holding it in place. These constitute a constellation of defense and protest. What this implies can be understood by recognizing that when an unsatisfying role was first imposed, the tendency to resist was almost overwhelming. People become extremely angry at role partners who try to impose unequal associations. Failing this, the impulse to isolate these unfair conditions becomes intense. What cannot be prevented may be compartmentalized in an effort to limit the damage. To illustrate, a caretaker-in-the-making can be furious at the impositions required of her. She may then repress her anger, allowing it to surface only in tangential and relatively innocuous ways.

When resocialization is underway, that which could not be resisted in the past may be challenged in the present. For instance, in reexperiencing abuse by a selfish parent, an adult caretaker may become agitated in ways that were impossible when she was young. As a child her righteous indignation would not only have fallen on deaf ears, it would probably have brought reprisals. As an adult, however, her objections to unfair treatment can elicit the respect they deserve. Having come to perceive more clearly how and why she was exploited, she can defend herself more articulately. This may ultimately enable her to discontinue the unconscious fights that kept her tied to her tormentors.   By the same token, an adult caretaker can extricate herself from the fears that tied her to people who seemed to be her protectors.   Long forgotten childhood terrors now recognized for what they are will no longer have the power to intimidate.

The repetition compulsion is, in a real sense, an effort to redo the negotiations in which dysfunctional roles were created. When this works and a person begins loosening the ligatures tying her to "lost" roles, she will eventually become capable of discarding them. Following a stormy period characterized by fits of rage and anxiety, she will become depressed. For most of us intense sadness is an experience we would rather avoid. And yet the seemingly bottomless pit of grief is, to paraphrase Freud, the royal road to happiness. As the mechanism that cuts our ties to insupportable cognitions, emotions, and volitions, it enables us to pass through a door to more verdant fields.   If handled carefully, and therefore slowly, melancholy does not eventuate in the death it seems to portend, but in a renewal of life. The irony is that those who allow themselves to tread the paths of their own misery usually find their way out, whereas those insistent upon feeling good become mired in a low-grade anguish that never ends.

Once the clouds surrounding the pain of loss begin to lift, it becomes possible to renegotiate new and more fruitful roles. Fair role partners can be sought out and mutually satisfactory behavior patterns worked through. Instead of lingering over what went wrong, untried possibilities can now be explored.   The final stage of resocialization is thus characterized by an acceptance of what one could not change, but also by an ability to leave it behind. New understandings, new plans of action, and fresh emotions all present themselves once depression has made a resurgent optimism possible. In the final analysis, successful role change does not guarantee a satisfying life, but it does free a person to take advantage of options not previously accessible.

INTRAPERSONAL CULTURAL CHANGE

At first blush painful personal roles so desperately cleaved to that they require therapeutic specialists to jettison seem to have little in common with race-related problems. The movement from a closed caste system to an open class society would seem to differ greatly from the journey from a debilitating neurosis to personal maturity. And yet there is a large area of overlap. Because cultural dysfunctions are perpetuated by many of the same mechanisms that perpetuate role dysfunctions, the means through which they are overcome have a great deal in common. With each set of dysfunctions held in place by cognitive, emotional, volitional, and social constraints, these must be addressed and disarmed before change can take place. Fortunately, once such cultural transformations occur, formidable limitations to structural change may also be reduced. The situation is this: since status mobility is frequently impeded by cultural patterns that prevent people from being as strong as their potential would otherwise permit, unless these impediments are diminished they are apt to lose those contests in which they must demonstrate their power vis-a-vis others. Until these cultural liabilities are removed, rather than being able to prove that they deserve the respect owed persons of enhanced rank, they are likely to act ineptly and improvidently.

The question is therefore how to remove such cultural dysfunctions, particularly given that there is no identifiable client, as there is in psychotherapy. Indeed, without a specific human being prepared to lie down on the couch, to identify his role problem, or to reexperience it, how can transformations occur? In this situation, whose anger or anxiety is supposed to be disarmed and whose soul undergo the liberating misery of a therapeutic depression? Indeed, who is supposed to renegotiate improved roles in the absence of a specifiable role holder? The answer lies in the fact that culture too has carriers. Its elements may be more broadly interjected than those of particular roles, but we are still dealing with beliefs, values, and norms held by real people.

In a sense, cultural changes result from the summed changes occurring within particular persons. As previously indicated, when a sufficient number of these think, feel, or act differently, their shared culture is thereby altered. The trouble is that cultural problems are rarely perceived as personal problems. In the case of role problems, it is the individual who suffers and who is presumably responsible. He or she is the one who misapprehends the world, experiences inappropriate emotions, and holds distorted values. As a scapegoat or caretaker his behaviors and attitudes are visibly distinct from those of others, hence more clearly worthy of blame. The result is that both he and his role partners can single him out for change.

Cultural problems, in contrast, are shared problems. Whole sets of beliefs may misapprehend the world, but because entire populations partake of them, no individual perceives himself as in error. On the contrary, people support one another's mistakes and even congratulate themselves on them. Nor do they recognize communal emotions as inappropriate no matter how intense or misplaced. The very fact of their being common validates them as normal. Likewise, monstrously dysfunctional values, if broadly held, appear essential rather than perverse. Thus when an entire society, such the Aztecs, celebrated blood sacrifice as life giving, few individuals felt guilty over reveling in the gore. The end product is that when cultures go wrong, those sustaining them are rarely motivated toward reform. Because all participate in an inertia born of a shared lack of personal responsibility, if anything, their peers discourage them from seeking alternatives.

This inertia is certainly in evidence vis-a-vis the culture of slavery. Those who perpetuate it do not perceive themselves as engaged in anything unusual or dysfunctional. Because when they look around, they do not detect themselves doing anything strange, it does not occur to them that internalized attitudes and beliefs are causing their distress. Just the opposite. In conjunction with role partners whose reactions are similar to their own, they attribute their difficulties to external forces. It is other people who are causing them pain and who need to change. They themselves are victims who will automatically be saved once these others undergo corrective transformations.

Let us consider some particular aspects of the culture of slavery that individuals might want to alter if they were recognized as being maintained by their own commitments. We can start with some commonly held beliefs. Many African-Americans today remain convinced that economic opportunities are denied them by the rapacity of whites. They are certain that they will not be hired for jobs because of race-based discrimination. Yet this is only a partial truth. Despite the fact that racism persists, conditions are better than they once were. Billson[14] tells the story of a teenage informant who never went to a local factory to seek employment. According to him, he "knew" this would be pointless, as his father had years earlier been turned down by the same employer. Billson, however, was aware that the plant had in recent years altered its hiring practices. What was now hindering the young man's job search was his own mind set. Had he been willing to reconsider what he thought he knew, he probably would have succeeded.

On a larger scale one sees an unwillingness to examine Korean shop ownership. In many African-American neighborhoods, Korean immigrants are a major economic factor. Rather than small grocery or liquor stores being owned by local residents, these "outsiders" have "taken over." This success is now resented by residents who often attribute it to unfair government subsidies. The fact is that the Koreans' competitive advantage comes from a strong work ethic and a proclivity to pool their meager resources. Blacks too have an opportunity to do these things, but do not. Instead they rationalize their failure with a variation of a belief held over from slavery. It will be recalled that one of the aspects of slavery was its paternalism. Since the benefits slaves received depended upon the good will of their masters, it makes sense to their descendants that if others are prospering it is because they have received a special benefit. How else could they succeed were they not subsidized by the "man"? Although it would be simple to verify the absence of such benefits, many blacks sustain a comforting fiction that fits well with a larger, historically derived, world view.

Turning now to emotions, a significant proportion of African-Americans sustain a variety of intense, and intensely dysfunctional, feelings originating in slavery, feelings that individually and collectively limit their potential for social mobility. The most important of these are anger and fear. By now it has become commonplace to acknowledge the depth of "black rage."[15] Yet the accumulated resentments of centuries of oppression are not an abstract legacy. They are a concrete encumbrance weighing down a host of individuals. Millions of people literally go about their daily rounds furiously angry, but not sure what they are angry about. Because their rage is not a direct product of slavery, but has been anonymously handed down from generation to generation, its provenance is obscure. Yet sadly, to be nameless is not equivalent to being benign. Too often a ferocity out of proportion to its immediate inspiration interferes with its bearers' capacity to think clearly and alienates others who might be helpful if given the opportunity. People then become the victims of their own unwavering determination not to be abused.

Excessive fear too can be culturally inherited. The violence and repression inherent in slavery awakened not only a desire to overcome it, but also an apprehension that one might not be able to. Because the master was too strong to defy and the limitations he imposed so numerous, the bondsmen's ability to cope was atrophied. Instead of acquiring a broad repertoire of skills with which to seek dominance, they and their progeny were condemned to relative impotence. Why then should not a pool of shared anxieties persist? In fact, one seems to have. As Shelby Steele[16] has pointed out, many contemporary African-Americans are petrified by the opportunities that the Civil Rights movement made available. Instead of embracing these, they appear intimidated by the prospect of failure.

Lastly, many African-Americans endure volitional deficits that exhibit a cultural pedigree. Their values, in particular, were distorted in unhelpful ways. To have come to believe that education, individual merit, and personal responsibility are inherently white aspirations is to renounce essential tools in the quest for prosperity. It is to fail to develop what economists call "cultural capital."[17] To value education, for instance, is to be predisposed to learn the skills needed in a technologically complex economy. It is to take pride in acquiring information and proficiencies useful when competing with others for commercial priority. Similarly, to value merit is to distinguish between what has quality and what has not. It is to recognize that some objects and activities are more beneficial than others, and hence have greater exchange value. Responsibility too, when it is accepted as a goal worth pursuing, confers advantages. He who is responsible can be trusted to complete essential tasks. He can, therefore, safely be delegated powers that the irresponsible cannot. In sum, to have failed to internalize the values that centuries of capitalism have validated as profitable is to exclude oneself from participation in the system.

Assuming for the moment that these cultural factors are disabilities, how would the individual who has adopted them proceed to something better? How would he or she facilitate the requisite personal change? By now it should be apparent that the mechanisms necessary shadow those of the resocialization process. Just as with social roles, dysfunctional cultural elements must be abandoned before more suitable ones can be adopted. This means that they too have to be reexperienced, reworked, relinquished, and renegotiated before a person can become what is desired. No matter how sincere one's intention to change, no matter how strong the appetite for improvements, these cannot occur without a dramatic internal reorganization of a person's beliefs, emotions, and values.

The individual who would extricate himself from the culture of slavery must first be willing to experience the inherent confusion of out-of-date beliefs, the disharmony of ferociously uncomfortable emotions, and the bewilderment of terribly misleading values, all the while doing so in a manner that enables them to be reevaluated. Although it may seem undeniable to his victims that the white man is a congenital villain, it must be possible to distinguish between the many varieties of Caucasians and their many incompatible motives. Similarly, although one's anger may feel completely justified, it must be calmed down and reconsidered. What was it that elicited one's rage and what is it that can be altered? Finally, although values feel God-given, one must determine their actual provenance and the spectrum of alternatives. To be committed to a particular goal, no matter how earnestly, does not prove its worth.

Intense emotions deserve special consideration. They, more than any other factor, fasten our commitments in place. Yet reexperiencing and reworking them can be traumatic. Because they are largely unresponsive to cognitive logic,[18] they are not dispelled by the simple expedient of recognizing when they are inappropriate. Nor are powerful emotions endured without risk. If allowed to get out of control, they can produce more damage than if they were subjected to continued repression. Rage can be especially destructive. In the guise of righteous indignation, particularly when embedded in a supportive cultural environment, it can be murderous.[19] In this case, instead of its objectives being reconsidered, it may seek vengeance and in the process leave behind a trail of destruction.

But assuming that all goes well and a person gains insight into why he thinks and feels as he does, the initial consequence of this awakening is not liberation, but a terrible despondency. To recognize that a culture in which one has been immersed had no possibility of satisfying one's needs is not a cause for rejoicing. Being betrayed by one's own hopes and emotions is among the worst experiences any human being can endure. It is to have one's entire world, both inside and outside, torn to shreds. It is to be deceived about the foundations of one's universe and to have its sands shift beneath one's feet. The pain can, in fact, be so profound that it seems impossible to survive.

Yet this is not the end of the ordeal. For personalized cultural change to eventuate in a positive outcome, its elements must be renegotiated with other human beings. These others must ratify newly renovated beliefs, emotions, and values, lest one be engulfed by solipsistic uncertainty. For new cultural patterns to have substance, they must be interpersonally endorsed; otherwise they are mere whims that can change at a moment's notice. Sharing gives them the possibility of being socially satisfying and fosters the cooperation essential for making them real. But the rub here is that we human beings never completely control each other. Collaboration may be essential to obtain the gratifications we seek, but our role partners can be obtuse and selfish. Rather than participate in a deal from which everyone profits, they may insist on conditions that undermine the entire effort, in which case, however far we have come, they may prevent the completion of the journey.

With all that can go wrong and all that must be endured, it is understandable why more people announce cultural changes than actually engage in them. Despite grand promises to themselves and others, they resist rather than welcome transformations. Time-worn patterns are repackaged as exciting breakthroughs and retreats into the past palmed off as final solutions. Amazingly, just as their courage fails them, people most loudly trumpet the valor of their efforts. The supreme irony here is that what has been responsible for their wretchedness is reinterpreted as the key to their survival and cleaved to more firmly than ever—witness the rhetorical celebration of the black family at the instant when its viability came into question. It is the unusual person, the one with strength and character, who undergoes the most substantial alterations. As with psychotherapy, those least in need of change are the most capable of it.

The upshot is that such cultural transformations as do occur are often unconscious achievements. Regardless of their proclaimed intentions, people are more apt to react to altered circumstances than to plan modifications in their beliefs, emotions, or values. What tends to occur can be apprehended by observing what transpired within the white community following World War II. Its receptivity to perceiving African-Americans differently had more to do with an emerging middle-class majority than with a determination to be kind to blacks. The pressures and opportunities made available by greater social mobility reduced white fears of black success at the same time that it increased their allegiance to universalistic market principles. They changed, not because they decided to, but because this meshed with their emerging needs.

The same principles apply to African-Americans. Should they individually resolve to relinquish the worst aspects of the culture of slavery, it will generally be because their personal circumstances have changed. Having obtained jobs that were not previously available, having completed college degrees that were once an impossible dream, or having engaged in personal interactions with whites under conditions in which their humanity is visible, they will reluctantly, and laboriously, modify their belief systems. Likewise, having become economically successful, a person may find it advantageous to renounce his rage lest it alienate co-workers, neighbors, or potential mates. In such a case, after years of wrestling with what seem to be personal demons, an individual may one day wake to realize his attitudes are not what they once were.

INTERPERSONAL/INTERGENERATIONAL CULTURAL CHANGE

But not all cultural change is personal change. Many ostensibly private modifications are initiated through the good offices of our role partners. Their influence can be the causative agent behind profound alterations in our beliefs and attitudes. If a significant proportion of those with whom we interact, especially when they are held in high esteem, have adjusted their cultural horizons, they can transmit these to us. Via a variety of mechanisms, some brutally coercive and others gently persuasive, they can induce a reappraisal of where we stand. If these others demand that we change the way we think, they may intimidate us into doing so. If they merely act in ways that are different, we may copy them in hopes of matching their success.

The central condition of interpersonal influence, however, is that it be exercised in areas of relative indifference.[20] People rarely alter strongly held beliefs or emotions, even when confronted with demands to do so. They may modify the expression of their true convictions so as to forestall reprisals, but deep within their psyches react just as they always have. It is in the cases where people do not care too strongly that they are most amenable to influence by opinion leaders or social movements. Since any of a multitude of positions would be acceptable to them, they comfortably take the path of least resistance. As applied to the culture of slavery, this pliability has induced many people to change their public postures as society has shifted its center of gravity. Many whites, for instance, lifted their objections to integrated lunch counters and interracial marriages once these became commonplace. More important to them than retaining a separation from blacks was being able to maintain their membership in the dominate clique. In like manner, for many blacks, their zone of indifference has included dressing in the common modalities when going to a newfound middle-class job. They might swap their suits for more casual attire when among friends, but in public pay homage to the prevailing styles.

The limitations inherent in interpersonal influences are thus quite significant. The pressures people place on one another may be able to alter the more obvious aspects of the cultural terrain, but its hidden recesses remain inaccessible. In fact, it will often appear to the participants that more change has occurred than actually has. The problem is that target populations routinely disguise those areas in which they refuse to conform. If these are not within their zones of indifference, they are motivated to prevent their discovery. Thus whites may continue to believe in the intellectual inferiority of blacks while at the same time asserting that they no longer subscribe to biological differences, whereas blacks may declare their allegiance to universal brotherhood while secretly assuming that few whites are genuinely human.

Then too, those individuals who are least inclined to engage in personal change will continue to exercise their influence in behest of cultural stasis. These may include both community "leaders" and community "losers." Those who benefit most from maintaining the culture of slavery intact, as well as those who have been most damaged by it, will each for their different reasons support the status quo. Since many community leaders derive their power from helping others overcome the impact of slavery, they would lose their positions if there were nothing left to overcome. Obviously being a hero for slaying dragons loses its luster when all the dragons are dead. Thus members of the Civil Rights establishment have often expended more energy in uncovering the remnants of racism than in fostering personal growth among their constituents.

But street thugs too resist change. More than this, they cultivate a counterrevolution. Making no pretense of encouraging racial progress—that is, unless they are members of an organization such as the Black Panthers[21]— in their rage to obtain a greater share of society's benefits, they are unconcerned with the damage they wreak. Yet it is through this damage that they set the clock back. In their very viciousness, they arouse a rage in their victims that prevents change. The fellow African-Americans whom they rob and pummel do not turn to the white community for an alternative example of how to live. They are instead inclined to turn inward and adopt familiar patterns, however limiting these may be. Rather than blame or ostracize the thugs, they identify with the aggressor and internalize beliefs and attitudes that might better be abandoned.[22]

Given these counterpressures, it can take longer to effect significant cultural modifications than most of the players relish. Not months or years, but decades and generations can pass before the causes of a grievance disappear. Often, it will literally be their children who are able to move past the snags that stymie them. Such changes as occur are therefore not in personally held beliefs and attitudes, but in those that separate the generations. Whereas individuals who grow to maturity in one decade are outraged by a particular form of prejudice, those coming of age in another may find it a non-issue. Just as the children of depression era parents failed to internalize the economic pessimism of their elders, they cannot understand, never mind emulate, the worries of those who preceded them.

Since structure often shapes culture, when sociopolitical conditions evolve, their consequences are modified. Put another way, different circumstances determine different responses. If a succeeding generation sustains no losses comparable to those of an earlier generations, these privations neither have to be protested nor grieved. To cite a simple illustration, stereotypes are not merely inherited from one generation to the next; they are also responsive to salient experiences from the present. This explains why our attitudes toward black quarterbacks have changed so dramatically. It also explains why contemporary images of black women are no longer dominated by the black mammy convention. With so few black women today employed as domestics, few Americans of either race have encountered one outside the movies.

To detect intergenerational change one must compare different periods rather than particular persons. As a nation becomes more prosperous, and its economy more technologically sophisticated, those living in altered times adopt new beliefs and values. Thus, whereas a higher education may have been a matter of indifference to their forebearers, they may find it a necessity. Likewise, although their parents hardly ever interacted with members of out-groups, they may find workplace diversity an established fact. In sum, as America becomes a more middle-class country, with an ever more efficient and specialized marketplace, those whose life prospects depend on where it is heading adapt as a matter of course.

THE ROLE OF THE CHANGE AGENT

If change occurs as has been outlined, what are the implications for race relations, and more particularly for eliminating the culture of slavery as an impediment to developing a genuinely open class society? For most of those concerned with racial questions, the issue is not what has happened, but what can be done to achieve their ideal. As potential change agents, they seek the most bang for the buck. This fixes their attention on interpersonal and intergenerational modes of engagement. In their mind's eye, they perceive themselves as actors who by dint of Herculean exertions will either influence others to change or, failing this, will modify the conditions under which they make their decisions. This makes the moral, social engineering, and clinical/educational strategies very appealing.

Nevertheless, as should be clear, there are limits on what outside instrumentalities can accomplish. If external influences are effectual only within zones of indifference and if the circumstances to which people react are beyond the manipulation of the change agents, then would-be reformers have fewer options than they suppose. It may even be that their most cherished schemes impede rather than foster change. What is often overlooked is that the reformers are human beings. They may be talented people whose powers of influence are superior to most, but they remain human. Those whom they seek to sway are, however, human too, and hence have the power to resist. Neither honeyed words, furious accusations, nor elaborate educational ploys are apt to make more than a marginal difference in their behaviors. Influence, it must be remembered, is not control. People may be momentarily moved, but their internal commitments and personal limitations ultimately assert themselves and they revert to a cultural conservatism. Idealists may dislike this propensity, but it is one of long standing.

Nor have the social engineers proven adept at managing the external conditions of society. The circumstances to which different generations respond have demonstrated a remarkable immunity to human orchestration. Evidence of this is readily available in the failure of our predictive powers. Each generation seems impelled to envision what the next will be like, but the self-appointed futurists have, with depressing regularity, proven a failure. General Motors 1939 World Fair projection of cities dominated by intersecting skyways was no more prescient than have been recent forecasts of how much Medicare would cost or how many people would get off welfare once its rules were tightened. Social engineers can, of course, alter conditions, with welfare reform being a convenient example, but here again there are limitations. Despite years of striving, the planners have not been conspicuously successful in inducing Americans to abandon their automobiles in favor of public transportation. The automobile, as a form of technology, has plainly enabled ordinary people to embrace social innovations that its creators, and would-be controllers, did not foresee.[23] These made it possible, among other things, for average citizens to elude the effects of forced busing.

This brings us back to the question of personal change. Assuming that the culture of slavery has consequences both for individuals and populations, to what degree is it possible to facilitate internal alterations in beliefs and attitudes? Is it possible for those concerned with accelerating social mobility to intervene in ways that accomplish this? The key concept here turns out to be "facilitate." Change agents, as outsiders, can no more control what occurs within individuals than therapists can dictate what happens inside their clients. They can, however, expedite developments. As long as they cooperate in helping people achieve what they themselves wish, they can hasten preferred outcomes.

Natural resocialization, to restate the obvious, is natural. It can unfold without the ministrations of technocrats. But these technicians can ease the process. Although they cannot prescribe the modifications made, they can make it easier for the affected individuals to make them. This can be achieved by providing a variety of supports. First among these is emotional support. Resocialization is intrinsically frightening. The feelings it arouses are inherently painful and the cognitions it stirs up inevitably confused. To be in the middle of the process is thus to be torn in conflicting directions while being pierced by emotional lighting bolts. As a consequence, having somebody nearby who understands the process, and is not terrified of it, can be very reassuring. The courage of this sort of helper can rub off and enable a person to endure what in his or her unaccompanied loneliness would be unendurable.

Second is physical support. Resocialization, whether natural or artificial, is time consuming and emotionally diverting. When in its midst, people are less able to take care of their personal needs. What they require is a degree of understanding. If the demands made of them are somewhat lessened, if they are offered a modicum of assistance in taking care of their responsibilities, they thereby obtain what has been called a "psychosocial moratorium."[24] While such moratoriums are never complete, and if taken too far can be debilitating, within limits they allow energies to be focused on change activities. Third, a competent helper can either provide, or assist in uncovering, vital information. Since resocialization is an unfamiliar venture for most people, an explanation of what is happening can be liberating. Instead of imagining that they are defective, what they are experiencing can be placed in context. In its predictability, it then becomes more manageable. A change agent can also participate in revealing information specific to a person's situation. The nature of her roles and cultural commitments can be explored, their origins examined, and attempted solutions assessed.

When cultural change is at issue, a change agent can begin by facilitating the reexperiencing of dysfunctional cultural elements. Given the discomfort inherent in these, the inclination to suppress them can be compelling. Someone less in their grip can point this out and provide the courage to confront them. Specifically, the culture of slavery includes a host of beliefs and attitudes that are either embarrassing or agitating. Who, for instance, is comfortable recognizing his racist proclivities? And who wants to acknowledge a tendency toward irresponsibility? These can so conflict with one's self-image that one will not admit them to oneself, never mind to others.[25]

Once the elements of a dysfunctional culture are acknowledged, and their unpleasantness allowed to sink in, they must be reworked. A person must understand how they came into existence and why they are maintained. The history of specific beliefs, feelings, and values must be scrutinized and their lack of inevitability recognized. This will gradually allow their victims to realize that there are alternatives. A change agent might, for example, encourage the exploration of how slavery actually operated. This might then eventuate in an understanding that the masters were neither superior beings, nor irredeemable devils, but people themselves caught in a peculiar social structure. Likewise, a helper might probe the nature of "black rage." Rather than leave this as terra incognita, the logic of the emotion can be exposed and the person introduced to techniques for taming it.[26]

After this working through process, a person may be ready to let go of dysfunctional commitments. Having passed through an extended period of desensitization and reprocessing, he or she may be able to withstand the agonies of acknowledging what was lost. But the sadness entailed in this can be so profound that it feels like a living death. This, in turn, can provoke attempts to escape back into a familiar, if noxious, past. In this case a would-be change agent must be able to exercise an almost superhuman restraint. Because attachments to what must be relinquished can be severed only in a crucible of intense grief, the person undergoing change must be allowed to become depressed. The helper must literally stand back and watch what develops without giving way to the natural impulse to interfere. By the same token, a depression cannot be allowed to become too deep. If is does, suicide is not improbable. This obligates the change agent to use his judgment in determining when to intercede and when to keep hands off. The point of balance can be difficult to ascertain and require a genuine expertise.

In the final stage of overcoming a cultural dysfunction, a person must establish alternative cultural elements. Because these are created in social negotiations, a would-be facilitator may be drafted into the position of role partner. He or she may be required to discuss, sometimes directly, sometimes indirectly, the respective advantages of a variety of options. She may also be required to validate new patterns of behavior as they emerge. With respect to the culture of slavery, this may entail confirming that a person has acquired powers and obligations not associated with slavery.

Would-be facilitators must also be cautious lest they perpetrate myths in the name of change. Since at all stages of resocialization reality can be a threat, the temptation to take a side track into a comforting daydream is substantial. Both the person attempting change and the helper can perceive this as a form of social support. Certainly it may prove an excellent, albeit temporary, anodyne to anxiety. The problem is that it may not be temporary. If myths are allowed to substitute for reality, they can delay, rather than expedite, the journey toward more functional beliefs and attitudes. Still, from the change agent's perspective, false promises are an enticing detour.

Because they may be welcomed as shortcuts, the helper may be lauded as a hero. Time will eventually disclose the truth, but in the meantime all involved may revel in a specious glory.

Chapter 10

The Black Middle Class

Not to demand that each member of the black community accept individual responsibility for her or his behavior—whether that behavior assumes the form of black-on-black homicide, violations by gang members against the sanctity of the church, unprotected sexual activity, gangster rap lyrics, misogyny and homophobia—is to function merely as ethnic cheerleaders selling woof tickets from the campus or the suburbs, rather than saying the difficult things that may be unpopular with our fellows. Henry Louis Gates, *The Future of the Race*

BLACK ENABLERS

Versions of the story are so common it has become apocryphal. 'It seems that after they were married, a woman discovered that her new husband had a problem with alcohol. A lack of sobriety she hitherto attributed to his proclivity to celebrate their relationship was evidently a regular feature of his life. Besides drinking for the sake of an evening's entertainment, he consumed large quantities of whiskey virtually every day. Most of the time he did not even wait for the evening and launched his efforts by imbibing his breakfast. The result was a perpetual haze that was occasionally broken by gales of violence. For her part, she tried to tame this intemperance. In the long run, she was sure he would honor his promises to be the kind of husband he was supposed to be. As time passed, however, the drinking increased. Even after they had children and mortgage payments to meet, he would periodically get too inebriated to go to work. But she gamely persisted. Despite the incessant complaints directed toward him by her friends, she stood by him. When he lost his job, she made sure that her employment was good enough to pay their bills. When he threatened to

249

assault the children, she interceded to quiet him down. To outsiders, all this was inexplicable. How could so good and reasonable a woman allow herself to be bamboozled by so obviously a lost cause? Why didn't she just leave him?

Eventually, even she lost patience. After one brawl too many, she laid down the law and vowed to move out unless he went for treatment. Reluctantly he agreed. Because his addiction was of long standing, an in-patient detoxification was prescribed. Two full months went by before he returned home. In the meantime, he went without a single drink. Continually supervised, and at long last motivated to correct his ways, upon graduation he was utterly sober. When he arrived back at the family dwelling, his wife eagerly awaited him with a huge grin on her face. Once they stopped kissing, she ushered him into the dining room to celebrate. There sitting in the middle of the table, in a place of honor, was a magnum of champagne. He had done so well, they simply had to drink to his success.

If this sounds like a joke, it is not to alcoholism counselors.[1] All too frequently they encounter spouses who speak passionately of the need to dry out their significant others only to be the ones who seduce them into resuming their habit. Sometimes this is achieved, as with the champagne incident, with illusory innocence, by making the outlawed potable physically available, sometimes by provoking a fight from which the alcoholic withdraws into a self-defeating high. Either way, the inducement to resume drinking is less inadvertent than it might seem. As professionals in the field learn, these incidents occur with dreary regularity. The reason is that many of the spouses are "co-dependent."[2] They may not be alcoholics themselves, but they obtain a payoff from being in a relationship with someone who is. Often their reward is the gratification of being a caretaker. Because in comparison with their partner, they are so clearly the "good one," they are able to imbibe massive amounts of sympathy from others who don't recognize what is going on.

Among alcoholism experts this sort of spouse is designated an "enabler." She may not herself drink, and will vigorously protest the excesses of her husband, but her behavior is such that she facilitates his addiction. If he is too inebriated to go to work, she calls in to make his excuses. If he alienates his relatives so badly that they swear to disown him, she pleads that he be given a second chance. Thanks to her, he has a roof over his head, food on his plate, and sufficient cash in his pocket to stay supplied with his favorite potable. Absent her ministrations, he might hit a bottom so profound that he would be forced to confront his mortality and seek a remedy. She, however, in the name of compassion, nourishes his habit and keeps it going.

The same sort of pattern can be found within the African-American community. There one encounters some people who are suffering from the after-effects of slavery and others who facilitate their continued travail. Members of the Civil Rights establishment, in particular, are prone to slowing down the emergence from bondage of those most afflicted by it. Ironically, they do so in the name of speeding up the journey toward freedom.[3] They too are enablers who make excuses for the frailties of their fellows and provide them with the resources to abstain from change. Instead of demanding that those trapped in failure carry out the work needed to get ahead, they shift the blame to others, for example, members of the white community. Change, their unflagging mantra proclaims, is the responsibility of those who initiated the difficulties, not of those who are its victims. It is the racists who must reform, not their targets; it is they, and not the victims, who should be blamed.

"Blaming the victim," say the enablers, is one of the most insidious effects of racism. It heaps insult upon injury and complicates the problems of the underdog. Yet theirs is a profoundly wrongheaded approach. It makes accusations that are untrue and propounds defenses that are debilitating. First, to claim that blacks must take responsibility for improving their situation is not ipso facto to "blame" the victim. It does not imply a moral failing, much less insist that its perpetrator be punished. To say that someone who was injured must himself undertake a series of actions if his impairment is to be overcome does not entail a belief that he is at fault. It no more blames him than does recommending to someone suffering from the flu that he stay home and drink plenty of fluids. Although it is not fair, those maimed by an external agency need the time to heal. Moreover, as the ones whose minds and bodies have been abused, they are best situated to provide relief. Indeed, there are certain forms of cure that only the victims can implement.

Second, using purported allegations of blame as a pretext to heap opprobrium on others is itself a form of moral turpitude. To begin with, the theory that when whites counsel blacks to be responsible, they thereby "blame the victim" is a moral hypothesis. It seeks to turn the tables on those urging African-Americans to change by asserting that they are the "real" transgressors who should feel guilty and themselves reform. In essence, a good guy/bad guy dichotomy is established with whites characterized as villains and blacks as innocents. In this state of absolute purity, as Steele[4] has explained, the "victims" are answerable for nothing. Their status provides them a blanket excuse that absolves them from taking actions they find onerous. The result is that blacks are not held accountable for failures which they, and often only they, have the possibility of correcting.

Blacks making excuses for the deficiencies of other blacks has become a cottage industry in some segments of the community. The most egregious example was surely the O.J. Simpson case. Millions of white Americans were suddenly made aware by the telecast of his trial that millions of other Americans were prepared to exonerate a brutal killer merely because he was perceived to be one of them. Not only were they ready to endorse jury nullification when a black was accused of violently murdering two whites, but they were eager to cheer a verdict of innocence where innocence had clearly not been proved. What was worse was that this was only the tip of the iceberg, with a multitude of other instances confirming a disposition to condone black transgressions. Johnnie Cochran may have been an eloquent advocate, but what was the justification for numerous well-placed blacks to rush to lionize his victory?

Other illustrations of this excuse machine are provided by protests against police brutality. Al Sharpton and his minions enthusiastically seize upon instances of police excess, whether typical or not, to vilify them.[5] Instead of seeking the means by which to assist those mandated to uphold the law, they insult them as "pigs" and "oppressors." No doubt some officers have earned these sobriquets, but in their readiness to believe the worst of all patrolmen, their detractors throw them on the defensive while at the same time offering comfort to genuine bad guys. Given the scourge of crime afflicting our innercities, one might imagine that those attempting to stem this tide would be feted as heroes.[6] That the opposite should be true, with criminality treated as a normal rite of passage in a community where one in three young men are involved in the criminal justice system, is disconcerting.[7] It declares, in no uncertain terms, that many black leaders would rather reject those perceived as outsiders than make common cause against the lawbreakers in their midst. Along with Congresswoman Waters, they prefer to find rationalizations for looting, rioting, and pimping.

What many seem not to realize is that when explanations are treated as forms of exoneration, the impact is to condone wrongdoing. When instead of denouncing those who steal and rape, their transgressions are blamed on others, the effect is to reinforce them. The perpetrators quickly learn that they will not be rejected by their peers and hence that criminality is a viable career move. When they also observe that the most prominent members of their community actively lobby to have the penalties for their actions reduced, the pressures toward self-improvement are further diminished. Why try to fix what the most important people in one's universe find unobjectionable? This certainly seems to be the result of efforts to get sentences for crack abuse lowered merely because a large proportion of blacks are subjected to them. When the deleterious effects of selling crack are ignored so that fewer blacks can be sent to prison, the message is that the damage caused to black addicts is of less weight than is thwarting white justice.

The same sort of mind set is evident in the excuses made for out-of-wedlock childbearing and lowered academic test scores. Rather than use community norms to ostracize those who irresponsibly bring unwanted children into the world, the single-parent family is justified as an alternative cultural choice. Its prevalence is not taken as a cause for alarm, but as an indicator that it is normal and hence authentically black. Likewise, if IQ tests continue to reveal a full standard deviation difference between whites and blacks, this is explained as due to a cultural bias in the test instruments even when no such bias is demonstrable. That this disparity is present in numerical, as well as verbal, tests is dismissed as irrelevant, rather than as evidence of a deficit than needs to be addressed.[8] There seems to be little recognition that that which is treated as standard quickly becomes the standard and that that which is tolerated as ordinary soon becomes ordinary, no matter how fundamentally intolerable.

Black enablers also foster the status quo by providing resources that make change less urgent. Not only do they fail to demand that people acquire the strengths to move ahead—either by excusing the inexcusable or alleging that it is someone else's fault—but they reduce the motivation for personal growth by providing the means of leading a comfortable life without having earned it. The number one culprit in this is affirmative action.[9] If people can be admitted to college without attaining the same academic credentials as others, or hired for jobs without demonstrating the same skills as their competitors, why bother to obtain these? That which is unearned is denominated in an inherently debased currency—its value having been reduced by its cheapness—but if it puts food on the table and a roof over one's head, this may be accepted as sufficient. Despite complaints that one is being disrespected, the impetus to do better—especially since this is not assured—is not adequate to encourage painful change. The end product is that people will not do what they are capable of doing because those who professedly care most about them have arranged things so that they do not have to. Very much in the same vein are easily obtained welfare checks which have fostered a dependency in their recipients,[10] a dependency so tenacious they fight for a continuation of the very conditions that prevent them from living up to their potential.

What those involved in this debacle need to understand is that equal status implies equal responsibilities. Those who wish to move ahead on the same basis as others must be willing to surmount the same obstacles as they. Special excuses, and special preferences, however justified by past injustices, constitute a velvet prison. By chaining people to their past, they prevent them from escaping their present. The champions of these measures, however pure their motives, perpetuate unnecessary weaknesses. Bedazzled, as some are, by the momentum of the Civil Rights movement, they fail to perceive what is happening. Instead of recognizing the centrality of social mobility, they cling to moral imperatives that no longer apply. Instead of addressing the cultural impediments that interfere with acquiring real strengths, they settle for appearances and perpetual inferiority.

A MIDDLE CLASS REVOLUTION

When in the 1940s E. Franklin Frazier[11] wrote about the black bourgeoisie, it was a tiny, embattled minority. It pretended to the same sorts of prestige as the white middle class, but had neither the education, nor the resources, to sustain it. As the Thernstroms[12] have documented, however, starting in at least the 1950s, blacks have surged forward both economically and socially. Even before the Civil Rights legislation of the 1960s came into play, they had begun a juggernaut of mobility that has not come to a halt.[13] Most important of all, they attained the power to transmit their successes intergenerationally. Whereas a 1962 survey revealed that neither the occupations nor the incomes of African-Americans were significantly correlated with their social class origins, by 1973 their mobility patterns differed little from that of whites. By then well-educated blacks could expect to raise well-educated children and anticipate that their move into the suburbs would not be followed by their offspring's plunge back into the ghetto.

In category after category evidence accumulated of the emergence of a stable black middle class. Thus between 1940 and 1990 the proportion of black men engaged in professional occupations vaulted from 1.8% to a respectable 9.4%. Black women did even better, rising from 4.3% to 15.9%. Overall by 1990 32% of black men had entered white-collar occupations, while 58.9% of black women had done so. Although over-represented in areas such as social work and the clergy, many were becoming physicians, attorneys, and engineers. On the education front, for persons between 25 and 29, in 1960 only 37.7% of blacks had high school degrees compared with 63.7% for whites. By 1995 this had changed so much that 86.5% of blacks and 87.4% of whites held these credentials, the difference having become statistically trivial. Even college attendance ballooned. Thus while only 7.2% entered higher education in 1960, by 1995 35.7% were doing so. This compared with the 49% of whites going to college at the latter date. Less encouraging, however, was the fact that by 1995 only 13.2% of blacks compared with 24% of whites were graduating from four-year schools. In the area of income too there were dramatic gains, with black male income rising from 41% that of whites in 1940 to 67% in 1995. Black females did substantially better. Their income rose from 36% to 89% that of white females. The bottom line is that whereas only 12% of blacks considered themselves middle class in 1949, by 1994 some 44% did. In contrast, the proportion of whites in this category rose from 34% to 64%, which is better, but proportionately not as good.

This historic transformation in status has been reflected in the way African-American academics characterize themselves and their problems. The sociologist William Julius Wilson[14] has gone so far as to declare that the major difficulty confronting blacks is a social class deficit rather than a racial barrier. Henry Louis Gates[15] has been more emphatic. Having hired Wilson away from the University of Chicago to bolster his African-American Studies department at Harvard, he has ratified the increasing significance of social class, and publicly admitted that he personally feels less in common with poor inner-city blacks than with his white colleagues. He has even affirmed that he finds it difficult to understand the thought processes of lower class blacks.

And yet this movement has not been accomplished without pain or disappointment. Becoming middle class has not been automatic, nor has it depended solely upon effort or ability. Gates tells the poignant stories of two of his classmates at Yale. Himself the parochial scion of rural West Virginia blacks, he was deeply impressed with two slightly elder peers, the one a social activist who seemed to have all the answers and the other a talented academic with an apparently unlimited horizon. Neither, lamentably, lived up to his potential. One, Glen DeChambert, was a charismatic student organizer. "With his impeccable attire and lordly way with a cigarette—[he] struck [Gates] as the perfect embodiment of black leadership.... Best of all DeChambert was a man with a plan. A very practical-sounding plan. What black America needed, he often said, was economic development, and the only way that was going to happen was if we did it ourselves." But this plan never came to fruition. DeChambert himself scarcely seemed able to move past the glory of giving speeches to Yale undergraduates. Far from being the one who demonstrated through his own success how economic development could be achieved, he lingered at Yale until there was no choice but to move on, first going to law school and then to an unspectacular career at the FCC. In the end, he impressed Gates as an unhappy chain-smoker bent on reviving the memories of his more promising youth.

The other model who inspired Gates, whom he considered one of his pair of aces, was Armstead Robinson. The scholar of the two, he was a "commanding picture of black intellection. Thin and ascetic in his unpressed dashiki... we knew [Robby] would change the way we understood our past and our present...." And at first he seemed likely to succeed. After all, he "founded, funded, and ran, superbly, the Carter G. Woodson Institute at the University of Virginia...[and was later] awarded the Yale Medal by President A. Bartlett Giamatti." But he too stalled out. "Robby, the most brilliant scholar of our set, completed his dissertation with difficulty; and then gave up the ghost. His book?... He never published the book...or anything much at all." Like tar babies caught in their own past, neither Robby nor DeCh proved capable of handling the larger world to which their abilities had provided access. Neither appeared to understand why and both foundered on the brink of their individual promised lands.

Dreams and plans are not the same as realities. Hopes and symbols are easier to manipulate than are obdurate facts. Real people and real groups do not cooperate as readily as fantasy role partners. Ideals may glow with a brilliant radiance,[16] and words may have the power to impress those as naive as ourselves, but they are poor appliances with which to extract social success. With its myriad of unexplained complications, the world is a much more difficult place to fathom than are our ambitions for it. Likewise, with their myriad of untamed emotions, our inner natures are less amenable to manipulation than one might expect. Those who do not come to grips with nasty truths, such as the culture of slavery, in the end are undone by them. Similarly, those who fail to appreciate the intense competition of an open market society find it hard to rise within it. Impervious to personal growth, they burn out before they discover that many of the difficulties they encounter are part of the way things work.

What has become apparent in recent decades is that many middle-class blacks have been frustrated by their achievements. Instead of reveling in success, they are bundles of complaint, ever prepared to find fault with the way the system is treating them. Whether on the job or at home, they feel disrespected and inexplicably refused the benefits they had supposed to be the normal accompaniment of prosperity. Ellis Cose[17] has described this phenomenon as the "rage of a privileged class." He notes that many of his peers find themselves shunted aside by white associates who do not perceive them as fully competent.[18] Yes, they may be hired to work in the newsroom, but they are palmed off with race-related stories instead of mainstream political ones. Yes, they are employed by Fortune 500 corporations, but they are assigned to the human resources department where it is believed they can do little damage.

Joe Feagin and Melvin Sikes[19] claim that the indignities wrought by American racism continue to be pervasive and that the personal affluence of successful blacks has not insulated them from these. Whether shopping in a department store, driving an upscale automobile down the wrong street, or seeking a house in a good neighborhood, the ordinary law-abiding black is likely to encounter skeptical stares and downright incivilities. In particular, if he is in business, he will find that many whites continue to doubt his abilities no matter how often these are proven. Rather than accept him as an equal, they refuse to purchase his services or to interact with him without being patronizing. For him, the American Dream has become a dream deferred. Feagin and Sikes suggest that for the ordinary middle-class black, racism entails the *lived experience* of being a visible minority in a white-dominated country and that the pain and stress this causes are cumulative and debilitating. To be thus surrounded by hostility and discrimination, they say, takes an inevitable, and tragically unfair, toll.

And yet these complaints may be an inescapable consequence of moving up. They may, in fact, be more symptomatic of progress than of failure. When a group of people succeed in freeing themselves from oppression, there is no guarantee they will have simultaneously learned how to exploit the possibilities that have opened up. Part of what may be necessary is the development of social capital.[20] A collection of skills and attitudes that facilitate economic and political advancement, this capital takes more time to internalize than may be apparent to those without it. Schooling alone, as Gates' classmates learned to their regret, does not provide all the insights and emotional strengths that are needed. Nor does moving up per se equip a person to recognize the realities of success. The normal human tendency to believe that those at the top lead tranquil lives, undisturbed by doubt or conflict, can lead the nouveau successful to conclude that the frustrations they experience are unique to themselves, and perhaps even a punishment for their achievements.

One of the most urgent adjustments a would-be member of the middle class must make is the adoption of a self-directed attitude. He who would assume a position in which he directs the activities of others, whether as a professional, a middle manager, or an entrepreneur, must be capable of making unaided decisions in an environment of uncertainty. Although consumed by perplexities, he must be able to keep his wits about him and arrive at a reasonable solution to most of the dilemmas tossed his way. This sort of level headedness, however, takes time to acquire. Those who have had decisions imposed on them from above may imagine that freedom alone bestows this capacity, but they are wrong. The curiosity to explore one's environment when an answer is not obvious, and the ability to be patient when success is not assured, are usually the product of a period of supportive learning. Nurturant others—who allow mistakes to be made—provide the environment in which a person determines both how to recover from a serious error and wherein his personal strengths lie. Those not so fortunate may find themselves in what feels like a pressure cooker. Their own insecurities, even though these are attributable to inexperience, induce them to increase their burdens by making intemperate demands of themselves. Not to overcome this handicap is to remove from view opportunities that others take for granted. It is to retreat to a position of inferior scope and inferior possibilities.

Members of the newly emerging black middle class are under a double handicap. A confluence of both structural and cultural liabilities increases their difficulties. In the quest for self-direction and social respect, they must conquer a host of historically imposed disadvantages. The first of these is starting out from a structurally subordinate location. Slaves and their progeny were poor; nor were they well connected. Indeed, slaves and their progeny were forced into an inferior status by laws that would not let them rise and fellow citizens who assumed their lowly station was decreed by nature. Thrust into the competition for social preferments without wealth, without natural allies, and without the respect of others, the battle to succeed was made all the more onerous by an ignorance of what was to come. Absent the guidance of associates who had already made the ascent, how were they to understand that success does not cancel out the need to prove oneself; that, if anything, it compounds it? How were they to recognize that the doubts others entertain of their competence are part of the process? That these should be perceived as an occasion to demonstrate one's superiority, rather than an inducement to further failure, was not in the cards. On the contrary, rage and shock filled the hearts of those who assumed that promises of equality were being broken.

Nor did culture come to their rescue. Unlike, let us say the Jews, they did not receive assurance that as God's chosen people success was a foregone conclusion. Nor did it encourage education, personal responsibility, or supportive family relationships. The lessons learned on the plantation did not even prepare the descendants of slaves for the pain of change. Their lack of familiarity with the resocialization process left them totally unready for the emotional exertions of self-improvement. That freedom should awaken a rage against their previous condition of servitude or that success should fill them with a sadness regarding what was long denied them was completely unanticipated. Rather, the traces of anger left over from the past, and the depression inherent in letting go of what was lost, were interpreted as a consequence of contemporary racism. This, to be sure, was facilitated by the continuing presence of discrimination and racism, but their role was overdrawn to the detriment of the change process itself.

Ironically, the middle-class revolution that so improved the condition of American blacks also increased their expectations. Thus their anger, when confronted with evidence of enduring unfairness, rose accordingly. Why, many wondered, in a nation where everyone was theoretically created equal, were they alone subjected to an asymmetrical burden? That the remnants of a caste society unfairly remained to encumber them is beyond doubt. But that this is an unavoidable consequence of the way things once were also needs to be recognized. This may not be nice; it is surely not equitable. It simply is. Failing to accept it may be a normal response to injustice, but it also has the unfortunate effect of retarding the change process.

THE CHANGE PROCESS

How then should American blacks respond to this situation? As a Caucasian American I am not in a position to give disinterested advice, but as a sociologist I can speculate on the likely course of natural resocialization. It seems evident that the steps necessary to reconfigure their status have, for many blacks, been set in motion by the middle-class revolution. This transformation has changed their circumstances so drastically that it has already instigated the efforts they need to make. To attain the self-assured flexibility of emotionally adult leadership,[21] blacks must overcome the inadequacies foisted upon them by an inequitable providence. If they, and not the generations that succeed them, are to achieve what has become possible, they need to enter upon voluntary modifications. But the inducements to do so are in place.

Fortunately—although it will not seem as such to those who must endure it—the process of becoming middle class can challenge people by confronting them with their own inadequacies. Because they are called upon to exercise an unaccustomed leadership, their difficulties in asserting themselves vis-a-vis others become painfully observable. Asked to make decisions with which others will comply, they will find that it is not enough to assert one is the "boss." They must either find, or develop, the strengths vital to asserting a nonstrident right to be heard. This discovery can make what they personally lack stand out in stark relief. They may not only notice that there are skills in which they are deficient, but can reexperience the interpersonal deficiencies of their earlier life with distressing clarity. There is nothing like having one's authority disputed to reawaken previous moments in which the same challenge was not met. Yet the sheer terror of coming face to face with unresolved weaknesses can have a sobering effect on those courageous enough to brave it. It can then become a powerful incentive to make sure these are overcome.

When a person is no longer able to deny a particular deficit, its dimensions need to be explored and worked through. Why was a subordinate's slight unnerving? Why, when the latter intimated by way of a demeaning joke that his leadership was inadequate, did this produce a shiver of recognition? Could it be that his parents, or childhood friends, made similar accusations? And if so, were they true? Those who are sufficiently strong to be honest not to retreat into exhibitions of immaturity may discover that they have abilities and potentialities they did not suspect. They may even find within themselves the capacity to develop fresh areas of expertise. Instead of allowing their fears to drive them into defensive postures, they can become what they have long wanted to be.

But such advances are not cost free. That which no longer works must be relinquished, and what is so abandoned must be done so by means of depression. Unfamiliar successes invariably arouse comparisons with previous losses. Strange to relate, on the verge of victory past insults and long gone disasters will reappear to test one's soul. Why, a person cannot help asking, was she treated so miserably when this was so unnecessary? And why was she excoriated as inferior, when she clearly was not? In a very real sense, the sweetness of today's luxuries makes the bitterness of past rejections all the deeper.

The good news is that this backward looking sadness opens the way to a more expansive future. It enables a person to deactivate emotions that were more appropriate to the past. Rather than wallow in the resurrection of recriminations that earlier role partners so richly deserved, more satisfying relationships can be pursued. Besides becoming more expert in technical matters, a person can learn to be a good ally by being one to others who are themselves good allies. The distrust that poisoned his previous relationships can be overcome in negotiations with peers who are given the opportunity to prove their trustworthiness. This will not only make the world a safer place, but it will also multiply his strengths by supplementing them with the strengths of these others.

In the end, natural resocialization can allow an African-American to become, not just a black leader, but an unhyphinated leader.[22] True social mobility is contingent upon rising not only within one's own community, but within the larger community as well. Genuine power—the sort that is truly fulfilling—crosses category boundaries and is respected because others have learned that it can be upheld. In particular, for a boss to be respected by subordinates who come from a different ethnic or racial stock, he must demonstrate that he has a better grasp of the situation than they. This requires that he not only understand where he is coming from, but where they are coming from as well. Orlando Patterson[23] puts the matter succinctly: "If and when Afro-Americans are to assume supervisory positions over Euro-Americans....[they will find that] a manager who speaks a different social and body language from the people he supervises—who knows and cares little for the intimate details of personal relationships, the myriad unverbalized gestures, signs, face cues, masking techniques, and other interaction rituals of everyday life among non-Afro-Americans—is a manager doomed to failure." Patterson recommends that the requisite knowledge of whites be acquired in interaction with them. Beginning at least in college and professional school, he urges them not to pass up relationships with Euro-Americans, arguing that these are "vital for the social capital, enhanced 'emotional intelligence,' and learning skills" they provide. In short, there are few better ways for African-Americans to learn the human quirks of white Americans than by dealing with them as people. Unless they do so, unless they voluntarily emerge from an all-black social cocoon, they disadvantage themselves.

One of the best examples of a person who afforded himself the opportunities to learn the necessary lessons is Colin Powell.[24] Although his cultural roots are not typical of most African-Americans, both of his parents having been immigrants from Jamaica,[25] he clearly had to surmount the stigma of being black in a nation dominated by white institutions. The institution in which he first made his mark was, of course, the U.S. Army. Beginning as a lowly reserve officer, he wound his way through a distinguished career capped by becoming the Chairman of the Joint Chiefs of Staff. Those who have read his autobiography will recognize in it a veritable handbook on how to become a leader. With sympathetic candor, he describes the many steps he had to take and, more importantly, the social facts he had to discover.

Leadership came almost by accident to Powell. While a geology student at the City College of New York he stumbled onto the Army Reserve Corps, where he quickly determined that he enjoyed the rigor of military discipline. He especially took pleasure in, first being a member of, and then commanding, the unit's award-winning drill team. Ultimately, after deciding to make the army his career, he was forced to adjust to numerous unanticipated circumstances. One of the earliest was segregation. The child of a mixed inner-city New York neighborhood, he had not personally experienced rejection in public accommodations until he was required to take training in Columbus, Georgia. Now he found that restaurant clerks and highway patrolman alike treated him not as a military officer, but as a black man who was where he shouldn't be. Although he wished to rebel, he recognized the limits of what was possible in the pre-Civil Rights South, and worked within them.

Subsequently Powell served several tours of duty in Vietnam. There he was constrained to learn the rudiments of small-unit leadership while under fire from a determined enemy. What is more, he had to do so while in liaison with troops from a culture different from his own. Instead of simply dismissing them as "gooks," he made special efforts to understand where they were coming from—just as he had with the Jewish storekeepers of the South Bronx and with the insensitive Rednecks of Alabama. Later when assigned administrative duties, he was exposed to the unique culture of military command. This forced him to develop the political skills that were ultimately to vault him to the top of the pyramid. Rather than be stiff necked, he sought to be a cooperative colleague and loyal ally, and in the long run this was rewarded by superiors who valued his support.

In many ways Powell's story is a fairy tale in which he benefited, not only from his personal talents, but also from being in the right place at the right time. As he would readily admit, he joined a service that was looking for able blacks to promote. When he was later assigned to advanced training at Fort Leavenworth or special duties at the White House, this was, in part, due to a policy decision that might be called affirmative action. But as Powell would also allow, he took advantage of these opportunities by turning in a superior performance. He not only attended his classes, he came out at their top. In other words, time and again he proved himself by delivering the goods.

Yet all was not perfect, even for a Colin Powell. He too had his share of fatuous commanding officers and jealous colleagues, but he out-maneuvered them by making friends in the right places. Among the insights that enabled him to persevere is that it is sometimes necessary to "pay the King his schilling." When a boss demands something foolish, rather than fight him at every turn, it is often advisable to do what is asked, then move on to other tasks. Making an issue of something within a superior's jurisdiction when that superior is determined to have his way is a waste of time. It is better to preserve one's energies for where they can make a difference. Similarly, Powell advises his readers that every day one must fight the dragon and that sometimes the dragon wins. To be a winner, one need not win all the time, only enough to obtain a respectable batting average.

Powell's resocialization, if we may call it that, took him from being a middling student with no idea of what to do in life to the guiding spirit of an international coalition that roundly defeated Saddam Hussein. Along the way he had to come to terms with circumstances that caused him considerable pain. Recognizing and accepting his own limitations was not easy; nor was accepting those of the society and individuals that surrounded him. In the end, he was able to let go of disabilities that would have mired down a lesser man. Instead of railing at the Gods for having made him a black man in white America, he worked through his distress at being refused the right to buy a hamburger from a roadside eatery or his chagrin at being mistaken for a railroad porter by a visiting dignitary. Whatever private torments he endured, he was strong enough to move forward and negotiate his own place on an historic stage with considerable success.

Part of the irony of this story is that Powell has become more a hero for whites than blacks. Condemned by his very success to being thought of as an honorary white man, he is not regarded as a model by many African-Americans, which is extremely sad. The skills he has exhibited and the journey he as navigated are precisely what they need to emulate. Paradoxically, many will do so, even though they do not realize it. It is no secret that the military has become an avenue to success for a disproportionate number of Afro-American males. Not only has it welcomed them into its ranks, and more or less evaluated them by the same rules as it has others, but it has had the additional advantage of providing discipline for those in need of it. As we have seen, among the disadvantages of the culture of slavery has been its lack of stress on self-discipline. To the extent that the rules applied to slaves were external, the emotional controls needed to make sound decisions, especially in an environment of uncertainty, remained underdeveloped. This gap has to a large extent been bridged by the military. Since its training methods stress the need to begin by accepting external discipline, it does not require potential leaders to commence with self-direction. On the contrary, they find themselves part of an institution that emphasizes obedience until one proves oneself capable of exercising greater initiative. In the long run this allows individuals who start with limited controls to handle enormous responsibilities.

The military has thus demonstrated an aptitude for supporting natural resocialization. Although it does not conceive of itself in these terms, recruits who successfully pass through its system are prepared to exercise greater responsibilities should they leave its close confines. They have, therefore, the opportunity for greater success in commercial endeavors than they would otherwise. Converted from passive victims to active players, they need no longer excuse their failures by blaming others. Nor need they perceive themselves along strictly racial lines. After having been permitted to direct the activities of a variety of subordinates, their skill at roletaking will have expanded. This will enable them—by putting themselves in others' shoes[26]—to obtain a more nuanced understanding of how the world works. As a consequence, their decisions are apt to be better informed and more successful.

The other great structural channel facilitating the natural resocialization of blacks has been the Civil Service. Whereas Gate's school chums were thrown into waters deeper than they could handle, government jobs, by contrast, because of their limited horizons and abundant red tape, provide their occupants the breathing space to develop their personal strengths. The fact that these positions are not entrepreneurial, but regulation bound, protects people from challenges they are not prepared to meet. They do, however, provide the responsibilities and resources for growth. Like the army, they allow people to learn how to make decisions and how to get along with others from different backgrounds. They also enable their occupants to pass these advances on to their children. Themselves almost surely operating within an environment that is less restrictive than the one in which they were raised, they can allow their youngsters the latitude to explore their own aptitudes. What is more, having themselves benefited from more information than they originally possessed, they can now encourage their children to reach out for additional knowledge.

Natural resocialization, when it works, enables people to change strongly held beliefs and attitudes. Because these transformations are genuine, those who undergo them can pass tests they once shunned. In the end, they do not need to resort to appearances to assert an enhanced status. In fact, newly emerging perspectives and expertises provide them the means for overcoming the stigma of affirmative action. To the extent that people are placed in positions they cannot manage, they invite exposure as frauds, but conversely when they can handle these, they attract respect. Internalized changes take time to evolve, but these stand up to the unpredictable wear and tear of a market-based class system better than the alternatives.

MOBILITY-FRIENDLY VALUES

Those who wish to get ahead, besides engaging in personal growth, do well to promote mobility-friendly values. For both themselves, and those they care about, a world in which most people favor rules that support a democratic, free-market society is to their advantage. Because such rules provide the scaffolding for an open social class system, they make advancement available for all. In particular, they open the possibility of taking tests even they can pass. No matter how capable individuals are, they will have difficulty becoming middle class in a society based on rigid traditions or organized around a command economy that they do not command. Only universalistic standards that encourage honest competition will enable them to do so. With regard to other members of the community—including their children—a freedom-based system has similar benefits. When a substantial proportion of a society internalizes market-oriented values, their futures too are enhanced.[27]

Sad to say, the area in which African-Americans have the most to gain is from a change in their value systems. Slavery, for the slaves, was hardly a hotbed of free enterprise or of democracy; hence the culture it produced was not marketplace friendly. This is evident not only in the current dearth of black entrepreneurs, but in the sorts of demands that blacks, especially black leaders, make. Ideals that stress victimization or a state-based redistribution of power[28] do not foster the sorts of effort needed in an open class system. When goals such as personal responsibility, individual merit, and family solidarity are downplayed, the result is individuals unequipped to compete against others who honor them. They will find that the legacy of slavery, instead of pointing toward genuine independence, promises a counterfeit equality.

Foremost among the values that a successful middle class must embrace is freedom. This master value of the American experiment has long since demonstrated its worth as a touchstone of economic prosperity and democratic decision making. The self-direction so characteristic of middle-class individuals is contingent upon an atmosphere of freedom. To make up their own minds, people must have the possibility of contradicting those above them. Those unable to express disagreement, and at least sometimes to make it stick, are ciphers, whatever their pretensions. Indeed, were they unable to develop, and act upon, an independent perspective, the flexibility necessary to operate within a complex, mass society could not exist. Not only would democracy be a fraud, but so would the vaunted capacity of capitalism to adjust to unanticipated circumstances.

Happily, entering upon a middle-class lifestyle, even in a rudimentary fashion, fosters an appreciation of freedom. Those who are thrust into situations where decisions are expected of them generally come to prize the latitude afforded by a system that celebrates individualism. The elbow room this invites provides them the space to experiment and the leeway to succeed. Although the prospect of being wrong can be terrifying, a pride in concocting winning formulae can offer ample compensation. Moreover, the novelties cultivated by a decentralized system can support a buoyant optimism. The unpredictable successes thereby made available provide an avenue to progress that comes to be cherished by those who benefit from it.

A similar alchemy can occur with regard to personal responsibility. To be responsible is, from the standpoint of some people, a vexatious burden. They do not wish to answer for their mistakes and would as soon foist them onto others. Yet the opposite of blame is credit, and those who have tasted victory are often willing to assume the onus of failure so as to reap the benefits of success. They calculate that if they are resilient enough to endure the opprobrium of defeat, they will be competent enough to ensure a surplus of praise. Instead of depending upon others to provide benefits they cannot govern, they opt to control their own destinies. For them, a paternalism parallel to that of slavery holds few charms. No longer feeling helpless, they prefer to depend on their own initiatives rather than the uncertain generosity of strangers. Nor are they intimidated by the rigors of self-discipline. Having learned through experience that good decisions result from self-possessed computations, they do not shrink from enforcing limits on themselves. Since the rules they follow are voluntarily incorporated, they are not tempted to rebel against them. To the contrary, they utilize their newly evolving emotional strengths to keep themselves on a track of which they approve.

A middle-class lifestyle likewise places a premium on personal merit. Those who find themselves in line to benefit from proficient performances have a stake in seeing that these are impartially evaluated. They want the best to be rewarded because the best is a standard to which everyone— including themselves—can have access. The best also translates into the most for all involved—at least most of the time. Products that are satisfying and procedures that are efficient tend to deliver the greatest gain for the largest number. The result is that a system which allows fair comparisons between competing objectives, and then favors the superior ones, is to everyone's advantage. Nor do the winners in such a situation evade efforts that, although onerous, they have learned are likely to pay off. Indeed, they acquire a tenacious work ethic precisely because they have discovered they too can profit from hard work.

Even the value of honesty is promoted by being middle class. This may seem counterintuitive in a capitalist society where sellers often try to deceive their customers about the quality of their products, yet the puffery of the marketplace exists within a fundamental ambiance of trust.[29] Were there not dependable limits on deceit, buying and selling would not be feasible. The impracticality of comparing value would make it absurd to exchange goods with others. Indeed, doing so would be a gamble in which one never knew if one were benefiting from the trade. Even the idea of money depends on a fundamental honesty. Paper currency would be impossible if those who accepted it were unsure it would be backed by "the full faith and credit" of a stable government. In business relationships too confidence is paramount. People prefer to engage in transactions with others whose behaviors are predictable. If these providers guarantee a due date, will they deliver? If they promise a level of performance, can it be counted upon? Unlike the assurances of the door-to-door salesman, those underlying more fundamental economic bargains assume integrity. This is why business people usually make deals with those with whom they have an established history. More particularly, as it relates to middle-class status, honesty is the bedrock of middle-class relationships. Although its appearance can be, and often is, manipulated for private gain, it is central to determining who to trust and, therefore, who is a dependable ally.

The worth of education is, of course, less controversial. In a world gripped by a technological fever, it is easy to appreciate the utility of schools in providing the necessary expertise. Similarly, in a marketplace characterized by diversity, the value of formal assistance in fathoming the motives of strangers is readily understood. Perhaps less elevated, but of more tangible worth is the professional credential. In a Gesellschaft society in which most people are strangers to one another,[30] expertise is often certified by academic degrees. This makes the importance of schooling self-evident to almost anyone who hopes to rise in an environment dominated by bureaucratic organizations.

Family values too have a middle-class connection. It was no accident that Victorian values emerged in England during its ascent to world economic hegemony.[31] The sort of domestic tranquillity exemplified by Victoria and Albert appealed to a broad swath of their subjects precisely because it suited the needs of a people anxious to claim their portion of a growing affluence. Christopher Lasch[32] has described the family as a potential "haven in a heartless world." It is at least a potential source of stability in a gigantic marketplace where increasing levels of specialization make it impossible to discern exactly what is going on. In the home, one can be known, and cared about, in a way that pecuniary exchanges do not allow. In the home, both parents and children can be afforded the emotional support that enables them to absorb the blows of strangers who perceive them as mere components in a system. All this is easy to appreciate for people caught in the middle of the game, hence their craving to be "loved."[33] Despite the increase in divorce rates, virtually everyone, including most African-Americans, dreams of a relationship that meets his or her emotional needs. Precisely because trust is imperiled by the impersonality of the marketplace, they seek compensation in the intimacy of the family abode.

Lastly, to return to a value that earlier led our list, a middle-class world is one in which physical violence is out of place. A society in which physical assaults are commonplace is not one in which people have the security to make deals with one another. The trust needed to exchange "goods" includes the confidence that one will not be beaten and robbed when one enters into interaction with others. Business simply cannot flourish in the midst of a war zone. This mandate is often described in middle-class circles as a need for "civility."[34] If Victorian prosperity placed a premium on the tight-knit nuclear family, the emergence during the European Middle Ages of a continental marketplace had a similar effect on personal "manners." It made "etiquette" the mark of the "gentlemen" and gave an assurance that the outstretched hand of a stranger was meant as a greeting, not the first step in a mugging. The same sort of logic applies no less to the African-American father who finds himself on an up economic escalator. When he greets potential customers or potential colleagues, he wants to make sure that his demeanor expresses his allegiance to the niceties of civil society, not the commotion of the inner-city back alley. By the same rationale, when he prepares his children to follow in his footsteps, he wants to be certain they too are aware of this distinction.[35] Whatever their peers may be doing in school, his aim is to have them internalize the conventions of successful citizens, not the tongue-piercing, tattoo-wearing, offense-taking rituals of the street.

In many ways the success of the African-American community depends on the pioneering efforts of middle-class blacks. It is vital that the lessons they learn be transmitted to those below them socially. Given that we are an hierarchical species, and that there is a sense of community among black Americans, successful blacks are in a unique position to influence those who are less successful. It is often asserted that prosperous Afro-Americans have a moral duty to share their good fortune with those left behind.[36] Typically this is envisioned in political terms, with the middle classes expected either to join in left-wing causes or to distribute their largess in the inner city. When they are warned not to forget where they came from, this implies that they must maintain an identification with roots that include an allegiance to the values derived from slavery. Whatever else they do, they must first and foremost remain "authentically" black.

It is much better for themselves, and those who have made less progress, if, when "they remember where they came from," they also recall what enabled them to get ahead. What middle-class blacks owe their less successful brethren are a model of what it takes to make it in an open class system and their best efforts in enforcing community standards. Hierarchical superiors almost inevitably furnish examples for those seeking to understand how to succeed. Their very presence serves as evidence that "people like us" have a chance. It is one of the best counters to stereotype vulnerability, particularly because their achievements make them salient and, therefore, effective stereotype busters. Likewise, the avenues of advancement they pioneer provide hints of where the openings lie. This is why if a value is good enough for them, others may give it a chance.[37]

Nor should the role of community standard bearer be neglected by the black middle classes. The rules that people live by, especially the moral rules, gain their legitimacy by being enforced by those with unequal power. If they do not use their disapproval to discourage negative behaviors, these are apt to flourish. As a consequence, they must have the courage of their convictions, even when these are resisted by a large proportion of ordinary folk. In the current context, this may entail following Gates' admonition to demand individual responsibility from other blacks.[38] When crime is not condemned, it is condoned. When violence is excused, it is permitted. No matter how valid the explanation or egregious the provocation, turning a blind eye to violations of one's central values has the effect of subsidizing them. Those who make O.J. a culture hero send the message that killers can find refuge among them, and thus, whatever their intentions, increase the probability that there will be killers among them.

Back on the plantation, the rules people were forced to live by were not mutual. When the culture of slavery encouraged rule-breaking it did so from the standpoint of the outsider. But members of the black middle class are not outsiders. If they continue to feel as if they are, this is a temporary condition. The longer their experience as part of the ruling elite, the more they will take it for granted and the less inclined they will be to doubt it. Sooner or later they will realize that the rules that enabled them to succeed are their rules. They may not have invented them, but in living them, they breathe life into them just as surely as do whites. When this happens, it will be easier for African-Americans to openly acknowledge their allegiance to middle-class values, and, for that matter, to the free market system, without feeling that they are "oreos" who are somehow disloyal to their origins. Once this day arrives, those who have internalized these rules will find that they constitute a ground upon which they can forge alliances with whites. Despite their difference in color, they will uncover a basis of trust in their shared attitudes. Like Gates, they will find it easier to understand, and feel sympathy for, Caucasian members of the middle class than Negroid members of the lower classes. In the end, an awareness of their joint humanity will overwhelm their history of conflict.

Today, successful African-Americans find themselves in an ambivalent position. Because the shift from a closed caste to an open class system is not complete, they have feet in both camps. As a result, they do not receive the respect they have earned. Nor is it widely appreciated that they hold the keys to a truly integrated society. Whatever whites do, or fail to do, middle-class blacks are leading the way to a society where everyone is free to move ahead, or fall back, based on their personal efforts. It is they who will be most responsible for our having achieved a color-blind society if we ever do.

Chapter 11

The White Middle Class

"Let freedom ring!"—the cry of democrats throughout the centuries—now echoes 'round the world. What do aggrieved peoples want? Freedom. When do they want it? Now.... But democratic freedom is a particular sort of freedom, tempered by centuries of hard wisdom that stretch from ancient Attica to the modern Western metropolis. It is decocted civic lore that tells us that human beings are not only capable of great deeds of courage and selfishness but are tempted by power, corrupted by greed, seduced by violence, and weakened by cowardice. Jean Bethke Elshtain, *Democracy on Trial*

WHITE ENABLERS

Some years ago a student came to me for academic advisement. Halfway through our session she stopped in mid-sentence to broach what she described as a sensitive subject. After several false starts, following each of which she profusely apologized for what she had been about to say, she asked my opinion regarding a campus job she held. One of her responsibilities, she explained, was to prepare materials for an impending conference, but she was dependent upon others to provide her with input before she could proceed. One of these, a black student leader, kept missing her deadlines. The problem had therefore become: Was it appropriate to say something to this student? Although my advisee experienced no difficulty in calling her white subordinates to account, she feared that saying something disapproving to a black person would be interpreted as "racist." When I asked her if she thought she was applying a harsher standard to this student than to the others, she indicated that she was not. When I further inquired what she would expect of her own child, if she had one, she replied that she would insist that deadlines be met. Nonetheless she felt guilty and concluded that it would be better to act as if nothing were wrong.

My student's dilemma has become commonplace among whites. Time and again they hold their tongues rather than criticize African-Americans. In situations where they would be demanding of fellow whites, they try to be "understanding" and will rehearse a series of possible excuses before responding. In the end, like a colleague of mine who agonized for days over giving an F to a black student, they wind up blaming themselves for these others' failures. In doing so, there can be little doubt that they are enabling them to get away with performances that would not be tolerated in Caucasians or Asians. Just as do black enablers, they absolve African-Americans from having to do their best and even provide them the resources to slide by. On the KSU campus one of the manifestations of this phenomenon was the budget allowed the African-American organization. Despite the fact that it was several times larger than that allocated any other student group—permitting it, for instance, to serve more lavish finger-foods at its functions—its leaders habitually claimed this was not enough and lobbied for an increase on the grounds of discrimination.

But the question remains: Is this disparity due to white guilt? On the basis of his personal observations, Steele[1] has speculated that blacks often seek to elicit a contrition that they can later convert into a material advantage. He believes that this was one of the major mechanisms that has enabled the Civil Rights movement to procure affirmative action programs. More recently he[2] has suggested that many whites, especially white liberals, are preoccupied with achieving "redemption." They are presumably so haunted by the sins of their ancestors that they will twist themselves into knots to expiate a deep-seated guilt that nonetheless resists being assuaged.

At first blush, this hypothesis has a surface plausibility—some whites surely do speak as if they harbored a gnawing guilt—but there are some difficulties with this explanation. Many Euro-American activists may utter the right words, but they do not seem to take them to heart. This was clearly the case with Jane Elliott and her KSU audience. Although she lambasted all whites, certainly all Southern whites, she did not include herself. And neither did her listeners include themselves. As their glistening eyes indicated, few of them were consumed by doubt. On the contrary, they were accusers. It was others, others not present in the auditorium, whom they believed to be guilty. It was these others who were in need of redemption. If only some day these intransigent racists would awaken to their faults, they might seek expiation. Only then would redemption be possible, for only they needed to transform themselves into moral human beings. Jim Sleeper[3] captures this attitude quite well when he says of the white liberal establishment that "what it wants...are ritual condemnations of its racism that implicitly credit its virtue." In other words, many whites proclaim their guilt in an effort to prove they have no reason to feel guilty. Far from redemption, they are seeking a superior moral status.

In fact, many whites seek to elevate their social positions by invoking unique moral credentials. Like black enablers, they wish to establish their innocence as a lever for achieving social power. Sleeper call this "innocence by association." If these whites can portray themselves as reliable allies of blacks, then doubtless they are entitled to the same privileges as they. Actually Steele[4] too is aware of this ploy, for as he notes, "the moral authority that redemptive liberalism is after is power." Thus, when politicians propose programs to benefit blacks, many are really in pursuit of credit for doing the right thing.

In instances such as this, when moral superiority lies in the balance, one must first determine who is likely to benefit. More specifically, what sorts of advantage are at stake and for whom? Before answering these queries, it is essential to recognize that a posture of moral excellence no more guarantees perfection than claims of superior intelligence certify a sharp mind. Who then are these white moralists comparing themselves with? Relative to whom are they asserting a social priority? The two most likely candidates are: (a) blacks and (b) white conservatives. And what sort of gain do they hope to reap? The rejoinder is surprisingly simple. It is none other than power. In the first case, that is, relative to blacks, a kind of jujitsu occurs in which those who claim to bestow moral status are thereby rewarded with a higher status. In the second, that is, relative to white conservatives, the assumption of moral purity is intended to be convertible into social domination. Instead of recognizing that they and their opponents often differ only in the means they recommend, persons who use this gambit vilify their rivals as classic examples of "bad guys" who ought to defer to them for protective guidance.

First, when white enablers utilize a feigned personal guilt to excuse the deficiencies of blacks, they thereby impute a special generosity to themselves. Since they assume that they are prepared to make allowances for blacks that others are not, they imply that they possess a uniquely forgiving spirit. Superficially, at least, they are ready to take a step back so that others can step forward. But appearances are deceptive. The reality is that those who provide these gifts are staking out a higher plane relative to their beneficiaries. In their magnanimity they get to set the standards and thus earn the right to expect gratitude. Those on the receiving end, in contrast, given their comparative dearth of excellence, are not supposed to criticize their benefactors. Their job is to be appropriately deferential and to make sure that this appreciation is known. But this sort of thankfulness is a small distance from groveling and therefore resented by those whom circumstances have forced into expressing it.[5]   Allowed a choice, they would much rather distribute charity than receive it.

Another way in which white superiority expresses itself is in what Smith and O'Connell[6] call "the sensitivity imperative." Liberals, in particular, seem to believe they have an obligation to treat African-Americans with special care. Given their long history of oppression, blacks are thought to have a right to be suspicious of Caucasians. Thus, when they take offense at being called "colored" or "Negro," it is up to whites to understand and defer to their desires. Similarly, if blacks invent a royal African lineage, claim to be working harder than others, or deny the dysfunctions of the black family, these assertions must be respected. What is insinuated is that blacks are too fragile to deal with the truth. Because so much that is unpleasant has happened to them, they have been overwhelmed, and must be protected from the resultant pain. Among themselves, many well-intentioned whites shake their heads at black inadequacies, but in public they stick to politically correct depictions of the situation. That this is patronizing, and assumes blacks are basically weak, is ignored, whereas the emotional superiority imputed to themselves is smugly accepted.

Relative to other whites, an assertion of moral excellence also functions as a power play. Although Steele[7] is primarily concerned with the concept of "innocence," many Caucasians who regard themselves as racially enlightened indulge in what is better referred to as "invidious goodness."[8] They go much farther than assert they have caused others no harm. In their own eyes, they are public benefactors who grant people services they cannot perform for themselves. They are convinced that they genuinely "care" about black welfare, whereas their rivals do not. These others, whatever their public rhetoric, are thought to be "mean-spirited" bigots. They may proclaim a desire for a "color-blind" society, but this is a code word whereby they communicate their determination to keep blacks suppressed. Proof of this is hypothetically found in their rejection of the policies advocated by the liberals. A failure to subscribe to the moral, the social engineering, or even the clinical/educational model is accepted as incontrovertible evidence of a negative disposition toward blacks. Comparatively speaking, this makes liberals "good" people. Their incessant proclamations that they "intend" to do what is right are taken as a conclusive demonstration of their unique worth.

Sometimes white enablers gain power by renouncing it. Instead of fighting for priority, they seek to avoid the damage that might be caused by a bruising battle. In ceding power in one area, they thereby hope to preserve it in another. These whites will allow blacks to call the tune regarding things they do not really care about so that they can devote their attention to the ones they do. This strategy might be called "tactical acquiescence." It is illustrated by what Sleeper[9] calls "mindless diversity." One of the oddest consequences of affirmative action programs is how strongly they have been embraced by business. Instead of fighting the quota systems imposed by the federal government, many corporations have developed training programs and hiring procedures meant to guarantee an ethnically diverse work force. In their press releases and internal documents alike, they proudly announce their allegiance to a multicultural society, while in private the chief concern is with avoiding lawsuits. Even though recent court decisions indicate that they might win a fair share of these, they conjecture that the possibility of adverse publicity makes it economically more feasible to pay what amounts to blackmail. Besides, business executives loathe uncertainty. From their perspective it is better to incur a cost they can calculate than to contract ones they cannot. Moreover, since their competitors are in precisely the same position as they, no one gains a competitive advantage.

Educators have shown a similar proclivity when they have altered school curricula to meet the criticisms of the racial entrepreneurs. Thus, when Hacker[10] complained that traditional educational strategies were not responsive to the uniquely "earthy" and "nonlinear" features of black culture, some members of the educational establishment rushed to make adjustments. Without subjecting these to the usual academic scrutiny, they hastened to adopt texts such as Asa Hilliard's[11] *Portland Baseline Essays.* Although these works made such questionable assertions as that "Egyptian culture had its developmental origins further south in the African interior" or that "Since Africa is widely believed to be the birthplace of the human race, it follows that Africa was the birthplace of mathematics and science," these went largely unchallenged. Indeed, Euro-Americans were said to have "invented the theory of 'white' Egyptians who were merely browned by the sun." Even Cleopatra,[12] though admittedly of Greek heritage, was alleged to have been sufficiently African that "She would probably be living in one of the Black communities of the United States."

Why this capitulation to shoddy scholarship? In part it seems to have been easier for administrators to co-opt their critics than defy them. Their power could as easily be preserved by including African-American representation as by excluding it. Less innocent is the possibility that these concessions have been applied to predominantly black school districts because those in charge are unconcerned about the quality of learning occurring within them. Perhaps from the white perspective, if Afro-American parents and teachers were intent on purveying myths to their own children, why not stand aside and let them? If, in the process, they wound up with an inferior education, Euro-American students would not be harmed.

In sum, from the perspective of the white enablers, these various strategies either fail to diminish their power or are more likely supplement it. They may claim to be advancing the interests of African-Americans, but as a consequence of their actions they push themselves farther ahead. In fact, they get to have things both ways. As the ostensible allies of blacks, they can call on them for assistance with their own agendas and as the social sponsors of blacks, they are able to stay a step ahead of them regardless of their progress. In a sense, being an enabler is an insurance policy against downward mobility. It is also an excellent balm against residual guilt.

A less distorted approach to black/white relations would surely recognize that true equality is characterized not by one-sided helpfulness, or overlysensitized communications, but by honest and sometimes even brutal exchanges. Unless whites feel free to tell blacks what they really think, the two cannot share a common status. And unless whites are allowed to say negative things to blacks without being labeled racist, they are not free to speak their minds. Genuine equity is between peers who recognize that both sides are able to take and dish it out. Their mutual respect is a product of approximately equal power that has been confirmed through the rough and tumble of social competition. Attempts to sidestep this requirement with a false niceness are habitually discredited by events. Far from expediting social advances, they breed distrust.

Let me underline this point. A society in which everyone has equal access to economic, social, and political mobility must be founded on *mutual trust*.[13] Just as is true of authentic friendships, people must be prepared to tolerate constructive criticism because they understand that it truly is intended to be constructive. Citizens of an open class society must have confidence in the fairness of their fellow citizens. It is no service for one group to try to protect another by denying its deficiencies, for unless people are aware of what they lack, they will not be motivated to make the necessary modifications. Gratuitous nastiness is, to be sure, unnecessary. People do not need to be vicious to be honest. But tactfulness need not be maudlin. Reality may sometimes be hard, but when all parties are committed to maintaining decent standards, all can benefit. As a plaque given to me by one of my clients proclaims, "The most beautiful gift we can give each other is the truth."

Especially unnecessary is the kind of reticence one sometimes encounters in the handling of such controversial political figures as Maxine Waters and Jesse Jackson. When Waters refused to condemn the riots that took place in the wake of the Rodney King decision, it was a national disgrace. But just as disgraceful was the silence of George Bush. Both may have intended to avoid tarring law-abiding African-Americans with the same brush as the rioters, yet the result was to pardon the barbarities. What was necessary was to distinguish those who had lost control from those who had not, and to roundly castigate the former. Although for their varying reasons neither Bush nor Waters did so, this omission spoke to the lack of trust between the communities they represented. By the same token the repeated failure of his political rivals to rebuke Jackson[14] for his "socialist" ideology bespeaks a discomfort in being too critical of an African-American. Indeed, from their rhetoric, one might not even suspect his socialistic bent. In a truly egalitarian society this would not be the case, for between real friends even jokes are tolerated. It may sound odd, but African-Americans will not have been accepted as on a par with other Americans until it is possible to make jests about them as naturally as we do today about Irish-Americans.

THE STEWARDSHIP ROLE

When George Bush (the elder) stood for reelection, millions of voters questioned his commitments. In the parlance of the time, the concern was with whether he had a grasp on "the vision thing." These Americans were not sure where he wanted to lead them and suspected him of marking time. Although in his speeches Bush sometimes alluded to a desire to be a "steward" of the nation, this did not resonate with his listeners. Mostly middle class, they could not identify with his upper-class mentality. Yet Bush was serious. His parents had taught him that as a child of privilege, it was his responsibility to protect what he had been given so as to pass this legacy on to others. His less well-off constituents, however, could not appreciate this as a valid goal. The vision of the future they sought was one in which they would be better off. Merely to conserve that which was already in place seemed an unworthy end, and perhaps even a way of preserving inequality.

The irony of this reaction is that as our nation matures, middle-class Americans more frequently find themselves called upon to be good stewards. They are discovering that the system that has enabled them to climb to positions of power and affluence is not self sustaining; that if it is to endure, they will have to defend its central premises. More particularly, if there is something in which white, middle-class Americans cannot afford to acquiesce, it is a dismantlement of the values that underlay an open class society. Democracy and economic freedom are fragile accomplishments. Their recent flowering may make them seem hardy perennials, but they are atypical of human civilization. To abdicate commitments to the standards that make a constitutional republic and an effective marketplace possible is thus to abandon their own interests. That nowadays many people seem willing to do so, albeit in the name of a more perfect commonwealth, is a supreme irony. Astonishingly, people seem not to recognize that total equality endangers the very conditions that make elementary freedoms possible.

Steele[15] is acutely aware of this predicament. He writes that "Because difficult principles [have] themselves [been] stigmatized as the demonic instruments of racism, white Americans and American institutions have had to *betray* the nation's best principles...." He bemoans their zeal to break faith with "such timeless American principles as self-reliance, hard work, moral responsibilities, sacrifice and initiative...." As a black man, he is especially disappointed that recent reforms "always [ask] *less* of blacks and [exempt] them from the expectations, standards, principles, and challenges that are considered demanding but necessary for the development of competence and character...." He is just as aware that such a renunciation imperils Caucasians; that in a society where competence and character are sacrificed for the sake of an imaginary millennium, everyone's happiness and security are endangered. Nor is Steele alone in this awareness. Sleeper[16] affirms that "As Glenn Loury and Randall Kennedy insist, society has an obligation to set and enforce basic standards and to punish their violation with stigma and shame, not in order to keep the historically disadvantaged down, but, if [their] judgments are sound, to give them firm moral footholds on the way to more freedom and power."

Too often in recent decades people have confused an uncritical tolerance of others with an equal access to society's benefits. They seem to imagine that if they allow others to do exactly as they want, this will automatically open a plethora of social opportunities. Nothing, however, can be further from the truth. A romantic relativism that equates all cultures, and all standards, does not bring about fairness. The fact is that not all cultures are equally functional and not all standards adequately meet human needs. Naive multiculturalists may assume that the greater the diversity within a society, the more equal the power and the more widespread the happiness,[17] but this is a fallacy. It is not a diversity of standards per se, but the nature of these standards that counts. Values that promote totalitarianism, ignorance, or apathy, no matter how diverse, tend toward the infelicitous.

The happy fact for contemporary America is that it is heir to the world's first, and most thoroughgoing, middle-class revolution. In no other human society have so many people been able to partake in their own governance. In no other have so many been able to benefit from a cornucopia of such fruitfulness. Although it is a cliché to describe the United States as a young nation, it is actually the world's oldest continuous representative democracy. Its founding fathers declared their independence from Britain and subsequently ratified a written Constitution on a globe dominated by kings and pashas. Likewise, although it is taken for granted that America has only newly emerged from frontier poverty, by the latter half of the nineteenth century the nation was already the world's wealthiest. These economic and political successes constitute a proud legacy, a legacy that its chief beneficiaries should have an interest in safeguarding.

Pivotal to this inheritance is, of course, its open class structure. A sophisticated marketplace and a representative government allow people the flexibility to migrate from one position to another, from one status to another. Those with the talent and energy to parlay the self-direction these permit into commercial or social success are free to reap the rewards of their efforts. The equities permitted by these arrangements may not be perfect, but they are the closest to unmitigated fairness that any mass society has ever managed.[18] Furthermore, because there is a greater than average prospect that those who produce the most will rise to its highest levels, the odds that society will be able to maximize its yield are optimized. To use what has by now become an archaic utilitarian formulation,[19] it will be a society that has the best chance of producing "the greatest good for the greatest number."

If all this is so, then the white middle class has no interest in securing a set percentage of positions for any segment of the community. Neither democracy nor economic rationality are promoted by ensuring that the number of blacks, women, or left-handed Albanians who enter particular jobs reflects their ratio in the larger population. As individuals, those in the upper ranks of society may care about the injuries visited upon those below them and wish to see these alleviated,[20] but they also have a larger responsibility. What is to their advantage, and to that of those for whose welfare they are accountable, is defending the assemblage of rules and values that enable democracy and economic flexibility to flourish. Above all, they need to promote a society in which trust is the norm. Not only must whites and blacks alike have confidence in each other's motives, but whites must also be able to trust themselves. If they cannot, the predictable schemas that enable them to plan orderly interactions collapse. As a consequence, the more broadly these standards are internalized, and the more universally they are enforced, the more secure will be the institutions upon which all depend. To put this bluntly, middle-class whites derive very little benefit from enforcing quotas for particular ethnic or racial groups; they derive a great deal more benefit from enforcing rules that enable anybody, regardless of his biological heritage, to compete for, and enter upon, any position for which he/she is qualified.

The key value in this arrangement, as should readily be apparent, is *freedom*. Freedom for all is the freedom to be one's best and the independence to contest one's comparative priority with others. Together with such subsidiary values as personal responsibility and interpersonal honesty, it forms the scaffolding of an open class system. One of the most dangerous errors of the postmodernists is the belief that freedom is an absolute.[21] The notion that unless a person can be completely spontaneous he has been enslaved by those constraining his behaviors is a delusion. What nineteenth century thinkers called "license" is not the royal road to self-actualization, but a detour into personal and social misery.[22] True freedom is dependent upon an infrastructure of norms and standards.[23] Without these, the world becomes—not a playland for those who seek an endless frolic—but a tangled undergrowth of hazards they must constantly guard against.

About a hundred years ago Emile Durkheim[24] made a crucial, but still underappreciated, observation. Reflecting on the theories of an earlier generation of social philosophers, he noted that their speculations about a "social contract" had overlooked a vital element. Whereas scholars such as John Locke[25] had assumed that human beings could impose civilization upon themselves by agreeing to abide by specific rules, Durkheim realized that their ability to formulate a contract depended upon the prior existence of a set of rules; that, for instance, an ability to enter a binding compact was contingent upon internalized norms of promise-keeping. The same reasoning applies today. Without an extensive set of informal rules, rules that have not been consciously decided upon, many ordinary social interactions could not take place.[26]

Let me illustrate. Baseball, like many sports, is governed by an extensive set of regulations. These may seem constraining in the sense that only a ball thrown in a certain place counts as a strike, but they are also liberating in that once the rules are accepted, the players have a wide range of options not previously available. The two battery mates can, for instance, work out a subtle series of pitches designed to fool the batter into swinging at an undesirable offering. The same logic applies to the marketplace. Absent rules against theft—rules that are by and large honored—it makes no sense to trade goods with others. The likelihood that any particular possession could be expropriated by more powerful persons would make it unwise to expose valuable items to the vicissitudes of public exchange. But once there are stable property rules, the creativity inherent in the marketplace is free to multiply exponentially. The utility of such regulations is, in fact, graphically on display in post-communist Russia. There the inadequacy of Soviet business law has put a serious crimp on economic reform. Without broadly respected civil codes to govern the conduct of entrepreneurs, an underground of corruption has erupted to fill the void. Even in the West, however, the rules must continuously evolve to fit changing circumstances. Thus we are currently witnessing an expansion in the legislation applicable to intellectual property; for example, as computer technologies have developed, the need for guidelines to regulate e-commerce has also.

If this is so, then fundamental to serving as good stewards in an open class society is honoring a collection of familiar values. The white middle classes, if they are to preserve the institutions upon which their ascendancy is dependent, must align themselves against racism and violence and for personal responsibility, individual merit, honesty, and family values. Moreover, as Paul Sniderman[27] and Talcott Parsons[28] before him have insisted, they must do so *universalistically*. To apply these principles only to themselves is to undermine their authority. Let us start with racism. No matter how strident the claims that whites are intrinsically racist, it is not to the advantage of middle class whites to promote racism. As professionals, middle managers, government administrators, and entrepreneurs, their role is to promote efficiency in the public and private sectors. While in specific cases it may profit particular individuals to cheat, for a class as a whole, the systematic cheating intrinsic to racial bigotry is not profitable. It does not allow talent to emerge and puts those who indulge in it at a disadvantage relative to those who do not. It also limits the alliances available and draws off energies to defend a structure with little payoff. Were this still a caste society in which one group could physically exploit another, or a zero sum economic game in which the resources are finite, racism might make sense, but it is neither. Because the power needed to suppress specific groups is more wisely expended elsewhere, and because the possibility of increasing the size of the pie is very real, it is more rational to ignore physiological differences in enforcing social precepts.

For similar reasons, it makes sense for middle-class whites to reject violence. Even when substantial force is directed only at repressing a pariah group, this has the effect of corrupting the entire polity. Just as antebellum plantation owners found their lives organized around the need to keep discipline in the slave quarters, so too would contemporary whites have to be on constant alert were they transfixed by a need to intimidate blacks. The claims of business and democracy would be of relatively less concern and would suffer accordingly. Moreover, the personal hardness required to impose violent measures would desensitize people to precisely the sort of human cues needed to engage in marketplace transactions.

Likewise, middle-class stewardship implies an allegiance to preserving social rules. With the spread of bureaucracy,[29] the myriad of rigidities thereby entailed has made rules anathema in many circles. Advertisers, for instance, now pander to fantasies of operating "outside the lines." Certainly old dictums about formal dress codes and vulgarity in mixed company have fallen upon hard times. Nonetheless, for a mass-market, democratic society to function a core of regulations must be firmly internalized. Not only promise-keeping, but also stepping aside when one loses an election, stopping for red lights, and not stealing from friends because the temptation has arisen must be virtually universal. Fortunately, despite recent upticks, crime has been contained within acceptable limits. For it to remain so, however, standards must be enforced. Just as the amount of graffiti in New York subways was reduced by its being removing without delay, so must rule-breakers confront reliable controls.[30] This means that the middle classes must be champions of law enforcement. Whoever's ox is gored, they must be committed to firm, even-handed constraints. Paradoxically, the very tenacity with which core rules are honored has permitted a loosening up of external symbols of rule-following—perhaps best exemplified by the dress codes. People no longer wear tightly starched collars to demonstrate their conformity with larger social pressures, not because conformity is irrelevant, but because it is assumed.

The implication here is that an allegiance to maintaining the rules goes hand in hand with personal responsibility. Because the most important social standards need to be effectively internalized, responsibility for respecting them resides with the individual. A large segment of the population must have sufficient self-discipline to do what is required even when not subject to external observation. This capacity demands early socialization. Children must learn from their parents that they can control themselves and must sometimes delay personal gratification. They must also learn that they will be asked to account for their lapses. Without a significant cadre of such persons, social order would be lost and a greedy opportunism become the mode. If they are present, however, vital standards can be enforced even upon those who do not internalize them.

When translated into how one treats others, a devotion to responsibility and self-discipline dictate a renunciation of paternalism. If others are to be allowed to function as full adults, they must not be treated as children. Even if they demand special benefits, when these are based upon the assumption that they are unable to perform up to the levels of others, they must be rejected. Steele[31] puts this responsibility as follows: "All social reform that hopes to initiate minorities into society should be based first and foremost on high expectations. The subliminal message of a high expectation is 'You *can* and you *must.' The high expectation is the only credible assertion of equality that society can make.*" When it comes to fostering change, this means that people must be allowed the time and space to learn and grow. Instead of interceding to protect them from the pain inherent in personal development, society must allow them to find their own way. To do less deprives them of the possibility of discovering their individual strengths, and, in essence, confirms their inferiority.

Implicit in this is, of course, a respect for individual merit. Standards that do not discriminate between what is better and what worse are not standards at all. When everything is of equal value, nothing has any value. Oddly, there has been a movement in some middle-class circles to eliminate competition in favor of cooperation.[32] Theoretically everyone is to work together for their mutual benefit with no one seeking precedence over any other. Thus, on the little league diamond everyone is supposed to be a winner, with everyone receiving a trophy at the conclusion of the season. Some go so far as to insist that score-keeping be abolished and that the players engage in the activity for the sheer joy of doing so.

All this, however, loses sight of the fact that we are an hierarchical species and that, in our eagerness to outdo each other, we have developed a host of technological and social advancements. It is true that competition creates winners *and* losers, and that merit implies flaws. This, sorry to say, poses the problem which, put more generally, is that superiority breeds inferiority and that inferiority imposes pain. The nasty secret buried herein is that the benefits of hierarchy do not come gratis and therefore some will fall to the bottom. And yet without pain to overcome, there can be little genuine pleasure. A false equality that overlooks our human strivings may seem fair, but it would drain the prospect of fulfillment from life. Like it or not, as a species we thrive on overcoming obstacles. A mobile system—such as our own—that enables people to seek their own levels is thus better than a sterile community of clones.

Some, such as Patterson,[33] insist that in reorganizing society, they do not intend to challenge the notion of merit. As he says, "Before I am wholly misunderstood,...let me make it clear that [a] redefinition of rules in no way entails a lessening of standards or the abandonment of the merit principle." Sad to say, this is wrong. Programs such as affirmative action not only change the rules, they cheapen our measures of success in the process. Because these new rules are designed to rank people according to their proportion in the population, relative skills are often ignored. This is described by Patterson as "a genuine universalization of the rules of conduct," but it is not. It is a particularism disguised as universalism. Moreover, despite his assumption of being value-neutral, he is not. Indeed, it is hard to imagine a more drastic change in goals than one from freedom to equality. For merit to survive, its defenders must see through such ploys. They must be able to distinguish between excellence and ambition, between liberty and a forced social balance.

Similar considerations apply to the middle-class commitment to a work ethic. Instead of placing "having fun" at the apex of their pantheon, successful people almost masochistically demand that effort be expended in pursuit of value. Those who only inherit a higher position are regarded as "drones" unless they too dig in and become producers. Even among the upper classes, the greatest respect goes to those who have "earned" it. Such an attitude refuses to make life easy, but has the virtue of increasing the goods available to everyone. An old adage has it that "Money does not grow on trees" and the same may be said of the products that make life worth living. The fact that that which is difficult to obtain feels more fulfilling has the practical effect of motivating people to keep working even when they become affluent.

This brings us to truth and honesty. Besides demanding an honest day's work for an honest day's pay, an open class system places a strong emphasis on honest communications. Both instrumental rationality and stable relationships depend on people knowing what is so and what is not. Unlike members of the working class, those in the middle specialize in working with people and data rather than things.[34] They are in this sense specialists in manipulating symbols. As such the possibility of deception is greater for them than for others. Indeed, people today seem to take delight in managing appearances.[35] Nevertheless, when it comes to personal relationships, most people despise mendacity. President Clinton may have survived in office, but his reputation as a moral leader was shredded by evidence that he lied to a Grand Jury. Where precisely the lines of honesty are to be drawn is still being fought out, but the question is not one of indifference.

Most members of the middle class are also aware of the power of education. Their experience on the job has convinced them of the utility of expertise and the advantage of credentials. They are therefore prepared to recommend education to their children and all others intent on upward mobility. What is less widely appreciated in the value of intelligence. Credentials, in fact, do not stand on their own. If, in the long run, they do not improve role performances, they must eventually fall into disrepute. Effective problem solving, whether in business, within one's family, or regarding social problems such as race relations, depends upon ascertaining facts and manipulating them logically.[36] Too widespread an inability to do so would endanger everyone's well being. Nor is there an advantage in concentrating incompetence within a minority community. If it cannot cooperate in solving shared social problems, these are bound to persist.

Finally, family values also fall within the compass of middle-class stewardship. To date, no social institution has proven as capable of producing happy, competent children as happy, competent nuclear families.[37] Besides the emotional support available in loving intimate relationships, no other arrangement fosters the caring needed to effectively socialize the young. It should also go without saying that sexual fidelity underlies the viable nuclear family. Without the trust encompassed by authentic sexual commitments, the strong bonds needed to withstand the battering sure to come from an uncertain world would be difficult to forge. Absent the fundamental emotional alliances that are possible in marriage, and the subsidiary alliances made possible by parenthood, people would be forced to fight lonelier, more desperate battles.

These considerations apply to blacks as well as whites. Thus, if middle-class whites are to be consistent and effective champions of the standards that underlay their open social class world, they must do so for blacks also. Although their own families are under assault from prosperity bred divorces,[38] they must not construct a moat around their suburban citadels. What is good for their relationships and children is likewise good for the relationships and children of the ghetto. To simply slough them off as having a different culture is to consign them to a permanent lower class status. Coercion, to be sure, is not an effectual means of proselytizing among the lower orders. Forcing people to pretend to adopt middle-class families is likely to beget resistance. But neither is renouncing one's fidelity to family values likely to work. At minimum, those serious about spreading viable standards, must provide a model for others seeking a path to success.

Nor, as stewards of history's premier form of social organization, ought the middle classes lose their nerve. Defending values that are sometimes misunderstood takes courage. When radical egalitarians and radical collectivists angrily accuse them of being insensitive, they must not fold their tents. Some, no doubt, will be tempted to monopolize their standards for themselves. They will reason that if others insist on suffering, it is better to move out of range and let them have their way. But this is short sighted. An open class society, to fulfill its promise, must be open to everyone. Those who do not understand how it operates should at least be given the opportunity to find out. Even when they ferociously attack the humanity of their would-be allies, social stewards must have the fortitude to endure these calumnies. Above all, those trapped by a slave, or a lower class, mentality must not be demonized. Whatever their limitations, their human potential remains intact. Then again, neither must the middle classes demonize themselves. They must not join in stigmatizing themselves as the primary cause of others' distress.

CHANGE AMONG WHITES

As the principal victims of slavery and the caste system, African-Americans carry more scars than most. As a result, they have more changes to undergo than others. Nevertheless, European-Americans are not exempt from a need to change. They too have been influenced by slavery and the caste system; hence they too need to learn the lessons of freedom and self-direction. But such instruction is already taking place. Like blacks, whites have had to confront a metamorphosing economic and political scene. As a consequence, they are not what they once were. Nor are they fully what they have the ability to become. The transformations that have occurred have not been total, but they are indisputable. Indeed, it is arguable that mutations have occurred more rapidly among them than among blacks and that these in turn have paved the way for black progress.

We have already reviewed some of the evidence for a surge in the ranks of middle-class blacks, that is, their increased incomes, professional status, and educational attainments, but these would not have been possible without the complicity of whites. If a working majority of European-Americans did not approve of, and in numerous cases participate in, these shifts, they would not have been possible. Black students would not have been admitted to previously all-white universities nor been allocated generous scholarships; neither would black administrators have been appointed to supervise white subordinates. The scope of these changes is evident, in part, in the dramatic shifts in opinion that have occurred among whites. As Schuman et al.[39] have documented, in category upon category, they now express more tolerance of blacks. Thus, most whites, in both the North and the South, currently approve of integrated public accommodations, schools, and neighborhoods. Of course, as Feagin and Sikes[40] point out, these attitudes are not always converted into action. Certainly this is true in residential living patterns[41] and in the eating arrangements in high school lunchrooms. In both cases, whites and blacks continue to lead separate lives. And yet this is not the whole story. As recently as 1963 only 20% of whites in the South, and little more than 40% in the North objected to laws against intermarriage. By 1993, however, more than 80% of whites disapproved of these statutes. More than this, whereas in 1958 fewer than 5% of all whites approved of intermarriage, by 1997 more than 60% did. In other words, not only were they now against legal restrictions on marriage, but were prepared to accept such marriages. And this has had an impact on their behavior. Back in the 1950s fewer than .5% of blacks married whites, but by the 1990s this had grown to between 4% and 9% (depending on the gender of the spouse)[42] with a doubling of the rate of intermarriage occurring for each decade following the Supreme Court ruling against miscegenation.

Those familiar with the South know that the changes in this region have been startling. Now referred to as the "New South" or the "Sunbelt," it is no longer a rural backwater. A commercial and industrial revolution has swept from Virginia through Texas to pull millions of people out of small agricultural towns and deposit them in rapidly growing urban enclaves. There they have been exposed to people and jobs that have dramatically altered their outlooks. In newly internationalized cities such as Atlanta, Charlotte, and Nashville, they find themselves under the influence, not of a provincial aristocracy, but of modern college educated executives running multibillion dollar corporations (e.g., Coca Cola). They likewise rub shoulders with a diverse company of co-workers, many of whom have migrated from places such as New York City and small towns in Nigeria.

If I may personalize this for a moment, recent carpetbaggers similar to myself are generally taken aback by the sophisticated, almost Northern, ambiance of places like Atlanta and their suburban strongholds such as Cobb County. At Kennesaw State University, in the heart of Cobb County, I am regularly confronted with thousands of students who have had a similar awakening. About half are transplanted Northerners who mistakenly expected to be immersed in a sea of unwashed rednecks. A large proportion of the others are transplanted from areas such as rural north Georgia. Of the latter, a significant proportion relate stories of change within their own families. Typically they tell of the shockingly variance between the student and his or her parents. The older generation is described as being trapped in a reflexive racism the younger finds hard to fathom. Having themselves attended integrated schools, and anticipating employment in integrated corporations, they have little difficulty in associating with blacks or in treating them respectfully.

The mechanisms of this transition were brought to my attention through the history of integration in Cobb County schools.[43] After Brown v. School Board something extraordinary occurred. Even before that, however, Cobb County was already being shaped by external forces. Most significantly, during World War II, Lockheed Aircraft opened a huge assembly plant in conjunction with Dobbins Airforce Base. To operate it, they recruited engineers from around the country and assembly workers mostly from the rural South. Together these collaborated on developing a cosmopolitan outlook that was different from the more pastoral areas in the region. Thus, when school integration loomed, and a statewide referendum asked for approval to privatize public schools, Cobb voters demurred. Unlike their more agrarian neighbors, they were on the way to acquiring a middle-class mindset and understood that without adequate schools—even integrated ones—the local economy might go into a tailspin.

For many other white Southerners the pain of adopting a tolerant middle class outlook has been as great as was that for blacks intent on moving past their racial resentments. In places such as Birmingham, Alabama, the resistance to integration was sometimes ferocious. Encouraged by leaders on the order of Governor George Wallace and Police Chief Bull Connor, they held out for decades. But even they have come around. Wallace, before he died, publicly reconciled with his African-American constituents, whereas Birmingham itself has leaped forward to become a modern commercial metropolis.

The North, to be sure, has been economically and politically ahead of the South. Transitions new to Dixie are old hat in places like New York City. This, unfortunately, has elicited an unseemly smugness. Many Northerners have assumed that they are totally without bigotry and therefore can serve as moral exemplars for others. What they have not taken into account is that further socioeconomic progress might demand additional changes of them. Northerners too have a great deal to learn about being middle class. Despite their head start, they too are capable of false steps. Paradoxically, whereas Southerners have been held back by an agrarian conservatism, Northerners have been impeded by an urban liberalism. Ironically, although they possess a set of ideals unlike those of the antebellum South, these are also inimical to racial advances.

Among the dysfunctional values to which Northerners cling are convictions that: (a) it is essential to be "nice" to the underdog and (b) government programs are critical to improving social conditions.[44] First, modern liberalism is committed to a moralistic interpretation of race relations. Most liberals truly believe that blacks are being held back almost entirely by white racism. The racism they have in mind is, to be sure, not their own, but they are convinced that its disappearance would instantly solve the problem. Second, most Northern liberals are certain that only the government has the power and munificence to dictate a moral reorganization. They assume that political control is inherently progressive. Fundamentally democrats (with a small "d"), they cannot imagine that a "government of the people, by the people and for the people" can be anything other than benign.

What many "Northern" whites do not realize is that they, and their chosen instruments, have less control than they would like. They may be able to reorganize some institutions, for example, by creating a Head Start program, but they cannot fully govern the consequences. Nor, as much as they may despise resistance to policies on the order of affirmative action, can they stamp out this opposition. More important still, they cannot facily manipulate cultural factors. What people think and feel are not available to the sorts of substitution they envision. This makes social engineering a dicey proposition. Indeed, the corruption and incompetence endemic to government programs are almost entirely absent from their calculations. Transfixed by their own moralism, they cannot imagine that idealism will not guide the day-to-day actions of government regulators.

Nor do most Northern liberals appreciate the need to maintain a variety of infrastructure controls. Mesmerized by a Rousseau-like belief in the essential "goodness" of mankind, they suppose that old-fashioned values can be jettisoned without peril. Fixated on collectivist visions of total human equality, they forget that freedom is a recent acquisition. Because we are an hierarchical species, in which contests for priority are eternal, and because we are a violent and creative species in which cheating is always possible, we need normative controls we are jointly prepared to enforce. Sometimes nice, but sometimes not; sometimes rational, but sometimes foolish, we cannot always predict the outcomes of our efforts. As a result, we require safeguards. Beyond our dreams of perfection, we need a hedge against our potential extremism.[45]

As the industrial, and now the information, revolution, gains impetus, the simple ideas that inspired collectivist reformers must be modified by a consciousness of the complexities of an advanced marketplace economy. Those at its helm, that is, the middle classes, whether North or South, must adjust to a loss of innocence. It may be painful to recognize that ideals of perfect equality and total cooperation are fatuous, but people must deal with this. Although it is confusing to accept a lack of micro-control, this is the reality. We must instead content ourselves with pursuing the possible. This, of course, means more piecemeal interventions and a ceding of decentralized controls to others.

What happened with school busing is a useful alarm. When Northern liberals decided that the only effective way to achieve integrated schools was the physical redistribution of students, they assumed that busing would do the trick. In retrospect it is clear that they did not calculate the revulsion of working class parents who, when picketing did not work, resorted to white flight. Shocked into passivity by years of roadblocks—roadblocks that ultimately removed the conditions necessary for physical integration—the liberal elites did not give up the busing ideal. Rather, they retreated into a moralistic denial. Busing came to be taken for granted in the urban landscape, even though it did not substantially increase integration or significantly improve the academic performance of black students. Nevertheless, to recognize the failure of the philosophy behind it was unthinkable. It would have required the rearrangement of an entire social perspective. Yet this is precisely the sort of painful change many Northerners have still to confront.

A SHARED HUMANITY

For several centuries, the American experiment has been dogged by racial conflicts. The oppression whites have visited on blacks, or the resentments of blacks feel toward whites, have fueled antagonisms that do not seem to die down. What many have concluded is that a blood feud has left the races natural enemies. But this enmity has the possibility of being ephemeral. Despite the millions of injuries which have been inflicted, and the millions of not yet healed wounds, African and European-Americans share a community of interest upon which they can erect a stable system of alliances. Collectivist philosophers may disparage the accomplishments of our market economy and democratic republic, but their successes have provided Americans—all Americans—with a legacy of freedom and prosperity that no other people has ever enjoyed. It is, therefore, in our interest not to kill the golden goose.

An open class system is an essential element of such a settlement. A modus operandi that freely enables people to rise and fall based upon their own efforts and abilities is an equitable arrangement and ultimately a color-blind one, for it depends on the humanity of those involved and not their racial origins. Since both blacks and whites are human beings, with comparable levels of intelligence and aggression, in the end their relative positions will depend on what they produce. This final consummation may be delayed by cultural and structural factors that interfere with optimal performances, but these can be overcome. Human nature may be such that people wish to tinker with the machinery in counterproductive ways, but ordinary human motives, coupled with commonplace socioeconomic forces, are poised to make this happen regardless of the ill-considered meddling.

The secret to a successful class system is treating people on the basis of their humanity. Rather than respond to social categories, one's role partners must be individuated. Each must be given credit for what he or she has individually accomplished and blame for what has been personally mangled. Jane Elliott, no doubt, would disparage this approach. She ridicules the possibility of whites being color-blind. According to her, when they claim this as their goal, they are being hypocritical.[46] But Elliott misses the point. Color-blind does not literally mean blind to color. It means not perceiving color as a discriminatory factor. Elijah Anderson's experience indicates that this is possible. He records cases of inner-city blacks perfectly capable of dealing with whites as human beings.[47] My experience seconds this. When I worked as a counselor at a methadone program where about half of my clients and colleagues were black, at one point someone asked me about the color of another. For a moment I was stymied. I had thought about this third party as a particular human being. It was necessary to close my eyes and visualize him before I could report his race. This is what I mean by color blind. It is a state in which the individual matters most and his racial affiliation is irrelevant.

Critics such as Elliott grossly underestimate what is possible for whites (and incidentally, blacks). Trapped in a moralistic universe, they routinely trash their rivals. Victimized by liberal stereotypes, they fail to individualize European-Americans. Yes, racism persists, but in a greatly attenuated form. And yes, some whites are viciously exploitive of blacks, but they have become the minority. Though change has been slow, it has been indefatigable. It may take centuries more before racism is completely eradicated, but long before this it will have become so diminished that ordinary African-Americans will not have to worry about it.

Notes and References

CHAPTER 1: MORAL INVISIBILITY

1. See: Gould, S.J. (1981) *The Mismeasure of Man*. New York: W.W. Norton.
2. The roots of this belief can probably be traced to anthropology. As Lee Baker notes "There is a rich and important history with regard to how generations of anthropologists have moved to a "no-race" position." See: Baker, L.D. (1998) *From Savage to Negro: Anthropology and the Construction of Race, 1896-1954*. Berkeley: University of California Press. Among the most active and influential in this effort was Ashley Montagu. His political acumen in influencing the United Nation's definition of race is a milestone of scientific advocacy. See: Montagu, M.F.A. (1942) *Man's Most Dangerous Myth: The Fallacy of Race*. New York: Columbia University Press.
3. Marger, M.N. (1997) *Race and Ethnic Relations: American and Global Perspectives:* 4th Edition. Belmont, CA: Wadsworth. pp.19-23.
4. In Ferrante, J. and Brown, P. (1998) *The Social Construction of Race and Ethnicity in the United States*. New York: Longman. See especially: Prince Brown, p.131-137.
5. Dyer, R. (1997) *White*. New York: Routledge. Broader discussions of how race has been defined in the United States can be found in: Haney Lopez, I.F. (1996) *White by Law: The Legal Construction of Race*. New York: New York University Press and Jacobson, M.F. (1998) *Whiteness of a Different Color: European Immigrants and the Alchemy of Race*. Cambridge, MA: Harvard University Press.
6. Aguirre, A. Jr., and Turner, J.H. (1998) *American Ethnicity: The Dynamics and Consequences of Discrimination*. 2nd Edition. New York: McGraw-Hill, p.2.
7. How sociologists have dealt with the concept of race during this past century is reviewed in McKee, J. B. (1993) *Sociology and the Race Problem: The Failure of a Perspective*. Urbana: University of Illinois Press.
8. Graham, R. (Ed.) (1990) *The Idea of Race in Latin America, 1870-(1940*. Austin: University of Texas Press.
9. The concept of race itself has a history. In the (19th century it was commonly used as we today employ that of "ethnicity," hence the references to "the British race" or "the Jewish race. Nowadays a similar elision is in the works, excepting that the common features thought to tie these concepts together are cultural rather than biological, hence the references to "African-Americans" and "European-Americans." See: Smedley, A. (1999) *Race in North America: Origin and Evolution of a Worldview*. Boulder, CO: Westview Press. Efforts, such as that of Lewontin, to demonstrate that race is a myth, have their own difficulties. They seem to rely more on ideology than hard empirical evidence. See: Lewontin, R.C., Rose, S., and Kamin, C.J. (1984) *Not In Our Genes: Biology, Ideology and Human Nature*. New York: Pantheon Books. Even Stephen J. Gould's estimable work on the mismeasure of race succumbs to a moralistic desire to disprove the existence of race. Gould, op. cit.
10. The philosopher Ludwig Wittgenstein described these continuums as "family resemblances." See: Wittgenstein, L. (1953) *Philosophical Investigations*. New York: MacMillan. Another example of this phenomenon would be color continuums wherein people make a distinction between orange and yellow despite the fact that there exists no determinate boundary between the two and despite the reality that some shades of orange are closer to yellow than to other shades of orange.
11. Money, J. and Ehrhardt, A. (1972) *Man and Woman; Boy and Girl*. Baltimore: Johns Hopkins University Press.
12. Entines succinct review of race theory is one of the best available. See: Entine, J. (2000) *Taboo: Why Black Athletes Dominate Sports and Why We Are Afraid to Talk About It*. New York: Public Affairs.

13. No less an authority than W.E.B. DuBois has affirmed the salience of these distinctions. He states that "there are differences—subtle, delicate, and elusive, though they may be—which have silently but definitely separated men into groups.... At all times...they have divided human beings into races, which while they perhaps transcended scientific definition, nevertheless, are clearly defined in the eye of the Historian and the Sociologist." How ironic this last gesture now seems! Quoted in: Huggins N. (Ed.) (1986) *W.E.B. Du Bois: Writings.* New York: Library of America.
14. Cavalli-Sforza, L., Menozzi, P., and Piazza. A. (1994) *The History and Geography of Human Genes.* Princeton, NJ: University of Princeton Press, and Cavalli-Sforza, L. and Cavalli-Sforza, F. (1995) *The Great Human Diasporas.* Reading, MA: Perseus Books. For a divergent view see: Wolpoff, M. and Caspari, R. (1997) *Race and Human Evolution: A Fatal Attraction.* New York: Simon & Schuster.
15. Wolpoff, M. and Caspari, R., Ibid.
16. As Entine puts it "between group variability is far larger than has been believed" with "genetic evidence [appearing] to point to three migratory waves out of Africa, one to Oceana, one to Asia and subsequently to America, and a third one predominately to Europe." Entine, op. cit.
17. Ellison, R. (1947) *Invisible Man.* New York: Random House.
18. Thernstrom, S. and Thernstrom, A. (1997) *America in Black and White: One Nation, Indivisible.* New York: Simon & Schuster.
19. Pat Bidol, along with a plethora of recent textbook writers is explicit about the connection. The formulation presented is: Power + Prejudice = Racism. See: Bidol, P.A. *Developing New Perspectives on Race.* As Larry Elder has noted, saying blacks are racist is now taboo. See: Elder, L. (2000) *The Ten Things You Can't Say in America.* New York: St. Martin's Press.
20. Asante, M.K. (1988) *Afrocentricity.* Trenton, NJ: Africa World Press.
21. Hardly an "Aunt Thomasa," Ladner has written such influential works as: Ladner, J. (1971) *Tommorow's Tomorrow: The Black Woman.* New York: Doubleday & Co; Ladner, J. (Ed.) (1973) *The Death of White Sociology.* New York: Random House.
22. Steele, S. (1998) *A Dream Deferred: The Second Betrayal of Black Freedom in America.* New York: HarperCollins.
23. Herrnstein, R.J. and Murray, C. (1994) *The Bell Curve: The Reshaping of American Life by Differences in Intelligence.* New York: Basic Books.
24. Peters, W. and Beutel, B. (1970) *The Eye of the Storm.* Mount Kisco, NY: ABC Media Concepts; Center for Humanities.
25. A scene in which the children energetically tore up their arm-bands at the conclusion of their period of isolation was especially evocative.
26. Sowell, T. (1984) *Civil Rights: Rhetoric or Reality?* New York: William Morrow. In *The Limits of Idealism* I have discussed this as the "civil rights ideal." See: Fein, M. (1999) *The Limits of Idealism: When Good Intentions Go Bad.* New York: Plenum Publishing.
27. Myrdal, G. (1944) *An American Dilemma: The Negro Problem and American Democracy.* New York: Harper & Row.
28. Farley, R. (1996) *The New American Reality: Who We Are, How We Got Here, Where We Are Going.* New York: Russell Sage Foundation.
29. Thernstrom, S. and Thernstrom, A. (1997) op. cit.
30. Sniderman, P.M. and Piazza, T. (1993) *The Scar of Race.* Cambridge, MA: The Belknap Press of Harvard University Press. Sniderman, P.M. and Carmines, E.G. (1998) *Reaching Beyond Race.* Cambridge, MA: Harvard University Press.
31. Steele, S. (1990) *The Content of Our Character: A New Vision of Race in America.* New York: St. Martin's Press.
32. Entine, J. (2000) op. cit.
33. How social work texts approach these matters is exemplified by: Zastrow, C. and Krist-Ashman, K. (1990). *Understanding Human Behavior and the Social Environment,* 2nd Edition. Chicago: Nelson-Hall. A clinical sociology approach is found in: Rebach, H. M. and Bruhn, J. G. (Eds.) (1991) *Clinical Sociology: An Agenda for Action.* New York: Plenum Publishing.

34. Demott, B. (1990) *The Imperial Middle: Why American Can't Think Straight About Class.* New Haven: Yale University Press.
35. Swartz, D. (1997) *Culture and Power: The Sociology of Pierre Bourdieu.* Chicago: University of Chicago Press; Bourdieu, P. (1980) *The Logic of Practice.* Stanford, CA: Stanford University Press; Shusterman, R. (Ed.) (1999) *Bourdieu: A Critical Reader.* Malden, MA: Blackwell.
36. Stampp, K.M. (1956) *The Peculiar Institution: Slavery in the Ante-Bellum South.* New York: Alfred A. Knopf. Blassingame, J.W. (1979) *The Slave Community: Plantation Life in the Antebellum South.* New York: Oxford University Press.
37. The concept of caste was probably introduced into the discussion of American race relations by the anthropologist W. Lloyd Warner. See: Warner, W.L. (1936) American caste and class. *American Journal of Sociology,* Sept. 42: pp. 234-37. See also: Dollard, J. (1937) *Caste and Class in a Southern Town.* New Haven: Yale University Press. Myrdal too recognized caste as a useful construct, as does Kenneth Stampp. See: Myrdal, G. (1944) *An American Dilemma: The Negro Problem and American Democracy.* New York: Harper & Row; and Stampp, K.M. (1965) *The Era of Reconstruction: 1865-1877.* New York: Vintage Books. The concept is nevertheless not without controversy. In some quarters its acceptance is contingent on the proviso that America has a "caste-like" system. See: Willie, C.V. (1979) *The Caste and Class Controversy.* New York: General Hall. For an overview from a conflict perspective see: Smaje, C. (2000) *Natural Hierarchies: The Historical Sociology of Race and Caste.* Malden, MA: Blackwell. And: Dumont, L. (1970) *Homo Hierarchicus: The Caste System and Its Implications.* Chicago: University of Chicago Press.
38. Bannister, R.C. (1979) *Social Darwinism: Science and Myth in Anglo-American Social Thought.* Philadelphia: Temple University Press.
39. Washington, B.T. (1901) [1985] *Up From Slavery.* New York: Oxford University Press.
40. Ellis, J.J. (1996) *American Sphinx: The Character of Thomas Jefferson.* New York: Alfred A. Knopf. Mapp, A.J. Jr. (1987) *Thomas Jefferson: A Strange Case of Mistaken Identity.* New York: Madison Books.
41. Putnam, R.D. (1993) *Making Democracy Work: Civic Traditions in Modern Italy.* Princeton, NJ: Princeton University Press.
42. de Tocqueville, A. (1966) *Democracy in America.* Trans. by George Lawrence. New York: Harper & Row.
43. See the issue of affirmative action in Meyers, S.L. (Ed.) (1997) *Civil Rights and Race Relations in the Post Reagan-Bush Era.* Westport, CT: Praeger.
44. Majors, R. and Billson, J.M. (1993) *The Cool Pose: The Dilemma of Black Manhood in America.* New York: Simon & Schuster.
45. Ravitch, D. and Finn, C.E. Jr. (1987) *What Do Our Seventeen-Year Olds Know?* New York: Harper & Row. For a further discussion see: Glazer, N. (1997) *We Are All Multiculturalists Now.* Cambridge, MA: Harvard University Press.
46. Gilbert, D. and Kahl, J.A. (1993) *The American Class Structure.* 4th Edition. Belmont, CA: Wadsworth Publishing. Kohn, M. (1969) *Class and Conformity: A Study in Values.* Homewood, IL.: The Dorsey Press.
47. Hochschild, J. (1995) *Facing Up to the American Dream.* Princeton, NJ: Princeton University Press. Cose, E. (1993) *The Rage of a Privileged Class.* New York: HarperCollins. —And references too numerous to cite.
48. Fein, M. (1993) *I.A.M.: A Common Sense Guide to Coping with Anger.* Westport, CT: Praeger.
49. Wolfe, A. (1998) *One Nation, After All.* New York: Viking.
50. McBride, J. (1996) *The Color of Water: A Black Man's Tribute to His White Mother.* New York: Riverhead Books.
51. DuBois, W.E.B. [1903] (1990) *The Souls of Black Folk.* New York: Vintage Books.
52. Ogburn, W. [1922] (1966) *Social Change with Respect to Culture and Original Nature.* New York: Heubsch.
53. Park, R. (1950) *Race and Culture.* Glencoe, IL: The Free Press.

54. The inability of Baby Doc Duvalier to sustain the Haitian dictatorship initiated by his father Papa Doc, despite the most careful grooming, is a case in point.
55. Not even Robert Park's contact-conflict-accommodation-assimilation model proved up to explicating the complexities inherent in assimilating a host of disparate immigrants. The difficulties in doing so have been discussed in numerous sources. For a sampling see: Park, R. (1950) op. cit; Alba, R.D. (1990) *Ethnic Identity: The Transformation of White America*. New Haven: Yale University Press; Alba, R. and Nee, V. (1997) Rethinking assimilation theory for a new era of immigration. *International Migration Review*. Vol.31, No.4, Winter, pp.826-874: Glazer, N. and Moynihan, D.P. (Ed.) (1975) *Ethnicity: Theory and Experience*. Cambridge, MA: Harvard University Press; Handlin, O. (1951) *The Uprooted*. Boston: Little, Brown and Co; Howe, I. (1976) *The World of Our Fathers*. New York: Harcourt, Brace, Jovanovich, Publishers; Gordon, M.M. (1964) *Assimilation in American Life: The Role of Race, Religion, and National Origins*. New York: Oxford University Press.

CHAPTER 2: MORAL ENEMIES

1. Carr, L.G. (1997) *"Color-Blind" Racism*. Thousand Oaks, CA: Sage.
2. McBride, J. (1996) *The Color of Water: A Black Man's Tribute to His White Mother*. New York: Riverhead Books.
3. Tamar Jacoby describes similar sensitivities among black reporters in a newsroom where she worked. Jacoby, T. (1998) *Someone Else's House: America's Unfinished Struggle for Integration*. New York: The Free Press.
4. D'Souza, D. (1995) *The End of Racism: Principles for a Multiracial Society*. New York: 1The Free Press.
5. See Chapter 3 for additional confirmation.
6. See Majors, R. and Billson, J.M. (1993) *The Cool Pose: The Dilemma of Black Manhood in America*. New York: Simon & Schuster. Anderson, E. (1999) *The Code of the Street: Decency, Violence and the Moral Life of the Inner City*. New York: W.W. Norton.
7. Loury, G.C. (1995) "The End of Relativism," *The Weekly Standard*, Sept. 25.
8. Monk, R.C. (1996) *Taking Sides: Race and Ethnicity, Second Edition*. Guilford, CT: Dushkin.
9. For examples see: Leo, J. (1994) *Two Steps Ahead of the Thought Police*. New York: Simon & Schuster; Kors, A.C. and Silverglate, H.A. (1998) *The Shadow University: The Betrayal of Liberty on America's Campuses*. New York: The Free Press.
10. Ignatiev, N. (1995) *How the Irish Became White*. New York: Routledge.
11. Jesse Jackson, among others, has also cited this calumny.
12. Sowell, T. (1984) *Civil Rights: Rhetoric or Reality?* New York: William Morrow.
13. Sowell, T. (1981) *Ethnic America*. New York: Basic Books.
14. Evidence for the existence of this elite can be found in: Benjamin, L. (1991) *The Black Elite: Facing the Color Line in the Twilight of the Twentieth Century*. Chicago: Nelson-Hall.
15. Whereas before World War II blacks were habitually held responsible for solving the "race problem," since the (1950's, especially in disciples such as sociology, the onus has decidedly switched to whites. See: McKee, J. B. (1993) *Sociology and the Race Problem: The Failure of a Perspective*. Urbana: University of Illinois Press.

16. One such work is: DuCille, A. (1996) *Skin Trade.* Cambridge, MA: Harvard University Press.
17. Among the attitudinal changes revealed by survey research are the following. Whereas in 1942 only 32% of whites favored integrated schools by 1995 96% said they did. Similarly in 1944 only 45% of whites advocated giving blacks equal job opportunity, but as early as 1972 97% did. Comparable shifts have also been documented in expressed attitudes toward segregated public facilities, residential housing patterns, and intermarriage. See: Schuman, H., Steeh, C., Bobo, L., and Kysman, M. (1997) *Racial Attitudes in America: Trends and Interpretations. Revised Edition.* Cambridge, MA: Harvard University Press.
18. One of the most extensive exposes of the calumnies to which whites are exposed is: Horowitz, D. (1999) *Hating Whitey and Other Progressive Causes.* Dallas: Spence Publishing. Rather revealingly, Horowitz relates that the white publishers of his best selling autobiography were so spooked by the subject that they refused to bring his new work to market. Seee also: Cheney, L.V. (1995) *Telling the Truth: Why Our Culture and Our Country Have Stopped Making Sense.* New York: Simon & Schuster, and MacDonald, H. (2000) *The Burden of Bad Ideas: How Modern Intellectuals Misshape Our Society.* Chicago: Ivan R. Dee.
19. National Education Association. (1973) *Education and Racism.*
20. Before World War II, it was blacks who were more likely to be castigated for their immorality. The virulence of these charges is attested in the words of Howard Odum. He authoritatively observed that: "nurtured with some hatred of whites, taught no morals, with a fanatical religion, itself leading to erratic actions, with little regard for common decency, and bred in filth and adultery, the negro is considered peculiarly liable to crime." See: Odum, H.W. (1910) *Social and Mental Traits of the Negro.* New York: Columbia University Press. The same attitude is on display in the textbooks of the era. See: Ellwood, C.A. (1924) *Sociology and Modern Social Problems.* New York: American Book.
21. *Ebony* (1992) *Who Get's Welfare?* December.
22. Jeanne Thornton and David Whitman with Dorian Friedman *U.S. News & World Report.* Whites' myths about blacks, Nov. 9, 1992, pp.41, 43-44.
23. For example in: Finsterbusch, K. (Ed.) (1997/98) *Annual Editions, Sociology.* Guilford, CT: Dushkin.
24. More recently the Amadou Diallo affair did the same. The publicity generated by Diallo's unjust death in a fusillade of police bullets was likewise used to impugn the motives of law enforcement agents. See MacDonald, H. op cit.
25. Cannon, L. (1997) *Official Negligence: How Rodney King and the Riots Changed Los Angeles and the LAPD.* New York: Times Books.
26. Sacks, D.O. and Thiel, P.A. (1995) *The Diversity Myth: "Multiculturalism" and the Politics of Intolerance at Stanford.* Oakland, CA: The Independent Institute.
27. Apparently other blacks, including law professors, are under this impression. See: Farber, D.A. and Sherry, S. (1997) *Beyond All Reason: The Radical Assault on Truth in American Law.* New York: Oxford University Press.
28. Lefkowitz, M. (1996) *Not Out of Africa: How Afrocentrism Became an Excuse to Teach Myth as History.* New York: Basic Books.
29. Numerous examples of this "gotcha" mentality have sprung up on American campuses of late. The best chroniclers of the phenomena are: Kors, A.C. and Silverglate, H.A. (1998) *The Shadow University: The Betrayal of Liberty on America's Campuses.* New York: The Free Press.
30. Schlesinger, A.M. (1992) *The Disuniting of America.* New York: W.W. Norton.

31. Steele, S. (1990) *The Content of Our Character: A New Vision of Race in America.* New York: St. Martin's Press.
32. Steele, S. (1998) *A Dream Deferred: The Second Betrayal of Black Freedom in America.* New York: HarperCollins.
33. Fein, M. (1997) *Hardball Without an Umpire: The Sociology of Morality.* Westport, CT: Praeger.
34. Fukuyama, F. (1999) The Great Disruption. *The Atlantic Monthly,* May, p.77.
35. Ellis, R.J. (1998) *The Dark Side of the Left: Illiberal Egalitarianism in America.* Lawrence, Kansas: University of Kansas Press.
36. Nietzsche, F. (1989) *Beyond Good and Evil.* (Translated by Helen Zimmern) New York: Prometheus Books.
37. Wolfe, A. (1998) *One Nation, After All.* New York: Viking.
38. Even legal scholars have taken to insisting that legal "truths" are determined by what "stories" one accepts. See: Farber, D.A. and Sherry, S. (1997) op. cit.
39. Durkheim, E. (1915) *The Elementary Forms of Religious Life.* New York: The Free Press; Durkheim, E. (1933) *The Division of Labor in Society.* New York: The Free Press; Durkheim, E. (1961) *Moral Education.* New York: The Free Press.
40. Fein, M. (1997) *Hardball Without an Umpire: The Sociology of Morality.* Westport, CT: Praeger.
41. See for instance: Gould, S.J. (1989) *Wonderful Life: The Burgess Shale and the Nature of Life.* New York: W.W. Norton Co.: Gould, S.J. (1993. *Eight Little Piggies: Reflections in Natural History.* New York: W.W. Norton.
42. Steele, S. (1990) op. cit; Steele, S. (1998) op cit.
43. Cayton, H.R. and Drake, St. C. (1946) *Black Metropolis.* London: Jonathan Cape.
44. Fisher, C.S., Hout, M., Sanchez Jankowski, M., Lucas, S.R., Swindler, A.. and Voss, K. (1996) *Inequality by Design: Cracking the Bell Curve Myth.* Princeton, NJ: Princeton University Press. Herrnstein missed the excitement, having unfortunately died before it got going.
45. See Becker, H. (Ed.) (1964) *The Other Side.* New York: Free Press; Becker, H. (1973) *The Outsiders: Studies in the Sociology of Deviance.* New York: The Free Press.
46. Sharpton, of course, has employed the same tactics many times, including in the Amadou Diallo affair.
47. Thernstrom, S. and Thernstrom, A. (1997) *America in Black and White: One Nation, Indivisible.* New York: Simon & Schuster.

CHAPTER 3: "DIED OF A THEORY"

1. See: Ballard, M.B. (1997) *The Long Shadow: Jefferson Davis and the Final Days of the Confederacy.* Athens: University of Georgia Press.
2. West, C. (1993) *Race Matters.* Boston: Beacon Press.
3. D'Souza, D. (1995) *The End of Racism: Principles for a Multiracial Society.* New York: The Free Press.
4. Brinkerhoff, D.B., White, L.K., and Riedmann, A.C. (1997) *Sociology,* 4th Edition. Belmont, CA: Wadsworth Press.
5. Appelbaum, R.P. and Chambliss, W.J. (1997) *Sociology,* 2nd Edition. New York: Longman.
6. Fong, T.P. (1998) *The Contemporary Asian American Experience: Beyond the Model Minority.* Upper Saddle River, NJ: Prentice-Hall.
7. Farley, J.E. (1995) *Majority-Minority Relations, Third Edition.* Englewood Cliffs, NJ: Prentice-Hall.

8. Allport, G. (1954) *The Nature of Prejudice*. Boston: Beacon Press.
9. Marger, M.N. (1997) *Race and Ethnic Relations: American and Global Perspectives:* 4th Edition. Belmont, CA: Wadsworth.
10. Shibutani, T. and Kwan, K. (1965) *Ethnic Stratification*. New York: MacMillan.
11. For other texts that come to similar conclusions see: Schaefer, R.T. (1996) *Racial and Ethnic Groups*, 6th Edition. New York: HarperCollins. Kitano, H.H. (1997) *Race Relations*, 5th Edition. Upper Saddle River, NJ: Prentice-Hall. Rose, P.I. (1997) *They and We: Racial and Ethnic Relations in the United States*, 5th Edition. New York: McGraw-Hill.
12. Mihesuah, D.A. (1996) *American Indians: Stereotypes and Realities*. Atlanta, GA: Clarity Press.
13. Luigi Luca Cavalli-Sforza would disagree. He presents genetic evidence to the contrary. See: Cavalli-Sforza, L. L. and Cavalli-Sforza, F. (1995) *The Great Human Diasporas*. Reading, MA: Perseus Books.
14. Called *Innovative Techniques for Teaching Sociological Concepts*, it is regularly updated by the ASA.
15. Leo, J. (1994) *Two Steps Ahead of the Thought Police*. New York: Simon & Schuster.
16. Park, R. (1950) *Race and Culture*. Glencoe, IL: The Free Press.
17. Aguirre, A., Jr., and Turner, J.H. (1998) *American Ethnicity: The Dynamics and Consequences of Discrimination*. 2nd Edition. New York: McGraw-Hill.
18. An anthropologist colleague, Wayne Van Horne, tells me that he gets similar results when he inquires into the stereotypes of Southerners versus Northerners. Van Horne, W. (1998) *Damn Yankees and Rednecks: Cultural Values, Communication Styles, and Stereotypes of Northerners and Southerners*. (unpublished paper)
19. D'Souza, D. (1995) *The End of Racism: Principles for a Multiracial Society*. New York: The Free Press.
20. Oliver, W. (1994) *The Violent Social World of Black Men*. New York: Lexington Books.
21. Richard Rodgers and Oscar Hammerstein's *South Pacific*. In: Rodgers, R. and Hammerstein, O. (1981) *Archives of Recorded Sound of Rodgers and Hammerstein*. Boston: G.R. Hall.
22. Wrong, D. (1961) The oversocialized conception of man in modern sociology. *American Sociological Review*, Vol.26, No.2.
23. West, T.G. (1997) *Vindicating the Founders: Race, Sex, Class, and Justice in the Origins of America*. Lanham, MD: Rowman & Littlefield Publishers.
24. Banaji, M.R. and Greenwald, A.G. (1994) Implicit stereotyping and prejudice. In: Zanna, M.P. and Olsen, J.M. (Eds.) *The Psychology of Prejudice: The Ontario Symposium*. Hillsdale, NJ: Lawrence Erlbaum Associates; Brewer, M.B. (1988) A dual process model of impression formation. In: Wyler, R.S., Jr., and Srull, T.K. (Eds.), *Advances in Social Cognition*, Vol.1. Hillsdale, NJ: Lawrence Erlbaum Associates; Devine, P.G. (1989) Stereotypes and prejudice: Their automatic and controlled components. *Journal of Personality and Social Psychology*, 56, 5-18; Paul, Anne Murphy (1998) Where bias begins: The truth about stereotypes. *Psychology Today*, 52-55, 82, May, June.
25. Schutz, A. (1970) *On Phenomenology and Social Relations*. Chicago: University of Chicago Press; Smith, T.A. and O'Connell, L. (1997) *Black Anxiety, White Guilt, and the Politics of Status Frustration*. Westport, CT: Praeger.
26. Parks, E.E. (1997) *White Racial Identity Attitudes and Stereotypes: An Empirical Investigation*. (unpublished dissertation) New York: Columbia University.

27. Mannheim, K. (1936) *Ideology and Utopia*. New York: Harcourt, Brace, and World.
28. Gouldner, A.W. (1970) *The Coming Crisis of Western Sociology*. New York: Basic Books.
29. Piattelli-Palmarini, M. (1994) *Inevitable Illusions: How Mistakes of Reason Rule Our Minds*. New York: John Wiley & Sons.
30. Sutherland, S. (1992) *Irrationality: Why We Don't Think Straight!* New Brunswick, NJ: Rutgers University Press.
31. Parks, E.E. (1997) op. cit.
32. de Tocqueville, A. (1966) *Democracy in America*. Trans. by George Lawrence. New York: Harper & Row.
33. Hirschfeld, L.A. (1996) *Race in the Making: Cognition, Culture, and the Child's Construction of Human Kinds*. Cambridge, MA: The MIT Press.
34. Hamilton, D.L., Stroessner, S.J. and Driscoll, D.M. (1994) Social cognition and the study of Stereotyping. In: Devine, P.G., Hamilton. D.L.. and Ostrom, T.M. (Eds.) *Social Cognition: Impact on Social Psychology*. San Diego, CA: Academic Press.
35. See Elliott's characterizations of Southerners and Baptists.
36. Toennies, F. (1966) [1887] *Community and Society*. New York: Harper & Row.
37. Anderson, E. (1990) *Streetwise: Race, Class and Change in an Urban Community*. Chicago: University of Chicago Press.
38. Goffman, E. (1959) *The Presentation of Self in Everyday Life*. Garden City, NY: Doubleday.
39. Pettigrew, T.F. (1979) The ultimate attribution error: Extending Allport's cognitive analysis of prejudice. *Personality and Social Psychology Bulletin* Vol.5, pp.461-476.
40. West, C. (1993) op. cit.
41. Illustrations of profiling can be found in: Egger, S.A. (1998) *Killers Among Us: An Examination of Serial Murders and Their Investigation*. Springfield: University of Illinois Press.
42. Steele, C.M., Spencer, S.J., and Lynch, M. (1993) Self-image, resilience and dissonance: The role of affirmational resources. *Journal of Personality and Social Psychology*, Vol.66: pp.885-896.
43. Steele, C.M. (1999) Thin ice: 'stereotype threat' and black college students. *The Atlantic Monthly*, August.
44. For the importance of salience see: Sutherland, S. (1992) *Irrationality: Why We Don't Think Straight!* New Brunswick, NJ: Rutgers University Press.
45. Jones, J.H. (1981) *Bad Blood: The Tuskegee Syphilis Experiment*. New York: The Free Press.
46. An explanation of "luminosity blindness" can be found in: Fein, M. (1999) *Idealism: When Good Intentions Go Bad*. New York: Plenum Publishing
47. Parks, E.E. (1997) op. cit.
48. Hamilton, D.L., Stroessner, S.J., and Driscoll, D.M. (1994) Social cognition and the study of stereotyping. In: Devine, P.G., Hamilton, D.L., and Ostrom, T.M. (Eds.) *Social Cognition: Impact on Social Psychology*. San Diego, CA: Academic Press.
49. Devine, P.G. (1989) Stereotypes and prejudice: Their automatic and controlled components. *Journal of Personality and Social Psychology*, Vol.56, pp.5-18. Helms, J.E. and Piper, R.E. (1994) Implications of racial identity theory for vocational psychology. *Journal of Vocational Behavior*, Vol.44, pp.124-138.
50. A lively review of these developments can be found in: Entine, J. (2000) *Taboo: Why Black Athletes Dominate Sports and Why We Are Afraid to Talk About It*. New York: Public Affairs.

51. Willes, quoted in John Leo, *U.S. News & World Report*, June 29, 1998, p.21.
52. A discussion of "individuating" is found in: Fiske, S.T. and Von Hendy, H.M. (1992) Personality feedback and situational norms can control stereotyping processes. *Journal of Personality and Social Psychology*, Vol.62, pp.577-596.
53. See: Powell, C. with Persico, J.E. (1995) *My American Journey*. New York: Random House.
54. See: Will, G.F. (1997) "Tale of Two Countries." *Newsweek*, Jan. 10. wherein he cites the work of a young inner-city teacher, Mark Gerson (1997), as evidence of what can be done. See also: Gerson, M. (1997) *In the Classroom: Dispatches from an Inner-City School that Works*. New York: The Free Press.

CHAPTER 4: THE AMERICAN CREED

1. Gibbon, E. (1960) *The Decline and Fall of the Roman Empire*. New York: Harcourt Brace.
2. Samuelson, R. (1996) *The Good Life and Its Discontents: The American Dream in the Age of Entitlement (1945-1995)* New York: Times Books.
3. Fukuyama, F. (1999) The Great Disruption. *The Atlantic Monthly*, May.
4. Himmelfarb, G. (1995) *The De-Moralization of Society: From Victorian Virtues to Modern Values*. New York: Alfred A. Knopf. And: Himmelfarb, G. (1999) *One Nation, Two Cultures*. New York: Alfred A. Knopf. Also: Hunter, J.D. (2000) *The Death of Character: Moral Education in an Age Without Good and Evil*. New York: Basic Books.
5. Moynihan, D.P. (1993) Defining deviancy down. *American Scholar*, Winter, Vol.62., No.1.
6. Coontz, S. (1992) *The Way We Never Were: American Families and the Nostalgia Trap*. New York: Basic Books.
7. Popenoe, D. (1996) *Life Without Father: Compelling New Evidence that Fatherhood and Marriage Are Indispensable for the Good of Children and Society*. New York: The Free Press.
8. Wilson, J.Q. and Kelling, G.L. (1982) Broken windows: The police and neighborhood safety. *Atlantic Monthly*, March.
9. Etzioni, A. (1993) *The Spirit of Community: The Reinvention of American Society*. New York: Simon & Schuster.
10. Wolfe, A. (1998) *One Nation, After All*. New York: Viking.
11. Bennett, W.J. (1998) *The Death of Outrage: Bill Clinton and the Assault on American Ideals*. New York: The Free Press.
12. Clinton, H.R. (1996) *It Takes a Village: and Other Lessons Children Teach Us*. New York: Simon & Schuster.
13. Etzioni, A. (1993) op. cit.
14. Wolfe, A. (1989) *Whose Keeper?* Berkeley, CA: University of California Press.
15. Hearn, F. (1997) *Moral Order and Social Disorder: The American Search for Civil Society*. New York: Aldine de Gruyter.
16. Durkheim, E. (1915) *The Elementary Forms of Religious Life*. New York: The Free Press.
17. Putnam, R.D. (1996) The strange disappearance of civic America. *The American Prospect*, Winter, pp.34-48.
18. Jackson, J.J. (1987) *Straight from the Heart*. (Edited by Roger D. Hatch and Frank E. Watkins). Philadelphia: Fortress Press.

19. A particularly noxious variation on the theme of moralism assures us that because science cannot be value-neutral, we can never rid ourselves of our biases. Thus in an appendix to his magnum opus Gunnar Myrdal informs us that "the attempt to eradicate biases by trying to keep out the valuations themselves is a hopeless and misdirected venture." Ironically, the biases of these moralists are themselves held to be harmless, whereas those of their opponents are subject to vigorous repression. See: Myrdal, G. (1944) *An American Dilemma: The Negro Problem and American Democracy*. New York: Harper & Row.

20. Myrdal, G. (1944) ibid.

21. Ellis, J.J. (1996) *American Sphinx: The Character of Thomas Jefferson*. New York: Alfred A. Knopf.

22. Thomas West in his *Vindicating the Founders: Race, Sex, Class, and Justice in the Origins of America* (1997), Lanham, MD: Rowman & Littlefield Publishers, puts this succinctly. Discussing the Declaration of Independence and several state ordinances, he affirms that, "Each of these formulas has the same meaning. All human beings are equal in the sense of possessing the same natural rights to life liberty and the pursuit of happiness."

23. Ellis, J.J. (1993) *Passionate Sage: The Character and Legacy of John Adams*. New York: W.W. Norton.

24. Hochschild, J. (1995) *Facing Up to the American Dream*. Princeton, NJ: Princeton University Press.

25. Coleman, J.S., Campbell, E.Q, Hobson, C.J., McPartland, J., Mood, A.M., Weinfeld, F.D., and York, R.L. (1966) *Equality of Educational Opportunity*. Washington, D.C.: U.S. Government Printing Office.

26. Marx, K. (1967) *Das Capital. Edited by F. Engels. Translated by Samuel Moore and Edward Aveling*. New York: International Publishing.

27. Sowell. T. (1999) *The Quest for Cosmic Justice*. New York: The Free Press.

28. Cruse, H. (1967) *The Crisis of the Negro Intellectual: A Historical Analysis of the Failure of Black Leadership*. New York: William Morrow.

29. Sniderman, P.M. and Carmines, E.G. (1998) *Reaching Beyond Race*. Cambridge, MA: Harvard University Press.

30. Parsons, T. (1951) *The Social System*. New York: The Free Press.

31. Staddon, J. (1995) On responsibility and punishment. *The Atlantic Monthly*, February, pp.88-94.

32. Rogers, C. (1951) *Client Centered Therapy*. Boston: Houghton-Mifflin.

33. Knight, R.H. (1998) *The Age of Consent: The Rise of Relativism and the Corruption of Popular Culture*. Dallas: Spence. It should be noted that, as Evertt Ladd's research confirms, Americans still place a higher valuation on individualism than most others. See: Ladd, E. C. (1999) *The Ladd Report*. New York: The Free Press.

34. Boas, F. (1928) *Anthropology and Modern Life*. New York: Dover.

35. Westermarck, E. (1960) *Ethical Relativity*. Paterson, NJ: Littlefield, Adams.

36. D'Souza, D. (1995) *The End of Racism: Principles for a Multiracial Society*. New York: The Free Press.

37. Loury, G.C. (1995) The end of relativism, *The Weekly Standard*, Sept. 25.

38. Hochschild, J. (1995) op. cit.

39. Chirot, D. (1994) *Modern Tyrants: The Power and Prevalence of Evil in Our Age*. Princeton: Princeton University Press.

40. Acton, J. (1956) *Essays on Freedom and Power. Introduction by G. Himmelfarb*. London: Thames and Hudson.

41. Rawls, J. (1971) *A Theory of Justice*. Cambridge, MA: The Belknap Press.

42. Most notably in *The Road to Serfdom* where he elaborated the dangers inherent in fascism. See: Hayek, F.A. von (1944) *The Road to Serfdom. With Foreward by John Chamberlain.* Chicago: University of Chicago Press.
43. West, T.G. (1997) op. cit.
44. Ellis, J.J. (1993) op. cit.
45. Madison, J., Hamilton, A. and Jay, J. (1966) *The Federalist Papers. (Eds.) W. Kendall and G.W. Carey.* New Rochelle, NY: Arlington House.
46. Ellis, J.J. (1993) op. cit.
47. Smith, A. (1776) *An Inquiry in the Nature and Causes of the Wealth of Nations.* London: W. Strahan & T. Cadell.
48. Friedman, M. (1962) *Capitalism and Freedom.* Chicago: University of Chicago Press.
49. de Tocqueville, A. (1966) *Democracy in America.* Trans. by George Lawrence. New York: Harper & Row.
50. Putnam, R.D. (1993) *Making Democracy Work: Civic Traditions in Modern Italy.* Princeton, NJ: Princeton University Press, p.167.
51. de Tocqueville, A. (1966) op. cit.
52. Chirot, D. (1994) *How Societies Change.* Thousand Oaks: Pine Forge Press.
53. Orlando Patterson places heavy emphasis on the reaction against slavery as the chief cause of Western allegiance to the value of freedom, but he seriously underestimates the role of the market place. He does not seem to recognize that the possibility of being a "free agent," who independently interacts with other free agents, through the process of buying and selling goods, is a necessary template for modern conceptions of freedom. See: Patterson, O. (1991) *Freedom: Freedom in the Making of Western Culture.* New York: Basic Books.
54. de Tocqueville, A. (1966) op. cit.
55. For an example of what happens when individualism is actively discouraged one can do no better than compare the way baseball is played in the United States and Japan. See: Whiting, R. (1989) *You Gatta Have WA.* New York: Vintage Books.
56. Lipset, S.M. (1996) *American Exceptionalism: A Double-Edged Sword.* New York: W.W. Norton.
57. Bellah, R.N., Madsen, R., Sullivan, W.M., Swindler, A., and Tipton, S.M. (1985) *Habits of the Heart: Individualism and Commitment in American Life.* Berkeley, CA: University of California Press.
58. Rogers, C. (1951) *Client Centered Therapy.* Boston: Houghton Mifflin.
59. Fein, M. (1999) *The Limits of Idealism: When Good Intentions Go Bad.* New York: Plenum Publishing.
60. Magnet, M. (1993) *The Dream and the Nightmare: The Sixties Legacy to the Underclass.* New York: William Morrow.
61. Wolfe, A. (1998) op. cit.
62. Olasky, M. (1992) *The Tragedy of American Compassion.* Washington, D.C.: Regnery.
63. Cantor, N.F. (1997) *Imagining the Law: Common Law and the Foundations of the American Legal System.* New York: HarperCollins.
64. Kennedy, R. (1997) *Race, Crime, and the Law.* New York: Random House.
65. Rothwax, H.J. (1995) *Guilty: The Collapse of Criminal Justice.* New York: Random House. See also Boot, M. (1998) *Out of Order: Arrogance, Corruption and Incompetence on the Bench.* New York: Basic Books.
66. Carter, S.L. (1998) *Civility: Manners, Morals, and Etiquette of a Democracy.* New York: Basic Books.

67. Fukuyama, F. (1995) *Trust: The Social Virtues and the Creation of Prosperity.* New York: The Free Press.
68. Ellis, J.J. (1996) *American Sphinx: The Character of Thomas Jefferson.* New York: Alfred A. Knopf.
69. Bowles, S. (1976) *Schooling in Capitalist America: Educational Reform and the Contradictions of Economic Life.* New York: Basic Books.
70. Herrnstein, R.J. and Murray, C. (1994) *The Bell Curve: The Reshaping of American Life by Differences in Intelligence.* New York: Basic Books.
71. Guy, M.E. (1997) Counterpoint: By thine own voice, shall thou be known. *Public Productivity and Management Review,* Vol.20, No.3, March, pp.237-242.
72. This and subsequent student quotes from Magnet, M. (1993) op. cit.
73. Orlando Patterson offers one of the more cogent defenses for this position. See: Patterson, O. (1997) *The Ordeal of Integration: Progress and Resentment in America's "Racial" Crisis.* Washington, D.C.: Civitas/Counterpoint.
74. Farber, D.A. and Sherry, S. (1997) *Beyond All Reason: The Radical Assault on Truth in American Law.* New York: Oxford University Press.
75. Bell, D. (1987) *And We Are Not Saved: The Elusive Quest for Racial Justice.* New York: Basic Books.
76. Farber, D.A. and Sherry, S. (1997) op. cit, p.4.
77. Some sociological theorists such as Pierre Bourdieu suggest a similar theory to explain how those at the top of the socio-economic heap maintain their dominance. See: Swartz, D. (1997) *Culture and Power: The Sociology of Pierre Bourdieu.* Chicago: University of Chicago Press; Bourdieu, P. (1980) *The Logic of Practice.* Stanford, CA: Stanford University Press.
78. Wolfe, A. (1998) op. cit.
79. Goffman, E. (1959) *The Presentation of Self in Everyday Life.* Garden City, NY: Doubleday.
80. Sutherland, S. (1992) *Irrationality: Why We Don't Think Straight!* New Brunswick, NJ: Rutgers University Press. Depuy, J.P. (Ed.) (1998) *Self-Deception and the Paradoxes of Rationality.* Stanford, CA: CSLI Publications; Gilovich, T. (1991) *How We Know What Isn't So: The Fallibility of Reason in Everyday Life.* New York: The Free Press.
81. Hamilton, R.F. (1996) *The Social Misconstruction of Reality: Validity and Verification in the Scholarly Community.* New Haven: Yale University Press.
82. Allan Bloom was probably the most influential critic of the depredations done to the so-called literary "canon." See: Bloom, A. (1987) *The Closing of the American Mind.* New York: Simon & Schuster.
83. Kimball, R. (1990) *Tenured Radicals: How Politics has Corrupted our Higher Education.* New York: HarperCollins.
84. Kors, A.C. and Silverglate, H.A. (1998) *The Shadow University: The Betrayal of Liberty on America's Campuses.* New York: The Free Press.
85. Mills, C.W. (1959) *The Sociological Imagination.* New York: Oxford University Press.
86. Farber, D.A. and Sherry, S. (1997) op. cit, p.31.
87. Moynihan, D.P. (1965) *The Negro Family: The Case for National Action.* Washington, D.C.: Department of Labor.
88. Coontz, S. (1992) *The Way We Never Were: American Families and the Nostalgia Trap.* New York: Basic Books.
89. Glenn, N. (1997) *Closed Hearts, Closed Minds: The Textbook Story of Marriage.* New York: Institute for American Values. See also Morehouse Research Institute

(1999) *Turning the Corner on Father Absence in Black America.* Atlanta: Morehouse University.

90. American Sociological Association. (1998) *Footnotes.* January.
91. Popenoe, D. (1996) op. cit.
92. Coltrane, S. (1996) *Family Man: Fatherhood, Housework, and Gender Equity.* New York: Oxford University Press. Coltrane, S. (1997) Scientific half-truths and postmodern parody in the family values debate. *Contemporary Sociology,* Vol. 26, No. 1, January pp.9-10.
93. Stacey, J. (1996) *In the Name of the Family: Rethinking Family Values in the Postmodern Age.* Boston, MA: Beacon Press.

CHAPTER 5: THE CULTURE OF SLAVERY: ORIGINS

1. An early, and rather tendentious, rendering of this observation comes from Charles Ellwood who noted that "slavery did not fit the individual or race for a life of freedom and did not raise moral standards much above those of Africa." See: Ellwood, C.A. (1924) *Sociology and Modern Social Problems.* New York: American Book. Robert Putnam makes the same point more felcitously. He says, "Slavery was, in fact, a social system *designed* to destroy social capital among slaves and between slaves and freemen. Well established networks of reciprocity among the oppressed would have raised the risk of rebellion, and egalitarian bonds of sympathy between slave and free would have undermined the very legitimacy of the system." Putnam, R.D. (2000) *Bowling Alone: The Collapse and Revival of American Community.* New York: Simon & Schuster. p. 294.
2. Blassingame, J.W. (1979) *The Slave Community: Plantation Life in the Antebellum South.* New York: Oxford University Press.
3. D'Souza, D. (1995) *The End of Racism: Principles for a Multiracial Society.* New York: The Free Press.
4. To quote Myrdal: "In practically all of its divergences, American Negro culture is not something independent of general American culture. It is a distorted development, or a pathological condition, of the general American Culture. The instability of the Negro family, the inadequacy of educational facilities for Negroes, the emotionalism of the Negro church, the insufficiency and underwholesomeness of Negro recreational activity, the plethora of Negro sociable organizations, the narrowness of interests of the average Negro, the provincialism of his political speculation, the high Negro crime rate, the cultivation of the arts to the neglect of other fields, superstition, personality difficulties, and other characteristic traits are mainly forms of social pathology which, for the most part, are created by the caste pressure." See: Myrdal, G. (1944) *An American Dilemma: The Negro Problem and American Democracy.* New York: Harper & Row.
5. Clark, K.B. (1965) *Dark Ghetto: Dilemmas of Social Power.* New York: Harper & Row.
6. Magnet, M. (1993) *The Dream and the Nightmare: The Sixties Legacy to the Underclass.* New York: William Morrow. For an overview of the dysfunctional consequences of culture for economic development see: Harrison, L.E. and Huntington, S.P. (Eds.) (2000) *Culture Matters: How Values Shape Human Progress.* New York: Basic Books.

7. Attitudes toward cultural explanations have been softening in recent years. There is still some bias against a "culture of slavery," but cultural constructs emanating from more recent events are better accepted. See: Lamont, M. (Ed.) (1999) *The Cultural Territories of race: Black and White Boundaries*. Chicago: University of Chicago Press; Patterson, O. (1998) *Rituals of Blood: Consequences of Slavery in Two American Centuries*. Washington, D.C.: Civitas/Counterpoint; Anderson, E. (1999) *The Code of the Street: Decency, Violence and the Moral Life of the Inner City*. New York: W.W. Norton; Fukuyama, F. (1999) The Great Disruption. *The Atlantic Monthly*, May; Massey, D.S. and Denton, N.A. (1993) *American Apartheid: Segregation and the Making of the Under Class*. Cambridge, MA: Harvard University Press. Harrison, L.E. and Huntington, S.P. (Eds.) (2000) op. cit.

8. Loury, G.C. (1995) The end of relativism, *The Weekly Standard*, Sept. 25.

9. Marger, M.N. (1997) *Race and Ethnic Relations: American and Global Perspectives:* 4th Edition. Belmont, CA: Wadsworth.

10. Hochschild, J. (1995) *Facing Up to the American Dream*. Princeton, NJ: Princeton University Press.

11. Anderson, E. (1990) *Streetwise: Race, Class and Change in an Urban Community*. Chicago: University of Chicago Press.

12. See also: Durneier, M. (1992) *Slim's Table: Race, Respectability and Masculinity*. Chicago: University of Chicago Press.

13. See: Hannerz, U. (1969) *Soul Side: Inquiries into Ghetto Culture and Community*. New York: Columbia University Press.

14. Wilson, W.J. (1987) *The Truly Disadvantaged: The Inner City, the Underclass and Public Policy*. Chicago: University of Chicago Press; Wilson, W.J. (1996) *When Work Disappears: The World of the New Urban Poor*. New York: Alfred A. Knopf.

15. Jencks, C. (1992) *Rethinking Social Policy: Race, Poverty and the Underclass*. Cambridge, MA: Harvard University Press.

16. Wilson, W.J. (1996) op. cit.

17. Massey too blames a concentration of poverty for exacerbating black problems, which he says essentially creates a "culture of segregation." See: Massey, D.S. and Denton, N.A. (1993) *American Apartheid: Segregation and the Making of the Under Class*. Cambridge, MA: Harvard University Press.

18. Park, R. (1950) *Race and Culture*. Glencoe, IL: The Free Press.

19. Washington, B.T. [1901] (1985) *Up From Slavery*. New York: Oxford University Press.

20. Ogburn, W. [1922] (1966) *Social Change with Respect to Culture and Original Nature*. New York: Heubsch.

21. Chirot, D. (1994) *Modern Tyrants: The Power and Prevalence of Evil in Our Age*. Princeton: Princeton University Press.

22. Merton, R.K. (1968) *Social Theory and Social Structure*. New York: The Free Press.

23. Hochschild, J. (1995) op. cit.

24. See especially: Fukuyama, F. (1999) *The Great Disruption: Human Nature and the Reconstitution of Social Order*. New York: Free Press; Patterson, O. (1998) op. cit; Anderson, E. (1999) op. cit.

25. For a special case see Hamilton, R.F. (1996) *The Social Misconstruction of Reality: Validity and Verification in the Scholarly Community*. New Haven: Yale University Press.

26. Fein, M. (1990) *Role Change: A Resocialization Perspective.* New York: Praeger; Biddle, B. (1979. *Role Theory: Expectations, Identities and Behaviors.* New York: Academic Press.

27. Chirot, D. (1994) op. cit.

28. Gerth, H. and Mills, C.W. (Eds.) (1946) *From Max Weber: Essays in Sociology.* New York: Oxford University Press.

29. Fukuyama, F. (1999) op. cit. A compelling example is also provided by: Putnam, R.D. (1993) *Making Democracy Work: Civic Traditions in Modern Italy.* Princeton, NJ: Princeton University Press.

30. Fein, M. (1990) op. cit.

31. Pierre Bourdieu's concept of habitas has similar implications. See: Swartz, D. (1997) *Culture and Power: The Sociology of Pierre Bourdieu.* Chicago: University of Chicago Press.

32. Some recent speculations about the impact of the emotions can be found in: Elster, J. (1999) *Alchemies of the Mind: Rationality and the Emotions.* New York: Cambridge University Press.

33. van der Kolk, B.A., McFarlane, A.C. and Weisaeth, L. (Eds.) (1996) *Traumatic Stress: The Effects of Overwhelming Experience on Mind, Body, and Society.* New York: Guilford.

34. For contemporary reflections on the nature of human agency see: Coleman, J.S. (1990b) *Foundations of Social Theory.* Cambridge MA: Belknap Press; Giddens, A. (1984) *The Constitution of Society.* Berkeley, CA: University of California Press.

35. Sumner, W.G. (1906) *Folkways.* Boston: Gin.

36. Gerson, M. (Ed.) (1996) *The Essential Neo-Conservative Reader.* Reading, MA: Addison-Wesley.

37. Gates, H.L. and West, C. (1996) *The Future of the Race.* New York: Vintage Books.

38. Lee, S. (1991) *Five for Five: The Films of Spike Lee.* New York: Stewart, Tabori and Chang.

39. Roth, C. (1970) *A History of the Jews.* New York: Schocken Books.

40. Gambino, R. (1974) *Blood of My Blood.* New York: Anchor Books. See as well: Putnam, R.D. (1993) *Making Democracy Work: Civic Traditions in Modern Italy.* Princeton, NJ: Princeton University Press. For a contemporaty comparison of Italians and Jews see: Rieder, J. (1985) *Canarsie: The Jews and Italians of Brooklyn Against Liberalism.* Cambridge, MA: Harvard University Press.

41. Sowell, T. (1996) *Migrations and Cultures: A World View.* New York: Basic Books.

42. Leyburn, J.G. (1962) *The Scotch-Irish: A Social History.* Chapel Hill, NC: University of North Carolina Press.

43. Lewis, O. (1966) *La Vida: A Puerto Rican Family in the Culture of Poverty.* New York: Random House; Howell, J. T. (1973) *Hard Living on Clay Street: Portraits of Blue Collar Families.* New York: Anchor Books.

44. Valentine, C.A. (1968) *Culture and Poverty.* Chicago: University of Chicago Press.

45. See the "culture of segregation" in Massey, D.S. and Denton, NA. (1993) op. cit.

46. Patterson, O. (1982) *Slavery and Social Death: A Comparative Study.* Cambridge, MA: Harvard University Press; Elkins, S.M. (1969) *Slavery.* Chicago: University of Chicago Press.

47. Blassingame, J.W. (1979) op. cit.

48. Zimbardo, P.G. (1972) The pathology of imprisonment. *Society.* April.

49. Early textbooks in sociology did sometimes refer to the "slave culture of the negro," but this was not the norm. See: Gillin, J.L., Dittmer, C.G., and Colbert, R.J. (1928) *Social Problems*. New York: Century. Much more common was the supposition that black culture was a pale, and often distorted replica, of white culture. See: Myrdal, G. (1944) op. cit.

50. Styron, W. (1967) *The Confessions of Nat Turner*. New York: Random House.

51. Ellis, J.J. (1996) *American Sphinx: The Character of Thomas Jefferson*. New York: Alfred A. Knopf.

52. It must not be assumed, however, that slave culture was exclusively reactive to white impositions. Holdovers from African cultural precursors, as well as slave creativity, also played a part. See: Genovese, E.D. (1974) *Roll, Jordan, Roll*. New York: Pantheon.

53. Locke, J. 1772) *Two Treaties on Government*. London: J. Whiston. See also: Aristotle (1941) *The Basic Works of Aristotle*. Edited by R. McKeon. New York: Random House. Orlando Patterson would surely agree that slavery has its origins in warfare. See: Patterson, O. (1991) *Freedom: Freedom in the Making of Western Culture*. New York: Basic Books.

54. Thomas, H. (1997) *The Slave Trade: The Story of the Atlantic Slave Trade: 1440-1870*. New York: Simon & Schuster.

55. Douglass, F. [1945] (1968) *Narrative of the Life of Fredrick Douglass*. New York: Signet Books.

56. Speaking of a later time period (the 1930s) John Dollard observed that "the hostility properly directed toward the white caste is deflected from it and focused within the Negro group itself." See: Dollard, J. (1937) *Caste and Class in a Southern Town*. New Haven: Yale University Press.

57. Blau, P.M. (1955) *The Dynamics of Bureaucracy: A Study of Interpersonal Relationships in Two Government Agencies*. Chicago: University of Chicago Press.

58. Hughes, E.C. (1958) *Men and Their Work*. Glencoe, IL: Free Press.

59. The Sally Hemmings case, wherein Thomas Jefferson has been demonstrated to have fathered several children by the slave half-sister of his deceased wife, is a vivid example.

60. Cherlin, A.J. (1992) *Marriage, Divorce, Remarriage*. Cambridge, MA: Harvard University Press. Anderson, E. (1999) *The Code of the Street: Decency, Violence and the Moral Life of the Inner City*. New York: W.W. Norton. Douglass, F. [1945] (1968) *Narrative of the Life of Fredrick Douglass*. New York: Signet Books.

61. Blassingame, J.W. (1979) op. cit.

CHAPTER 6: THE CULTURE OF SLAVERY: OUTCOMES

1. Neugarten, B. (1946) Social class and friendship among school children. *American Journal of Sociology*. Vol.51, pp.3105-13.

2. DuCille, A. (1996) *Skin Trade*. Cambridge, MA: Harvard University Press.

3. Clausen, J.A. (1968) *Socialization and Society*. Boston: Little, Brown & Co.

4. Rodgers, R and Hammerstein, O. (1981) *Archives of Recorded Sound of Rodgers and Hammerstein*. Boston: G.R. Hall.

5. Fein, M. (1997) *Hardball Without an Umpire: The Sociology of Morality*. Westport, CT: Praeger.

6. Bolman, L.G. and Deal, T.E. (1991) *Reframing Organizations: Artistry, Choice, and Leadership.* San Francisco: Jossey-Bass.
7. Gelles, R.J. (1997) *Intimate Violence in Families,* 3rd Edition. Thousand Oaks, CA: Sage
8. Anderson, E. (1999) *The Code of the Street: Decency, Violence and the Moral Life of the Inner City.* New York: W.W. Norton.
9. Freud, A. (1966) *The Ego and the Mechanisms of Defense.* New York: International Universities Press.
10. Rainwater, L. (1970) *Behind Ghetto Walls: Family Life in a Federal Slum.* Chicago: Aldine.
11. Blassingame, J.W. (1979) *The Slave Community: Plantation Life in the Antebellum South.* New York: Oxford University Press.
12. Boas, F. (1928) *Anthropology and Modern Life.* New York: Dover.
13. Darwin, C. (1979) *The Origin of Species.* New York: Avnel Books.
14. Guttman, H.G. (1977) *The Black Family in Slavery and Freedom, 1750-1925.* New York: Vintage Books.
15. Ellis, J.J. (1993) *Passionate Sage: The Character and Legacy of John Adams.* New York: W.W. Norton.
16. Fred Matthews makes a similar point with regard to the philosophy of Robert E. Park. He writes "the mark of scientific neutrality, to Park, was not a total abstinence from moral judgment, or from social action, but rather a willingness to face the facts of social resistance to change." See: Matthews, F.R. (1977) *Quest for an American Sociology: Robert E. Park and the Chicago School.* Montreal: McGill-Queen's University Press.
17. Gouldner, A.W. (1970) *The Coming Crisis of Western Sociology.* New York: Basic Books.
18. Fein, M. (1999) *The Limits of Idealism: When Good Intentions Go Bad.* New York: Plenum Publishing.
19. Thernstrom, S. and Thernstrom, A. (1997) *America in Black and White: One Nation, Indivisible.* New York: Simon & Schuster.
20. Frazier, E.F. (1957) *Black Bourgeoisie.* New York: The Free Press.
21. Gans, H.J. (1999) The possibility of a new racial hierarchy in the twenty-first-century United States. In: Lamont, M. (Ed.) (1999) *The Cultural Territories of Race: Black and White Boundaries.* Chicago: University of Chicago Press.
22. Bannister, R.C. (1979) *Social Darwinism: Science and Myth in Anglo-American Social Thought.* Philadelphia: Temple University Press.
23. Herrnstein, R.J. and Murray, C. (1994) *The Bell Curve: The Reshaping of American Life by Differences in Intelligence.* New York: Basic Books; Fisher, C.S., Hout, M., Sanchez Jankowski, M., Lucas, S.R., Swindler, A., and Voss, K. (1996) *Inequality by Design: Cracking the Bell Curve Myth.* Princeton, NJ: Princeton University Press.
24. Ellis, J.J. (1996) *American Sphinx: The Character of Thomas Jefferson.* New York: Alfred A. Knopf.
25. Writing from the vantage point of the 1930' John Dollard describes the situation thusly: "Southern white people...show the greatest sensitivity to aggression from the side of the Negro, and, in fact, to the outside observer, often seem to be reacting to it when it is not there.... Only constant watchfulness, it is believed, and a solid front against potential Negro attack maintain the *status quo*." In: Dollard, J. (1937) *Caste and Class in a Southern Town.* New Haven: Yale University Press.
26. Lowe, D. (1967) *Ku Klux Klan: The Invisible Empire.* New York: W.W. Norton.

27. Patterson, O. (1998) *Rituals of Blood: Consequences of Slavery in Two American Centuries.* Washington, DC: Civitas/Counterpoint.
28. Lee, H. (1960) *To Kill a Mockingbird.* Philadelphia; Lippincott.
29. Larson, E.J. (1995) *Sex, Race and Science: Eugenics in the Deep South.* Baltimore: Johns Hopkins University Press.
30. Douglass, F. [1945] (1968) *Narrative of the Life of Fredrick Douglass.* New York: Signet Books.
31. DuBois, W.E.B. [1899] (1996) *The Philadelphia Negro: A Social Study.* Philadelphia: University of Pennsylvania Press.
32. Butterfield, F. (1995) *All God's Children: The Bosket Family and the Tradition of Violence.* New York: Alfred A. Knopf.
33. Patterson, O. (1998) op. cit.
34. Quadagno, J. (1994) *The Color of Welfare: How Racism Undermined the War on Poverty.* New York: Oxford University Press; Williams, J. (1998) *Thurgood Marshall: American Revolutionary.* New York: Times Books.
35. Stampp, K.M. (1965) *The Era of Reconstruction: 1865-1877.* New York: Vintage Books; Lemann, N. (1991) *The Promised Land: The Great Black Migration and How It Changed America.* New York: Alfred A. Knopf.
36. Dollard, J. (1937) op. cit; DuBois, W.E.B. [1903] (1990) *The Souls of Black Folk.* New York: Vintage Books.
37. Cayton, H.R. and Drake, St. C. (1946) *Black Metropolis.* London: Jonathan Cape.
38. Ball, E. (1998) *Slaves in the Family.* New York: Farrar, Straus and Giroux.
39. Mitchell, M. (1939) *Gone with the Wind.* New York: MacMillan.
40. The validity of utilizing these categories is seconded by scholars with very different agendas. Massey, for instance, employs them to illustrate his "culture of segregation." Massey, D.S. and Denton, N.A. (1993) *American Apartheid: Segregation and the Making of the Under Class.* Cambridge, MA: Harvard University Press.
41. Dawson, M.C. (1999) 'Dis beat disrupts': Rap, ideology and black political attitudes. In: Lamont, M. (Ed.) (1999) *The Cultural Territories of Race: Black and White Boundaries.* Chicago: University of Chicago Press.
42. Steele, S. (1990) *The Content of Our Character: A New Vision of Race in America.* New York: St. Martin's Press.
43. See in contrast: Waters, M.C. (1999) Explaining the comfort factor: West Indian immigrants confront American race relations. In: Lamont, M. (Ed.) (1999) *The Cultural Territories of Race: Black and White Boundaries.* Chicago: University of Chicago Press.
44. Collier, P. and Horowitz, D. (Eds.) (1997) *The Race Card: White Guilt, Black Resentment, and the Assault on Truth and Justice.* Rocklin, CA: Forum.
45. Jones, J.H. (1981) *Bad Blood: The Tuskegee Syphilis Experiment.* New York: The Free Press.
46. Ladner, J. (1979) Transracial Adoption: Can White Parents Bring Up a Healthy Black Child? In: Blumberg, R.G. and Roye, W.J. *Interracial Bonds.* New York: General Hall.
47. For the extent of the problem see Patterson, O. (1998) op. cit; Anderson, E. (1999) op. cit; Wolfe, A. (1996) *Marginalized in the Middle.* Chicago: University of Chicago Press.
48. Oliver, W. (1994) *The Violent Social World of Black Men.* New York: Lexington Books.
49. Billson, J.M. (1998) *Pathways to Manhood: Young Black Males Struggle for Identity.* 2nd Edition. New Brunswick, NJ: Transaction.

50. Shakur, S. (aka Monster Kody Scott) (1993) *Monster: The Autobiography of an L.A. Gang Member.* New York: Penguin Books.
51. McCall, N. (1994) *Makes Me Want to Holler: A Young Black Man in America.* New York: Vintage Books.
52. See also Haley, A. and Malcolm X. (1964) *The Autobiography of Malcolm X.* New York: Grove Press.
53. Butterfield, F. (1995) op. cit.
54. Dash, L. (1996) *Rosa Lee: A Mother and Her Family in Urban America.* New York: Basic Books.
55. Horowitz, D. (1998) *The Politics of Bad Faith: The Radical Assault on America's Future.* New York: The Free Press.
56. Fanon, F. (1967) *Black Skin, White Masks.* New York: Grove Press.
57. Hooks, B. (1995) *Killing Rage: Ending Racism.* New York: Henry Holt.
58. Cose, E. (1993) *The Rage of a Privileged Class.* New York: HarperCollins.
59. Fein, M. (1999) op cit.
60. Rainwater, L. (1970) op. cit.
61. Bennett, W.J. (Ed.) (1993) *The Book of Virtues: A Treasury of Great Moral Stories.* New York: Simon & Schuster.
62. Anderson, E. (1999) op cit.
63. Butler, P. (1995) Racially based jury nullification: black power in the criminal justice system, Vol.105 *Yale Law Review*, p.677.
64. Kennedy, R. (1997) *Race, Crime, and the Law.* New York: Random House.
65. The Amadou Diallo case, in which a brouhaha arose in reaction to an African immigrant's death in a fusillade of police bullets, is a recent instance, and one in which the officers were accused of murder.
66. D'Souza, D. (1995) *The End of Racism: Principles for a Multiracial Society.* New York: The Free Press.
67. Massey, D.S. and Denton, N.A. (1993) op. cit.
68. Anderson, E. (1999) op. cit.
69. DuBois, W.E.B. [1899] (1996) op. cit.
70. Anderson, E. (1999) op. cit.
71. Dollard, J. (1937) op. cit.
72. Wilson, W.J. (1996) *When Work Disappears: The World of the New Urban Poor.* New York: Alfred A. Knopf.
73. Landry, B. (1987) *The New Black Middle Class.* Berkeley: University of California Press.
74. Oliver, M.L. and Shapiro, T.M. (1995) *Black Wealth? White Wealth: A New Perspective on Racial Inequality.* New York: Routledge.
75. Thernstrom, S. and Thernstrom, A. (1997) op. cit. The tendency, however, is to blame government policies and legal restrictions for discouraging black entrpreeurship. While this may well have been true during reconstruction, today African-Americans face no more structural limitations than do Korean-Americans. For the case that continuing descrimination is at fault see: Oliver, M.L. and Shapiro, T.M. (1995) ibid.
76. As was so often the case in his less politically correct era, John Dollard was not bashful in asserting this in print. He unfortunately associated this alleged impulsivity with freedom and personal happiness. See: Dollard, J. (1937) op. cit.
77. Merton, R.K. (1968) *Social Theory and Social Structure.* New York: The Free Press.
78. Billson, J.M. (1998) op. cit.

79. Kinder, R.R. and Sanders, L.M. (1996) *Divided by Color: Racial Politics and Democratic Ideals*. Chicago: University of Chicago Press.
80. Guy, M.E. (1997) Counterpoint: By thine own voice, shall thou be known. *Public Productivity and Management Review*, Vol.20, No.3, March, pp.237-242. A stinging indictment of black anti-intellectualism can be found in: McWhorter, J.H. (2000) *Losing the Race: Self-Sabotage in Black America*. New York: The Free Press. He also provides an excellent illustration of how teasing can inculcate anti-intellectual values. Reasons why our school systems have failed to address this attitude can be found in Ravitch, D. (1974) *The Great School Wars: A History of the New York City Public Schools*. New York: Basic Books.
81. Wolfe, A. (1998) *One Nation, After All*. New York: Viking.
82. Kors, A.C. and Silverglate, H.A. (1998) *The Shadow University: The Betrayal of Liberty on America's Campuses*. New York: The Free Press.
83. Carter, S.L. (1991) *Reflections of an Affirmative Action Baby*. New York: Basic Books.
84. Ogbu, J.U. (1974) *The Next Generation: An Ethnography of Education in an Urban Neighborhood*. New York: Academic Press.
85. Kinder, R.R. and Sanders L.M. (1996) op. cit.
86. DuBois, W.E.B. [1899] (1996) op. cit.
87. Dollard, J. (1937) op. cit.
88. Wilson, for instance, cites research in which inner-city employers describe African-American workers as lacking work motivation, but like most others he ultimately attributes this to the employer's biases. The dnager here is that a uniform empirical finding is casually dismissed on unsubstantiated moral grounds. See: Wilson, W.J. (1996) *When Work Disappears: The World of the New Urban Poor*. New York: Alfred A. Knopf. See also: Wilson, W.J. (1978) *The Declining Significance of Race: Blacks and Changing American Institutions*. Chicago: University of Chicago Press.
89. Sniderman, P.M. and Carmines, E.G. (1998) *Reaching Beyond Race*. Cambridge, MA: Harvard University Press.
90. Newman, K.S. and Ellis, C. (1999) 'There's no shame in my game': Status and stigma among Harlem's working poor." In: Lamont, M. (Ed.) (1999) *The Cultural Territories of Race: Black and White Boundaries*. Chicago: University of Chicago Press.
91. Jencks, C. (1992) *Rethinking Social Policy: Race, Poverty and the Underclass*. Cambridge, MA: Harvard University Press.
92. Cayton, H.R. and Drake, St. C. (1946) op. cit.
93. Frazier, E.F. (1957) op. cit.
94. Richburg, K.B. (1997) *Out of America: A Black Man Confronts Africa*. San Diego: Harcourt, Brace.
95. Binder, A. (1999) Friend and foe: Boundary work and collective identity in the Afrocentric and multicultural curriculum movements in American public education." In: Lamont, M. (Ed.) (1999) *The Cultural Territories of Race: Black and White Boundaries*. Chicago: University of Chicago Press.
96. Van Sertima, I. (1976) *They Came Before Columbus*. New York: Random House; Van Sertima, I. (1998) *Early America Revisited*. New Brunswick, NJ: Transaction Publishers.
97. Kaplan, J. and Bernays, A. (1997) *The Language of Names: What We Call Ourselves and Why It Matters*. New York: Simon & Schuster.
98. Oliver, W. (1994) op cit.

99. Rainwater, L. (1970) op. cit.
100. The "trickster" role is especially beloved in Black folklore. See: Harris, J.C. (1904) *The Tar Baby*. New York: Appleton & Co.
101. St. John, N.H. (1975) *School Desegregation: Outcomes for Children*. New York: John Wiley & Sons; Ogbu, J.U. (1978) *Minority Education and Caste: The American System in Cross-Cultural Perspective*. New York: Academic Press.
102. Anderson, E. (1999) op. cit.
103. Moynihan, D.P. (1965) *The Negro Family: The Case for National Action*. Washington, D.C.: Department of Labor.
104. Blankenhorn, D. (1995) *Fatherless America: Confronting Our Most Urgent Social Problem*. New York: Basic Books.
105. Morehouse Research Institute (1999) *Turning the Corner on Father Absence in Black America*. Atlanta: Morehouse University.
106. Waller, M.R. (1999) Meanings and motives in new family stories: The separation of reproduction and marriage among low-income black and white parents. In: Lamont, M. (Ed.) (1999) *The Cultural Territories of Race: Black and White Boundaries*. Chicago: University of Chicago Press.
107. Michael, R.T., Gagnon, J.H., Laumann, E.O. and Kolata. G. (1994) *Sex in America*. New York: Warner Books.
108. Patterson, O. (1998) op. cit.
109. Franklin, D. L. (1997) *Ensuring Inequality: The Structural Transformation of the African-American Family*. New York: Oxford University Press. For an overview of the roots of teenage childbearing see Constance Willard Williams: Williams, C.W. (1991) *Black Teenage Mothers: Pregnancy and Child Rearing from Their Perspective*. Lexington, MA: Lexington Books.
110. Lemann, N. (1991) *The Promised Land: The Great Black Migration and How It Changed America*. New York: Alfred A. Knopf.
111. Guttman, H.G. (1977) op. cit.
112. Patterson, O. (1998) op. cit.
113. Waller, M.R. (1999) op. cit.
114. Murray, C. (1984) *Losing Ground: American Social Policy (1950-1986)*. New York: Basic Books.
115. Anderson, E. (1999) op. cit.
116. Anderson, E. (1999) ibid.
117. Majors, R. and Billson, J.M. (1993) *The Cool Pose: The Dilemma of Black Manhood in America*. New York: Simon & Schuster.
118. Gates, H.L. (1994) *Colored People: A Memoir*. New York: Vintage Books.
119. Oliver, W. (1994 *The Violent Social World of Black Men*. New York: Lexington Books.
120. Dollard talks was well of the "indulgent behavior permitted the Negro." See: Dollard, J. (1937) op. cit.

CHAPTER 7: RACIAL "EMPOWERMENT"

1. Patterson, O. (1997) *The Ordeal of Integration: Progress and Resentment in America's "Racial" Crisis*. Washington, D.C.: Civitas/Counterpoint.
2. Gouldner, A.W. (1954) *Pattern of Industrial Bureaucracy: A Case Study of Modern Factory Administration*. New York: The Free Press.

3. Robert E. Park certainly believed this. According to Matthews "Park assumed that changes were not *granted* but *won*; the dynamic forces must come from the oppressed themselves." See: Matthews, F.R. (1977) *Quest for an American Sociology: Robert E. Park and the Chicago School*. Montreal: McGill-Queen's University Press.
4. See: Gould, J.L. and Gould, C. (1989) *Sexual Selection*. New York: Scientific American Library.
5. For a persuasive case that we human beings are by nature hierarchical see Francis Fukuyama. He calls us "homo hierarchicus" and argues that stratification is built into our emotional system. Fukuyama, F. (1999) *The Great Disruption: Human Nature and the Reconstitution of Social Order*. New York: The Free Press.
6. Norbert Elias has provided one of the best conceptual accounts of tests of strength among human beings. He calls them "primal contests" and explains how they vary under different circumstances. See: Elias, N. (1978) *What is Sociology?* (Trans. by Stephen Mennell and Grace Morissey). New York: Columbia University Press; Elias, N. (1998) *On Civilization, Power, and Knowledge*. (Edited by Stephen Mennell and Johan Goudsblom.) Chicago: University of Chicago Press. A very different conflict theory account can be found in: Tilly, C. (1998) *Durable Inequality*. Berkeley: University of California Press.
7. Whyte, W.F. (1943) *Street Corner Society*. Chicago: University of Chicago Press.
8. Anderson, E. (1999) *The Code of the Street: Decency, Violence and the Moral Life of the Inner City*. New York: W.W. Norton.
9. Pierre Bourdieu discusses this phenomenon under the rubric of different "fields." See: Swartz, D. (1997) *Culture and Power: The Sociology of Pierre Bourdieu*. Chicago: University of Chicago Press.
10. Anderson, E. (1999) op. cit.
11. Bolman, L.G. and Deal, T.E. (1991) *Reframing Organizations: Artistry, Choice, and Leadership*. San Francisco: Jossey-Bass.
12. Max Weber was among the first to make this observation. See: Gerth, H. and Mills, C.W. (Eds.) (1946) *From Max Weber: Essays in Sociology*. New York: Oxford University Press.
13. Gerth, H. and Mills, C.W. (Eds.) (1946) op. cit.
14. Anderson, E. (1999) op. cit. A particularly well researched manner in which alliances can increase one's power is in searching for a job. So called "weak bonds" are a primary source of job referrals. See: Granovetter, M.S. (1974) *Getting a Job*. Cambridge, MA: Harvard University Press.
15. See Serif, M. (1936) *The Psychology of Social Norms*. New York: Harper & Brothers.
16. Steele, C.M. (1999) Thin ice: 'Stereotype threat' and black college students. *The Atlantic Monthly*, August.
17. Robert Park made a comparable point with regard to prejudice. He described as "a conservative force, a sort of spontaneous conservation which tends to preserve the social order and the social distances upon which that order rests." See: Park, R. (1950) *Race and Culture*. Glencoe, IL: The Free Press.
18. See their earlier described attitude toward merit.
19. Patterson, O. (1998) *Rituals of Blood: Consequences of Slavery in Two American Centuries*. Washington, D.C.: Civitas/Counterpoint.
20. Steele, S. (1998) *A Dream Deferred: The Second Betrayal of Black Freedom in America*. New York: HarperCollins.
21. Goffman, E. (1959) *The Presentation of Self in Everyday Life*. Garden City, NY: Doubleday.

22. Gans, H.J. (1999) The possibility of a new racial hierarchy in the twenty-first-century United States. In: Lamont, M. (Ed.) (1999. *The Cultural Territories of Race: Black and White Boundaries*. Chicago: University of Chicago Press.
23. Baker, L.D. (1998) *From Savage to Negro: Anthropology and the Construction of Race, 1896-1954*. Berkeley: University of California Press.
24. Landry, B. (1987) *The New Black Middle Class*. Berkeley: University of California Press.
25. Schuman, H., Steeh, C., Bobo, L., and Kysman, M. (1997) *Racial Attitudes in America: Trends and Interpretations*, Revised Edition. Cambridge, MA: Harvard University Press.
26. West, T.G. (1997) *Vindicating the Founders: Race, Sex, Class, and Justice in the Origins of America*. Lanham, MD: Rowman & Littlefield.
27. Stampp, K.M. (1956) *The Peculiar Institution: Slavery in the Ante-Bellum South*. New York: Alfred A. Knopf.
28. Stampp, K.M. (1965) *The Era of Reconstruction: 1865-1877*. New York: Vintage Books.
29. Washington, B.T. [1901] (1985) *Up From Slavery*. New York: Oxford University Press.
30. Lemann, N. (1991) *The Promised Land: The Great Black Migration and How It Changed America*. New York: Alfred A. Knopf.
31. Cruse, H. (1967) *The Crisis of the Negro Intellectual: A Historical Analysis of the Failure of Black Leadership*. New York: William Morrow.
32. Stein, J. (1986) *The World of Marcus Garvey: Race and Class in Modern Society*. Baton Rouge: Louisiana State University Press.
33. Williams, J. (1998) *Thurgood Marshall: American Revolutionary*. New York: Times Books.
34. Landry, B. (1987) op. cit.
35. Thernstrom, S. and Thernstrom, A. (1997) *America in Black and White: One Nation, Indivisible*. New York: Simon & Schuster.
36. John Dollard is quite explicit about this connection. He writes "The effect of the social set-up [of the South] seems to be to keep Negroes infantile, to grant them infantile types of freedom and responsibility, and also to exercise the autocratic control over them which is the prerogative of the patriarchal father." Dollard, J. (1937) *Caste and Class in a Southern Town*. New Haven: Yale University Press.
37. Gould, S.J. (1981) *The Mismeasure of Man*. New York: W.W. Norton.
38. Dollard unfortunately seems to argue that enforced immaturity was as functional for blacks as it was for whites. No such implication is intended here. See: Dollard, J. (1937) op. cit.
39. Howell, J.T. (1973) *Hard Living on Clay Street: Portraits of Blue Collar Families*. New York: Anchor Books.
40. Douglass, F. [1945] (1968) *Narrative of the Life of Fredrick Douglass*. New York: Signet Books; McFeely, W.S. (1991) *Fredrick Douglass*. New York: W.W. Norton.
41. Washington, B.T. [1901] (1985) op. cit.
42. Horney, K. (1945) *Our Inner Conflicts: A Constructive Theory of Neurosis*. New York: W.W. Norton.
43. Washington, B.T. [1901] (1985) op. cit.
44. Blauner, R. (1972) *Racial Oppression in America*. New York: Harper & Row.
45. Majors, R. and Billson, J.M. (1993) *The Cool Pose: The Dilemma of Black Manhood in America*. New York: Simon & Schuster.

46. Davis, S. Jr., with J. and B. Boyar (1965) *Yes, I Can.* New York: Farrar, Straus, and Giroux.
47. Williams, J. (1998) op. cit.
48. Erikson, E. (1968) *Identity: Youth and Crisis.* New York: W.W. Norton.
49. Salzman, J. and West, C. (Eds.) (1997) *Struggles in the Promised Land: Toward a History of Black-Jewish Relations in the United States.* New York: Oxford University Press.
50. Fein, M. (1999) *The Limits of Idealism: When Good Intentions Go Bad.* New York: Plenum Publishing.
51. Sowell, T. (1984) *Civil Rights: Rhetoric or Reality?* New York: William Morrow.
52. West, T.G. (1997) op. cit.

CHAPTER 8: CHANGE STRATEGIES

1. Franklin, J.H. (1969) *From Slavery to Freedom.* New York: Vintage Books.
2. Maraniss, D. (1995) *First in His Class: The Biography of Bill Clinton.* New York: Simon & Schuster.
3. Shepard, S. (1998) Race panel prompts different responses. *Atlanta Journal Constitution.* A11, Sept. 19.
4. Aronson, E. (1988) *The Social Animal,* 5th Edition. New York: W.H. Freeman, p. 266.
5. This, of course, was Gunnar Myrdal's primary strategy. See: Myrdal, G. (1944) *An American Dilemma: The Negro Problem and American Democracy.* New York: Harper & Row.
6. Pettigrew, T.F. (1961) Social psychology and desegregation research. *American Psychologist,* Vol.16, pp.105-112.
7. Deutsch, M. and Collins, M.E. (1951) *Interracial Housing: A Psychological Evaluation of a Social Experiment.* Minneapolis: University of Minnesota Press.
8. Myrdal, G. (1944) op. cit.
9. Some commentators, it must be noted, perceive morality as an exercise in repressing evil. Their objective is to force people to do good. See: Fein, M. (Ed.) (2000) Race Relations. *Sociological Practice,* Vol.2, No.3.
10. Fein, M. (1997) *Hardball Without an Umpire: The Sociology of Morality.* Westport, CT: Praeger.
11. Steele, S. (1990) *The Content of Our Character: A New Vision of Race in America.* New York: St. Martin's Press.
12. In June (1998) in Washington D.C.
13. Merton, R.K. (1968) *Social Theory and Social Structure.* New York: The Free Press.
14. Feagin, J.R. and Feagin, C.B. (1999) *Racial and Ethnic Relations,* 6th Edition. Upper Saddle River, NJ: Prentice-Hall.
15. In Wolfe's words, "reluctant to pass judgment, [Americans] are [now] tolerant to a fault.... Above all moderate in their outlook on the world, they believe in the importance of leading a virtuous life but are reluctant to impose values they understand as virtuous for themselves on others...." See: Wolfe, A. (1998) *One Nation, After All.* New York: Viking.
16. Boas, F. (1928) *Anthropology and Modern Life.* New York: Dover.
17. Rogers, C. (1951) *Client Centered Therapy.* Boston: Houghton-Mifflin.

18. Fein, M. (1997) op. cit.
19. Johnson, P. (1997) *A History of the American People.* New York: HarperCollins.
20. Festinger, L. (1957) *A Theory of Cognitive Dissonance.* Stanford, CA: Stanford University Press.
21. Fukuyama, F. (1999) *The Great Disruption: Human Nature and the Reconstitution of Social Order.* New York: The Free Press.
22. Fishman, R. (1983) *Bourgeois Utopias: The Rise and Fall of Suburbia.* New York: Basic Books.
23. Jackson, J.J. (1987) *Straight from the Heart.* (Edited by Roger D. Hatch and Frank E. Watkins). Philadelphia: Fortress Press.
24. Terrill, R. (1980) *A Biography: Mao.* New York: Harper & Row.
25. Fein, M. (1999) *The Limits of Idealism: When Good Intentions Go Bad.* New York: Plenum Publishing.
26. See: Fein, M. (Ed.) (2000) Race relations interventions. *Sociological Practice,* Vol.2, No.3. The zeal to condemn unwanted behaviors as deviant can be remarkable. Even seasoned clinical sociologists are vulneable to it.
27. A social engineering mentality has been a prominent feature of sociology since its founding by August Comte. See: Collins, R. and Makowsky, M. (1998) *The Discovery of Society,* 6th Edition. New York: McGraw-Hill.
28. Hayek, F.A. von (1944) *The Road to Serfdom. With Forward by John Chamberlain.* Chicago: University of Chicago Press.
29. Graglia, F.C. (1998) *Domestic Tranquility: A Brief Against Feminism.* Dallas, TX: Spence.
30. Horowitz, D. (1998) *The Politics of Bad Faith: The Radical Assault on America's Future.* New York: The Free Press, pp.180-181.
31. Gerson, M. (Ed.) (1996) *The Essential Neo-Conservative Reader.* Reading, MA: Addison-Wesley.
32. Simon, H.A. (1947) *Administrative Behavior.* New York: MacMillan.
33. Since World War II many sociologists have been surprised by the depth of the unanticipated resistance to their recommendations for racial reform. See: McKee, J.B. (1993) *Sociology and the Race Problem: The Failure of a Perspective.* Urbana: University of Illinois Press.
34. Entwisle, D.R, Alexander, K.L., and Olson, L.S. (1997) *Children, Schools, and Inequality.* Boulder, CO: Westview Press.
35. Rossi, P. (1989) *Down and Out in America: The Origins of Homelessness.* Chicago: University of Chicago Press; Jencks, C. (1994) *The Homeless.* Cambridge, MA: Harvard University Press.
36. There are a variety of proposals on the table regarding how reparations might be delivered, not all of which depend on a single financial outlay, yet all of which seem to be problematic. In any event, reparations represent a quintessential dream of rescue. It seems fair to say that they have been an obsession which, at the very least, has diverted black attention from more worthwhile self-help projects. See: Robinson, R. (2000) *The Debt: What America Owes Blacks.* New York: Dutton.
37. Dawes, C.G. (1950) *A Journal of the McKinley Years.* Chicago: Lakeside Press.
38. Clark, K.B. (1965) *Dark Ghetto: Dilemmas of Social Power.* New York: Harper & Row.
39. Hewitt, J.P. (1998) *The Myth of Self-Esteem: Finding Happiness and Solving Problems in America.* New York: St. Martin's Press. Murl, C. (1995) *Self-Esteem: Research, Theory and Practice.* New York: Springer.

40. St. John, N.H. (1975) *School Desegregation: Outcomes for Children*. New York: John Wiley & Sons; Crain, R.L. and Mahard, R.E. (1982) *Desegregation Plans that Raise Black Achievement: A Review of the Research*. Santa Monica: The Rand Corporation.

41. Coleman, J.S. (1990) *Equality and Achievement in Education*. Boulder, CO: Westview Press.

42. Greenhouse, L. (1995) Justices say lower courts erred in orders in desegregation case. New York: *The New York Times*, June 13. Efforts to establish bilingual education have travelled a parallel unsuccessful course. See: Porter, R.P. (1997) The politics of bilingual education. *Society*, Vol.34, No.6.

43. Coleman, J.S., Campbell, E.Q, Hobson, C.J., McPartland, J., Mood, A.M., Weinfeld, F.D., and York, R.L. (1966) *Equality of Educational Opportunity*. Washington, D.C.: U.S. Government Printing Office.

44. Cose, E. (1997) *Color Blind: Seeing Beyond Race in a Race Obsessed World*. New York: Harper Collins.

45. Hochschild, J. (1999) Affirmative action as culture War. In: Lamont, M. (Ed.) (1999) *The Cultural Territories of Race: Black and White Boundaries*. Chicago: University of Chicago Press. The case against affirmative action is most passionately argued in: Connerly, W. (2000) *Creating Equal: My Fight Against Race Preferences*. San Francisco: Encounter Books.

46. Patterson, O. (1997) *The Ordeal of Integration: Progress and Resentment in America's "Racial" Crisis*. Washington, D.C.: Civitas/Counterpoint.

47. Thernstrom, S. and Thernstrom, A. (1997) *America in Black and White: One Nation, Indivisible*. New York: Simon & Schuster.

48. Smith, T.A. and O'Connell, L. (1997) *Black Anxiety, White Guilt, and the Politics of Status Frustration*. Westport, CT: Praeger.

49. Sniderman, P.M. and Carmines, E.G. (1998) *Reaching Beyond Race*. Cambridge, MA: Harvard University Press.

50. Wolfe, A. (1998) op. cit.

51. Carter, S.L. (1991) *Reflections of an Affirmative Action Baby*. New York: Basic Books.

52. Steele, S. (1998) *A Dream Deferred: The Second Betrayal of Black Freedom in America*. New York: HarperCollins.

53. Patterson suggests that "only 7 percent of Euro-Americans can actually claim that they have been affected unfavorably by affirmative action." Patterson, O. (1997) op. cit., p. 160. This would be as many as ten million persons, but Patterson treats it as a modest price to pay for justice.

54. Hochschild, J. (1999) op. cit.

55. Patterson, O. (1997) op. cit.

56. Schlesinger, A.M. (1992) *The Disuniting of America*. New York: W.W. Norton.

57. In sociology calls for a "cultural pluralism" have become modal. These generally assume that group distinctiveness can be maintained without causing a threat to democracy and without introducing invidious distinctions. Thus Robin Williams states that he "envisions an end-situation in which (1) a considerable portion of cultural distinctiveness of various groups will be retained, but (2) there will be extensive interaction among all groups, and (3) at least a minimum body of shared values and traditions will be emphasized." See: Williams, R.M., Jr. (1951) *American Society: A Sociological Interpretation*. New York: Alfred A. Knopf. See also: Davis, A. and Dollard J. (1940) *Children of Bondage: The Personality Development of Negro*

Youth in the Urban South. Washington, D.C.: American Council on Education. In fact, at least as regards European ethnics, assimilation seems to be proceeding apace, with each successive generation voluntarily relinquishing significant aspects of their unique traditions. See: Alba, R.D. (1990) *Ethnic Identity: The Transformation of White America*. New Haven: Yale University Press.

58. Fishman, R. (1983) op. cit.
59. An influential archetype of this orientation was provided by Theodore Adorno and his colleagues. They eagerly labeled prejudice a "disease" for which a cure must be found. In their words, "Techniques for overcoming resistance, developed mainly in the field of psychotherapy, can be improved and adapted to use with groups and even on a mass scale." See: Adorno, T., et al. (1950) *The Authoritarian Personality*. New York: Harper.
60. Adorno, T., et al. (1950) ibid.
61. American Psychiatric Association; Task Force on DSM-IV. (1994) *Diagnostic and Statistical Manual of Mental Disorders*, 4th Edition. Washington, D.C.
62. Billson, J.M. (1998) *Pathways to Manhood: Young Black Males Struggle for Identity*, 2nd Edition. New Brunswick, NJ: Transaction.
63. Scott, W.R. (1999) Use-of-self in social constructionist therapy: Some guidelines for a multicultural practice. In: Fu, V.R and Stremmel, A.J. (Eds.) *Affirming Diversity Through Democratic Conversations*. Upper Saddle River, NJ: Prentice-Hall. See also: Worchel, S. (1999) *Written in Blood: Ethnic Identity and the Struggle for Human Harmony*. New York: Worth.
64. Herrnstein, R.J. and Murray, C. (1994) *The Bell Curve: The Reshaping of American Life by Differences in Intelligence*. New York: Basic Books.
65. Alexander, F. (1948) Fundamentals of Psychoanalysis. New York: W.W. Norton.
66. Goffman, E. (1963) *Stigma: Notes on the Management of Spoiled Identity*. Englewood Cliffs, NJ: Prentice-Hall.
67. Stampp, K.M. (1956) *The Peculiar Institution: Slavery in the Ante-Bellum South*. New York: Alfred A. Knopf.
68. Somewhere between the clinical and the educational approaches lies the "socialization" model. It assumes that prevention is the best cure and hence aims to correct patterns of socialization which lead to later problems. The classic statement of this position was provided by Allison Davis and John Dollard. In their case studies of Negro socialization, they came to the conclusion that blacks needed to be socialized along more middle class lines. See: Davis, A. and Dollard J. (1940) op. cit.
69. Goleman, D. (1995) *Emotional Intelligence: Why It Can Matter More Than IQ*. New York: Bantam Books.
70. Park, R. (1950) *Race and Culture*. Glencoe, IL: The Free Press. See also: Raushenbush, W. (1979. *Robert E. Park: Biography of a Sociologist*. Durham, NC: Duke University Press.
71. Frazier, E.F. (1960) [1939] *The Negro Family in the United States*. Chicago: University of Chicago Press.
72. Moynihan, D.P. (1965) *The Negro Family: The Case for National Action*. Washington, D.C.: Department of Labor.Sowell, T. (1981) *Ethnic America*. New York: Basic Books.
73. Sowell, T. (1984) *Civil Rights: Rhetoric or Reality?* New York: William Morrow; Sowell, T. (1994) *Race and Culture: A World View*. New York: Basic Books; Sowell, T. (1996) *Migrations and Cultures: A World View*. New York: Basic Books.

320 Notes and References

74. Smith, T.A. and O'Connell, L. (1997) *Black Anxiety, White Guilt, and the Politics of Status Frustration*. Westport, CT: Praeger.
75. Patterson, O. (1982) *Slavery and Social Death: A Comparative Study*. Cambridge, MA: Harvard University Press; Patterson, O. (1997) op. cit; Patterson, O. (1998) *Rituals of Blood: Consequences of Slavery in Two American Centuries*. Washington, D.C.: Civitas/Counterpoint.
76. Steele, S. (1990) op. cit; Steele, S. (1998) op. cit.
77. Burke, J. (1978) *Connections*. Boston: Little, Brown.
78. Marx, K. (1967) *Das Capital*. Edited by F. Engels. *Translated by Samuel Moore and Edward Aveling*. New York: International Publishing.
79. Popper, K. (1961) *The Poverty of Historicism*. London: Routledge.
80. Lindbergh, A.M. (1940) *The Wave of the Future: A Confession of Faith*. New York: Harcourt, Brace.
81. Darwin, C. (1979) *The Origin of Species*. New York: Avnel Books.
82. Fein, M. (1990) *Role Change: A Resocialization Perspective*. New York: Praeger.

CHAPTER 9: NATURAL RESOCIALIZATION

1. Parsons, T. (1951) *The Social System*. New York: The Free Press.
2. Stone, I.F. (1988) *The Trial of Socrates*. Boston: Little, Brown.
3. Sutherland, S. (1992) *Irrationality: Why We Don't Think Straight!* New Brunswick, NJ: Rutgers University Press.
4. Freud, S. (1953-1974) *The Standard Edition of the Complete Psychological Works of Sigmund Freud*. (Edited by J. Strachey) London: Hogarth Press and Institute for Psychoanalysis.
5. Stryker, S. (1980) *Symbolic Interactionism*. Menlo Park, CA: Benjamin/Cummings.
6. Fein, M. (1990) *Role Change: A Resocialization Perspective*. New York: Praeger.
7. van der Kolk, B.A., McFarlane, A.C., and Weisaeth, L. (Eds.) (1996) *Traumatic Stress: The Effects of Overwhelming Experience on Mind, Body, and Society*. New York: Guilford.
8. Frank, J. (1973) *Persuasion and Healing: A Comparative Study of Psychotherapy*. Baltimore: Johns Hopkins University Press.
9. For an interpretation of the sorts of tasks performed by therapists who subscribe to a variety of therapeutic traditions see: Fein, M. (1992) *Analyzing Psychotherapy: A Social Role Interpretation*. New York: Praeger.
10. See van der Kolk, B.A., McFarlane, A.C., and Weisaeth, L. (Eds.) (1996) op. cit.
11. Kubler-Ross, E. (1969) *On Death and Dying*. New York: MacMillan.
12. Bowlby, J. (1969) *Attachment*. New York: Basic Books; Bowlby, J. (1973) *Separation: Anxiety and Anger*. New York: Basic Books; Bowlby, J. (1980) *Loss: Sadness and Depression*. New York: Basic Books.
13. Alexander, F. (1948) Fundamentals of Psychoanalysis. New York: W.W. Norton.
14. Billson, J.M. (1998) *Pathways to Manhood: Young Black Males Struggle for Identity*, 2nd Edition. New Brunswick, NJ: Transaction.
15. Cose, E. (1993) *The Rage of a Privileged Class*. New York: Harper/Collins; Fanon, F. (1967) *Black Skin, White Masks*. New York: Grove Press.
16. Steele, S. (1998) *A Dream Deferred: The Second Betrayal of Black Freedom in America*. New York: HarperCollins.

17. Fukuyama, F. (1999) *The Great Disruption: Human Nature and the Reconstitution of Social Order.* New York: The Free Press.
18. Fein, M. (1993) *I.A.M.: A Common Sense Guide to Coping with Anger.* Westport, CT: Praeger.
19. Chirot, D. (1994) *Modern Tyrants: The Power and Prevalence of Evil in Our Age.* Princeton: Princeton University Press.
20. Barnard, C. (1938) *The Function of the Executive.* Cambridge, MA: Harvard University Press.
21. Horowitz, D. (1998) *The Politics of Bad Faith: The Radical Assault on America's Future.* New York: The Free Press.
22. Freud, A. (1966) *The Ego and the Mechanisms of Defense.* New York: International Universities Press.
23. Fishman, R. (1983) *Bourgeois Utopias: The Rise and Fall of Suburbia.* New York: Basic Books.
24. Erikson, E. (1968) *Identity: Youth and Crisis.* New York: W.W. Norton.
25. Festinger, L. (1957) *A Theory of Cognitive Dissonance.* Stanford, CA: Stanford University Press.
26. Fein, M. (1993) op. cit.

CHAPTER 10: THE BLACK MIDDLE CLASS

1. Bratter, T.E. and Forrest G.G. (1985) *Alcoholism and Substance Abuse: Strategies for Clinical Intervention.* New York: The Free Press.
2. Beattie, M. (1987) *Codependent No More.* San Francisco: Harper & Row.
3. Donald Young as described the situation very aptly. "Man is an impatient animal, eager for the solution of social ills and disdainful of academicians' surveys, hypotheses, analyses, and theories. Action, not cautious and laborious research, is demanded of those who would lead the populace." See: Young, D. (1932) *American Minority Peoples: A Study of Racial and Cultural Conflicts in the United States.* New York: Harper and Brothers.
4. Steele, S. (1990) *The Content of Our Character: A New Vision of Race in America.* New York: St. Martin's Press.
5. In the Amadou Diallo case, this meant that the police continued to be vilified even after they were exonerated.
6. Certainly New York City's mayor Rudi Guilliani was execrated for the measures he employed to lower the crime rate. Despite the fact that most of the beneficiaries were black, it was black leaders who were most vociferous in condemning him.
7. Anderson, E. (1999) *The Code of the Street: Decency, Violence and the Moral Life of the Inner City.* New York: W.W. Norton.
8. Herrnstein, R.J. and Murray, C. (1994) *The Bell Curve: The Reshaping of American Life by Differences in Intelligence.* New York: Basic Books.
9. Steele, S. (1998) *A Dream Deferred: The Second Betrayal of Black Freedom in America.* New York: HarperCollins.
10. Murray, C. (1984) *Losing Ground: American Social Policy (1950-1986)* New York: Basic Books.
11. Frazier, E.F. (1957) *Black Bourgeoisie.* New York: Free Press.
12. Thernstrom, S. and Thernstrom, A. (1997) *America in Black and White: One Nation, Indivisible.* New York: Simon & Schuster.

13. Landry, B. (1987) *The New Black Middle Class*. Berkeley: University of California Press.
14. Wilson, W.J. (1978) *The Declining Significance of Race: Blacks and Changing American Institutions*. Chicago: University of Chicago Press.
15. Gates, H.L. and West, C. (1996) *The Future of the Race*. New York: Vintage Books.
16. Fein, M. (1999) *The Limits of Idealism: When Good Intentions Go Bad*. New York: Plenum Publishing.
17. Cose, E. (1993) *The Rage of a Privileged Class*. New York: HarperCollins.
18. Cose, E. (1997) *Color Blind: Seeing Beyond Race in a Race Obsessed World*. New York: HarperCollins.
19. Feagin, J.R. and Sikes, M.P. (1994) *Living with Racism: The Black Middle-Class Experience*. Boston: Beacon Press.
20. Hearn, F. (1997) *Moral Order and Social Disorder: The American Search for Civil Society*. New York: Aldine de Gruyter. See also: Putnam, R.D. (1993) *Making Democracy Work: Civic Traditions in Modern Italy*. Princeton, NJ: Princeton University Press and Bourdieu, P. (1980) *The Logic of Practice*. Stanford, CA: Stanford University Press.
21. Goleman, D. (1995) *Emotional Intelligence: Why It Can Matter More Than IQ*. New York: Bantam Books.
22. Anderson, E. (1999) The social situation of the black executive. In: Lamont, M. (Ed.) (1999) *The Cultural Territories of Race: Black and White Boundaries*. Chicago: University of Chicago Press.
23. Patterson, O. (1997) *The Ordeal of Integration: Progress and Resentment in America's "Racial" Crisis*. Washington, D.C.: Civitas/Counterpoint.
24. Powell, C. with Persico, J.E. (1995) *My American Journey*. New York: Random House.
25. Waters, M.C. (1999) Explaining the comfort factor: West Indian immigrants confront American race relations. In: Lamont, M. (Ed.) (1999) *The Cultural Territories of Race: Black and White Boundaries*. Chicago: University of Chicago Press.
26. Berger, D. (1987) *Clinical Empathy*. Northvale, NJ.: Jason Aronson.
27. Fukuyama, F. (1999) *The Great Disruption: Human Nature and the Reconstitution of Social Order*. New York: The Free Press.
28. Jackson, J.J. (1987) *Straight from the Heart*. (Edited by Roger D. Hatch and Frank E. Watkins). Philadelphia: Fortress Press.
29. Fukuyama, F. (1995) *Trust: The Social Virtues and the Creation of Prosperity*. New York: Free Press; Putnam, R.D. (1993. op. cit.
30. Toennies, F. (1966) [1887] *Community and Society*. New York: Harper & Row.
31. Himmelfarb, G. (1995) *The De-Moralization of Society: From Victorian Virtues to Modern Values*. New York: Alfred A. Knopf.
32. Lasch, C. (1979) *The Culture of Narcissism: American Life in an Age of Diminishing Expectations*. New York: Warner Books.
33. Michael, R.T., Gagnon, J.H., Laumann, E.O., and Kolata. G. (1994) *Sex in America*. New York: Warner Books.
34. Elias, N. (1983) *The Court Society*. New York: Pantheon Books.
35. Anderson, E. (1999) op. cit.
36. Wilson, W.J. (1987) *The Truly Disadvantaged: The Inner City, the Underclass and Public Policy*. Chicago: University of Chicago Press.
37. Ashe, A. (1988) *A Hard Road to Glory: A History of the African-American Athlete*. New York: Warner Books.

38. Gates, H.L. and West, C. (1996) *The Future of the Race.* New York: Vintage Books.

CHAPTER 11: THE WHITE MIDDLE CLASS

1. Steele, S. (1990) *The Content of Our Character: A New Vision of Race in America.* New York: St. Martin's Press.
2. Steele, S. (1998) *A Dream Deferred: The Second Betrayal of Black Freedom in America.* New York: HarperCollins.
3. Sleeper, J. (1997) *Liberal Racism.* New York: Viking.
4. Steele, S. (1998) op. cit.
5. Ellison R. (1947) *Invisible Man.* New York: Random House; Cruse, H. (1967) *The Crisis of the Negro Intellectual: A Historical Analysis of the Failure of Black Leadership.* New York: William Morrow.
6. Smith, T.A. and O'Connell, L. (1997) *Black Anxiety, White Guilt, and the Politics of Status Frustration.* Westport, CT: Praeger.
7. Steele, S. (1990) op. cit.
8. Fein, M. (1997) *Hardball Without an Umpire: The Sociology of Morality.* Westport, CT: Praeger.
9. Sleeper, J. (1997) op. cit.
10. Hacker, A. (1995) *Two Nations: Black and White, Separate, Hostile, Unequal.* New York: Ballantine Books.
11. Collier, P. and Horowitz, D. (Eds.) (1997) *The Race Card: White Guilt, Black Resentment, and the Assault on Truth and Justice.* Rocklin, CA: Forum. See also: Schlesinger, A.M. (1992) *The Disuniting of America.* New York: W.W. Norton, and Lefkowitz, M. (1996) *Not Out of Africa: How Afrocentrism Became an Excuse to Teach Myth as History.* New York: Basic Books.
12. The nature of the logic used is illustrated by Randall Robinson. He suggests that because one of Cleopatra's grandparents is unknown, this person was probably black, and therefore so was she. See: Robinson, R. (2000) *The Debt: What America Owes Blacks.* New York: Dutton.
13. Fukuyama, F. (1995) *Trust: The Social Virtues and the Creation of Prosperity.* New York: The Free Press. Sadly as Robert Putnam has observed, "In America, blacks express less social trust than whites...." and, furthermore, a more general decline in social trust has coincided with the rise of the civil rights movement. See: Putnam, R.D. (2000) *Bowling Alone: The Collapse and Revival of American Community.* New York: Simon & Schuster.
14. Jackson, J.J. (1987) *Straight from the Heart.* (Edited by Roger D. Hatch and Frank E. Watkins). Philadelphia: Fortress Press.
15. Steele, S. (1998) op. cit, p 124.
16. Sleeper, J. (1997) op. cit, p. 178.
17. Coontz, S. (1992) *The Way We Never Were: American Families and the Nostalgia Trap.* New York: Basic Books.
18. Fukuyama, F. (1992) *The End of History and the Last Man.* New York: The Free Press.
19. Bentham, J. (1948) [1789] *Introduction to the Principles of Morals and Legislation.* Oxford: Blackwell.

20. Sennett, R. and Cobb, J. (1972) *The Hidden Injuries of Class.* New York: Vintage Books.
21. Foucault, M. (1979) *Discipline and Punish: The Birth of the Prison.* New York: Random House; Hamilton, R.F. (1996) *The Social Misconstruction of Reality: Validity and Verification in the Scholarly Community.* New Haven: Yale University Press.
22. Mill, J.S. (1956) [1859] *On Liberty.* New York: Liberal Arts Press.
23. Friedman, M. (1962) *Capitalism and Freedom.* Chicago: University of Chicago Press.
24. Durkheim, E. (1915) *The Elementary Forms of Religious Life.* New York: The Free Press; Durkheim, E. (1933) *The Division of Labor in Society.* New York: The Free Press.
25. Locke, J. (1772) *Two Treaties on Government.* London: J. Whiston.
26. Fein, M. (1997) op. cit.
27. Sniderman, P.M. and Carmines, E.G. (1998) *Reaching Beyond Race.* Cambridge, MA: Harvard University Press.
28. Parsons, T. (1951) *The Social System.* New York: The Free Press.
29. Gerth, H. and Mills, C.W. (Eds.) (1946) *From Max Weber: Essays in Sociology.* New York: Oxford University Press.
30. Wilson, J.Q. and Kelling, G.L. (1982) Broken windows: The police and neighborhood safety. *Atlantic Monthly,* March.
31. Steele, S. (1998) op. cit, p.112.
32. Samuelson, R. (1996) *The Good Life and Its Discontents: The American Dream in the Age of Entitlement (1945-(1995)* New York: Times Books.
33. Patterson, O. (1997) *The Ordeal of Integration: Progress and Resentment in America's "Racial" Crisis.* Washington, D.C.: Civitas/Counterpoint.
34. Kohn, M.L. and Schooler, C. (1983) *Work and Personality: An Inquiry Into the Impact of Social Stratification.* Norwood, NJ: Ablex.
35. Goffman, E. (1959) *The Presentation of Self in Everyday Life.* Garden City, NY: Doubleday.
36. Gilovich, T. (1991) *How We Know What Isn't So: The Fallibility of Reason in Everyday Life.* New York: The Free Press.
37. Blankenhorn, D. (1995) *Fatherless America: Confronting Our Most Urgent Social Problem.* New York: Basic Books.
38. Cherlin, A.J. (1992) *Marriage, Divorce, Remarriage.* Cambridge, MA: Harvard University Press.
39. Schuman, H., Steeh, C., Bobo, L., and Kysman, M. (1997) *Racial Attitudes in America: Trends and Interpretations. Revised Edition.* Cambridge, MA: Harvard University Press.
40. Feagin, J.R. and Sikes, M.P. (1994) *Living with Racism: The Black Middle-Class Experience.* Boston: Beacon Press.
41. Massey, D.S. and Denton, N.A. (1993) *American Apartheid: Segregation and the Making of the Under Class.* Cambridge, MA: Harvard University Press.
42. Black men turn out to be more than twice as likely to enter an inter-racial marriage as are black women. White, J.E. (1997) I'm just who I am. *Time,* May 5.
43. I am indebted to Robert Brand, a student in my graduate course on *Diversity in Business,* for having decided to do a term paper on the integration of Cobb County schools. A life-long resident of the county, he wondered how it had responded to the Brown v. School Board decision outlawing segregation in public schools.
44. Sleeper, J. (1997) op. cit.

45. Fein, M. (1999) *The Limits of Idealism: When Good Intentions Go Bad.* New York: Plenum Publishing.
46. It remains odd that those who declare it is impossible for people to be color blind, also deny that there is such a thing as race.
47. Anderson, E. (1999) *The Code of the Street: Decency, Violence and the Moral Life of the Inner City.* New York: W.W. Norton.

Bibliography

Acton, J. (1956) *Essays on Freedom and Power. Introduction by G. Himmelfarb.* London: Thames and Hudson.

Adams, J. (1770) Argument in Defense of British Soldiers in the Boston Massacre.

Adorno, T., et al. (1950) *The Authoritarian Personality.* New York: Harper.

Aguirre, A. Jr. and Turner, J.H. (1998) *American Ethnicity: The Dynamics and Consequences of Discrimination.* 2nd Edition. New York: McGraw-Hill.

Alba, R.D. (1988) *Ethnicity and Race in the USA.* New York: Routledge.

Alba, R.D. (1990) *Ethnic Identity: The Transformation of White America.* New Haven: Yale University Press.

Alba, R. and Nee, V. (1997) Rethinking assimilation theory for a new era of immigration. *International Migration Review,* Vol.31, No.4, Winter, pp. 826-874.

Alexander, F. (1948) Fundamentals of Psychoanalysis. New York: W.W. Norton.

Allport, G. (1954) *The Nature of Prejudice.* Boston: Beacon Press.

American Psychiatric Association; Task Force on DSM-IV. (1994) *Diagnostic and Statistical Manual of Mental Disorders;* 4th Edition. Washington, D.C.

American Sociological Association. (1998) Footnotes January.

Anderson, E. (1990) *Streetwise: Race, Class and Change in an Urban Community.* Chicago: University of Chicago Press.

Anderson, E. (1999a) *The Code of the Street: Decency, Violence and the Moral Life of the Inner City.* New York: W.W. Norton.

Anderson, E. (1999b) The social situation of the black executive. In Lamont, M. (Ed.) (1999) *The Cultural Territories of Race: Black and White Boundaries.* Chicago: University of Chicago Press.

Ansell, A.E. (1997) *New Right, New Racism: Race and Reaction in the United States and Britain.* New York: New York University Press.

Appelbaum, R.P. and Chambliss, W.J. (1997) *Sociology, Second Edition.* New York: Longman.

Aristotle (1941) *The Basic Works of Aristotle.* Edited by R. McKeon. New York: Random House.

Aronson, E. (1988) *The Social Animal,* 5th Edition. New York: W.H. Freeman & Co.

Asante, M.K. (1988) *Afrocentricity.* Trenton, NJ: Africa World Press.

Ashe, A. (1988) *A Hard Road to Glory: A History of the African-American Athlete.* New York: Warner Books.

Baker, L.D. (1998) *From Savage to Negro: Anthropology and the Construction of Race, 1896-1954.* Berkeley: University of California Press.

Ball, E. (1998) *Slaves in the Family.* New York: Farrar, Straus and Giroux.

Ball, T. and Dagger, R. (1999) *Political Ideologies and the Democratic Ideal,* 3rd Edition. New York: Longman.

Ballard, M.B. (1997) *The Long Shadow: Jefferson Davis and the Final Days of the Confederacy.* Athens: University of Georgia Press.

Banaji, M.R. and Greenwald, A.G. (1994) Implicit stereotyping and prejudice. In Zanna, M.P. and Olsen, J. M. (Eds.) *The Psychology of Prejudice: The Ontario Symposium.* Hillsdale, NJ: Lawrence Erlbaum Associates.

Banaji, M.R., Hardin, C., and Rothman, A.J. (1993) Implicit stereotyping in person judgment. *Journal of Personality and Social Psychology*, Vol. 65, pp. 272-281.

Bannister, R.C. (1979) *Social Darwinism: Science and Myth in Anglo-American Social Thought*. Philadelphia: Temple University Press.

Barnard, C. (1938) *The Function of the Executive*. Cambridge, MA: Harvard University Press.

Beattie, M. (1987) *Codependent No More*. San Francisco: Harper & Row.

Becker, H. (Ed.) (1964) *The Other Side*. New York: Free The Free Press.

Becker, H. (1973) *The Outsiders: Studies in the Sociology of Deviance*. New York: The Free Press.

Bell, D. (1987) *And We Are Not Saved: The Elusive Quest for Racial Justice*. New York: Basic Books.

Bellah, R.N., Madsen, R., Sullivan, W.M., Swindler, A., and Tipton, S.M. (1985) *Habits of the Heart: Individualism and Commitment in American Life*. Berkeley, CA: University of California The Free Press.

Benjamin, L. (1991) *The Black Elite: Facing the Color Line in the Twilight of the Twentieth Century*. Chicago: Nelson-Hall.

Bennett, W.J. (Ed.) (1993) *The Book of Virtues: A Treasury of Great Moral Stories*. New York: Simon & Schuster.

Bennett, W.J. (1998) *The Death of Outrage: Bill Clinton and the Assault on American Ideals*. New York: The Free Press.

Bentham, J. (1948) [1789] *Introduction to the Principles of Morals and Legislation*. Oxford: Blackwell.

Berger, D. (1987) *Clinical Empathy*. Northvale, NJ: Jason Aronson.

Berger, P.L. and Luckman, F. (1966) *Social Construction of Reality: A Treatise in the Sociology of Knowledge*. New York: Doubleday.

Bergmann, B.R. (1996) *In Defense of Affirmative Action*. New York: Basic Books.

Bernstein, R. (1994) *Dictatorship of Virtue: Multiculturalism and the Battle for America's Future*. New York: Alfred A. Knopf.

Biddle, B. (1979) *Role Theory: Expectations, Identities and Behaviors*. New York: Academic The Free Press.

Billson, J.M. (1998) *Pathways to Manhood: Young Black Males Struggle for Identity*. 2nd Edition. New Brunswick, NJ: Transaction.

Binder, A. (1999) Friend and foe: Boundary work and collective identity in the Afrocentric and multicultural curriculum movements in American public education. In: Lamont, M. (Ed.) (1999) *The Cultural Territories of Race: Black and White Boundaries*. Chicago: University of Chicago The Free Press.

Blankenhorn, D. (1995) *Fatherless America: Confronting Our Most Urgent Social Problem*. New York: Basic Books.

Blassingame, J.W. (1979) *The Slave Community: Plantation Life in the Antebellum South*. New York: Oxford University The Free Press.

Blau, P.M. (1955) *The Dynamics of Bureaucracy: A Study of Interpersonal Relationships in Two Government Agencies*. Chicago: University of Chicago The Free Press.

Blauner, R. (1969) Internal colonialism and ghetto revolt." *Social Problems*, Vol. 16, pp. 393-408.

Blauner, R. (1972) *Racial OpThe Free Pression in America*. New York: Harper & Row.

Bloom, A. (1987) *The Closing of the American Mind*. New York: Simon & Schuster.

Blumberg, R.G. and Roye, W.J. (1979) *Interracial Bonds*. New York: General Hall.

Boas, F. (1928) *Anthropology and Modern Life.* New York: Dover.

Bolman, L.G. and Deal, T.E. (1991) *Reframing Organizations: Artistry, Choice, and Leadership.* San Francisco: Jossey-Bass.

Boot, M. (1998) *Out of Order: Arrogance, Corruption and Incompetence on the Bench.* New York: Basic Books.

Bourdieu, P. (1980) *The Logic of Practice.* Stanford, CA: Stanford University The Free Press.

Bowlby, J. (1969) *Attachment.* New York: Basic Books.

Bowlby, J. (1973. *Separation: Anxiety and Anger.* New York: Basic Books.

Bowlby, J. (1980) *Loss: Sadness and DeThe Free Pression.* New York: Basic Books.

Bowles, S. (1976) *Schooling in Capitalist America: Educational Reform and the Contradictions of Economic Life.* New York: Basic Books.

Bratter, T.E. and Forrest G.G. (1985) *Alcoholism and Substance Abuse: Strategies for Clinical Intervention.* New York: The Free The Free Press.

Brewer, M.B. (1988) A dual process model of impression formation. In; Wyler, Jr., R.S. and Srull, T.K. (Eds.), *Advances in Social Cognition,* Vol. 1. Hillsdale, NJ: Lawrence Erlbaum Associates.

Brinkerhoff, D.B., White, L.K., and Riedmann, A.C. (1997.) *Sociology, Fourth Edition.* Belmont, CA: Wadsworth The Free Press.

Brodkin, K. (1999) *How Jews Became White Folks and What that Says about Race in America.* New Brunswick. NJ: Rutgers University The Free Press.

Bryson, B. (1999) Multiculturalism as a moving moral boundary: Literature professors redefine racism." In: Lamont, M. (Ed.) (1999) *The Cultural Territories of Race: Black and White Boundaries.* Chicago: University of Chicago The Free Press.

Buckley, K.W. (1989) *Mechanical Man: John Broadus Watson and the Beginnings of Behaviorism.* New York: Guilford.

Burke, J. (1978) *Connections.* Boston: Little, Brown.

Butler, P. (1995) Racially based jury nullification: Black power in the criminal justice system. Vol. 105. *Yale Law Review,* p. 677.

Butterfield, F. (1995) *All God's Children: The Bosket Family and the Tradition of Violence.* New York: Alfred A. Knopf.

Cannon, L. (1997) *Official Negligence: How Rodney King and the Riots Changed Los Angeles and the LAPD.* New York: Times Books.

Cantor, N.F. (1997) *Imagining the Law: Common Law and the Foundations of the American Legal System.* New York: HarperCollins.

Carr, L.G. (1997) *"Color-Blind" Racism.* Thousand Oaks, CA: Sage.

Carroll, L. (1963) *Alice's Adventures in Wonderland an Through the Looking Glass.* New York: MacMillan.

Carter, S.L. (1991) *Reflections of an Affirmative Action Baby.* New York: Basic Books.

Carter, S.L. (1996) *Integrity.* New York: Basic Books.

Carter, S.L. (1998) *Civility: Manners, Morals, and Etiquette of a Democracy.* New York: Basic Books.

Cavalli-Sforza, L.L., Menozzi, P. and Piazza. A. (1994) *The History and Geography of Human Genes.* Princeton, NJ: University of Princeton Press.

Cavalli-Sforza, L.L. and Cavalli-Sforza, F. (1995) *The Great Human Diasporas.* Reading, MA: Perseus Books.

Cayton, H.R. and Drake, St. C. (1946) *Black Metropolis.* London: Jonathan Cape.

Cheney, L.V. (1995) *Telling the Truth: Why Our Culture and Our Country Have Stopped Making Sense.* New York: Simon & Schuster.

Cherlin, A.J. (1992) *Marriage, Divorce, Remarriage.* Cambridge, MA: Harvard University Press.

Chirot, D. (1994a) *How Societies Change.* Thousand Oaks: Pine Forge The Free Press.

Chirot, D. (1994b) *Modern Tyrants: The Power and Prevalence of Evil in Our Age.* Princeton: Princeton University Press.

Clark, K.B. (1965) *Dark Ghetto: Dilemmas of Social Power.* New York: Harper & Row.

Clausen, J.A. (1968) *Socialization and Society.* Boston: Little, Brown.

Clinton, H.R. (1996) *It Takes a Village: and Other Lessons Children Teach Us.* New York: Simon & Schuster.

Coleman, J.S. (1990a) *Equality and Achievement in Education.* Boulder CO: Westview Press.

Coleman, J.S. (1990b) *Foundations of Social Theory.* Cambridge, MA: Belknap Press.

Coleman, J.S., Campbell, E.Q, Hobson, C.J., McPartland, J., Mood, A.M., Weinfeld, F.D. and York, R.L. (1966) *Equality of Educational Opportunity.* Washington: U.S. Government Printing Office.

Collier, P. and Horowitz, D. (Eds.) (1997) *The Race Card: White Guilt, Black Resentment, and the Assault on Truth and Justice.* Rocklin, CA: Forum.

Collins, R, and Makowsky, M. (1998) *The Discovery of Society:* 6th Edition. New York: McGraw-Hill.

Coltrane, S. (1996) *Family Man: Fatherhood, Housework, and Gender Equity.* New York: Oxford University Press.

Coltrane, S. (1997) *Scientific Half-Truths and Postmodern Parody in the Family Values Debate.* Contemporary Sociology, Vol. 26, No. 1, January, pp.7-10.

Connerly, W. (2000) *Creating Equal: My Fight Against Race Preferences.* San Francisco: Encounter Books.

Cooley, C.H. (1902) *Human Nature and the Social Order.* New York: Scribner's Sons.

Coontz, S. (1992) *The Way We Never Were: American Families and the Nostalgia Trap.* New York: Basic Books.

Cose, E. (1993) *The Rage of a Privileged Class.* New York: HarperCollins.

Cose, E. (1997) *Color Blind: Seeing Beyond Race in a Race Obsessed World.* New York: HarperCollins.

Crain, R.L. and Mahard, R.E. (1982) *Desegregation Plans that Raise Black Achievement: A Review of the Research.* Santa Monica: The Rand Corporation.

Cranston, M. (1982) *Jean-Jacques.* New York: W.W. Norton.

Cross, June (1998) Secret Daughter. Frontline, PBS. December, 28.

Crozier, M. (1964) *The Bureaucratic Phenomenon.* Chicago: University of Chicago Press.

Cruse, H. (1967) *The Crisis of the Negro Intellectual: A Historical Analysis of the Failure of Black Leadership.* New York: William Morrow.

Dahrendorf, R. (1968) *Essays in the Theory of Society.* Stanford, CA: Stanford University Press.

Darwin, C. (1974) *The Descent of Man, and Selection in Relation to Sex.* Detroit: Gale Research.

Darwin, C. (1979) *The Origin of Species.* New York: Avnel Books.

Dash, L. (1996) *Rosa Lee: A Mother and Her Family in Urban America.* New York: Basic Books.

Davis, A. and Dollard J. (1940) *Children of Bondage: The Personality Development of Negro Youth in the Unban South.* Washington, D.C.: American Council on Education.

Davis, S. Jr., with J. and B. Boyar (1965) *Yes, I Can.* New York: Farrar, Straus, and Giroux.

Dawes, C.G. (1950) *A Journal of the McKinley Years.* Chicago: Lakeside Press.

Dawson, M.C. (1999) 'Dis beat disrupts': Rap, ideology and black political attitudes. In: Lamont, M. (Ed.) (1999) *The Cultural Territories of Race: Black and White Boundaries.* Chicago: University of Chicago Press.

Demott, B. (1990) *The Imperial Middle: Why American Can't Think Straight About Class.* New Haven: Yale University Press.

Dennis, R.M. (Ed.) (1997) *The Black Intellectuals.* Greenwich, CT: JAI Press.

Depuy, J. P. (Ed.) (1998) *Self-Deception and the Paradoxes of Rationality.* Stanford, CA: CSLI Publications.

Deutsch, M. and Collins, M.E. (1951) *Interracial Housing: A Psychological Evaluation of a Social Experiment.* Minneapolis: University of Minnesota Press.

Devine, P.G. (1989) Stereotypes and prejudice: Their automatic and controlled components. *Journal of Personality and Social Psychology,* Vol.56, pp.5-18.

Dodoo, E.N. (1997) Assimilation differences among Africans in America. *Social Forces,* Vol.76, No.2, pp.527-46.

Dollard, J. (1937) *Caste and Class in a Southern Town.* New Haven: Yale University Press.

Douglass, F. (1945) (1968) *Narrative of the Life of Fredrick Douglass.* New York: Signet Books.

D'Souza, D. (1995) *The End of Racism: Principles for a Multiracial Society.* New York: The Free Press.

DuBois, W.E.B. [1899] (1996) *The Philadelphia Negro: A Social Study.* Philadelphia: University of Pennsylvania Press.

DuBois, W.E.B. [1903] (1990) *The Souls of Black Folk.* New York: Vintage Books.

DuBois, W.E.B. (1935) *Black Reconstruction.* New York: Harcourt Brace.

DuCille, A. (1996) *Skin Trade.* Cambridge, MA: Harvard University Press.

Dumont, L. (1970) *Homo Hierarchicus: The Caste System and Its Implications.* Chicago: University of Chicago Press.

Durkheim, E. (1915) *The Elementary Forms of Religious Life.* New York: The Free Press.

Durkheim, E. (1933) *The Division of Labor in Society.* New York: The Free Press.

Durkheim, E. (1961) *Moral Education.* New York: The Free Press.

Durkheim, E. (1951) *Suicide: A Study in Sociology.* Glencoe, IL: The Free Press.

Durneier, M. (1992) *Slim's Table: Race, Respectability and Masculinity.* Chicago: University of Chicago Press.

Dyer, R. (1997) *White.* New York: Routledge.

Ebony (1992) *Who Get's Welfare?* December.

Edgerton, R.B.. (1992) *Sick Societies: Challenging the Myth of Primitive Harmony.* New York: The Free Press.

Egger, S.A. (1998) *Killers Among Us: An Examination of Serial Murders and Their Investigation.* Springfield: University of Illinois Press.

Elder, L. (2000) *The Ten Things You Can't Say in America.* New York: St. Martin's Press.

Elias, N. (1978) *What is Sociology?* (Trans. by Stephen Mennell and Grace Morissey). New York: Columbia University Press.

Elias, N. (1983) *The Court Society.* New York: Pantheon Books.

Elias, N. (1998) *On Civilization, Power, and Knowledge.* (Edited by Stephen Mennell and Johan Goudsblom.) Chicago: University of Chicago The Free Press.

Elkins, S.M. (1969) *Slavery*. Chicago: University of Chicago Press.

Ellis, J.J. (1993) *Passionate Sage: The Character and Legacy of John Adams*. New York: W.W. Norton.

Ellis, J.J. (1996) *American Sphinx: The Character of Thomas Jefferson*. New York: Alfred A. Knopf.

Ellis, J.M. (1997) *Literature Lost: Social Agendas and the Corruption of the Humanities*. New Haven: Yale University Press.

Ellis, R.J. (1998) *The Dark Side of the Left: Illiberal Egalitarianism in America*. Lawrence, Kansas: University of Kansas Press.

Ellison, R. (1947) *Invisible Man*. New York: Random House.

Ellwood, C.A. (1924) *Sociology and Modern Social Problems*. New York: American Book.

Elster, J. (1999) *Alchemies of the Mind: Rationality and the Emotions*. New York: Cambridge University Press.

Entine, J. (2000) *Taboo: Why Black Athletes Dominate Sports and Why We Are Afraid to Talk About It*. New York: Public Affairs.

Entwisle, D.R, Alexander, K.L., and Olson, L.S. (1997) *Children, Schools, and Inequality*. Boulder, CO: Westview Press.

Erikson, E. (1968) *Identity: Youth and Crisis*. New York: W.W. Norton.

Etzioni, A. (1993) *The Spirit of Community: The Reinvention of American Society*. New York: Simon & Schuster.

Fanon, F. (1967) *Black Skin, White Masks*. New York: Grove Press.

Farber, D.A. and Sherry, S. (1997) *Beyond All Reason: The Radical Assault on Truth in American Law*. New York: Oxford University Press.

Farley, J.E. (1995) *Majority-Minority Relations, Third Edition*. Englewood Cliffs, NJ: Prentice-Hall.

Farley, R. (1996) *The New American Reality: Who We Are, How We Got Here, Where We Are Going*. New York: Russell Sage Foundation.

Feagin, J.R. and Sikes, M.P. (1994) *Living with Racism: The Black Middle-Class Experience*. Boston: Beacon Press.

Feagin, J.R. and Feagin, C.B. (1999) *Racial and Ethnic Relations*, 6th Edition Upper Saddle River, NJ: Prentice-Hall.

Fein, M. (1990) *Role Change: A Resocialization Perspective*. New York: Praeger.

Fein, M. (1992) *Analyzing Psychotherapy: A Social Role Interpretation*. New York: Praeger.

Fein, M. (1993) *I.A.M.: A Common Sense Guide to Coping with Anger*. Westport, CT: Praeger.

Fein, M. (1997) *Hardball Without an Umpire: The Sociology of Morality*. Westport, CT: Praeger.

Fein, M. (1999) *The Limits of Idealism: When Good Intentions Go Bad*. New York: Plenum Publishing.

Fein, M. (2000) Race relations: A survey of intervention strategies. *Sociological Practice*, Vol.2, No.3.

Ferrante, J. and Brown, P. (1998) *The Social Construction of Race and Ethnicity in the United States*. New York: Longman.

Festinger, L. (1957) *A Theory of Cognitive Dissonance*. Stanford, CA: Stanford University Press.

Festinger, L., Riecken, and Schacter, S. (1956) *When Prophecy Fails*. Minneapolis: University of Minnesota Press.

Fine, M., Weis, L., Powell, L.C., and Wong, L.M. (Eds.) (1997) *Off White: Readings on Race, Power, and Society*. New York: Routledge.

Finsterbusch, K. (Ed.) (1997/98) *Annual Editions, Sociology*. Guilford, CT: Dushkin.

Fischer, D.H. (1970) *Historians Fallacies: Toward a Logic of Historical Thought*. New York: HarperPerennial.

Fisher, C.S., Hout, M., Sanchez Jankowski, M., Lucas, S.R., Swindler, A., and Voss, K. (1996) *Inequality by Design: Cracking the Bell Curve Myth*. Princeton, NJ: Princeton University Press.

Fisher, H.E. (1982) *The Sex Contract: The Evolution of Human Behavior*. New York: William Morrow.

Fisher, H.E. (1992) *Anatomy of Love: The Natural History of Monogamy, Adultery and Divorce*. New York: W.W. Norton.

Fishman, R. (1983) *Bourgeois Utopias: The Rise and Fall of Suburbia*. New York: Basic Books.

Fiske, S.T. and Von Hendy, H.M. (1992) Personality feedback and situational norms can control stereotyping processes. *Journal of Personality and Social Psychology*, Vol.62, pp.577-596.

Fong, T.P. (1998) *The Contemporary Asian American Experience: Beyond the Model Minority*. Upper Saddle River, NJ: Prentice-Hall.

Forbes, H.D. (1997) *Ethnic Conflict: Commerce, Culture, and the Contact Hypothesis*. New Haven, CT: Yale University Press.

Foucault, M. (1973) *Madness and Civilization*. New York: Random House.

Foucault, M. (1979) *Discipline and Punish: The Birth of the Prison*. New York: Random House.

Frank, J. (1973) *Persuasion and Healing: A Comparative Study of Psychotherapy*. Baltimore: Johns Hopkins University Press.

Franklin, D.L. (1997) *Ensuring Inequality: The Structural Transformation of the African-American Family*. New York: Oxford University Press.

Franklin, J.H. (1969) *From Slavery to Freedom*. New York: Vintage Books.

Frazier, E.F. (1957) *Black Bourgeoisie*. New York: The Free Press.

Frazier, E.F. (1960) [1939] *The Negro Family in the United States*. Chicago: University of Chicago Press.

Freud, A. (1966) *The Ego and the Mechanisms of Defense*. New York: International Universities Press.

Freud, S. (1953-1974) *The Standard Edition of the Complete Psychological Works of Sigmund Freud*. Edited by J. Strachey. London: Hogarth Press and Institute for Psychoanalysis.

Friedman, M. (1962) *Capitalism and Freedom*. Chicago: University of Chicago Press.

Fu, V.R. and Stremmel, A.J. (Eds.) (1999) *Affirming Diversity Through Democratic Conversations*. Upper Saddle River, NJ: Prentice-Hall.

Fukuyama, F. (1992) *The End of History and the Last Man*. New York: The Free Press.

Fukuyama, F. (1995) *Trust: The Social Virtues and the Creation of Prosperity*. New York: The Free Press.

Fukuyama, F. (1999a) *The Great Disruption: Human Nature and the Reconstitution of Social Order*. New York: The Free Press.

Fukuyama, F. (1999b) The great disruption. *The Atlantic Monthly*, May.

Gaines, K.K. (1996) *Uplifting the Race: Black Leadership, Politics, and Culture in the Twentieth Century*. Chapel Hill: University of North Carolina Press.

Gambino, R. (1974) *Blood of My Blood*. New York: Anchor Books.

Gans, H.J. (1999) The possibility of a new racial hierarchy in the twenty-first-century United States." In: Lamont, M. (Ed.) (1999) *The Cultural Territories of Race: Black and White Boundaries*. Chicago: University of Chicago Press.

Gates, H.L. (1994) *Colored People: A Memoir*. New York: Vintage Books.

Gates, H.L. and West, C. (1996) *The Future of the Race*. New York: Vintage Books.

Gelles, R.J. (1997) *Intimate Violence in Families*, 3rd Edition. Thousand Oaks, CA: Sage

Genovese, E.D. (1974) *Roll, Jordan, Roll*. New York: Pantheon.

Gerson, M. (Ed.) (1996) *The Essential Neo-Conservative Reader*. Reading, MA: Addison-Wesley.

Gerson, M. (1997) *In the Classroom: Dispatches from an Inner-city School that Works*. New York: The Free Press

Gerth, H. and Mills, C.W. (Eds.) (1946) *From Max Weber: Essays in Sociology*. New York: Oxford University Press.

Gibbon, E. (1960) *The Decline and Fall of the Roman Empire*. New York: Harcourt Brace.

Giddens, A. (1984) *The Constitution of Society*. Berkeley, CA: University of California Press.

Gilbert, D. and Kahl, J.A. (1993) *The American Class Structure*, 4th Edition. Belmont, CA: Wadsworth.

Gillin, J.L., Dittmer, C.G., and Colbert, R.J. (1928) *Social Problems*. New York: Century.

Gilovich, T. (1991) *How We Know What Isn't So: The Fallibility of Reason in Everyday Life*. New York: The Free Press.

Glazer, N. (1995) Levin, Jeffries, and the fate of academic freedom. *The Public Interest*, Vol.120, Summer, pp.14-40.

Glazer, N. (1997) *We Are All Multiculturalists Now*. Cambridge, MA: Harvard University Press.

Glazer, N. and Moynihan, D.P. (1963) *Beyond the Melting Pot*. Cambridge: The MIT Press.

Glazer, N. and Moynihan, D.P. (Eds.) (1975) *Ethnicity: Theory and Experience*. Cambridge, MA: Harvard University Press.

Glendon, M.A. (1991) *Rights Talk: The Impoverishment of Political Discourse*. New York: The Free Press.

Glendon, M.A. and Blankenhorn, D. (Eds.) (1995) *Seedbeds of Virtue: Sources of Competence, Character, and Citizenship in American Society*. Lanham, MD: Madison Books.

Glenn, N. (1997) *Closed Hearts, Closed Minds: The Textbook Story of Marriage*. New York: Institute for American Values.

Goffman, E. (1959) *The Presentation of Self in Everyday Life*. Garden City, NY: Doubleday.

Goffman, E. (1963) *Stigma: Notes on the Management of Spoiled Identity*. Englewood Cliffs, NJ: Prentice-Hall.

Goleman, D. (1995) *Emotional Intelligence: Why It Can Matter More Than IQ*. New York: Bantam Books.

Goode, E. and Ben-Yehuda, N. (1994) *Moral Panics: The Social Construction of Deviance*. Cambridge: Blackwell.

Goolishian, H.A. and Anderson, H. (1992) Strategy and intervention versus nonintervention: A matter of theory? *Journal of Marital and Family Therapy*, Vol.18, pp.5-15.

Gordon, M. M. (1964) *Assimilation in American Life: The Role of Race, Religion, and National Origins.* New York: Oxford University Press.

Gould, J.L. and Gould, C. (1989) *Sexual Selection.* New York: Scientific American Library.

Gould, M. (1999) Race and theory: Culture, poverty and adaptation to discrimination in Wilson and Ogbu. *Sociological Theory*, July, Vol.17, No.2, p. 171.

Gould, S.J. (1981) *The Mismeasure of Man.* New York: W.W. Norton.

Gould, S.J. (1989) *Wonderful Life: The Burgess Shale and the Nature of Life.* New York: W.W. Norton.

Gould, S.J. (1993) *Eight Little Piggies: Reflections in Natural History.* New York: W.W. Norton.

Gouldner, A.W. (1954) *Pattern of Industrial Bureaucracy: A Case Study of Modern Factory Administration.* New York: The Free Press.

Gouldner, A.W. (1970) *The Coming Crisis of Western Sociology.* New York: Basic Books.

Graglia, F.C. (1998) *Domestic Tranquillity: A Brief Against Feminism.* Dallas, TX: Spence.

Graham, L.O. (1999) *Our Kind of People: America's Black Upper Class.* New York: HarperCollins.

Graham, R. (Ed.) (1990) *The Idea of Race in Latin America, 1870-1940.* Austin: University of Texas Press.

Granovetter, M.S. (1974) *Getting a Job.* Cambridge, MA: Harvard University Press.

Greenhouse, L. (1995) Justices say lower courts erred in orders in desegregation case, New York: *The New York Times*, June 13.

Guttman, H.G. (1977) *The Black Family in Slavery and Freedom, 1750-1925.* New York: Vintage Books.

Guy, M.E. (1997) Counterpoint: By thine own voice, shall thou be known. *Public Productivity and Management Review*, Vol.20, No.3, March, pp.237-242.

Hacker, A. (1995) *Two Nations: Black and White, Separate, Hostile, Unequal.* New York: Ballantine Books.

Haley, A. and Malcolm X. (1964) *The Autobiography of Malcolm X.* New York: Grove Press.

Hamilton, D.L., Stroessner, S.J., and Driscoll, D.M. (1994) Social cognition and the study of stereotyping. In: Devine, P.G., Hamilton, D.L., and Ostrom, T.M. (Eds.) *Social Cognition: Impact on Social Psychology.* San Diego, CA: Academic Press.

Hamilton, R.F. (1996) *The Social Misconstruction of Reality: Validity and Verification in the Scholarly Community.* New Haven: Yale University Press.

Handlin, O. (1951) *The Uprooted.* Boston: Little, Brown.

Handlin, O. (1959) *The Newcomers: Negroes and Puerto Ricans in a Changing Metropolis.* New York: Doubleday.

Haney Lopez, I.F. (1996) *White by Law: The Legal Construction of Race.* New York: New York University Press.

Hannerz, U. (1969) *Soul Side: Inquiries into Ghetto Culture and Community.* New York: Columbia University Press.

Harris, J.C. (1904) *The Tar Baby.* New York: Appleton.

Harrison, L.E. and Huntington, S.P. (Eds.) (2000) *Culture Matters: How Values Shape Human Progress.* New York: Basic Books.

Hayek, F.A. von (1944) *The Road to Serfdom. With Forward by John Chamberlain.* Chicago: University of Chicago Press.

Hearn, F. (1997) *Moral Order and Social Disorder: The American Search for Civil Society.* New York: Aldine de Gruyter.

Helms, J.E. and Piper, R.E. (1994) Implications of racial identity theory for vocational psychology. *Journal of Vocational Behavior,* Vol.44, pp.124-138.

Herrnstein, R.J. and Murray, C. (1994) *The Bell Curve: The Reshaping of American Life by Differences in Intelligence.* New York: Basic Books.

Hewitt, J.P. (1998) *The Myth of Self-Esteem: Finding Happiness and Solving Problems in America.* New York: St. Martin's.

Himmelfarb, G. (1995) *The De-Moralization of Society: From Victorian Virtues to Modern Values.* New York: Alfred A. Knopf.

Himmelfarb, G. (1999) *One Nation, Two Cultures.* New York: Alfred A. Knopf.

Hirschfield, L.A. (1996) *Race in the Making: Cognition, Culture, and the Child's Construction of Human Kinds.* Cambridge, MA: The MIT Press.

Hochschild, J. (1995) *Facing Up to the American Dream.* Princeton, NJ: Princeton University Press.

Hochschild, J. (1999) Affirmative action as culture war. In: Lamont, M. (Ed.) (1999) *The Cultural Territories of Race: Black and White Boundaries.* Chicago: University of Chicago Press.

Hooks, B. (1995) *Killing Rage: Ending Racism.* New York: Henry Holt.

Horney, K. (1945) *Our Inner Conflicts: A Constructive Theory of Neurosis.* New York: W.W. Norton.

Horowitz, D. (1997) *Radical Son: A Generational Odyssey.* New York: The Free Press.

Horowitz, D. (1998) *The Politics of Bad Faith: The Radical Assault on America's Future.* New York: The Free Press.

Horowitz, D. (1999) *Hating Whitey and Other Progressive Causes.* Dallas, TX: Spence.

Howard, P.K. (1995) *The Death of Common Sense: How Law Is Suffocating America.* New York: Random House.

Howe, I. (1976) *The World of Our Fathers.* New York: Harcourt, Brace, Jovanovich.

Howell, J. T. (1973) *Hard Living on Clay Street: Portraits of Blue Collar Families.* New York: Anchor Books.

Huggins, N.I. (Ed.) (1986) *W.E.B. Du Bois: Writings.* New York: Library of America.

Huggins, N.I., Kilson, M., and Fox, D.M. (Eds.) (1971) *Key Issues in the Afro-American Experience.* San Diego: Harcourt, Brace, Jovanovich.

Hughes, E.C. (1958) *Men and Their Work.* Glencoe, Ill.: The Free Press.

Hume, D. (1961) [1739] *A Treatise on Human Nature.* New York: Dolphin Books.

Hunter, J.D. (2000) *The Death of Character: Moral Education in an Age Without Good and Evil.* New York: Basic Books.

Hurst, C.E. (1995) *Social Inequality: Forms, Causes, and Consequences.* 2nd Edition. Boston: Allyn and Bacon.

Ignatiev, N. (1995) *How the Irish Became White.* New York: Routledge.

Jackson, J.J. (1987) *Straight from the Heart.* (Edited by Roger D. Hatch and Frank E. Watkins). Philadelphia: Fortress Press.

Jacobson, M.F. (1998) *Whiteness of a Different Color: European Immigrants and the Alchemy of Race.* Cambridge, MA: Harvard University Press.

Jacoby, T. (1998) *Someone Else's House: America's Unfinished Struggle for Integration.* New York: The Free Press.

Jay, T. (1998) *Cursing in America.* Philadelphia: John Benjamins.

Jencks, C. (1992) *Rethinking Social Policy: Race, Poverty and the Underclass.* Cambridge, MA: Harvard University Press.

Jencks, C. (1994) *The Homeless*. Cambridge, MA: Harvard University The Free Press.

Johnson, P. (1997) *A History of the American People*. New York: HarperCollins.

Jones, J.H. (1981) *Bad Blood: The Tuskegee Syphilis Experiment*. New York: The Free Press.

Jourard, S.M. (1964) *The Transparent Self: Self Disclosure and Well Being*. Princeton, NJ: Van Nostrand.

Judd, C.M., Ryan C.S., and Park, B. (1991) Accuracy in the judgment of ingroup and outgroup variability. *Journal of Personality and Social Psychology*, Vol.61, pp.366-379.

Kain, E.L. and Neas, R. (Eds.) (1993) *Innovative Techniques for Teaching Sociological Concepts*. Washington, D.C.: American Sociological Association.

Kaplan, J. and Bernays, A. (1997) *The Language of Names: What We Call Ourselves and Why It Matters*. New York: Simon & Schuster.

Katz, J. (1988) *Seductions of Crime: Moral and Sensual Attraction in Doing Evil*. New York: Basic Books.

Kennedy, R. (1997) *Race, Crime, and the Law*. New York: Random House.

Kerbo, H.R. (1996) *Social Stratification and Inequality*. Third Edition. New York: McGraw-Hill.

Kimball, R. (1990) *Tenured Radicals: How Politics has Corrupted our Higher Education*. New York: HarperCollins.

Kinder, R.R. and Sanders, L.M. (1996) *Divided by Color: Racial Politics and Democratic Ideals*. Chicago: University of Chicago Press.

Kitano, H.H. (1997) *Race Relations*, 5th Edition. Upper Saddle River, NJ: Prentice-Hall.

Knight, R.H. (1998) *The Age of Consent: The Rise of Relativism and the Corruption of Popular Culture*. Dallas, TX: Spence.

Kohn, M.L. (1969) *Class and Conformity: A Study in Values*. Homewood, IL.: The Dorsey Press.

Kohn, M.L. and Schooler, C. (1983) *Work and Personality: An Inquiry Into the Impact of Social Stratification*. Norwood, NJ: Ablex.

Kors, A.C. and Silverglate, H.A. (1998) *The Shadow University: The Betrayal of Liberty on America's Campuses*. New York: The Free Press.

Kozol, J. (1967) *Death at an Early Age*. Boston: Houghton, Mifflin.

Kubler-Ross, E. (1969) *On Death and Dying*. New York: MacMillan.

Kuran, T. (1997) *Private Truths, Public Lies: The Social Consequences of Preference Falsification*. Cambridge, MA: Harvard University Press.

Ladd, E. C. (1999) *The Ladd Report*. New York: The Free Press.

Ladner, J. (1971) *Tommorow's Tomorrow: The Black Woman*. New York: Doubleday.

Ladner, J. (Ed.) (1973) *The Death of White Sociology*. New York: Random House.

Ladner, J. (1979) Transracial adoption: Can white parents bring up a healthy black child? In: Blumberg, R.G. and Roye, W.J., *Interracial Bonds (Eds.)*. New York: General Hall.

Lamont, M. (Ed.) (1999) *The Cultural Territories of Race: Black and White Boundaries*. Chicago: University of Chicago Press.

Landry, B. (1987) *The New Black Middle Class*. Berkeley: University of California Press.

Larson, E.J. (1995) *Sex, Race and Science: Eugenics in the Deep South*. Baltimore: Johns Hopkins University Press.

Lasch, C. (1979) *The Culture of Narcissism: American Life in an Age of Diminishing Expectations*. New York: Warner Books.

Lee, H. (1960) *To Kill a Mockingbird*. Philadelphia; Lippincott.

Lee, S. (1991) *Five for Five: The Films of Spike Lee*. New York: Stewart, Tabori and Chang.

Lefkowitz, M. (1996) *Not Out of Africa: How Afrocentrism Became an Excuse to Teach Myth as History*. New York: Basic Books.

Lemann, N. (1991) *The Promised Land: The Great Black Migration and How It Changed America*. New York: Alfred A. Knopf.

Lemert, E. (1997) *The Trouble with Evil: Social Control at the Edge of Morality*. Albany: State University of New York Press.

Lenski, G. (1966) *Power and Privilege: A Theory of Social Stratification*. New York: McGraw-Hill.

Leo, J. (1994) *Two Steps Ahead of the Thought Police*. New York: Simon & Schuster.

Lewis, M. and Saarni, C. (Eds.) (1993) *Lying and Deception in Everyday Life*. New York: Guilford Press.

Lewis, O. (1961) *The Children of Sanchez*. New York: Random House.

Lewis, O. (1966) *La Vida: A Puerto Rican Family in the Culture of Poverty*. New York: Random House.

Lewontin, R.C., Rose, S., and Kamin, C.J. (1984) *Not In Our Genes: Biology, Idiology and Human Nature*. New York: Pantheon Books.

Leyburn, J.G. (1962) *The Scotch-Irish: A Social History*. Chapel Hill, NC: University of North Carolina Press.

Liebow, E. (1967) *Talley's Corner: A Study of Negro Streetcorner Men*. Boston: Little, Brown.

Lindbergh, A.M. (1940) *The Wave of the Future: A Confession of Faith*. New York: Harcourt, Brace.

Lindzey, G. and Aronson, E. (Eds.) (1985) *Handbook of Social Psychology*, 3rd Edition. New York: Random House.

Lipset, S.M. (1996) *American Exceptionalism: A Double-Edged Sword*. New York: W.W. Norton.

Litwack, L.F. (1979) *Been in the Storm So Long*. New York: Alfred A. Knopf.

Locke, J. (1959) [1765] *An Essay Concerning Human Understanding*. New York: Dover.

Locke, J. (1772) *Two Treaties on Government*. London: J. Whiston.

Loury, G.C. (1995a) *One by One, from the Inside Out: Essays and Reviews on Race and Responsibility in America*. New York: The Free Press.

Loury, G.C. (1995b) The end of relativism, *The Weekly Standard*, Sept. 25.

Love, S. (1996) *One Blood: The Death and Resurrection of Charles R. Drew*. Chapel Hill: University of North Carolina Press.

Lowe, D. (1967) *Ku Klux Klan: The Invisible Empire*. New York: W.W. Norton.

Lynch, F.R. (1997) *The Diversity Machine*. New York: The Free Press.

MacDonald, H. (2000) *The Burden of Bad Ideas: How Modern Intellectuals Misshape Our Society*. Chicago: Ivan R. Dee.

MacDougall, H.A. (1982) *Racial Myth in English History: Trojans, Teutons, and Anglo-Saxons*. Hanover, NH: University Press of New England.

McBride, J. (1996) *The Color of Water: A Black Man's Tribute to His White Mother*. New York: Riverhead Books.

McCall, N. (1994) *Makes Me Want to Holler: A Young Black Man in America*. (1994) New York: Vintage Books.

McFeely, W.S. (1991) *Fredrick Douglass*. New York: W.W. Norton.

McGoldrick, M., Pearce, J.K., and Giordano, J. (1982) *Ethnicity and Family Therapy.* New York: Guilford.

McKee, J.B. (1993) *Sociology and the Race Problem: The Failure of a Perspective.* Urbana: University of Illinois Press.

Macrae, C.N., Bodenhausen, G.V., Milne, A.B., and Jetten, J. (1994) Out of mind but back in sight: Stereotypes on the rebound. *Journal of Personality and Social Psychology,* Vol. 67, pp.808-817.

Macrae, C.N., Milne, A.B., and Bodenhausen, G.V. (1994) Stereotypes as energy saving devices: A peek inside the cognitive toolbox. *Journal of Personality and Social Psychology,* Vol.66, pp.37-47.

McWhorter, J.H. (2000) *Losing the Race: Self-Sabotage in Black America.* New York: The Free Press.

Madison, J., Hamilton, A., and Jay, J. (1966) *The Federalist Papers.* Kendall, W. and Carey, G.W.(Eds.) New Rochelle, NY: Arlington House.

Magnet, M. (1993) *The Dream and the Nightmare: The Sixties Legacy to the Underclass.* New York: William Morrow.

Majors, R. and Billson, J.M. (1993) *The Cool Pose: The Dilemma of Black Manhood in America.* New York: Simon & Schuster.

Mannheim, K. (1936) *Ideology and Utopia.* New York: Harcourt, Brace, and World.

Mapp, A.J., Jr. (1987) *Thomas Jefferson: A Strange Case of Mistaken Identity.* New York: Madison Books.

Maraniss, D. (1995) *First in His Class: The Biography of Bill Clinton.* New York: Simon & Schuster.

Marger, M.N. (1997) *Race and Ethnic Relations: American and Global Perspectives,* 4th Edition. Belmont, CA: Wadsworth.

Marx, K. (1967) *Das Capital.* Edited by F. Engels. Translated by Samuel Moore and Edward Aveling. New York: International Publishing.

Massey, D.S. and Denton, N.A. (1993) *American Apartheid: Segregation and the Making of the Under Class.* Cambridge, MA: Harvard University Press.

Matthews, F.R. (1977) *Quest for an American Sociology: Robert E. Park and the Chicago School.* Montreal: McGill-Queen's University Press.

Mayer, S. (1997) *What Money Can't Buy: Family Income and Children's Life Chances.* Cambridge: Harvard University Press.

Merton, R.K. (1968) *Social Theory and Social Structure.* New York: The Free Press.

Meyers, S.L. (Ed.) (1997) *Civil Rights and Race Relations in the Post Reagan-Bush Era.* Westport, CT: Praeger.

Michael, R.T., Gagnon, J.H., Laumann, E.O., and Kolata. G. (1994) *Sex in America.* New York: Warner Books.

Mihesuah, D.A. (1996) *American Indians: Stereotypes and Realities.* Atlanta, GA: Clarity Press.

Mill, J.S. (1956) [1859] *On Liberty.* New York: Liberal Arts Press.

Mills, C.W. (1959) *The Sociological Imagination.* New York: Oxford University Press.

Mitchell, M. (1939) *Gone with the Wind.* New York: MacMillan.

Money, J. and Ehrhardt, A. (1972) *Man and Woman; Boy and Girl.* Baltimore: Johns Hopkins University Press.

Monk, R.C. (1996) *Taking Sides: Race and Ethnicity, Second Edition.* Guilford, CT: Dushkin.

Montagu, M.F.A. (1942) *Man's Most Dangerous Myth: The Fallacy of Race.* New York: Columbia University Press.

Morehouse Research Institute (1999) *Turning the Corner. on Father Absence in Black America.* Atlanta: Morehouse University.

Moskos, C.C. and Butler, J.S. (1996) *All That We Can Be: Black Leadership and Racial Integration The Army Way.* New York: Basic Books.

Mosteller, F. and Moynihan, D.P. (1972) *On Equality of Educational Opportunity.* New York: Random House.

Moynihan, D.P. (1965) *The Negro Family: The Case for National Action.* Washington, D.C.: Department of Labor.

Moynihan, D.P. (1993) Defining deviancy down. *American Scholar,* Winter, Vol.62, No1.

Murl, C. (1995) *Self-Esteem: Research, Theory and Practice.* New York: Springer.

Murray, C. (1984) *Losing Ground: American Social Policy (1950-1986.* New York: Basic Books.

Myrdal, G. (1944) *An American Dilemma: The Negro Problem and American Democracy.* New York: Harper & Row.

National Education Association. (1973) *Education and Racism.*

Neugarten, B. (1946) Social class and friendship among school children. *American Journal of Sociology,* Vol.51, pp.105-113.

Newman, K.S. and Ellis, C. (1999) 'There's no shame in my game': Status and stigma among Harlem's working poor. In: Lamont, M. (Ed.) (1999) *The Cultural Territories of Race: Black and White Boundaries.* Chicago: University of Chicago Press.

Nietzsche, F. (1989) *Beyond Good and Evil.* (Translated by Helen Zimmern) New York: Prometheus Books.

Nightingale, C.H. (1993) *On the Edge: A History of Poor Black Children and Their American Dream.* New York: Basic Books.

Odum, H.W. (1910) *Social and Mental Traits of the Negro.* New York: Columbia University Press.

Ogbu, J.U. (1974) *The Next Generation: An Ethnography of Education in an Urban Neighborhood.* New York: Academic Press.

Ogbu, J.U. (1978) *Minority Education and Caste: The American System in Cross-Cultural Perspective.* New York: Academic Press.

Ogburn, W. [1922] (1966) *Social Change with Respect to Culture and Original Nature.* New York: Heubsch.

Olasky, M. (1992) *The Tragedy of American Compassion.* Washington, D.C.: Regnery.

Oliver, M.L. and Shapiro, T.M. (1995) *Black Wealth? White Wealth: A New Perspective on Racial Inequality.* New York: Routledge.

Oliver, W. (1994) *The Violent Social World of Black Men.* New York: Lexington Books.

Olmsted, F.L. (1969) *The Cotton Kingdom.* New York: Modern Library.

Park, R. (1950) *Race and Culture.* Glencoe, IL: The Free Press.

Parks, E.E. (1997) *White Racial Identity Attitudes and Stereotypes: An Empirical Investigation.* (unpublished dissertation). New York: Columbia University.

Parsons, T. (1951) *The Social System.* New York: The Free Press.

Patterson, O. (1982) *Slavery and Social Death: A Comparative Study.* Cambridge, MA: Harvard University Press.

Patterson, O. (1991) *Freedom: Freedom in the Making of Western Culture.* New York: Basic Books.

Patterson, O. (1997) *The Ordeal of Integration: Progress and Resentment in America's "Racial" Crisis.* Washington, D.C.: Civitas/Counterpoint.

Patterson, O. (1998) *Rituals of Blood: Consequences of Slavery in Two American Centuries.* Washington, D.C.: Civitas/Counterpoint.
Paul, A.M. (1998) Where bias begins: The truth about stereotypes. *Psychology Today,* Vol. 82, pp.52-55, May, June.
Peters, W. and Beutel, B. (1970) *The Eye of the Storm.* Mount Kisco, NY: ABC Media Concepts; Center for Humanities.
Pettigrew, T.F. (1961) Social psychology and desegregation research. *American Psychologist,* Vol.16, pp.105-112.
Pettigrew, T.F. (1979) The ultimate attribution error: Extending Allport's cognitive analysis of prejudice. *Personality and Social Psychology Bulletin,* Vol.5, pp.461-476.
Pettigrew, T.F. (1980) *The Sociology of Race Relations.* New York: The Free Press.
Piattelli-Palmarini, M. (1994) *Inevitable Illusions: How Mistakes of Reason Rule Our Minds.* New York: John Wiley & Sons.
Pinderhughes, H. (1997) *Race in the Hood: Conflict and Violence among Urban Youth.* Minneapolis: University of Minnesota Press.
Plato (1945) *The Republic of Plato.* Translated by Francis MacDonald Cornford. New York: Oxford University Press.
Popenoe, D. (1996) *Life Without Father: Compelling New Evidence that Fatherhood and Marriage Are Indispensable for the Good of Children and Society.* New York: The Free Press.
Popper, K. (1961) *The Poverty of Historicism.* London: Routledge.
Porter, R.P. (1997) The politics of bilingual education. *Society.* Vol.34, No.6.
Powell, C. with Persico, J.E. (1995) *My American Journey.* New York: Random House.
Pruitt, D.J. (1981) *Negotiation Behavior.* New York: Academic Press.
Putnam, R.D. (1993) *Making Democracy Work: Civic Traditions in Modern Italy.* Princeton, NJ: Princeton University Press.
Putnam, R.D. (1995) Bowling alone: America's declining social capital. *Journal of Democracy,* January.
Putnam, R.D. (1996) The strange disappearance of civic America. *The American Prospect,* Winter, pp.34-48.
Putnam, R.D. (2000) *Bowling Alone: The Collapse and Revival of American Community.* New York: Simon & Schuster.
Quadagno, J. (1994) *The Color of Welfare: How Racism Undermined the War on Poverty.* New York: Oxford University Press.
Rainwater, L. (1970) *Behind Ghetto Walls: Family Life in a Federal Slum.* Chicago: Aldine .
Rankin, D.C. (1977) The impact of the Civil War on the Free Colored Community of New Orleans. In: *Perspectives in American History,* Vol XI.
Rand, A. (1957) *Atlas Shrugged.* New York: Random House.
Raushenbush, W. (1979) *Robert E. Park: Biography of a Sociologist.* Durham, NC: Duke University Press.
Ravitch, D. (1974) *The Great School Wars: A History of the New York City Public Schools.* New York: Basic Books.
Ravitch, D. and Finn, C.E., Jr. (1987) *What Do Our Seventeen-Year Olds Know?* New York: Harper & Row.
Ravitch, D. (2000) *Left Back: A Century of Failed School Reforms.* New York: Simon & Schuster.
Rawls, J. (1971) *A Theory of Justice.* Cambridge, MA: The Belknap Press.

Rebach, H.M. and Bruhn, J.G. (Eds.) (1991) *Clinical Sociology: An Agenda for Action.* New York: Plenum.

Reuter, E.B. (1927) *The American Race Problem: A Study of the Negro.* New York: Thomas Y. Crowell.

Richburg, K.B. (1997) *Out of America: A Black Man Confronts Africa.* San Diego: Harcourt, Brace.

Rieder, J. (1985) *Canarsie: The Jews and Italians of Brooklyn Against Liberalism.* Cambridge, MA: Harvard University Press.

Robinson, R. (2000) *The Debt: What America Owes Blacks.* New York: Dutton.

Rodgers, R. and Hammerstein, O. (1981) *Archives of Recorded Sound of Rodgers and Hammerstein.* Boston: G.R. Hall.

Rogers, C. (1951) *Client Centered Therapy.* Boston: Houghton-Mifflin.

Rose, P.I. (1997a) *They and We: Racial and Ethnic Relations in the United States,* 5th Edition. New York; McGraw-Hill.

Rose, P.I. (1997b) *Tempest-Tost: Race, Immigration, and the Dilemmas of Diversity.* New York: Oxford University Press.

Ross, M. and Fletcher, G.J.O. (1985) Attribution and social perception. In: Lindzey, G. and Aronson, E. (Eds.) *Handbook of Social Psychology,* 3rd Edition. New York: Random House.

Rossi, P. (1989) *Down and Out in America: The Origins of Homelessness.* Chicago: University of Chicago Press.

Roth, C. (1970) *A History of the Jews.* New York: Schocken Books.

Rothwax, H.J. (1995) *Guilty: The Collapse of Criminal Justice.* New York: Random House.

Rousseau, J.J [1762] (1913) *The Social Contract.* In: Cole, G.D.H.(Ed.), *The Social Contract and Discourses.* London: Dent.

Rousseau, J.J. [1762] (1979) *Emile.* Trans. A. Bloom. New York: Basic Books.

Rubin L.B. (1972) *Busing & Backlash: White Against White in an Urban School District.* Berkeley: University of California Press.

Sacks, D.O. and Thiel, P.A. (1995) *The Diversity Myth: "Multiculturalism" and the Politics of Intolerance at Stanford.* Oakland, CA: The Independent Institute.

St. John, N.H. (1975) *School Desegregation: Outcomes for Children.* New York: John Wiley & Sons.

Salzman, J. and West, C. (Eds.) (1997) *Struggles in the Promised Land: Toward a History of Black-Jewish Relations in the United States.* New York: Oxford University Press.

Samuelson, R. (1996) *The Good Life and Its Discontents: The American Dream in the Age of Entitlement (1945-1995.* New York: Times Books.

Schaefer, R.T. (1996) *Racial and Ethnic Groups,* 6th Edition. New York: HarperCollins.

Schlesinger, A.M. (1992) *The Disuniting of America.* New York: W.W. Norton.

Schulz, D.A. (1969) *Coming Up Black: Patterns of Ghetto Socialization.* Englewood Cliffs, NJ: Prentice-Hall.

Schuman, D. and Oluf, D. (1995) *Diversity on Campus.* Boston: Allyn & Bacon.

Schuman, H., Steeh, C., Bobo, L., and Kysman, M. (1997) *Racial Attitudes in America: Trends and Interpretations*, Revised Edition. Cambridge, MA: Harvard University Press.

Schutz, A. (1970) *On Phenomenology and Social Relations*. Chicago: University of Chicago Press.

Scott, W.R. (1999) Use-of-self in social constructionist therapy: Some guidelines for a multicultural practice. In: Fu, V.R, and Stremmel, A.J., (Eds.) *Affirming Diversity Through Democratic Conversations*. Upper Saddle River, NJ: Prentice-Hall.

Seligman, A.B. (1992) *The Idea of Civil Society*. Princeton, NJ: Princeton University Press.

Sennett, R. and Cobb, J. (1972) *The Hidden Injuries of Class*. New York: Vintage Books.

Shakur, S. (aka Monster Kody Scott) (1993) *Monster: The Autobiography of an L.A. Gang Member*. New York: Penguin Books.

Shepard, S. (1998) Race panel prompts different responses. *Atlanta Journal Constitution*. A11, Sept. 11.

Sherif, M. (1936) *The Psychology of Social Norms*. New York: Harper & Brothers.

Sherif, M. (1967) *Social Interaction Process and Products: Selected Essays*. Chicago: Aldine.

Shibutani, T. and Kwan, K. (1965) *Ethnic Stratification*. New York: MacMillan.

Shusterman, R. (Ed.) (1999) *Bourdieu: A Critical Reader*. Malden, MA: Blackwell.

Sigelman, L. and Tuch, S.A. (1997) Metastereotypes: Blacks' perceptions of whites' stereotypes of blacks. *Public Opinion Quarterly*, Vol,61, pp.87-101, Spring.

Simon, H.A. (1947) *Administrative Behavior*. New York: MacMillan.

Skocpol, T. (2000) *The Missing Middle: Working Families and the Future of American Social Policy*. New York: W.W. Norton.

Skrentny, J.L. (1996) *The Ironies of Affirmative Action: Politics, Culture, and Justice in America*. Chicago: University of Chicago Press.

Sleeper, J. (1997) *Liberal Racism*. New York: Viking.

Smaje, C. (2000) *Natural Hierarchies: The Historical Sociology of Race and Caste*. Malden, MA: Blackwell.

Smedley, A. (1999) *Race in North America: Origin and Evolution of a Worldview*. Boulder, CO: Westview Press.

Smith, A. (1776) *An Inquiry in the Nature and Causes of the Wealth of Nations*. London: W. Strahan & T. Cadell.

Smith, T.A. and O'Connell, L. (1997) *Black Anxiety, White Guilt, and the Politics of Status Frustration*. Westport, CT: Praeger.

Sniderman, P.M. and Piazza, T. (1993) *The Scar of Race*. Cambridge, MA: The Belknap Press of Harvard University Press.

Sniderman, P.M. and Carmines, E.G. (1998) *Reaching Beyond Race*. Cambridge, MA: Harvard University Press.

Snyder, M. and Miene, P. (1994) On the functions of stereotypes and prejudice. In: Zanna, M.P. and Olsen, J.M., (Eds.) *The Psychology of Prejudice: The Ontario Symposium*. Hillsdale, NJ: Lawrence Erlbaum Associates.

Sowell, T. (1981) *Ethnic America*. New York: Basic Books.

Sowell, T. (1984) *Civil Rights: Rhetoric or Reality?* New York: William Morrow.

Sowell, T. (1994) *Race and Culture: A World View*. New York: Basic Books.

Sowell, T. (1996) *Migrations and Cultures: A World View*. New York: Basic Books.

Sowell, T. (1999) *The Quest for Cosmic Justice*. New York: The Free Press.

Stacey, J. (1996) *In the Name of the Family: Rethinking Family Values in the Postmodern Age.* Boston, MA: Beacon Press.

Staddon, J. (1995) On responsibility and punishment. In: *The Atlantic Monthly,* February, pp.88-94.

Stampp, K.M. (1956) *The Peculiar Institution: Slavery in the Ante-Bellum South.* New York: Alfred A. Knopf.

Stampp, K.M. (1965) *The Era of Reconstruction: 1865-1877.* New York: Vintage Books.

Steele, C.M. (1999) Thin ice: 'Stereotype threat' and black college students." *The Atlantic Monthly,* August.

Steele, C.M., Spencer, S.J., and Lynch, M. (1993) "Self-image, resilience and dissonance: The role of affirmational resources." *Journal of Personality and Social Psychology,* Vol.66, pp.885-896.

Steele, S. (1990) *The Content of Our Character: A New Vision of Race in America.* New York: St. Martin's Press.

Steele, S. (1998) *A Dream Deferred: The Second Betrayal of Black Freedom in America.* New York: HarperCollins.

Stein, J. (1986) *The World of Marcus Garvey: Race and Class in Modern Society.* Baton Rouge: Louisiana State University Press.

Stone, I.F. (1988) *The Trial of Socrates.* Boston: Little, Brown.

Stryker, S. (1980) *Symbolic Interactionism.* Menlo Park, CA: Benjamin/Cummings.

Styron, W. (1967) *The Confessions of Nat Turner.* New York: Random House.

Sumner, W.G. (1906) *Folkways.* Boston: Gin.

Sutherland, S. (1992) *Irrationality: Why We Don't Think Straight!* New Brunswick, NJ: Rutgers University Press.

Suttles, G.D. (1968) *The Social Order of the Slum: Ethnicity and Territory in the Inner City.* Chicago: University of Chicago Press.

Swartz, D. (1997) *Culture and Power: The Sociology of Pierre Bourdieu.* Chicago: University of Chicago The Free Press.

Terrill, R. (1980) *A Biography: Mao.* New York: Harper & Row.

Thernstrom, S. and Thernstrom, A. (1997) *America in Black and White: One Nation, Indivisible.* New York: Simon & Schuster.

Thomas, H. (1997) *The Slave Trade: The Story of the Atlantic Slave Trade: 1440-1870.* New York: Simon & Schuster.

Thomas, W.I. and Znaniecki, Z. (1918-20) *The Polish Peasant in Europe and America.* Boston: Richard Badger.

Thornton, J., Whitman, D., and Friedman, D. (1992) Whites' Myths about Blacks. *U.S. News & World Report,* Nov.9, pp.41, 43-44.

Tilly, C. (1998) *Durable Inequality.* Berkeley: University of California Press.

Toennies, F. (1966) [1887] *Community and Society.* New York: Harper & Row.

de Tocqueville, A. (1966) *Democracy in America.* Trans. by George Lawrence. New York: Harper & Row.

Trout, P.E. (1998) Incivility in the classroom breeds 'education lite.' *The Chronicle of Higher Education.* July, p.24.

Tuch, S.A. and Martin, J.K. (Eds.) (1998) *Racial Attitudes in the 1990s: Continuity and Change.* Westport, CT: Praeger.

Valentine, C.A. (1968) *Culture and Poverty.* Chicago: University of Chicago Press.

van der Kolk, B.A., McFarlane, A.C., and Weisaeth, L. (Eds.) (1996) *Traumatic Stress: The Effects of Overwhelming Experience on Mind, Body, and Society.* New York: Guilford Press.

Van Horne, W. (1998) *Damn Yankees and Rednecks: Cultural Values, Communication Styles, and Stereotypes of Northerners and Southerners.* (unpublished paper)

Van Sertima, I. (1976) *They Came Before Columbus.* New York: Random House.

Van Sertima, I. (1998) *Early America Revisited.* New Brunswick, NJ: Transaction.

de Waal, F.B.M. (1982) *Chimpanzee Politics: Power and Sex among Apes.* New York: Harper & Row.

Wagner, D. (1997) *The New Temperance: The American Obsession with Sin and Vice.* Boulder, CO: Westview Press.

Waller, J. (1998) *Face to Face: The Changing State of Racism Across America.* New York: Insight.

Waller, M.R. (1999) Meanings and motives in new family stories: The separation of reproduction and marriage among low-income black and white parents. In: Lamont, M. (Ed.) (1999) *The Cultural Territories of Race: Black and White Boundaries.* Chicago: University of Chicago Press.

Warner, W.L. (1936) American caste and class. *American Journal of Sociology*, Sept. Vol.42, pp.234-37.

Washington, B.T. [1901] (1985) *Up From Slavery.* New York: Oxford University Press.

Waters, M.C. (1999) Explaining the comfort factor: West Indian immigrants confront American race relations." In: Lamont, M. (Ed.) (1999) *The Cultural Territories of Race: Black and White Boundaries.* Chicago: University of Chicago Press.

Weber, M. (1958) *The Protestant Ethic and the Spirit of Capitalism.* New York: Charles Scribner's Sons.

West, C. (1993) *Race Matters.* Boston: Beacon Press.

West, T.G. (1997) *Vindicating the Founders: Race, Sex, Class, and Justice in the Origins of America.* Lanham, MD: Rowman & Littlefield.

Westermann, W.L. (1955) *The Slave Systems of Greek and Roman Antiquity.* Philadelphia: The American Philosophical Society.

Westermarck, E. (1960) *Ethical Relativity.* Paterson, NJ: Littlefield, Adams.

White, J.E. (1997) I'm just who I am. *Time Magazine*, May 5, PP.32-36.

Whiting, R. (1989) *You Gatta Have WA.* New York: Vintage Books.

Whyte, W.F. (1943) *Street Corner Society.* Chicago: University of Chicago Press.

Will, G.F. (1997) Tale of two countries." *Newsweek*, Jan. 10.

Williams, C.W. (1991) *Black Teenage Mothers: Pregnancy and Child Rearing from Their Perspective.* Lexington, MA: Lexington Books.

Williams, J. (1998) *Thurgood Marshall: American Revolutionary.* New York: Times Books.

Williams, R.M., Jr. (1951) *American Society: A Sociological Interpretation.* New York: Alfred A. Knopf.

Willie, C.V. (1979) *Caste and Class Controversy.* New York: General Hall.

Wilson, W.J. (1978) *The Declining Significance of Race: Blacks and Changing American Institutions.* Chicago: University of Chicago Press.

Wilson, W.J. (1987) *The Truly Disadvantaged: The Inner City, the Underclass and Public Policy.* Chicago: University of Chicago Press.

Wilson, W.J. (1996) *When Work Disappears: The World of the New Urban Poor.* New York: Alfred A. Knopf.

Wilson, J.Q. (1997) *Moral Judgment.* New York: The Free The Free Press.

Wilson, J.Q. and Kelling, G.L. (1982) Broken windows: The police and neighborhood safety. *Atlantic Monthly*, March, Vol.249, No.3.

Wittgenstein, L. (1953) *Philosophical Investigations.* New York: MacMillan.

Wolfe, A. (1989) *Whose Keeper?* Berkeley, CA: University of California Press.

Wolfe, A. (1996) *Marginalized in the Middle*. Chicago: University of Chicago Press.

Wolfe, A. (1998) *One Nation, After All*. New York: Viking.

Wolpoff, M. and Caspari, R. (1997) *Race and Human Evolution: A Fatal Attraction*. New York: Simon & Schuster.

Worchel, S. (1999) *Written in Blood: Ethnic Identity and the Struggle for Human Harmony*. New York: Worth.

Wrong, D. (1961) The oversocialized conception of man in modern sociology. *American Sociological Review*, Vol.26, No.2.

Wuthnow, R. (1996) *Poor Richard's Principle: Recovering the American Dream Through the Moral Dimension of Work, Business, & Money*. Princeton, NJ: University of Princeton Press.

Young, D. (1932) *American Minority Peoples: A Study of Racial and Cultural Conflicts in the United States*. New York: Harper and Brothers.

Zimbardo, P.G. (1972) The pathology of imprisonment. *Society*. April.

Zweigenhaft, R.L. and Domhoff, G.W. (1991) *Blacks in the White Establishment: A Study of Race and Class in America*. New Haven: Yale University Press.

Index